Canon® EOS
Rebel T3i/600D
FOR
DUMMIES®

by Julie Adair King

WILEY

Wiley Publishing, Inc.

Canon® EOS Rebel T3i/600D For Dummies®

Published by
Wiley Publishing, Inc.
111 River Street
Hoboken, NJ 07030-5774

www.wiley.com

WILEY

About the Author

Julie Adair King is the author of many books about digital photography and imaging, including the best-selling *Digital Photography For Dummies*. Her most recent titles include a series of *For Dummies* guides to popular digital SLR cameras, including the *Canon EOS Rebel T2i/550D, T1i/500D, XSi/450D, XS/1000D,* and *XTi/400D,* and *Nikon D7000, D5000, D3100, D3000, D300s, D90, D60,* and *D40/D40x.* Other works include *Digital Photography Before & After Makeovers, Digital Photo Projects For Dummies, Julie King's Everyday Photoshop For Photographers, Julie King's Everyday Photoshop Elements,* and *Shoot Like a Pro!: Digital Photography Techniques.* When not writing, King teaches digital photography at such locations as the Palm Beach Photographic Centre. A graduate of Purdue University, she resides in Indianapolis, Indiana.

Author's Acknowledgments

I am deeply grateful for the chance to work once again with the wonderful publishing team at John Wiley and Sons. Kim Darosett, Jennifer Webb, Steve Hayes, Heidi Unger, and Katie Crocker are just some of the talented editors and designers who helped make this book possible. And finally, I am also indebted to technical editor Dave Hall, without whose insights and expertise this book would not have been the same.

Publisher's Acknowledgments

We're proud of this book; please send us your comments at http://dummies.custhelp.com. For other comments, please contact our Customer Care Department within the U.S. at 877-762-2974, outside the U.S. at 317-572-3993, or fax 317-572-4002.

Some of the people who helped bring this book to market include the following:

Acquisitions and Editorial

Project Editor: Kim Darosett

Executive Editor: Steven Hayes

Copy Editor: Heidi Unger

Technical Editor: David Hall

Editorial Manager: Leah Cameron

Editorial Assistant: Amanda Graham

Sr. Editorial Assistant: Cherie Case

Cartoons: Rich Tennant
(www.the5thwave.com)

Composition Services

Project Coordinator: Katherine Crocker

Layout and Graphics: Samantha K. Cherolis, Corrie Socolovitch

Proofreader: Penny L. Stuart

Indexer: BIM Indexing & Proofreading Services

Publishing and Editorial for Technology Dummies

Richard Swadley, Vice President and Executive Group Publisher

Andy Cummings, Vice President and Publisher

Mary Bednarek, Executive Acquisitions Director

Mary C. Corder, Editorial Director

Publishing for Consumer Dummies

Diane Graves Steele, Vice President and Publisher

Composition Services

Debbie Stailey, Director of Composition Services

Contents at a Glance

Table of Contents

Introduction

In 2003, Canon revolutionized the photography world by introducing the first digital SLR camera to sell for less than $1,000, the EOS Digital Rebel/300D. And even at that then-unheard-of price, the camera delivered exceptional performance and picture quality, earning it rave reviews and multiple industry awards. No wonder it quickly became a best seller.

That tradition of excellence and value lives on in the EOS Rebel T3i/600D. Like its ancestors, this baby offers the range of advanced controls that experienced photographers demand plus an assortment of tools designed to help beginners be successful as well. Adding to the fun, the T3i/600D also offers the option to record full high-definition video, plus an articulating monitor that's not only useful but also just plain cool.

This Rebel is so feature-packed, in fact, that sorting out everything can be a challenge, especially if you're new to digital photography or SLR photography, or both. For starters, you may not even be sure what SLR means, let alone have a clue about all the other techie terms you encounter in your camera manual — resolution, aperture, white balance, and ISO, for example. And if you're like many people, you may be so overwhelmed by all the controls on your camera that you haven't yet ventured beyond fully automatic picture-taking mode. That's a shame because it's sort of like buying a Porsche Turbo and never pushing it past 50 miles per hour.

Therein lies the point of *Canon EOS Rebel T3i/600D For Dummies*. In this book, you can discover not only what each bell and whistle on your camera does but also when, where, why, and how to put it to best use. Unlike many photography books, this one doesn't require any previous knowledge of photography or digital imaging to make sense of concepts, either. In classic *For Dummies* style, everything is explained in easy-to-understand language, with lots of illustrations to help clear up any confusion.

In short, what you have in your hands is the paperback version of an in-depth photography workshop tailored specifically to your Canon picture-taking powerhouse. Whether your interests lie in taking family photos, exploring nature and travel photography, or snapping product shots for your business, you'll get the information you need to capture the images you envision.

A Quick Look at What's Ahead

This book is organized into four parts, each devoted to a different aspect of using your camera. Although chapters flow in a sequence that's designed to take you from absolute beginner to experienced user, I also tried to make each chapter as self-standing as possible so that you can explore the topics that interest you in any order you please.

Here's a quick look at what you can find in each part:

✏ **Part I: Fast Track to Super Snaps:** This part contains four chapters that help you get up and running with your Rebel T3i/600D. Chapter 1 offers a brief overview of camera controls and walks you through initial setup and customization steps. Chapter 2 explains basic picture-taking options, such as shutter-release mode and image quality settings, and Chapter 3 shows you how to use the camera's simplest exposure modes, including Scene Intelligent Auto and Creative Auto. Chapter 4 explains the ins and outs of using Live View, the feature that lets you compose pictures on the monitor, and also covers movie recording.

✏ **Part II: Working with Picture Files:** As its title implies, this part discusses after-the-shot topics. Chapter 5 explains picture playback features, and Chapter 6 guides you through the process of transferring pictures from your camera to your computer and then getting pictures ready for print and online sharing. You can also get help with converting pictures shot in the Canon Raw file format (CR2) to a standard format in Chapter 6.

✏ **Part III: Taking Creative Control:** Chapters in this part help you unleash the full creative power of your camera by moving into semi-automatic or manual photography modes. Chapter 7 covers the all-important topic of exposure, and Chapter 8 offers tips for manipulating focus and color. Chapter 9 wraps up the part with a quick-reference guide to the camera settings and shooting strategies that produce the best results for specific types of pictures: portraits, action shots, landscape scenes, close-ups, and more.

✏ **Part IV: The Part of Tens:** In famous *For Dummies* tradition, the book concludes with two top-ten lists containing additional bits of information and advice. Chapter 10 shows you how to fix less-than-perfect images using the free software provided with your camera. Chapter 11 closes out the book with a review of camera features that, though not found on most "Top Ten Reasons I Bought My Rebel T3i/600D" lists, are nonetheless interesting, useful on occasion, or a bit of both.

Icons and Other Stuff to Note

If this isn't your first *For Dummies* book, you may be familiar with the large, round icons that decorate its margins. If not, here's your very own icon-decoder ring:

✏ A Tip icon flags information that saves you time, effort, money, or another valuable resource, including your sanity.

 ✔ This icon highlights information that's especially worth storing in your brain's long-term memory or to remind you of a fact that may have been displaced from that memory by another pressing fact.

 ✔ When you see this icon, look alive. It indicates a potential danger zone that can result in much wailing and teeth-gnashing if it's ignored.

 ✔ Lots of information in this book is of a technical nature — digital photography is a technical animal, after all. But if I present a detail that's useful mainly for impressing your geeky friends, I mark it with this icon.

Additionally, I need to point out a few other details that will help you use this book:

 ✔ **Other margin art:** Replicas of some of your camera's buttons and onscreen graphics also appear in the margins of some paragraphs and in some tables. I include these images to provide quick reminders of the appearance of the button or option being discussed.

 ✔ **Software menu commands:** In sections that cover software, a series of words connected by an arrow indicates commands you choose from the program menus. For example, if a step tells you, "Choose File⇨Export," click the File menu to unfurl it and then click the Export command on the menu.

 ✔ **Camera firmware:** *Firmware* is the internal software that controls many of your camera's operations. This book was written using version 1.0.0 of the firmware, which was the most current at the time of publication.

 Occasionally, Canon releases firmware updates, and you should check its website (www.canon.com) periodically to find out whether any updates are available. (Chapter 1 tells you how to determine which firmware version your camera is running.) If you download an update, be sure to read the accompanying description of what it accomplishes so that you can adapt this book's instructions as necessary.

About the Software Shown in This Book

In chapters that cover picture downloading and editing, I show you how to get things done using the free Canon software that ships on one of the two CDs in your camera box. (The other CD contains the software manuals in electronic form.) Rest assured, though, that the tools used in these programs work similarly in other programs, so you should be able to easily adapt the steps to whatever software you use.

eCheat Sheet

As an added bonus, you can find an electronic version of the *For Dummies* Cheat Sheet at www.dummies.com/cheatsheet/canoneosrebelt3i600d. The Cheat Sheet contains a quick-reference guide to all the buttons, dials, switches, and exposure modes on your camera. Log on, print it out, and tuck it in your camera bag for times when you don't want to carry this book with you.

Practice, Be Patient, and Have Fun!

To wrap up this preamble, I want to stress that if you initially think that digital photography is too confusing or too technical for you, you're in very good company. *Everyone* finds this stuff a little mind-boggling at first. Take it slowly, experimenting with just one or two new camera settings or techniques at first. Then, every time you go on a photo outing, make it a point to add one or two more shooting skills to your repertoire. With some time, patience, and practice, you'll soon wield your camera like a pro, dialing in the necessary settings to capture your creative vision almost instinctively.

So without further ado, I invite you to grab your camera and a cup of whatever it is you prefer to sip while you read and then start exploring the rest of this book. Your Rebel T3i/600D is the perfect partner for your photographic journey, and I thank you for allowing me, in this book, to serve as your tour guide.

Part I
Fast Track to Super Snaps

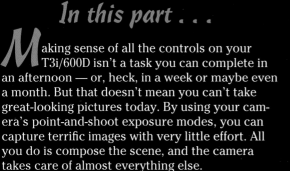

In this part . . .

Making sense of all the controls on your T3i/600D isn't a task you can complete in an afternoon — or, heck, in a week or maybe even a month. But that doesn't mean you can't take great-looking pictures today. By using your camera's point-and-shoot exposure modes, you can capture terrific images with very little effort. All you do is compose the scene, and the camera takes care of almost everything else.

This part shows you how to take best advantage of your camera's most-automatic photography modes and also addresses some basic setup steps, such as adjusting the viewfinder to your eyesight and getting familiar with the camera menus, buttons, and dials. In addition, chapters in this part explain a few picture-taking settings that come into play in any exposure mode and show you how to use your camera's Live View and movie-making features.

Getting the Lay of the Land

For many people, getting your first *serious* camera means moving from a point-and-shoot to an SLR (single-lens reflex) model. As with any growth spurt, the excitement of the move is often tempered with a bit of anxiety. Sure, you'll be able to do lots of new things with your dSLR (digital SLR), but along with that newfound capability comes a barrage of new buttons, knobs, LCD menus, and mechanical knickknacks. Heck, this may be the first time you've even changed lenses on a camera — a big step in itself.

If the Rebel T3i/600D is both your first SLR *and* your first digital camera, you're getting something of a double-whammy in the New Stuff department. But fear not: With some practice and the help of this chapter, which introduces you to each external control, explains how to adjust camera settings, and offers advice on a few setup options, you'll quickly get comfortable with your new camera.

Adjusting the Monitor Position

One of the many cool features of the T3i/600D is its articulating monitor. When you first take the camera out of its box, the monitor is positioned with the screen facing the back of the body, as shown on the left in Figure 1-1, protecting the screen from scratches and smudges. (It's a good idea to place the monitor in this position when you're not using the camera.) When you're ready to start shooting or reviewing your photos, you can lock the monitor in the traditional position on the camera back, as shown on the right in Figure 1-1. Or for more flexibility, you can swing the monitor out and away from the camera body and then rotate it to find the best viewing angle, as shown in Figure 1-2.

Figure 1-1: Here you see just two of the possible monitor positions.

Because playing with the monitor is no doubt one of the first things you did after unpacking your new camera, I won't waste space here walking you through the process of adjusting the screen. (If you need help, the camera manual shows you what to do.) But I want to offer a few monitor-related tips:

- ✔ **Don't force things.** Although the monitor assembly is sturdy, treat it with respect as you adjust the screen position. The monitor twists only in certain directions, and it's easy to forget which way it's supposed to move. So if you feel resistance, don't force things — you could break the monitor. Instead, rely on that feeling of resistance to remind you to turn the screen the other way.

- ✔ **Watch the crunch factor.** When positioning the monitor back into the camera (whether face in or face out), take care that nothing gets in the way. Use a lens brush or soft cloth to clean the monitor housing on the camera back so there's nothing in the way that could damage the monitor.

✔ **Clean smart.** It's virtually impossible to keep nose prints and finger-prints off the monitor — well, it is for me, anyway. When you get the urge to clean the screen, use only the special cloths and cleaning solu-tions made for this purpose. (You can find them in any camera store.) *Do not* use paper products such as paper towels because they can con-tain wood fibers that can scratch the surface of the LCD. And never try to use a can of compressed air to blow dust off the camera — the air is cold and can crack the monitor.

✔ **Live View photography has some drawbacks.** *Live View* is the feature that enables you to compose your photos using the monitor rather than the viewfinder. You switch the feature on and off by pressing the Live View button, which is found to the right of the viewfinder and looks like the icon shown in the margin here.

Live View may feel more comfortable than using the viewfinder if you're stepping up to the T3i/600D from a point-and-shoot camera that didn't have a viewfinder. But the monitor is one of the biggest drains on bat-tery power, and autofocusing in Live View mode is slower than when you use the viewfinder. For these reasons and a few others you can explore in Chapter 4, I stick with the viewfinder for most regular pho-tography and reserve Live View for movie recording. (You can't use the viewfinder in Movie mode.) Whatever you decide, note that if Live View is enabled and you orient the monitor to face the same direction as the lens, the monitor may display a mirror image of your subject.

Figure 1-2: You also can unlock the monitor from the body and then rotate the screen to get the best view of things.

Getting Comfortable with Your Lens

One of the biggest differences between a point-and-shoot camera and an SLR camera is the lens. With an SLR, you can swap lenses to suit different photographic needs, going from an extreme close-up lens to a super-long telephoto, for example. Additionally, an SLR lens has a movable focusing ring that lets you focus manually instead of relying on the camera's autofocus mechanism. Even this basic difference extends your picture-making opportunities in big ways.

Of course, those added capabilities mean that you need a little background information to take full advantage of your lens. To that end, the next several sections explain the process of attaching, removing, and using this critical part of your camera.

Attaching a lens

Your camera accepts two categories of Canon lenses: those with an EF-S design and those with a plain-old EF design.

 The EF stands for *electro focus;* the S, for *short back focus.* And *that* simply means the rear element of the lens is closer to the sensor than with an EF lens. And no, you don't need to remember what the abbreviation stands for — just make sure that if you buy a Canon lens other than the one sold with the camera, it carries either the EF or EF-S specification. If you want to buy a non-Canon lens, check the lens manufacturer's website to find out which lenses work with the Rebel T3i/600D.

Whatever lens you choose, follow these steps to attach it to the camera body:

1. **Remove the cap that covers the lens mount on the front of the camera.**

2. **Remove the cap that covers the back of the lens.**

3. **Locate the proper lens mounting index on the camera body.**

   A *mounting index* is simply a marker that tells you where to align the lens with the camera body when connecting the two. Your camera has two of these markers, one red and one white, as shown in Figure 1-3.

   Which marker you use to align your lens depends on the lens type:

   - *Canon EF-S lens:* The white square is the mounting index.
   - *Canon EF lens:* The red dot is the mounting index.

   If you buy a non-Canon lens, check the lens manual for help with this step.

EF-S mounting index

EF mounting index

Figure 1-3: Which index marker you should use depends on the lens type.

4. **Align the mounting index on the lens with the correct one on the camera body.**

   The lens also has a mounting index. Figure 1-4 shows the one that appears on the so-called *kit lens* — the EF-S 18–55mm IS (Image Stabilizer) zoom lens that Canon sells as a unit with the Rebel T3i/600D. If you buy a different lens, the index marker may be red or some other color, so again, check the lens instruction manual.

5. **Keeping the mounting indexes aligned, position the lens on the camera's lens mount.**

6. **Turn the lens in a clockwise direction until the lens clicks into place.**

   In other words, turn the lens toward the lens-release button, as indicated in Figure 1-4.

Always attach (or switch) lenses in a clean environment to reduce the risk of getting dust, dirt, and other contaminants inside the camera or lens. Changing lenses on the beach on a windy day, for example, isn't a good idea. For added safety, point the camera body slightly down when performing this maneuver, as shown in the figure. Doing so helps prevent any flotsam in the air from being drawn into the camera by gravity.

Removing a lens

To detach a lens from the camera body, take these steps:

1. **Locate the lens-release button on the front of the camera, labeled in Figure 1-4.**

2. **Grip the rear collar of the lens.**

   In other words, hold onto the stationary part of the lens that's closest to the camera body.

3. **Press the lens-release button while turning the lens away from the lens-release button (counterclockwise).**

   You can feel the lens release from the mount at this point. Lift the lens off the mount to remove it.

4. **Place the rear protective cap onto the back of the lens.**

   If you aren't putting another lens on the camera, cover the lens mount with the protective cap that came with your camera, too. These steps help keep your lens and camera interior dust-free.

EF-S mounting indexes

Lens-release button

Figure 1-4: Place the lens in the lens mount with the mounting indexes aligned.

Using an IS (image stabilizer) lens

The 18–55mm lens sold with the Rebel T3i/600D camera offers *image stabilization*. On Canon lenses, this feature is indicated by the initials *IS* in the lens name.

Image stabilization attempts to compensate for small amounts of camera shake that are common when photographers handhold their cameras and use a slow shutter speed, a lens with a long focal length, or both. Camera shake is a problem because it can result in blurry images, even when your focus is dead-on. Although image stabilization can't work miracles, it does enable most people to capture sharp handheld shots in many situations that they otherwise couldn't.

WARNING!

However, when you use a tripod, image stabilization can have detrimental effects because the system may try to adjust for movement that isn't actually occurring. Although this problem shouldn't be an issue with most Canon IS lenses, if you do see blurry images while using a tripod, try setting the Stabilizer switch (shown in Figure 1-5) to Off. You also can save battery power by turning off image stabilization when you use a tripod. If you use a monopod, leave image stabilization turned on so that it can help compensate for any accidental movement of the monopod. (I never can keep those things perfectly still, no matter how hard I try — but then again, I drink way too much coffee.)

Focusing ring   Zoom ring   Focal length indicator   Auto/Manual focus switch

Image Stabilizer switch

Figure 1-5: Image stabilization can help ensure sharper handheld shots.

If you use a non-Canon lens, the image stabilization feature may go by another name: *anti-shake, vibration compensation,* and so on. In some cases, the manufacturers may recommend that you leave the system turned on or select a special setting when you use a tripod, so be sure to check the lens manual for information.

Whatever type of lens you use, image stabilization isn't meant to eliminate the blur that can occur when your subject moves during the exposure. That problem is related to shutter speed, a topic you can explore in Chapter 7. Chapter 8 offers more tips for blur-free shots and explains focal length and its effect on your pictures.

Shifting from autofocus to manual focus

Your Rebel T3i/600D offers an excellent autofocusing system, which you can find out how to exploit to its best advantage in Chapter 8. With some subjects, however, autofocusing can be slow or impossible, which is why your camera also offers manual focusing.

Make the shift from auto to manual focus as follows:

1. **Set the AF/MF switch on the side of the lens to the MF position.**

   This switch sets the focus operation to either auto (AF) or manual (MF). Figure 1-5 shows you the switch as it appears on the Rebel T3i/600D kit lens. The switch should be in a similar location on other Canon lenses. If you use a lens from another manufacturer, check the lens instruction manual.

2. **Look through the viewfinder and twist the focusing ring until your subject comes into focus.**

   On the kit lens, the focusing ring is at the far end of the lens barrel, as indicated in Figure 1-5. If you use another lens, the focusing ring may be located elsewhere, so check your lens manual.

   If you have trouble focusing, you may be too close to your subject; every lens has a minimum focusing distance. (For the kit lens, the minimum close-focus range is about 10 inches; for other lenses, check the specifications in the lens manual.) You also may need to adjust the viewfinder to accommodate your eyesight; see the next section for details.

Some lenses enable you to use autofocusing to set the initial focusing point and then fine-tune focus manually. Check your lens manual for information on how to use this option, if available. (This option isn't offered on the kit lens.)

Zooming in and out

If you bought a zoom lens, it sports a movable zoom ring. On the kit lens, the zoom ring is behind the focusing ring, as shown in Figure 1-5, but again, the relative positioning of the two components depends on your lens. With the kit lens, you rotate the lens barrel to zoom. A few zoom lenses use a push-pull motion to zoom instead.

The numbers around the edge of the zoom ring, by the way, represent *focal lengths.* Chapter 8 explains focal lengths in detail. In the meantime, just note that when the lens is mounted on the camera, the number that's aligned with the white focus-length indicator, labeled in Figure 1-5, represents the current focal length. In Figure 1-5, for example, the focal length is 24mm.

Adjusting the Viewfinder Focus

Perched on the top-right edge of the viewfinder is a tiny black knob, labeled in Figure 1-6. Officially known as a *dioptric adjustment control,* this knob enables you to adjust the magnification of the viewfinder to mesh with your eyesight.

Viewfinder adjustment knob   Autofocus point

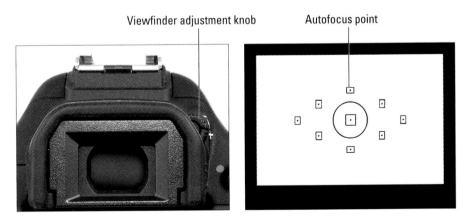

Figure 1-6: Roll the little knob to set the viewfinder focus for your eyesight.

Adjusting the viewfinder to your eyesight is critical: If you don't, scenes that appear out-of-focus through the viewfinder may actually be sharply focused through the lens, and vice versa.

Follow these steps to adjust your viewfinder:

1. **Remove the lens cap from the front of the lens.**

2. **Look through the viewfinder, aim the lens at a plain surface (such as a white wall), and concentrate on the focusing screen shown on the right side of Figure 1-6.**

   The *focusing screen* is the collective name assigned to the group of nine autofocus points that appears in the viewfinder — the little squares with the dots inside. One of the little guys is labeled in Figure 1-6. (The circle that surrounds the center autofocus point is related to exposure metering, a subject you can explore in Chapter 7.)

3. **Rotate the dioptric adjustment knob until the autofocus points appear to be in focus.**

   Don't worry about focusing the actual picture now; just pay attention to the sharpness of the autofocus points.

If your eyesight is such that you can't get the autofocus points to appear sharp by using the dioptric adjustment knob, you can buy an additional eyepiece adapter. This accessory, which you pop onto the eyepiece, enables further adjustment of the viewfinder display. Prices range from about $15–$30 depending on the magnification you need. Look for an E-series dioptric adjustment lens adapter.

Working with Memory Cards

Instead of recording images on film, digital cameras store pictures on *memory cards*. Your Rebel T3i/600D uses a specific type of memory card — an *SD card* (for *Secure Digital*), shown in Figures 1-7 and 1-8. You can also use *high-capacity* SD cards, which carry the label SDHC and come in capacities ranging from 4–32GB (gigabytes), and *extended-capacity* (SDXC) cards, which offer capacities higher than 32GB.

Memory cards also are rated according to *speed class,* which refers to how quickly data can be written to and read from the card. A higher-speed card helps ensure the smoothest movie recording and playback. Currently, the fastest cards have a speed rating of 10. For movie recording, Canon recommends that you purchase a card with a speed class of 6 or higher.

Whatever the speed or capacity, safeguarding your memory cards — and the images on them — requires a few precautions:

✔ **Inserting a card:** Turn the camera off and then put the card in the card slot with the label facing the back of the camera, as shown in Figure 1-7. Push the card into the slot until it clicks into place.

✔ **Formatting a card:** The first time you use a new memory card, take a few seconds to format it by choosing the Format option on Setup Menu 1. This step ensures that the card is properly prepared to record your pictures. See the upcoming section "Setup Menu 1" for details.

✔ **Removing a card:** First, check the status of the memory card access light, labeled in Figure 1-7. After making sure that the light is off, indicating that the camera has finished recording your most recent photo, turn off the camera. Open the memory card door, as shown in Figure 1-7. Depress the memory card slightly until you hear a little click and then let go. The card pops halfway out of the slot, enabling you to grab it by the tail and remove it.

✔ **Handling cards:** Don't touch the gold contacts on the back of the card. (See the left card in Figure 1-8.) When cards aren't in use, store them in the protective cases they came in or in a memory card wallet. Keep cards away from extreme heat and cold as well.

✔ **Locking cards:** The tiny switch on the left side of the card, labeled *lock switch* in Figure 1-8, enables you to lock your card, which prevents any data from being erased or recorded to the card. Press the switch toward the bottom of the card to lock the card contents; press it toward the top of the card to unlock the data.

Memory card access light

Figure 1-7: Insert the card with the label facing the camera back.

Don't touch!   Lock switch

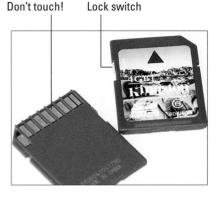

Figure 1-8: Avoid touching the gold contacts on the card.

Exploring External Camera Controls

Scattered across your camera's exterior are a number of buttons, dials, and switches that you use to change picture-taking settings, review and edit your photos, and perform various other operations. Later chapters discuss all your camera's functions in detail and provide the exact steps to follow to access those functions. The next few sections provide just a basic introduction to the external controls.

Topside controls

Your virtual tour begins on the top of the camera, as shown in Figure 1-9.

The items of note here are

✓ **On/Off switch:** Okay, you probably already figured this one out, but here's a side tip that may be new to you: By default, the camera automatically shuts itself off after 30 seconds of inactivity to save battery power. To wake up the camera, press the shutter button halfway or press the Menu, Disp, or Playback buttons. You can adjust the auto shutdown timing via Setup Menu 1, covered later in this chapter.

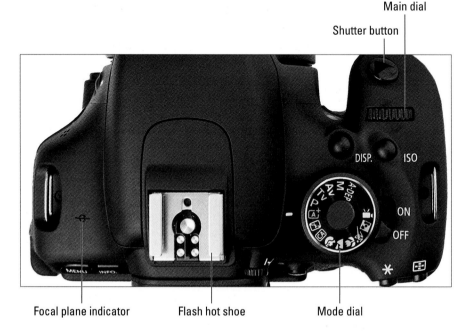

Figure 1-9: The tiny pictures on the Mode dial represent special automatic shooting modes.

✔ **Mode dial:** Rotate this dial to select an *exposure mode,* which determines whether the camera operates in fully automatic, semi-automatic, or manual exposure mode when you take still pictures. To shoot a movie, you set the dial to Movie mode. Chapter 2 provides an overview of the exposure modes.

✔ **Main dial:** Just forward of the Mode dial, you see a black dial that has the official name *Main dial.* You use this dial when selecting many camera settings. (Specifics are provided throughout the book.) In fact, this dial plays such an important role that you'd think it might have a more auspicious name, but Main dial it is.

✔ **ISO button:** This button provides one way to access the ISO setting, which determines how sensitive the camera is to light. Chapter 7 details this critical exposure setting.

✔ **Disp button:** Use this button to toggle the Shooting Settings display on and off. The section "Using the Shooting Settings display" talks more about this feature.

✔ **Shutter button:** You probably already understand the function of this button, too. But what you may not realize is that when you're using autofocusing and autoexposure, you can mess up your picture if you don't press the button in two stages: Press halfway, pause to let the camera set focus and exposure, and then press the rest of the way to capture the image. You'd be surprised how many people mess up their pictures because they press that button with one quick jab, denying the camera the time it needs to set focus and exposure.

✔ **Flash hot shoe:** A *hot shoe* is a connection for attaching an external flash head. The contacts on the shoe are covered by a little black insert when you take the camera out of its shipping box; when you're ready to attach a flash head, remove the insert to reveal the contacts, as shown in Figure 1-9.

✔ **Focal plane indicator:** Should you ever need to know the exact distance between your subject and the camera, the *focal plane indicator* labeled in Figure 1-9 is key. This mark indicates the plane at which light coming through the lens is focused onto the negative in a film camera or the image sensor in a digital camera. Basing your measurement on this mark produces a more accurate camera-to-subject distance than using the end of the lens or some other external point on the camera body as your reference point.

Back-of-the-body controls

Traveling over the top of the camera to its back, you encounter a smorgasbord of buttons and controls, including the knob you use to adjust the viewfinder to your eyesight, as discussed earlier in this chapter. Figure 1-10 gives you a look at the layout of the backside controls.

AF Point Selection

Speaker

AE Lock

Set button and cross keys

Figure 1-10: Having lots of external buttons makes accessing the camera's functions easier.

Don't let the abundance of buttons intimidate you. Having all those external controls actually makes operating your camera easier. On cameras that have only a few buttons, you have to dig through menus to access the camera features, which is a pain. On the T3i/600D, you can access almost every critical shooting setting via external buttons, which is much more convenient.

Throughout this book, pictures of some of these buttons appear in the margins to help you locate the button being discussed. So even though I provide the official control names in the following list, don't worry about getting all those straight right now. The list is just to get you acquainted with the *possibility* of what you can accomplish with all these features.

Do note, however, that many of the buttons have multiple names because they serve multiple purposes depending on whether you're taking pictures, reviewing images, recording a movie, or performing some other function. In this book, I refer to these buttons by the first label you see in the following list to simplify things. For example, I refer to the AF Point Selection/Magnify button as the AF Point Selection button. Again, though, the margin icons help you know exactly which button is being described.

And here's another tip: If the label or icon for a button is blue, it indicates a function related to viewing, printing, or downloading images. Labels that indicate a shooting-related function are white, and the sole red label indicates a button purpose related to Live View and movie shooting.

With that preamble out of the way, it's time to explore the camera back, starting at the top-right corner and working westward (well, assuming that your lens is pointing north, anyway):

- **AF Point Selection/Magnify button:** When you use certain advanced shooting modes, you press this button to specify which of the nine autofocus points you want the camera to use when establishing focus. Chapter 8 tells you more. In Playback, Live View, and Movie mode, you use this button to magnify the image display (thus the plus sign in the button's magnifying glass icon). See Chapter 5 for help with that function.

- **AE Lock/FE Lock/Index/Reduce button:** As you can guess from the official name of this button, it serves many purposes. The first two are related to still-image capture functions: You use the button to lock in the autoexposure (AE) settings and to lock flash exposure (FE). Chapter 7 details both issues. When using Live View and Movie modes, covered in Chapter 4, this button serves only as an autoexposure lock.

  This button also serves two image-viewing functions: It switches the display to Index mode, enabling you to see multiple image thumbnails at once, and it reduces the magnification of images when displayed one at a time. Chapter 5 explains picture playback.

- **Speaker:** When you play a movie that contains an audio track, the sound comes wafting through these little holes, which lead to the camera's internal speakers.

- **Live View/Movie button:** You press this button to shift the camera into Live View mode and, when shooting movies, to start and stop recording. (For the latter, you must first set the Mode dial to Movie mode.) Chapter 4 offers the pertinent details.

- **Exposure Compensation/Aperture button:** When you work in M (manual) exposure mode, you press this button and rotate the Main dial to choose the aperture setting, better known as the *f-stop.* In the other advanced exposure modes (P, Tv, Av, and A-DEP), you instead use the button and dial to apply *Exposure Compensation,* a feature that enables you to adjust the exposure selected by the camera's autoexposure mechanism. Chapter 7 discusses both issues.

✏ **Quick Control/Direct Print button:** You press this button to display the Quick Control screen, which gives you one way to adjust picture settings. As for the Direct Print button, it's used to print directly from the camera to a compatible printer. Chapter 6 covers this printing function. (Hint: It's not one that most people need to use.)

✏ **Set button and cross keys:** Figure 1-10 points out the Set button and the four surrounding buttons, known as *cross keys.* These buttons team up to perform several functions, including choosing options from the camera menus. You use the cross keys to navigate through menus and then press the Set button to select a specific menu setting. You can find out more about ordering from menus later in this chapter.

In this book, the instruction "Press the left cross key" means to press the one that sports the left-pointing arrowhead. "Press the up cross key" means to press the one with the up-pointing arrowhead, and so on.

The cross keys and the Set button also have nonmenu responsibilities, as follows:

- *After displaying the Quick Control screen (via the Quick Control button) and choosing a function, press the Set button to enter the respective setting screen.* Get the full story in the upcoming section "Taking Advantage of the Quick Control screen."

- *Press the right cross key to adjust the AF mode.* This option controls one aspect of the camera's autofocus behavior, as outlined in Chapter 8.

- *Press the left cross key to change the Drive mode.* The Drive mode settings enable you to switch the camera from single-frame shooting to continuous capture or self-timer/remote-control shooting. See Chapter 2 for details.

- *Press the down cross key to change the Picture Style.* Chapter 8 explains Picture Styles, which you can use to adjust color, contrast, and sharpness of your pictures.

- *Press the up cross key to change the White Balance setting.* The White Balance control, explained near the end of Chapter 8, enables you to ensure that your photo colors are accurate and not biased by the color of the light source.

You can customize the function of the Set button; Chapter 11 explains how. But while you're working with this book, stick with the default setup, just described. Otherwise, the instructions I give won't work.

✏ **Playback button:** Press this button to switch the camera into picture-review mode. Chapter 5 details playback features.

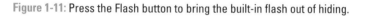

✔ **Erase button:** Sporting a trash can icon, the universal symbol for delete, this button lets you erase pictures from your memory card during playback. Chapter 5 has specifics. In Live View and Movie mode, also covered in Chapter 4, this button is involved in the focusing process.

✔ **Menu button:** Press this button to access the camera menus. See the next section for details on navigating menus.

✔ **Info button:** In Live View, Movie, and Playback modes, pressing this button changes the picture-display style, as outlined in Chapters 4 and 5, respectively. But when the Shooting Settings display is active, you can press the Info button to toggle between that display and the Camera Settings display. (Both displays are explained in detail later in this chapter.)

Front odds and ends

On the front of the camera, you find the following features, labeled in Figure 1-11:

Figure 1-11: Press the Flash button to bring the built-in flash out of hiding.

- ✓ **Flash button:** Press this button to use the built-in flash in the advanced exposure modes (P, Tv, Av, M, or A-DEP). See Chapter 2 for a flash primer; flip to Chapters 7 and 9 for more tips on flash photography.

- ✓ **Microphone:** When recording movies, you can attach an external microphone or record audio via the built-in microphone. If you opt for the latter, be careful not to cover up the little holes that lead to the microphone, labeled in the left photo in Figure 1-11. See Chapter 4 for details on sound recording.

- ✓ **Lens-release button:** Press this button to disengage the lens from the lens mount so that you can remove it from the camera. See the first part of this chapter for details on mounting and removing lenses.

- ✓ **Depth-of-Field Preview button:** When you press this button, the image in the viewfinder offers an approximation of the depth of field that will result from your selected aperture setting, or f-stop. *Depth of field* refers to how much of the scene will be in sharp focus. Chapter 8 provides details.

- ✓ **Red-Eye Reduction/Self-Timer Lamp:** When you set your flash to Red-Eye Reduction mode, this little lamp (see the right side of Figure 1-11) emits a brief burst of light prior to the real flash — the idea being that your subjects' pupils will constrict in response to the light, thus lessening the chances of red-eye. If you use the camera's standard, 10-second self-timer feature, the lamp blinks to provide you with a visual countdown to the moment at which the picture will be recorded. See Chapter 2 for more details about Red-Eye Reduction flash mode and the self-timer function.

- ✓ **Remote-control sensor:** Labeled in the right image in Figure 1-11, the sensor can pick up the signal from an optional Canon wireless remote-control shutter release accessory.

Connection ports

Hidden under the two little covers on the left side of the camera, you find the following inputs for connecting the camera to various devices. The left side of Figure 1-12 shows you what lurks beneath the first cover; the right side of the figure shows the connections found under the second cover. Starting with the left side, the available connections are as follows:

- ✓ **Remote-control terminal:** As an alternative to using a wireless remote controller to trigger the shutter release, you can attach the Canon Remote Switch RS-60E3 wired controller here.

The controller currently sells for about $30 and is a very worthwhile investment if you do a lot of long-exposure shooting (such as nighttime shots and fireworks). By using the remote control, you eliminate the chance that the action of your finger on the shutter button moves the camera enough to blur the shot, which is especially problematic during long exposures. And unlike a wireless remote, which must be positioned so that the signal reaches the sensor on the front of the camera, a wired remote can be operated from behind the camera (which is why it's my remote controller of choice).

Wired remote-control terminal   A/V and USB port

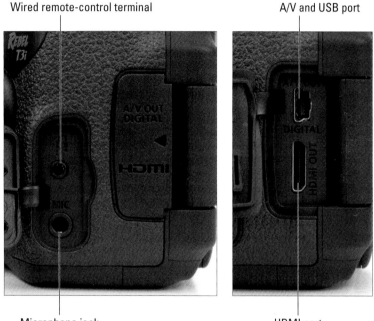

Microphone jack   HDMI port

Figure 1-12: These two rubber covers conceal terminals for connecting the camera to other devices.

🖙 **Microphone jack:** If you're not happy with the audio quality provided by the internal microphone, you can plug in an external microphone here. The jack accepts a 3.5mm stereo microphone miniplug. See Chapter 4 for all things movie-related.

🖙 **A/V and USB connection terminal:** This connection point serves two purposes: You can connect your camera to a standard-definition televi-sion for picture playback via an A/V (audio/video) cable, which ships with the camera. Chapter 5 explains this option. You use the same termi-nal to connect the camera to a computer via the supplied USB cable for picture downloading (although using a memory-card reader is usually a better alternative, for reasons you can explore in Chapter 6).

✔ **HDMI terminal:** For picture or movie playback on a high-definition television or screen, you can connect the camera via this terminal, using an optional HDMI cable HTC-100 (HDMI male to mini-C connectors). You'll pay about $70 if you buy the cable from Canon. (You can use other manufacturer's cables, but be sure they are of high quality.) Again, see Chapter 5 for details on connecting the camera to a TV.

If you turn the camera over, you find a tripod socket, which enables you to mount the camera on a tripod that uses a ¼-inch screw, plus the battery chamber. And finally, tucked just above the battery chamber, on the right side of the camera, is a little flap that covers a connection for attaching an optional AC power adapter; Canon sells the adapter for about $65. See the camera manual for specifics on running the camera on AC power.

Viewing and Adjusting Camera Settings

You've no doubt already deduced that your Rebel T3i/600D is loaded with options. Your camera also gives you several ways to monitor the current settings and adjust them if needed. The next sections provide just a quick introduction to viewing and changing settings; later chapters explain exactly how and where to access individual options. (Note, too, that the information here relates to regular shooting modes — if you switch to Live View or Movie mode, some things work a little differently. You can get the scoop on those two modes in Chapter 4.)

Ordering from menus

You access many of the camera's features via internal menus, which, conveniently enough, appear on the monitor when you press the Menu button, located atop the upper-left corner of the camera back. Features are grouped into the menus described in Table 1-1.

The exact assortment of menus and options depends on your exposure mode. Some menu functions and even entire menus appear only when you set the Mode dial to one of the advanced exposure modes (P, Tv, Av, M, and A-DEP). Similarly, the three Movie menus appear only when the Mode dial is set to the Movie setting.

In case you didn't notice, the icons that represent the menus are color-coded. The Shooting and Movie menus have red icons; the Setup menus sport yellow icons; the Playback menus have a blue symbol; and the My Menu icon is green. (Chapter 11 explains the My Menu feature, through which you can create your own, custom menu.)

Table 1-1		Rebel T3i/600D Menus
Symbol	*Open This Menu*	*To Access These Functions*
	Shooting Menu 1	Picture Quality settings, Red-Eye Reduction flash mode, and a few other basic camera settings
	Shooting Menu 2	Additional shooting options in advanced exposure modes; Live View options in other exposure modes.
	Shooting Menu 3*	Options for enabling the Dust Delete Data and Auto ISO features
	Shooting Menu 4*	Live View photography options
	Playback Menu 1	Rotate, protect, and erase pictures, as well as the Creative Filters and image-resizing features
	Playback Menu 2	Additional playback features, including picture rating, slide shows, histogram display, image jump, and HDMI control
	Setup Menu 1	Memory card formatting plus basic customization options, such as the file-numbering system and auto shutdown timing
	Setup Menu 2	More customization options and maintenance functions, such as sensor cleaning
	Setup Menu 3*	Custom Functions, Copyright Embedding, firmware information, and options for resetting camera functions to factory defaults
	My Menu*	User-customized menu setup
	Movie Menu 1**	Movie exposure and focusing options, plus remote-control option
	Movie Menu 2**	More movie settings, including recording size, sound recording, and video snapshot (enable or disable)
	Movie Menu 3**	Additional movie exposure and color settings

*Menu appears only when Mode dial is set to P, Tv, Av, M, or A-DEP

**Menu appears only when Mode dial is set to Movie

After you press the Menu button, a screen similar to the one shown on the left in Figure 1-13 appears. Along the top of the screen, you see the icons shown in Table 1-1, each representing a menu. (Remember that which icons appear depends on the setting of the Mode dial.)

Figure 1-13: Use the cross keys to navigate menus; press Set to access available settings.

The highlighted icon marks the active menu; options on that menu appear automatically on the main part of the screen. In Figure 1-13, Shooting Menu 1 is active, for example.

I explain all the important menu options elsewhere in the book; for now, just familiarize yourself with the process of navigating menus and selecting options. After pressing the Menu button to display the menus, use these techniques:

- **To select a different menu:** Press the right or left cross keys or rotate the Main dial to cycle through the available menus.

- **To select and adjust a function on the current menu:** Press the up or down cross key to highlight the feature you want to adjust. On the left side of Figure 1-13, the Quality option is highlighted, for example. Next, press the Set button. Settings available for the selected item then appear either right next to the menu item or on a separate screen, as shown on the right side of the figure. Either way, use the cross keys to highlight your preferred setting and then press Set again to lock in your choice.

Using the Shooting Settings display

As shown in Figure 1-14, the Shooting Settings screen displays the most critical photography settings — aperture, shutter speed, ISO, and the like. Note that the display is relevant only to regular still-photography shooting, though. When you switch to Live View mode or Movie mode, you can choose to see some settings superimposed over your image in the monitor, but the process of adjusting settings and customizing the display is different. (See Chapter 4 for details.)

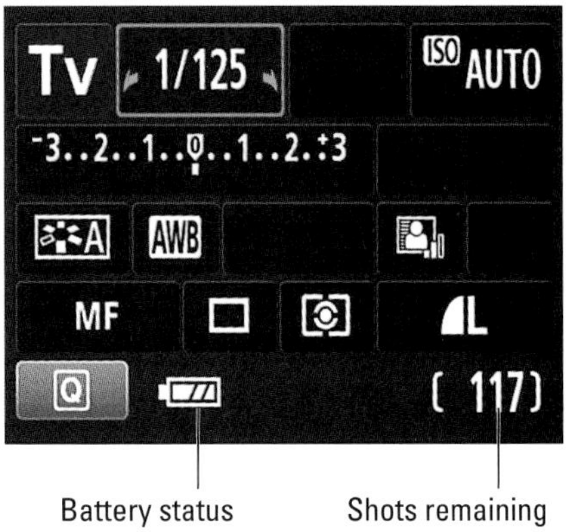

The types of data shown in the Shooting Settings display depend on the exposure mode you select. The figure shows data that's included when you work in one of the advanced modes, such as Tv (shutter-priority autoexposure). In the fully automatic modes as well as in Creative Auto mode, you see far fewer settings, because you can control fewer settings in those modes. Figure 1-14 labels two key points of data that are helpful in any mode, though: how many more pictures can fit on your memory card at the current settings and the status of the battery. A "full" battery icon like the one in the figure shows that the battery is fully charged. When the icon appears empty, you better have your spare battery handy if you want to keep shooting.

Battery status   Shots remaining

Figure 1-14: The Shooting Settings display gives you an easy way to monitor current picture settings.

If you're running low and don't have a charger or spare battery handy, you can preserve the last few bits of battery juice by turning off the features that are the biggest power hogs: the monitor, image stabilization, and flash. Also avoid keeping the shutter button pressed halfway for long periods, because the exposure and focusing processes that are activated with a half-press also consume battery power.

Back to the Shooting Settings display: You use it to both view and adjust certain picture-taking settings. Here's what you need to know:

- **Turning on the Shooting Settings display:** The display appears automatically when you turn on the camera. After the display shuts off (usually after 30 seconds), you can turn it on again by pressing the shutter button halfway and releasing it or by pressing the Disp button. You also can use the shutter-button technique to shift from the menu displays to the Shooting Settings display.

- **Turning off the Shooting Settings display:** To turn off the display before the automatic shutoff occurs, press the Disp button again. The display also turns off when you press the shutter button halfway, but then reappears as soon as you release the button. (You can change this behavior, though, through an option on Setup Menu 2; for details, look for the section discussing that menu toward the end of this chapter.)

If you use the Disp button to turn off the display, press the button again to bring the display back to life; pressing the shutter button halfway doesn't do the trick.

✓ **Adjusting settings:** While the Shooting Settings display is active, you can change some shooting settings by rotating the Main dial alone or by using the dial in combination with one of the camera buttons.

For example, in the shutter-priority autoexposure mode (Tv, on the Mode dial), rotating the Main dial changes the shutter speed. And if you press and hold the Exposure Compensation button, the Exposure Compensation meter becomes highlighted, as shown on the left in Figure 1-15, and you can rotate the Main dial to adjust the setting. Release the button to continue shooting.

In some cases, the camera displays a screen full of options instead of the curved arrows when you press a control button. Pressing the ISO button in the advanced exposure modes, for example, takes you to the screen you see on the right in Figure 1-15. You can then release the button and either rotate the Main dial or use the cross keys to select the setting you want to use. Press the Set button to lock in your choice and bring back the full Shooting Settings display.

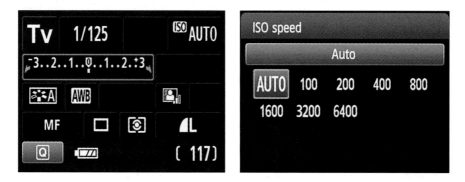

Figure 1-15: Pressing a control button either activates the highlighted setting (left) or takes you to a screen of available settings (right).

Taking advantage of the Quick Control screen

The Quick Control screen enables you to change certain shooting settings without using the control buttons (ISO button, the Exposure Compensation button, and so on) or menus. You can use this technique to adjust settings in any exposure mode, but the settings that are accessible depend on the mode you select. To try it out, set the Mode dial to Tv so that what you see on your screen looks like what you see in the upcoming figures. Then follow these steps:

1. **Display the Shooting Settings screen.**

   Either press the shutter button halfway and then release it, or press the Disp button.

2. **Press the Quick Control button.**

   The screen shifts into Quick Control mode, and one of the options on the screen becomes highlighted. For example, the White Balance option is highlighted on the left in Figure 1-16. A text bar showing the current setting appears at the bottom of the screen for some options.

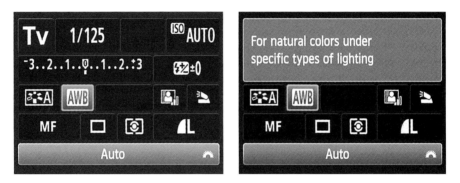

Figure 1-16: Press the Quick Control button to shift to Quick Control mode; the active option appears highlighted.

3. **Press the cross keys to move the highlight over the setting you want to adjust.**

   When you first choose a setting, a little text tip reminds you of the purpose of the active setting, as shown on the right in Figure 1-16.

   If you find the text tips annoying, you can get rid of them by disabling the Feature Guide option on Setup Menu 2.

4. **Adjust the setting.**

   In general, you can use either of these two techniques:

   - Rotate the Main dial to scroll through the possible settings.

   - Press the Set button to display a screen that contains all the possible settings, as shown in Figure 1-17; then rotate the Main dial or use the cross keys to select an option. In some cases, the screen contains a brief explanation or note about the option, as shown in the figure, regardless of the setting of the Feature Guide option. After selecting your choice, press Set again to return to the Quick Control screen.

A few controls require a slightly different approach, but don't worry — I spell out all the needed steps throughout the book.

5. **To exit Quick Control mode, press the shutter button halfway and release it or press the Quick Control button again.**

You're returned to the normal Shooting Settings display.

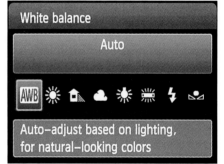

Figure 1-17: From the Quick Control screen, press Set to display all settings available for the currently selected option.

To help you remember which button to press to enter the Quick Control mode, a little Q appears in a blue square in the lower-left corner of the Shooting Settings display. (Refer to the left screen in Figure 1-15.)

Decoding viewfinder data

When the camera is turned on, you can view critical exposure settings and a few other pieces of information in the viewfinder. Just put your eye to the viewfinder and press the shutter button halfway to activate the display.

The viewfinder data changes depending on what action you're undertaking and what exposure mode you're using. For example, if you set the Mode dial to Tv (for shutter-priority autoexposure), you see the basic set of data shown in Figure 1-18: shutter speed, f-stop (aperture setting), Exposure Compensation setting, and ISO setting. Additional data displays when you enable certain features, such as flash.

Again, I detail each viewfinder readout as I explain your camera options throughout the book. But I want to explain now one often-confused value: The number at the far right end of the viewfinder (9, in Figure 1-18) shows you the number of *maximum burst frames*. This number relates to shooting in the Continuous capture mode, where the camera fires off multiple shots in rapid succession as long as you hold down the shutter button. (Chapter 2 has details.) Although the highest number that the viewfinder can display is 9, the actual number of maximum burst frames may be higher. At any rate, you don't really need to pay attention to the number until it starts dropping toward 0, which indicates that the camera's *memory buffer* (its temporary internal data-storage tank) is filling up. If that happens, just give the camera a moment to catch up with your shutter-button finger.

While you're looking through the viewfinder, you can adjust some shooting settings by using the Main dial alone or in conjunction with the function buttons, as you do with the Shooting Settings screen. For example, if you're working in one of the advanced exposure modes (P, Tv, Av, M, or A-DEP) and press the ISO button, all data but the current ISO setting dims, and you can then rotate the Main dial to change the setting. Press the shutter button halfway to return to the normal viewfinder display after changing the setting.

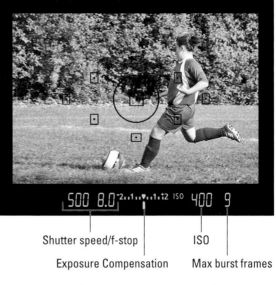

Shutter speed/f-stop   ISO

Exposure Compensation   Max burst frames

Figure 1-18: You also can view some camera information at the bottom of the viewfinder.

Checking the Camera Settings display

In addition to the Shooting Settings display, you can view a collection of additional settings data via the Camera Settings display, as shown in Figure 1-19. This screen is purely an informational tool, however; you can't actually adjust any of the reported settings from this screen.

To display the Camera Settings screen, first display the Shooting Settings display by pressing the shutter button halfway and releasing it or by pressing the Disp button. Then press the Info button.

Figure 1-19 shows the settings that you can monitor when shooting in the advanced exposure modes. Again, that's P, Tv, Av, M, and A-DEP. Here are the details you can glean from the display, with settings listed in the order they appear on the screen.

Freespace	931 MB
Color space	sRGB
WB Shift/BKT	0,0/±0
Live View shoot.	Enable
Enable	Disable
30 sec.	On
Enable	
	03/14/2011 10:09:12

Figure 1-19: Press the Info button when the Shooting Settings screen is active to switch to this screen.

✓ **Freespace:** This value indicates how much storage space is left on your camera memory card. How many pictures you can fit into that space depends on the Quality setting you select. Chapter 2 explains this issue.

✓ **Color Space:** This value tells you whether the camera is capturing images in the sRGB or Adobe RGB color space, an advanced option that you can investigate in Chapter 8.

✓ **White Balance Shift/Bracketing:** Add this to the list of advanced color options covered in Chapter 8.

✓ **Live View Shooting:** Chapter 4 details this feature, which enables you to use your monitor instead of the viewfinder to compose your shots.

✓ **Auto Sensor Cleaning and Red-Eye Reduction flash mode:** (These two functions share a line in the screen.) See the section "Setup Menu 2," later in this chapter, for more about automatic sensor cleaning; check out Chapter 2 for information about Red-Eye Reduction flash mode.

✓ **Auto Power Off and Auto Rotate:** For information on these two settings, which also live together on the display, see the upcoming section, "Setup Menu 1."

✓ **Beep:** The status of this setting tells you whether the camera will beep after certain operations; you can adjust the setting via Shooting Menu 1, as I explain later in this chapter.

✓ **Date/Time:** The section "Setup Menu 2" also explains how to adjust the date and time.

In exposure modes other than P, Tv, Av, M, and A-DEP, the Color Space and White Balance Shift/Bracketing information items don't appear in the Camera Settings display, because those other modes prevent you from adjusting those two features.

Of course, with the exception of the free card space value, you also can simply go to the menu that contains the option in question to check its status. The Camera Settings display just gives you a quick way to monitor some of the critical functions without hunting through menus.

Reviewing Basic Setup Options

One of the many advantages of investing in the Rebel T3i/600D is that you can customize its performance to suit the way *you* like to shoot. Later chapters explain options related to actual picture taking, such as those that affect flash behavior and autofocusing. The rest of this chapter details options related to initial camera setup.

Setup Menu 1

At the risk of being conventional, start your camera customization by opening Setup Menu 1, shown in Figure 1-20.

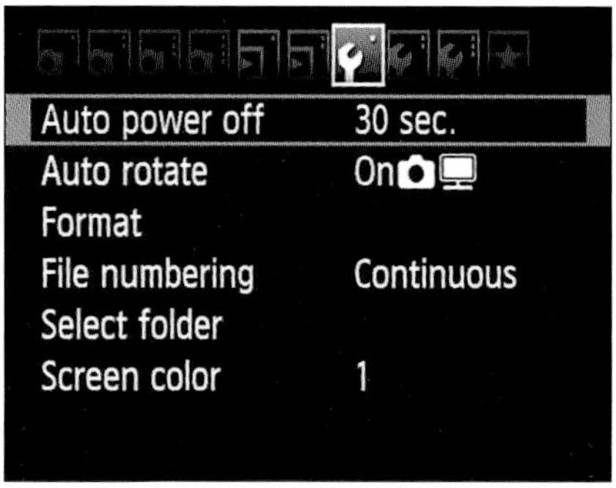

Here's a quick rundown of each menu item:

Auto power off	30 sec.
Auto rotate	On 🅾️ 💻
Format	
File numbering	Continuous
Select folder	
Screen color	1

Figure 1-20: Options on Setup Menu 1 deal mainly with basic camera behavior.

- **Auto Power Off:** To help save battery power, your camera automatically powers down after a certain period of inactivity. By default, the shutdown happens after 30 seconds, but you can change the shutdown delay to 1, 2, 4, 8, or 15 minutes. Or you can disable auto shutdown altogether by selecting the Off setting, although even at that setting, the monitor still turns itself off if you ignore the camera for 30 minutes. Just give the shutter button a quick half-press and release or press the Disp button to bring the monitor out of hibernation.

- **Auto Rotate:** If you enable this feature, your picture files include a piece of data that indicates whether the camera was oriented in the vertical or horizontal position when you shot the frame. Then, when you view the picture on the camera monitor or on your computer, the image is automatically rotated to the correct orientation. Chapter 5 details this playback option, which is enabled by default.

- **Format:** The first time you insert a new memory card, use this option to *format* the card, a maintenance function that wipes out any existing data on the card and prepares it for use by the camera.

If you previously used your card in another device, such as a digital music player, be sure to copy those files to your computer before you format the card. You lose *all* data on the card when you format it, not just picture files.

When you choose the Format option from the menu, you can opt to perform a normal card formatting process or a *low-level* formatting by pressing the Erase button to select the Low Level Format box. This option gives your memory card a deeper level of cleansing than ordinary formatting and thus takes longer to perform. Normally, a regular formatting will do, although performing a low-level formatting can be helpful if your card seems to be running more slowly than usual. However — and this is a however for anyone with a high-security clearance who's shooting pictures that should *never* fall into enemy hands — a regular-level formatting leaves enough bits of data intact that a determined computer wiz could recover your images. To prevent that possibility, do a low-level formatting or crush the card under your heel. Or run over it with your car. You can never be too safe, with all these spies running around looking just like your mild-mannered neighbor.

✔ **File Numbering:** This option controls how the camera names your picture files.

- *Continuous:* This is the default; the camera numbers your files sequentially, from 0001 to 9999, and places all images in the same folder. The initial folder name is 100Canon; when you reach image 9999, the camera creates a new folder, named 101Canon, for your next 9,999 photos. This numbering sequence is retained even if you change memory cards, which helps to ensure that you don't wind up with multiple images that have the same filename.

- *Auto Reset:* If you switch to this option, the camera restarts file numbering at 0001 each time you put in a different memory card or create a new folder, an option discussed next. Enabling this option isn't a good idea, for the reason I stated already.

Beware of one gotcha that applies both to the Continuous and Auto Reset options: If you swap memory cards and the new card already contains images, the camera may pick up numbering from the last image on the new card, which throws a monkey wrench into things. To avoid this problem, format the new card before putting it into the camera.

- *Manual Reset:* Select this setting if you want the camera to begin a new numbering sequence, starting at 0001, for your next shot. The camera then returns to whichever mode you previously used (Continuous or Auto Reset).

✔ **Select Folder:** You need to worry about this option only if your memory card contains more than one image-storage folder. Again, the camera creates folders for you automatically, starting with folder 100Canon and then creating a new folder when the existing one is full. But you can create your own folders, too, by following the instructions laid out in Chapter 11.

If your card does contain multiple folders, use the Select Folder option *before* you begin shooting to tell the camera which folder to use to store your photos.

✔ **Screen Color:** If you don't like the default color scheme of the Shooting Settings display, which is the one used for the screens shown in this book, you can choose from three other schemes via the Screen Color option.

✓ **Eye-Fi Settings:** The T3i/600D works with Eye-Fi memory cards, which are special cards that enable you to transmit images from the camera to the computer over a wireless network. It's a cool option, but the cards themselves are more expensive than regular cards and require some configuring that I don't have room to cover in this book. Additionally, Canon doesn't guarantee that everything will work smoothly with Eye-Fi cards, and directs you to the Eye-Fi support team if you have trouble. All that said, if an Eye-Fi card is installed in the camera, you see this menu option, which leads to some settings that come into play for the image-transmission process. When no Eye-Fi card is installed, the menu option is hidden, as it is in Figure 1-20. For more details, visit www.eye.fi.

Setup Menu 2

Setup Menu 2, posing in Figure 1-21, offers an additional batch of customization options:

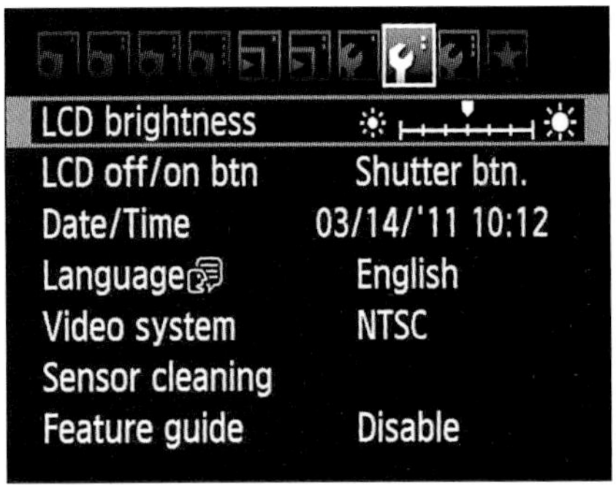

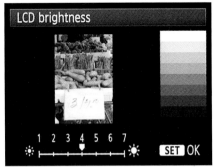

Figure 1-21: Setup Menu 2 offers more ways to customize basic operations.

✓ **LCD Brightness:** This option enables you to make the camera monitor brighter or darker. After highlighting the option on the menu, as shown in Figure 1-21, press the Set button to display a screen similar to what you see in Figure 1-22. The camera displays a picture from your memory card; if the card is empty, you see a black box instead. Press the right and left cross keys to adjust the brightness setting. Press Set to finish the job and return to the menu.

If you take this step, what you see on the display may not be an accurate rendition of the actual exposure of your image. Crank up the monitor brightness, for example, and an underexposed photo may look just fine. So keeping the brightness at its default center position is a good idea unless you're shooting in very bright or dark conditions. As an

Figure 1-22: If you adjust monitor brightness, don't rely on the screen to gauge picture exposure.

alternative, you can gauge exposure when reviewing images by displaying a Brightness histogram, a tool that I explain in Chapter 5.

✔ **LCD Off/On Btn:** This option determines what buttons you press to turn the Shooting Settings display on and off. Your choices are as follows:

- *Shutter btn (button):* At this setting, things work as I describe earlier in this chapter, in the section "Using the Shooting Settings display." The display turns on when you press the shutter button halfway and release it; the display turns off when you press and hold the button halfway. You also can turn the display on and off via the Disp button, but if you use Disp to turn the display off, you have to press that button again to bring the screen back to life.

- *Shutter/Disp:* The display turns off and stays off when you press the shutter button halfway. Press Disp to turn the display on again.

- *Remains on:* The display turns off only when you press Disp. Press the button again to wake the monitor up again.

✔ **Date/Time:** When you turn on your camera for the very first time, it automatically displays this option and asks you to set the date and time.

Keeping the date/time accurate is important because that information is recorded as part of the image file. In your photo browser, you can then see when you shot an image and, equally handy, search for images by the date they were taken. Chapter 6 shows you where to locate the date/time data when browsing your picture files.

✔ **Language:** This option determines the language of any text displayed on the camera monitor. Screens in this book display the English language, but I find it entertaining on occasion to hand the camera to a friend after changing the language to, say, Swedish. Or sometimes if I'm sitting on a plane next to a really nosy but really handsome guy, I set the language to French to make myself seem more exotic. (It helps if the nosy hottie can't really speak French, because about all I can recall from my high-school French class is how to say "Open your French books, please" and "Pierre met Marie at the library.")

If you change the camera language (intentionally or by accident) to something freaky, you'll appreciate the little *speech bubble* next to the Language setting; this bubble helps you find the Language setting — so that you can get back to English — even when you can't read the word for *Language.*

✔ **Video System:** This option is related to viewing your images and movies on a television, a topic I cover in Chapter 5. Select NTSC if you live in North America or other countries that adhere to the NTSC video standard; select PAL for playback in areas that follow that code of video conduct.

✓ **Sensor Cleaning:** Highlight this option and press the Set button to access some options related to the camera's internal sensor-cleaning mechanism. These work like so:

- *Auto Cleaning:* By default, the camera's sensor-cleaning mechanism activates each time you turn the camera on and off. This process helps keep the image sensor — which is the part of the camera that captures the image — free of dust and other particles that can mar your photos. You can disable this option, but it's hard to imagine why you would choose to do so unless you turn your camera on and off a lot between shots, in which case the cleaning routine can get in the way of catching a fleeting moment.

- *Clean Now:* Select this option and press Set to initiate a cleaning cycle.

- *Clean Manually:* In the advanced exposure modes (P, Tv, Av, M, and A-DEP), you can access this third option, which prepares the camera for manual cleaning of the sensor. I don't recommend this practice; sensors are delicate, and you're really better off taking the camera to a good service center for cleaning.

✓ **Feature Guide:** When this option is enabled and you switch exposure modes (via the Mode dial) or choose certain other camera options, little text notes appear on the monitor to explain the feature you're about to use. For example, Figure 1-23 shows the text that appears when you first set the Mode dial to Tv (shutter-priority autoexposure). The guide screens disappear as soon as you press a camera button or rotate the Main dial.

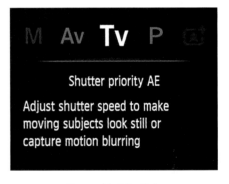

Figure 1-23: To get rid of the Help screens that appear when you select certain camera options, disable the Feature Guide.

Although the Feature Guide screens are helpful at first, having them appear every time you select the options is a pain after you get familiar with your camera. So I leave this option set to Disable — and for the sake of expediency in this book, I assume that you keep the option turned off as well. (If not, just don't be concerned when my instructions don't mention the screens in the course of showing you how to work the camera controls.)

Setup Menu 3

Setup Menu 3, shown in Figure 1-24, contains the following offerings, which you can access only in the advanced exposure modes. Again, those modes are P, Tv, Av, M, and A-DEP. Chapter 7 introduces you to each mode.

Figure 1-24: To display Setup Menu 3, you must set the Mode dial to an advanced exposure mode.

- ✔ **Custom Functions:** Selecting this option opens the door to *Custom Functions,* a set of customization features that either relate to advanced exposure options or are otherwise designed for people with some photography experience. Check this book's index to find out where to locate details about the various functions.

- ✔ **Copyright Information:** Using this menu option, explained in Chapter 11, you can embed your personal copyright information in the image metadata. *Metadata* is invisible text data that doesn't appear on the photo itself but can be read in many photo-viewer programs. Chapter 6 shows you how to view the metadata in the free Canon software that ships with your camera.

- ✔ **Clear Settings:** Via this menu option, you can restore the default shooting settings. You also can reset all the Custom Functions settings to their defaults through this option.

- ✔ **Firmware Ver.:** This screen tells you the version number of the camera firmware (internal operating software). At the time of publication, the current firmware version was 1.0.0.

Keeping your camera firmware up-to-date is important, so visit the Canon website (www.canon.com) regularly to find out whether your camera sports the latest version. Follow the instructions given on the website to download and install updated firmware if needed.

Three more customization options

Shooting Menu 1, shown in Figure 1-25, offers two more basic setup options:

- ✔ **Beep:** By default, your camera beeps after certain operations, such as after it sets focus when you use autofocusing. If you need the camera to hush up, set this option to Off.

✓ **Release Shutter without Card:**
Setting this option to Disable
prevents shutter-button release
when no memory card is in the
camera. If you turn on the option,
you can take a picture and then
review the results for a few seconds in the camera monitor. The
image isn't stored anywhere,
however; it's temporary.

If you're wondering about the
point of this option, it's designed
for use in camera stores, enabling
salespeople to demonstrate
cameras without having to keep

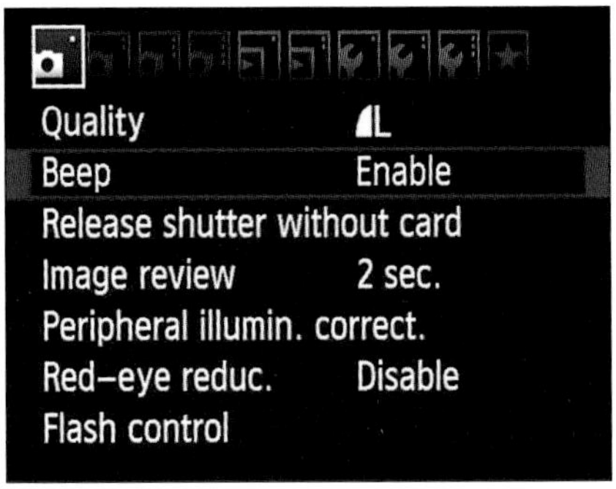

Figure 1-25: You can silence the camera via
Shooting Menu 1.

a memory card in every model. Unless that feature somehow suits your
purposes, keep this option set to Disable.

Why does this camera have two names?

You may notice that your camera manual, as
well as this book, refers to your camera by
two different names — EOS Rebel T3i and EOS
600D. What gives? The answer is that Canon
assigns different names to a single camera
model depending on the part of the world where
it's sold.

The *EOS* part, by the way, stands for Electro
Optical System, the core technology used in

Canon's autofocus SLR (single-lens reflex)
cameras. According to Canon, the proper pro-
nunciation is *EE-ohs,* which is also how you
pronounce the name *Eos,* the goddess of dawn
in Greek mythology.

With apologies to the goddess, I elected to
save a little room in this book by shortening the
camera name to simply T3i/600D.

2

Choosing Basic Picture Settings

In This Chapter

▷ Spinning the Mode dial

▷ Changing the shutter-release mode

▷ Adding flash

▷ Understanding the Quality setting (resolution and file type)

*E*very camera manufacturer strives to provide a good out-of-box experience — that is, to ensure that your first encounter with the camera is a happy one. To that end, the camera's default (initial) settings are selected to make it as easy as possible for you to take a good picture the first time you press the shutter button.

On the T3i/600D, the default settings ensure that the camera works about the same way as any automatic, point-and-shoot camera you may have used in the past: You frame the subject in the viewfinder, press the shutter button halfway to focus, and then press the button the rest of the way to take the shot.

Although you can get a good picture using the default settings in many cases, they're not designed to give you optimal results in every shooting situation. You may be able to use the defaults to take a decent portrait, for example, but will probably need to tweak a few settings to capture fast action. And adjusting a few options can also help you turn that decent portrait into a stunning one, too.

So that you can start fine-tuning camera settings to your subject, this chapter explains the most basic picture-taking options, such as the exposure mode, shutter-release mode (also called Drive mode), and the picture quality. They're not the sexiest or most exciting options to explore (don't think I didn't notice you stifling a yawn), but they make a big difference in how easily you can capture the photo you have in mind.

Choosing an Exposure Mode

The very first picture-taking setting to consider is the exposure mode, which you select via the Mode dial, shown in Figure 2-1. Your choice determines how much control you have over two critical exposure settings — aperture and shutter speed — as well as many other options, including those related to color and flash photography.

Canon categorizes the various exposure modes as follows:

✔ **Basic Zone:** The Basic Zone category includes the following point-and-shoot modes, represented on the Mode dial with the icons shown in the margins:

- *Scene Intelligent Auto:* This is the most basic mode; the camera analyzes the scene in front of the lens, determines what settings would best capture that scene, and then handles everything but framing and focusing for you.

- *Flash Off:* This one works just like Scene Intelligent Auto except that the flash is disabled.

- *Creative Auto:* This mode is like Scene Intelligent Auto on steroids, taking control of most settings but giving you an easy way to tweak some picture qualities, such as how much the background blurs.

- *Image Zone modes:* This subgroup includes five modes that are geared to capturing specific types of scenes:

Portrait, for taking traditional portraits

Landscape, for capturing scenic vistas

Close-up, for shooting flowers and other subjects at close range

Sports, for capturing moving subjects (whether they happen to be playing a sport or not)

Night Portrait, for outdoor photographs of people at night. (Note the star over the person's head in the icon.)

Advanced exposure modes

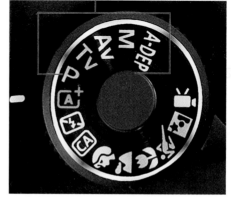

Figure 2-1: Settings on the Mode dial determine the exposure mode.

Chapter 3 tells you more about these modes, but be forewarned: To remain easy to use, all these automatic modes prevent you from taking advantage of most of the camera's exposure, color, and autofocusing controls. You can still adjust the options discussed in this chapter, but the camera takes control of most everything else.

✏ **Creative Zone:** When you're ready to take full control over the camera, step up to one of the Creative Zone modes. This category includes the advanced exposure modes (P, Tv, Av, M, and A-DEP), which I detail in Chapter 7.

✏ **Movie:** Movie mode is outside the zoning limits, because it stands on its own, with no zone moniker. Before you can begin recording a movie or access the movie options on the menus, you must set the dial to this mode. Chapter 4 explains everything you need to know about movie-making with the T3i/600D.

Keeping track of all these *zones* is a little confusing, especially because the modes in the Image Zone category are often referred to generically in photography discussions as *creative scene modes* or *creative modes.* So to keep things a little simpler, I use the generic terms *fully automatic exposure modes* or *point-and-shoot modes* to refer to the Basic Zone modes — because, in a nutshell, that is the type of photography those zones provide — and *advanced exposure modes* to refer to the Creative Zone modes. For Creative Auto mode, which straddles the line between fully automatic and advanced, I use its full name to avoid inserting confusion into the mix. Okay, to avoid inserting any *additional* confusion.

One very important and often misunderstood aspect about all the exposure modes: Although your access to exposure and color controls, as well as to some other advanced camera features, depends on the setting of the Mode dial, it has *no* bearing on your *focusing* choices. You can choose from manual focusing or autofocusing in any mode, assuming that your lens offers auto-focusing. (Chapter 1 shows you how to set the lens to manual or autofocus-ing.) However, access to options that modify how the autofocus system works is limited to the advanced exposure modes.

Changing the Drive Mode

Setting the Drive mode tells the camera what to do when you press the shut-ter button: Record a single frame, record a series of frames, or record one or more shots after a short delay. Your camera offers the following Drive mode settings, which are represented in the camera displays by the symbols you see in the margin:

✔ **Single:** This setting records a single image each time you press the shutter button. In other words, this is normal photography mode. It's the default setting for all exposure modes except Portrait and Sports.

✔ **Continuous:** Sometimes known as *burst mode,* this mode records a continuous series of images as long as you hold down the shutter button. The camera can capture roughly 3.7 frames per second, but your mileage may vary, for the following reasons:

  • The number of frames per second depends in part on your shutter speed. At a slow shutter speed, the camera may not be able to reach the maximum frame rate. (See Chapter 7 for an explanation of shutter speed.)

  • Some other functions can slow down the continuous capture rate. For example, when you use flash, the frame rate slows because the flash needs time to recycle between shots. Enabling the High ISO Noise Reduction feature (explained in Chapter 7) also typically prevents you from achieving the highest burst rate. Finally, the speed of your memory card also plays a role in how fast the camera can transfer data to the card, which in turn affects the burst rate. In other words, consider 3.7 shots per second a best-case scenario.

Continuous Drive mode is the default setting for Portrait and Sports modes. Having continuous capture available for portraits may seem odd, but it can actually help you capture the perfect expression on your subject's face — or, at least, a moment between blinks! (But if you use flash for your portrait, keep the previous tip in mind.)

✔ **Self-Timer: 10 second/remote control:** Want to put yourself in the picture? Select this mode, depress the shutter button, and run into the frame. You have 10 seconds to get yourself in place and pose before the image is recorded.

You can also use the self-timer function to avoid any possibility of camera shake. The mere motion of pressing the shutter button can cause slight camera movement, which can blur an image. Put the camera on a tripod and then activate the self-timer function. This enables "hands-free" — and therefore motion-free — picture taking. This is great for close-up or macro work in which camera shake is magnified. Anything that magnifies the subject also magnifies camera shake, including the use of telephoto lenses and shooting close-ups, where small subjects are rendered large on the sensor.

As an alternative, you can trigger the shutter release with either a wireless remote control or one that plugs into the remote-control terminal on the left side of the camera. (If you don't buy a remote made by Canon, be sure that it's compatible with your camera.) Set the Drive mode to this option when using a remote control. (For some remotes, you also may be able to use the following two self-timer settings; check your remote's instruction manual to find out which options work with the unit.)

$\circlearrowright_2$ ✏ **Self-Timer: 2 second:** This mode works just like the regular Self-Timer mode, but the capture happens just two seconds after you fully press the shutter button. Unfortunately, this mode is available only in the P, Tv, Av, M, or A-DEP exposure modes.

$\circlearrowright_C$ ✏ **Self-Timer: Continuous:** With this option, the camera waits 10 seconds after you press the shutter button and then captures a continuous series of images. You can set the camera to record 2 to 10 images per each shutter release.

You can check the current Drive mode on the Shooting Settings screen. The icon representing the Drive mode appears in a different area depending on your exposure mode; the left screen in Figure 2-2 shows you where to look when shooting in Scene Intelligent Auto, for example, and the right screen shows where the icon hangs out when the Mode dial is set to one of the advanced exposure modes.

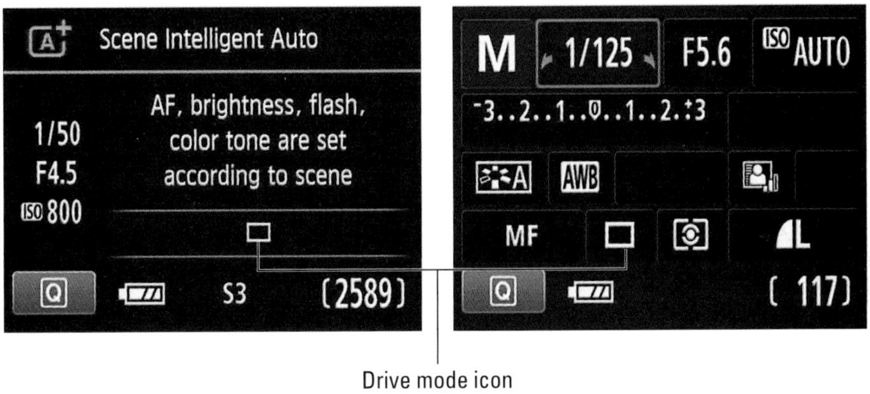

Drive mode icon

Figure 2-2: The Shooting Settings screen displays an icon indicating the current Drive mode.

To change the Drive mode, you have two options:

✏ **Press the left cross key.** Notice that the key is marked by three little Drive mode icons to help you remember its function, as shown on the left in Figure 2-3. After you press the cross key, you see the screen shown on the right in the figure. Highlight your choice and press Set.

For the Self-Timer: Continuous mode, selected in the right screen of Figure 2-3, press the up or down cross key to set the number of continuous shots you want the camera to capture.

✔ **Use the Quick Control screen.** You also can adjust the Drive mode via the Quick Control screen. After you highlight the Drive mode icon, the name of the current setting appears at the bottom of the screen, as shown in Figure 2-4. Rotate the Main dial to cycle through the available Drive mode settings. Or press Set to access the selection screen shown on the right in Figure 2-3. (See Chapter 1 if you need help using the Quick Control screen.)

Press to access Drive mode settings

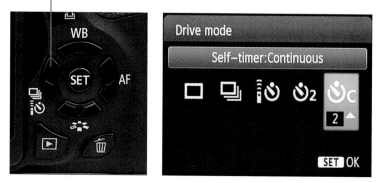

Figure 2-3: The fastest way to get to the Drive mode setting is to press the left cross key.

Whichever route you go to change the Drive mode, remember these key points:

✔ **To access all Drive modes, you must use the P, Tv, Av, M, or A-DEP exposure mode.** In Creative Auto mode, you lose the 2-second self-timer option. And in all the other exposure modes, you get only the default Drive mode — either Single or Continuous — plus the 10-second and continuous self-timer options.

Figure 2-4: But you also can change the setting via the Quick Control screen.

✏ **Check the Drive mode before each shoot.** Your selected Drive mode remains in force until you change it or switch to an exposure mode for which the selected Drive mode isn't available. So put this setting on the list of options to review every time you set out with your camera.

✏ **Cover the viewfinder for self-timer or remote shooting.** Any time you take a picture without your eye to the viewfinder, light can seep in through the viewfinder and mess with exposure metering. For that reason, Canon includes a little viewfinder cover on the camera strap. Chapter 4 shows you how to install the cover, which is also recommended for Live View shooting.

✏ **To cancel self-timer shooting after the countdown starts, press the Drive mode button (left cross key).** If you're like me, though, the camera will take the shot long before you remember this trick. Well, no worries — that's why the camera has an Erase button.

✏ **Consider using Mirror Lock-Up for long exposures.** Although using the self-timer or remote-control Drive modes to shoot "hands-free" ensures that the action of pressing the shutter button doesn't shake the camera enough to blur the photo, you can add another layer of security by enabling Mirror Lock-Up.

Here's the deal: The camera's optical assembly includes a little mirror whose job it is to reflect the scene coming through the lens onto the viewfinder. When you press the shutter button, the mirror moves out of the optical path so that the scene can be recorded by the image sensor. With a long exposure time, the mirror action can be enough to create a slight blur, so the camera enables you to delay the shutter release until after the mirror movement is complete. This feature, called Mirror Lock-Up, requires a special shooting technique; Chapter 11 provides details.

Using the Flash

The built-in flash on your camera offers an easy, convenient way to add light to a too-dark scene. But whether you can use flash — or opt to go flash-free — depends on your exposure mode, as outlined in the next few sections.

Before you skip off to digest that information, note these universal tips:

✏ **The viewfinder offers two cues regarding flash status.** A little lightning bolt in the lower-left corner of Figure 2-5 tells you that the flash is enabled. The word "Busy" along with the lightning bolt means that the flash needs a few moments to recharge. When the flash is ready to go, the "Busy" message disappears. Flash recycling status also appears on the monitor.

✓ **The effective range of the built-in flash is about 16 feet.** If you need to illuminate a subject that's farther away, you'll have to attach an external flash head.

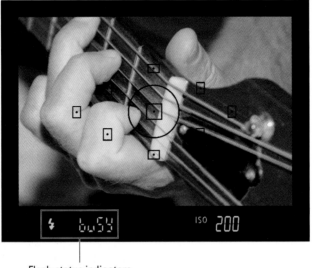

Flash status indicators

Figure 2-5: A Busy signal means that the flash is recharging.

Using flash in the fully automatic modes

In the following exposure modes, you have zero control over whether the flash fires. And whether flash is even a possibility depends on the exposure mode. Here's how things shake out:

✓ **Scene Intelligent Auto, Portrait, Close-up, and Night Portrait:** If the camera thinks extra light is needed, it automatically raises and fires the built-in flash. Otherwise, the flash remains closed, and nothing you can do will coax it out of its cave.

If flash is available, you have the option of enabling Red-Eye Reduction flash, which is designed to help eliminate those "devil eyes" that often plague flash portraits. You can find details on the pros and cons of that option a little later in this chapter.

✓ **Landscape, Sports, and Flash Off modes:** Flash is disabled.

Disabling flash in the Flash Off mode makes sense, of course. But why no flash in Sports and Landscape mode, you ask? Well, Sports mode is designed to enable you to capture moving subjects, and the flash can make that more difficult because it needs time to recycle between shots. On top of that, the maximum shutter speed that's possible with the built-in flash is 1/200 second, which often isn't fast enough to ensure a blur-free subject. Finally, action photos usually aren't taken at a range close enough for the flash to reach the subject, which is also the reason why flash is disabled for Landscape mode.

Using flash in Creative Auto mode

 Although Creative Auto mode is like Scene Intelligent Auto in many respects, it gives you some input over various picture characteristics, including whether flash is used. In fact, you can choose from three flash modes:

 ✓ **Auto flash:** The camera decides when to fire the flash, basing its decision on the lighting conditions.

✓ **On:** The flash fires regardless of the lighting conditions. You may hear this flash mode referred to as _force_ flash because the camera is forced to trigger the flash even if its exposure brain says there's plenty of ambient light. This flash mode is sometimes also called _fill_ flash because it's designed to fill in shadows that can occur even in bright light. Whatever you call it, this option causes the built-in flash to pop up as soon as you press the shutter button halfway. The flash will continue to fire for all subsequent shots until you change the flash mode to Auto or Off.

✓ **Off:** The flash does not fire, no way, no how. Even if the built-in flash is raised because you used it on the previous shot, it still won't fire until you shift the flash mode to Auto or On. (If you're not planning to use the flash, just press it down gently to close it.)

You can view the current flash setting in the Shooting Settings screen, which appears as shown in Figure 2-6 in the Creative Auto exposure mode. (Chapter 3 explains the other stuff you see on the screen.)

To change the flash mode, press the Quick Control button and navigate to the flash setting, as shown on the left in Figure 2-7. Then press Set to display a screen showing all three flash options, as shown on the right in the figure. Select your choice and press Set again.

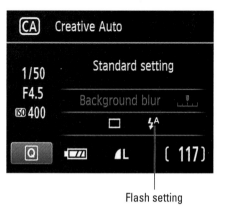

Figure 2-6: In Creative Auto mode, use the Quick Control screen to set the flash to Auto, On, or Off firing modes.

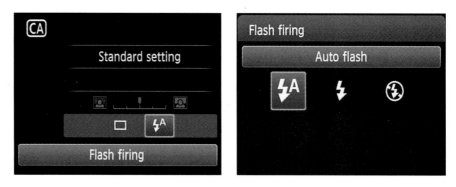

Figure 2-7: Use the Quick Control screen to change the flash setting.

If you use flash, also see the upcoming section related to Red-Eye Reduction flash, which may improve flash portraits.

Enabling flash in the advanced exposure modes

 In the P, Tv, Av, M, and A-DEP modes, you don't choose from the Auto, On, and Off flash modes available in Creative Auto mode. Instead, if you want to use the built-in flash, you simply press the Flash button on the side of the camera. (Refer to Figure 2-8.) The flash unit pops up, and the flash fires on your next shot. Don't want flash? Just close the flash unit. There is no such thing as auto flash in these exposure modes — but don't worry, because using flash (or not) is one picture-taking setting you definitely want to control, for reasons you can explore in Chapter 7.

You do, however, have access to several flash options that aren't available in the fully automatic exposure modes or Creative Auto mode. Until you're ready to dig into all those features — again, head to Chapter 7 to explore them — just make sure that when you enable the flash, the Quick Control screen displays a Built-in Flash Function symbol that looks like the one shown

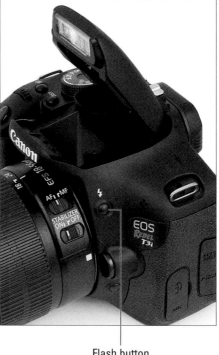

Flash button

Figure 2-8: In the advanced exposure modes, press the Flash button to raise the built-in flash.

in Figure 2-9. That symbol — note that it doesn't appear until you raise the flash — represents the Normal flash firing setting. If another symbol appears, use the Quick Settings screen to select the Normal setting; the other two options set the flash to trigger off-camera flash units.

Using Red-Eye Reduction flash

Red-eye is caused when flash light bounces off a subject's retinas and is reflected back to the camera lens. Red-eye is a human phenomenon, though; with animals, the reflected light usually glows yellow, white, or green.

Built-in Flash Function setting

Figure 2-9: Select this option unless you want to use the built-in flash as a wireless trigger for other flash units.

Man or beast, this issue isn't nearly the problem with the type of pop-up flash found on your T3i/600D as it is on non-SLR cameras. Your camera's flash is positioned above the lens, a position that lessens the chances of red-eye. However, red-eye may still be an issue when you use a lens with a long focal length (a telephoto lens) or you shoot subjects from a distance.

If you do notice red-eye in your flash photos, you can try enabling Red-Eye Reduction flash. When you turn on this feature, the Red-Eye Reduction Lamp on the front of the camera lights up when you press the shutter button halfway. The purpose of this light is to attempt to shrink the subject's pupils, which helps reduce the amount of light that enters the eye and, thus, the chances of that light reflecting and causing red-eye. The flash itself fires when you press the shutter button the rest of the way. (Be sure to warn your subjects to wait for the flash, or they may step out of the frame or stop posing after they see the light from the Red-Eye Reduction Lamp.)

You can enable this feature in any exposure mode that permits flash. The control for turning it on and off lives on Shooting Menu 1, as shown in Figure 2-10.

Quality	▪L
Beep	Enable
Release shutter without card	
Image review	2 sec.
Peripheral illumin. correct.	
Red−eye reduc.	Disable
Flash control	

Figure 2-10: Turn Red-Eye Reduction flash mode on and off via Shooting Menu 1.

The viewfinder and Shooting Settings display don't offer any indication that Red-Eye Reduction is enabled. The Camera Settings screen shows the current status, however; look for the little eyeball icon and the word *Enable* or *Disable,* shown in Figure 2-11. You can get to this screen by displaying the Shooting Settings screen and then pressing the Info button — but frankly, I find it just as easy to check the feature status on Shooting Menu 1.

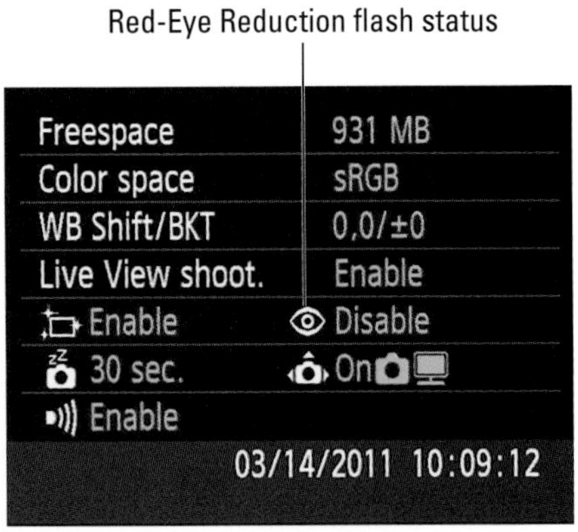

Red-Eye Reduction flash status

Freespace	931 MB
Color space	sRGB
WB Shift/BKT	0,0/±0
Live View shoot.	Enable
⌂ Enable	◉ Disable
⏲ 30 sec.	🗗 On📷🖥
�))) Enable	
	03/14/2011 10:09:12

TIP

After you press the shutter button halfway in Red-Eye Reduction flash mode, a row of vertical bars appears in the center of the viewfinder display,

Figure 2-11: You can view the Red-Eye Reduction status in the Camera Settings screen as well as on Shooting Menu 1.

just to the left of the ISO value. A few moments later, the bars turn off one by one. For best results, wait until all the bars are off to take the picture. (The delay gives the subject's pupils time to constrict in response to the Red-Eye Reduction Lamp.)

Controlling Picture Quality

Almost every review of the T3i/600D contains glowing reports about the camera's top-notch picture quality. As you've no doubt discovered for yourself, those claims are true: This baby can create large, beautiful images.

Getting the maximum output from your camera, however, depends on choosing the right capture settings. Chief among them is the appropriately named Quality setting. This critical control determines two important aspects of your pictures: *resolution,* or pixel count; and *file format,* which refers to the type of computer file the camera uses to store your picture data.

Resolution and file format both play a large role in the quality of your photos, so selecting from the Quality settings on your camera is an important decision. Why not just dial in the setting that produces the maximum quality level and be done with it? Well, that's the right choice for some photographers. But because choosing that maximum setting has some disadvantages, you may find that stepping down a notch or two on the quality scale is a better option, at least for some pictures.

To help you figure out which Quality setting meets your needs, the rest of this chapter explains exactly how resolution and file format affect your pictures. Just in case you're having quality problems related to other issues, though, the following section provides a handy defect-diagnosis guide.

Diagnosing quality problems

When I use the term *picture quality,* I'm not talking about the composition, exposure, or other traditional characteristics of a photograph. Instead, I'm referring to how finely the image is rendered in the digital sense.

Figure 2-12 illustrates the concept: The first example is a high-quality image, with clear details and smooth color transitions. The other examples show five common digital-image defects. Each defect is related to a different issue, and only two are affected by the Quality setting. So if you aren't happy with your image quality, first compare your photos with those in the figure to properly diagnose the problem. Then try these remedies:

High quality   Pixelation   JPEG artifacts

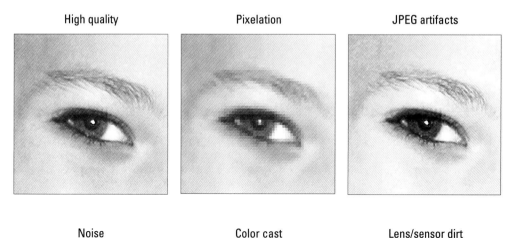

Noise   Color cast   Lens/sensor dirt

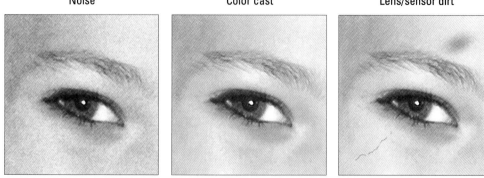

Figure 2-12: Refer to this symptom guide to determine the cause of poor image quality.

✔ **Pixelation:** When an image doesn't have enough *pixels* (the colored tiles used to create digital images), details aren't clear, and curved and diagonal lines appear jagged. The fix is to increase image resolution, which you do via the Quality setting. See the upcoming section, "Considering Resolution: Large, Medium, or Small?" for details.

✔ **JPEG artifacts:** The "parquet tile" texture and random color defects that mar the third image in Figure 2-12 can occur in photos captured in the JPEG *(JAY-peg)* file format, which is why these flaws are referred to as *JPEG artifacts.* This defect is also related to the Quality setting; see the "Understanding File Type (JPEG or Raw)" section, later in this chapter, to find out more.

✔ **Noise:** This defect gives your image a speckled look, as shown in the lower-left example in Figure 2-12. Noise is most often caused by a high ISO setting (an exposure control) or by long exposure times (shutter speeds longer than one second). Chapter 7 explores these topics in detail.

✔ **Color cast:** If your colors are seriously out of whack, as shown in the lower-middle example in Figure 2-12, try adjusting the camera's White Balance setting. Chapter 8 covers this control and other color issues.

✔ **Lens/sensor dirt:** A dirty lens is the first possible cause of the kind of defects you see in the last example in Figure 2-12. If cleaning your lens doesn't solve the problem, dust or dirt may have made its way onto the camera's image sensor.

Your T3i/600D offers an automated, internal sensor-cleaning mechanism. (Chapter 1 has details.) But if you frequently change lenses in a dirty environment, the internal cleaning mechanism may not be adequate, in which case a manual sensor cleaning is necessary. You can do this job yourself, but I don't recommend it. Image sensors are pretty delicate, and you can easily damage them or other parts of your camera if you aren't careful. Instead, find a local camera store that offers this service. In my area (central Indiana), sensor cleaning costs between $30–$50.

One important point regarding Figure 2-12: I took some mild image-processing liberties to exaggerate the flaws in the examples to make the symptoms easier to see. With the exception of an unwanted color cast or a big blob of lens or sensor dirt, these defects may not even be noticeable unless you print or view your image at a very large size. And the subject matter of your image may camouflage some flaws; most people probably wouldn't detect a little JPEG artifacting in a photograph of a densely wooded forest, for example.

In other words, don't consider Figure 2-12 as an indication that your camera is suspect in the image quality department. First, *any* digital camera can produce these defects under the right circumstances. Second, by following the guidelines in this chapter and the others mentioned in the preceding list, you can resolve any quality issues that you may encounter.

Decoding the Quality options

Your camera's Quality setting determines both the image resolution and file format of the pictures you shoot. Your options for changing the setting depend on your exposure mode, as follows:

- ✔ **Quick Control screen (P, Tv, Av, M, and A-DEP modes only):** After highlighting the setting, as shown on the left in Figure 2-13, rotate the Main dial to cycle through the available Quality settings. (The current setting appears in the text bar at the bottom of the screen.) Or if you prefer, press the Set button to display the screen shown on the right in Figure 2-13, which contains all the possible Quality options. Rotate the Main dial or press the right/left cross keys to select a setting; then press Set to exit the screen.

- ✔ **Shooting Menu 1 (any exposure mode):** You also can adjust the Quality setting through this menu, as illustrated in Figure 2-14.

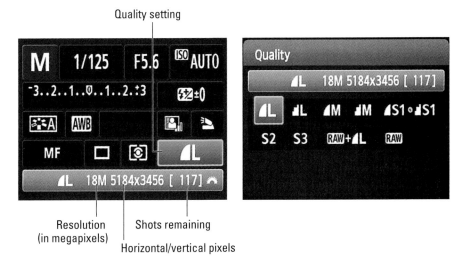

Quality setting

Resolution (in megapixels)   Shots remaining

Horizontal/vertical pixels

Figure 2-13: In the advanced exposure modes, you can change the Quality setting via the Quick Control screen.

If you're new to digital photography, the Quality settings won't make much sense to you until you read the rest of this chapter, which explains format and resolution in detail. But even if you're schooled in those topics, you may need some help deciphering the way that the settings are represented on your camera. As you can see from Figures 2-13 and 2-14, the options are presented in rather cryptic fashion, so here's your decoder ring:

Figure 2-14: You also can select the Quality option via Shooting Menu 1.

✔ At the bottom of the Quick Settings screen, you see three bits of information about the current Quality setting, as labeled in Figure 2-13: the *resolution,* or total pixel count (measured in megapixels), the horizontal and vertical pixel count, and the number of subsequent shots you can fit on your current memory card if you select that Quality setting. (The Main dial icon to the right of the Quality settings is a reminder to use that dial to change settings.) The next section explains pixels and megapixels.

✔ This same informational bar (less the Main dial icon) appears at the top of the screen when you change the setting via Shooting Menu 1 or press Set after highlighting the Quality option on the Quick Settings screen. (See the right screens in Figures 2-13 and 2-14.) The next two rows of both screens show icons representing the eight Quality settings.

✔ The settings marked with the little arc symbols capture images in the JPEG file format, as do the S2 and S3 settings. The arc icons represent the level of JPEG *compression,* which affects picture quality and file size. You get two JPEG options: Fine and Normal. The smooth arcs represent the Fine setting; the jagged arcs represent the Normal setting. Both S2 and S3 use the JPEG Fine recording option. And no, I don't know why they don't sport the arc icons — maybe the arc-supplier guy was sick the day that S2 and S3 got added to the Quality mix. At any rate, check out the upcoming section "JPEG: The imaging (and web) standard" for details about all things JPEG.

✔ Within the JPEG category, you can choose from five resolution settings, represented by L, M, and S1, S2, and S3 *(large, medium,* and *small, smaller, smallest).* See the next section for information that helps you select the right resolution.

✓ You also can capture images in the Raw file format. All Raw files are created at the Large resolution setting, giving you the maximum pixel count. One of the two Raw settings also records a JPEG Fine version of the image, also at the maximum (Large) resolution. The upcoming section "Raw (CR2): The purist's choice" explains the benefits and downsides to using the Raw format.

Which Quality option is best depends on several factors, including how you plan to use your pictures and how much time you care to spend processing your images on your computer. The rest of this chapter explains these and other issues related to the Quality settings.

Considering Resolution: Large, Medium, or Small?

To decide upon a Quality setting, the first decision you need to make is how many pixels you want your image to contain. *Pixels* are the little square tiles from which all digital images are made; *pixel* is short for *pic*ture *el*ement. You can see some pixels close up in the right image in Figure 2-15, which shows a greatly magnified view of the eye area in the left image. (If your photo viewer has a zoom tool that enables you to greatly magnify an image, you can inspect the pixels in your own photos.)

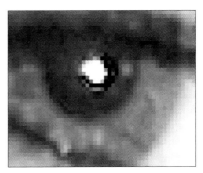

Figure 2-15: Pixels are the building blocks of digital photos.

The number of pixels in an image is referred to as its *resolution*. Your camera offers five resolution levels, which are assigned the generic labels Large, Medium, and Small (1–3) and are represented on the list of Quality settings by the initials L, M, and S (1–3). Table 2-1 shows you the pixel count that results from each option. (If you select Raw as your Quality setting, images are always captured at the Large resolution value.)

Table 2-1	The Resolution Side of the Quality Settings	
Symbol	*Setting*	*Pixel Count*
L	Large	5184 x 3456 (18 MP)
M	Medium	3456 x 2304 (8 MP)
S1	Small 1	2592 x 1728 (4.5 MP)
S2	Small 2	1920 x 1280 (2.5 MP)
S3	Small 3	720 x 480 (0.35 MP)

In the table, the first pair of numbers shown for each setting in the Pixel Count column represents the image *pixel dimensions* — that is, the number of horizontal pixels and the number of vertical pixels. The values in parentheses indicate the total resolution, which you get by multiplying the horizontal and vertical pixel values. This number is usually stated in *megapixels,* or MP for short. The camera displays the resolution value using only one letter M, however. (Refer to Figures 2-13 and 2-14.) Either way, 1 MP equals 1 million pixels.

To choose the right setting, you need to understand the three ways that pixel count affects your pictures:

✓ **Print size:** Pixel count determines the size at which you can produce a high-quality print. If you don't have enough pixels, your prints may exhibit the defects you see in the pixelation example in Figure 2-12, or worse, you may be able to see the individual pixels, as in the right example in Figure 2-15.

How many pixels you need depends on your photo printer, but a good minimum threshold is 200 pixels per linear inch, or *ppi,* of the print. To produce an 8 x 10 print at 200 ppi, for example, you need a pixel count of 1600 x 2000, or just less than 2 MP. For professional publication, you may be required to submit photos at a higher ppi — the publishers of this book, for example, require 300-ppi images. If you're printing your own photos, experiment to see whether you get better results at a higher ppi; in some cases, you won't see any difference at all.

Even though many photo-editing programs enable you to add pixels to an existing image, doing so isn't a good idea. For reasons I won't bore you with, adding pixels — known as *upsampling* — doesn't enable you to successfully enlarge your photo. In fact, resampling typically makes matters worse. The printing discussion in Chapter 6 includes some example images that illustrate this issue.

✔ **Screen display size:** Resolution doesn't affect the quality of images viewed on a monitor, television, or other screen device the way it does for printed photos. Instead, resolution determines the *size* at which the image appears. This issue is one of the most misunderstood aspects of digital photography, so I explain it thoroughly in Chapter 6. For now, just know that you need *way* fewer pixels for onscreen photos than you do for printed photos. In fact, the smallest resolution setting available on your camera, 720 x 480 pixels (S3), is plenty for e-mail sharing.

✔ **File size:** Every additional pixel increases the amount of data required to create a digital picture file. So a higher-resolution image has a larger file size than a low-resolution image.

Large files present several problems:

• You can store fewer images on your memory card, your computer's hard drive, and removable storage media such as a CD-ROM.

• The camera needs more time to process and store the image data on the memory card after you press the shutter button. This extra time can hamper fast-action shooting.

• When you share photos online, larger files take longer to upload and download.

• When you edit your photos in your photo software, your computer needs more resources and time to process large files.

As you can see, resolution is a bit of a sticky wicket. What if you aren't sure how large you want to print your images? What if you want to print your photos *and* share them online? I take the better-safe-than-sorry route, which leads to the following recommendations about which resolution setting to use:

✔ **Always shoot at a resolution suitable for print.** You then can create a low-resolution copy of the image for use online. In fact, your camera has a built-in Resize tool that can do the job for you. Chapter 6 shows you how to use that feature as well as the resizing option found in the free Canon photo software.

✔ **For everyday images, Medium is a good choice.** Keep in mind that even at the Medium setting, your pixel count (3456 x 2304) is far more than you need to produce an 8 x 10" print at 200 ppi, and almost exactly what you need for an 8 x 10" print at 300 ppi.

✔ **Choose Large for an image that you plan to crop, print very large, or both.** The benefit of maxing out resolution is that you have the flexibility to crop your photo and still generate a decent-sized print of the remaining image. Figure 2-16 offers an example. I wanted to fill the frame with the butterfly, but couldn't do so without getting so close that I risked scaring it away. So I kept my distance and took the picture at the Large setting, resulting in the composition shown on the left in the figure. Because I had oodles of pixels in that photo, I could crop it and still have enough pixels left to produce a great print, as you see in the right image. In fact, I could have printed it at a much larger size than you see here, but then I would have had to cut some of my fascinating prose, which is simply too painful to consider. For me, anyway.

How many pictures fit on my memory card?

Image resolution (pixel count) and file format (JPEG or Raw) together contribute to the size of the picture file which, in turn, determines how many photos fit in a given amount of camera memory. The following table shows you the approximate size of the files, in megabytes (MB), that are generated at each of the possible resolution/format combinations on your T3i/600D. (The actual file size of any image also depends on other factors, such as the subject, ISO setting, and Picture Style setting.) In the Image Capacity column, you see approximately how many pictures you can store at the setting on a 4GB (gigabyte) memory card.

Picture Capacity of a 4GB Memory Card			
Symbol	**Quality Setting**	**File Size**	**Image Capacity**
◢L	Large/Fine	6.4MB	570
◢L	Large/Normal	3.2MB	1120
◢M	Medium/Fine	3.4MB	1070
◢M	Medium/Normal	1.7MB	2100
◢S1	Small 1/Fine	2.2MB	1670
◢S1	Small 1/Normal	1.1MB	3180
S2	Small 2/Fine	1.3MB	2780
S3	Small 3/Fine	0.3MB	10780
RAW	Raw	24.5MB	150
RAW ◢L	Raw+Large/Fine	30.9MB*	110

Combined size of the two files produced at this setting.

Figure 2-16: When you can't get close enough to fill the frame with the subject, capture the image at the Large resolution setting and crop later.

Understanding File Type (JPEG or Raw)

In addition to establishing the resolution of your photos, the Quality setting determines the *file type*, which simply refers to the type of image file that the camera produces. Your T3i/600D offers two file types — JPEG and Raw (sometimes seen as *raw* or *RAW)*, with a couple variations of each. The next sections explain the pros and cons of each setting.

File type is also sometimes referred to as file *format.* Don't confuse that use of the word with the Format option on Setup Menu 1, which erases all data on your memory card.

JPEG: The imaging (and web) standard

This format is the default setting on your camera, as it is for most digital cameras. JPEG is popular for two main reasons:

- **Immediate usability:** JPEG is a longtime standard format for digital photos. All web browsers and e-mail programs can display JPEG files, so you can share them online immediately after you shoot them. You also can get JPEG photos printed at any retail outlet, whether it's an online or a local printer. Additionally, any program that has photo capabilities, from photo-editing programs to word-processing programs, can handle your files.

- **Small files:** JPEG files are smaller than Raw files. And smaller files mean that your pictures consume less room on your camera memory card and on your computer's hard drive.

The downside — you knew there had to be one — is that JPEG creates smaller files by applying *lossy compression.* This process actually throws away some image data. Too much compression leads to the defects you see in the JPEG artifacts example in Figure 2-12, earlier in this chapter.

On your camera, the amount of compression that's applied depends on whether you choose a Quality setting that carries the label Fine or Normal. The difference between the two breaks down as follows:

- **Fine:** At this setting, very little compression is applied, so you shouldn't see many compression artifacts, if any. Canon uses the symbol that appears in the margin here to indicate the Fine compression level; how-ever, the S2 and S3 settings both use the Fine level even though they don't sport the symbol.

- **Normal:** Switch to Normal, and the compression amount rises, as does the chance of seeing some artifacting. Notice the jaggedy-ness of the Normal icon, as shown in the margin? That's your reminder that all may not be "smooth" sailing when you choose a Normal setting.

Note, though, that even the Normal setting doesn't result in anywhere near the level of artifacting that you see in the example in Figure 2-12. Again, that example is exaggerated to help you recognize artifacting defects and under-stand how they differ from other image-quality issues. In fact, if you keep your image print or display size small, you aren't likely to notice a great deal of quality difference between the Fine and Normal compression levels. The differences become apparent only when you greatly enlarge a photo.

Given that the differences between Fine and Normal aren't all that easy to spot until you really enlarge the photo, is it okay to shift to Normal and enjoy the benefits of smaller files? Well, only you can decide what level of quality your pictures demand. For most photographers, the added file sizes produced by the Fine setting aren't a huge concern, given that the prices of memory cards fall all the time. Long-term storage is more of an issue; the larger your files, the faster you fill your computer's hard drive and the more DVDs or CDs you need for archiving purposes. But in the end, I prefer to take the storage hit in exchange for the lower compression level of the Fine set-ting. You never know when a casual snapshot is going to be so great that you want to print or display it large enough that even minor quality loss becomes a concern. And of all the defects that you can correct in a photo editor, arti-facting is one of the hardest to remove. So I stick with Fine when shooting in the JPEG format.

To make the best decision, do your own test shots, carefully inspect the results in your photo editor, and make your own judgment about what level of artifacting you can accept. Artifacting is often much easier to spot when you view images onscreen. It's difficult to reproduce artifacting here in print because the printing press obscures some of the tiny defects caused by compression. Your inkjet prints are more likely to reveal these defects.

If you don't want *any* risk of artifacting, bypass JPEG altogether and change the file type to Raw (CR2). Or consider your other option, which is to record two versions of each file, one Raw and one JPEG. The next section offers details.

Raw (CR2): The purist's choice

The other picture-file type that you can create on your T3i/600D is *Camera Raw,* or just *Raw* (as in, uncooked) for short.

Each manufacturer has its own flavor of Raw files; Canon's are CR2 files (or, on some older cameras, CRW). You'll see that three-letter designation at the end of your picture filenames on your computer.

Raw is popular with advanced, very demanding photographers, for two reasons:

- **Greater creative control:** With JPEG, internal camera software tweaks your images, adjusting color, exposure, and sharpness as needed to produce the results that Canon believes its customers prefer (or according to settings you chose). With Raw, the camera simply records the original, unprocessed image data. The photographer then copies the image file to the computer and uses special software known as a *raw converter* to produce the actual image, making decisions about color, exposure, and so on, at that point. The upshot is that "shooting Raw" enables you, not the camera, to have the final say on the visual characteristics of your image.

- **Higher bit depth:** *Bit depth* is a measure of how many distinct color values an image file can contain. JPEG files restrict you to 8 bits each for the red, blue, and green color components, or *channels,* that make up a digital image, for a total of 24 bits. That translates to roughly 16.7 million possible colors. On the EOS T3i/600D, a Raw file delivers a higher bit count, collecting 14 bits per channel.

  Although jumping from 8 to 14 bits sounds like a huge difference, you may not really ever notice any difference in your photos — that 8-bit palette of 16.7 million values is more than enough for superb images. Where having the extra bits can come in handy is if you really need to adjust exposure, contrast, or color after the shot in your photo-editing program. In cases where you apply extreme adjustments, having the extra original bits sometimes helps avoid a problem known as *banding* or *posterization,* which creates abrupt color breaks where you should see smooth, seamless transitions. (A higher bit depth doesn't always prevent the problem, however, so don't expect miracles.)

✔ **Best picture quality:** Because Raw doesn't apply the destructive compression associated with JPEG, you don't run the risk of the artifacting that can occur with JPEG.

But of course, as with most things in life, Raw isn't without its disadvantages. To wit:

✔ **You can't do much with your pictures until you process them in a Raw converter.** You can't share them online, for example, or put them into a text document or multimedia presentation. You can print them immediately if you use the Canon-provided software, but most other photo programs require you to convert the Raw files to a standard format first. Ditto for retail photo printing. So when you shoot Raw, you add to the time you must spend in front of the computer instead of behind the camera lens. Chapter 6 gets you started processing your Raw files using your Canon software.

✔ **Raw files are larger than comparable JPEGs.** Unlike JPEGs, Raw doesn't apply lossy compression to shrink files. This means that Raw files are significantly larger than JPEGs, so they take up more room on your memory card and on your computer's hard drive or other picture-storage devices.

Whether the upside of Raw outweighs the down is a decision that you need to ponder based on your photographic needs, schedule, and computer-comfort level. If you decide to try Raw shooting, you can select from the following Quality options:

✔ **RAW:** This setting produces a single Raw file at the maximum resolution (18 MP).

✔ **RAW+Large/Fine:** This setting produces two files: the Raw file plus a JPEG file captured at the Large/Fine setting. The advantage is that you can share the JPEG online or get prints made immediately and then process your Raw files when you have time. The downside, of course, is that creating two files for every image eats up substantially more space on your memory card and your computer's hard drive. I leave it up to you to decide whether the pluses outweigh the minuses.

My take: Choose Fine or Raw

At this point, you may be finding all this technical goop a bit much, so allow me to simplify things until you have time or energy to completely digest all the ramifications of JPEG versus Raw:

- ✔ If you require the absolute best image quality and have the time and interest to do the Raw conversion process, shoot Raw.

- ✔ If great photo quality is good enough for you, you don't have wads of spare time, or you aren't that comfortable with the computer, stick with one of the Fine JPEG settings.

- ✔ If you want to enjoy the best of both worlds, consider Raw+Large/Fine — assuming, of course, that you have an abundance of space on your memory card and your hard drive. Otherwise, creating two files for every photo on a regular basis isn't really practical.

- ✔ Select JPEG Normal if you aren't shooting pictures that demand the highest quality level and you aren't printing or displaying the photos at large sizes. The smaller file size also makes JPEG Normal the way to go if you're running seriously low on memory card space during a shoot.

- ✔ Finally, remember that the format and resolution together determine the ultimate picture quality. So if you capture an image at the S1/Normal setting, for example, and then print the photo at a large size, the combination of a lower pixel count and a higher level of JPEG compression may produce disappointing picture quality.

3

Taking Great Pictures, Automatically

*A*re you old enough to remember the Certs television commercials from the 1960s and '70s? "It's a candy mint!" declared one actor. "It's a breath mint!" argued another. Then a narrator declared the debate a tie and spoke the famous catchphrase: "It's two, two, two mints in one!"

Well, that pretty much describes the EOS T3i/600D. On one hand, it provides a range of powerful controls, offering just about every feature a serious photographer could want. On the other, it also offers fully automated exposure modes that enable people with absolutely no experience to capture beautiful images. "It's a sophisticated photographic tool!" "It's as simple as 'point and shoot'!" "It's two, two, two cameras in one!"

Of course, you probably bought this book for help with your camera's advanced side, so that's what other chapters cover. This chapter, however, is devoted to your camera's point-and-shoot side, explaining how to get the best results from the fully automatic exposure modes.

As Easy As It Gets: Auto and Flash Off

For the most automatic of automatic photography, set your camera's Mode dial to one of the following two settings:

Scene Intelligent Auto

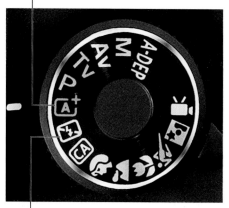

Flash Off

Figure 3-1: These two modes are identical except one disables flash.

- **Scene Intelligent Auto:** The name of this mode, labeled in Figure 3-1, refers to the fact that the camera analyzes the scene in front of the lens and selects the picture-taking options that it thinks will best capture the subject.

- **Flash Off:** Also labeled in the figure, this mode does the exact same thing as Scene Intelligent Auto, except flash is disabled. This mode provides an easy way to ensure that you don't break the rules when shooting in locations that don't permit flash.

In either mode, follow these steps to take a picture:

1. **Set the focusing switch on the lens to the AF (autofocus) position, as shown in Figure 3-2.**

   The figure features the 18–55mm kit lens. If you own a different lens, the switch may look and operate differently; check your lens manual for details.

2. **Unless you're using a tripod, set the Stabilizer switch to the On setting, as shown in Figure 3-2.**

   The switch controls image stabilization, which helps produce sharper images by compensating for camera movement that can occur when you handhold the camera. If you're using a tripod, you can save some battery power by turning stabilization off. Again, if you use a lens other than the kit lens, check your lens manual for details about using its stabilization feature, if provided.

3. **Check the Drive mode on the Shooting Settings display.**

By default, the camera sets the Drive mode to Single, which means that you capture one picture with each press of the shutter button. But you can choose the 10-second or continuous self-timer options if you prefer.

You can view the current Drive mode in the Shooting Settings display, as shown in Figure 3-3. To adjust the Drive mode, press the left cross key; see Chapter 2 if you need more help understanding your options.

The screen also briefly displays three exposure settings (f-stop, shutter speed, and ISO), as shown in the figure. Chapter 7 details these settings, if you want to know more.

4. **Select the Quality setting via Shooting Menu 1.**

   Chapter 2 spells out the intricacies of this setting. If you're not up for digesting the topic, keep the setting at the default (Large/Normal). The icon representing that Quality setting looks like the one shown in Figure 3-3.

5. **Looking through the viewfinder, frame the image so that your subject appears under an autofocus point.**

   The *autofocus points* are those nine tiny rectangles clustered in the center of the viewfinder, as shown in Figure 3-4.

   Framing your subject so that it falls under the center autofocus point typically produces the fastest and most accurate autofocusing.

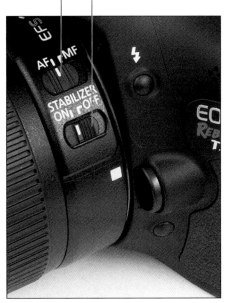

Auto/Manual focus switch

Image Stabilizer switch

Figure 3-2: Set the lens switch to AF to use autofocusing.

Exposure settings

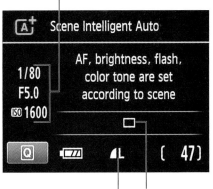

Single Drive mode

Large/Fine Quality setting

Figure 3-3: In Scene Intelligent Auto and Flash Off modes, you can adjust only the Drive mode via the Quick Control screen.

Autofocus points

Figure 3-4: The tiny rectangles in the viewfinder indicate autofocus points.

6. Press and hold the shutter button halfway down.

The camera's autofocus and autoexposure meters begin to do their thing. In dim light, the flash pops up if the camera thinks light is needed when you use the Scene Intelligent Auto exposure mode. Additionally, the flash may emit an *AF-assist beam,* a few rapid pulses of light designed to help the autofocusing mechanism find its target. (The *AF* stands for autofocus.)

After the camera meters exposure, it displays its chosen aperture (f-stop) and shutter speed settings at the bottom of the viewfinder. In Figure 3-5, for example, the shutter speed is 1/200 second, and the f-stop is f/5.6. You also see the current ISO setting and the maximum burst rate (in this case, 100 and 9, respectively). (Chapter 7 details shutter speed, f-stops, and ISO; see Chapter 1 for information about the maximum burst rate.)

If the shutter speed value blinks, the camera needs to use a slow shutter speed to expose the picture. Because any movement of the camera or subject can blur the picture at a slow shutter speed, use a tripod and tell your subject to remain as still as possible.

7. Pause to give the camera time to set focus.

This step is critical! If you simply press the shutter button down in one continuous motion, the camera may not be able to set focus correctly.

When focus is established, one or more of the autofocus points blink red to indicate which areas of the frame are in focus. For example, in Figure 3-5, all points except the one on the far left are lit, showing that everything under those points are in focus.

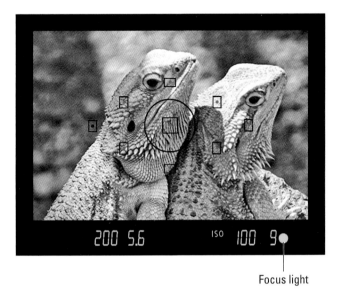

Focus light

Figure 3-5: When you photograph stationary subjects, the green focus indicator lights when the camera locks focus.

In most cases, you also hear a tiny beep, and the focus indicator in the viewfinder lights, as shown in Figure 3-5. Focus is now locked as long as you keep the shutter button halfway down. Typically, the camera focuses on the closest object; if you want to set focus elsewhere, your easiest option is to use manual focusing. (Chapter 1 shows you how.)

These focus signals vary if the camera senses motion in front of the lens, however. If so, you may hear a series of small beeps, and the focus lamp may not light. Both signals mean that the camera switched to an autofo-cusing option that enables it to adjust focus as necessary up to the time you take the picture. (This continuous-autofocusing option is called AI Servo; Chapter 8 has details.) As long as you keep the subject within one of the autofocus points, focus should be correct.

8. Press the shutter button the rest of the way down to record the image.

While the camera sends the image data to the camera memory card, the memory card access lamp on the lower-right corner of the camera back lights. Don't turn off the camera or remove the memory card while the lamp is lit, or you may damage both camera and card.

When the recording process is finished, the picture appears briefly on the camera monitor. By default, the review period is two seconds; you can adjust the timing via Shooting Menu 1. (See Chapter 5 to find out more about picture playback.)

I need to add just a few more pointers about the Scene Intelligent Auto and Flash Off modes:

 ✔ **Exposure:** In dim lighting, the camera may need to use a very high ISO setting, which increases the camera's sensitivity to light, or very slow shutter speed (longer exposure time), especially if you use the Flash Off mode. Unfortunately, both can create *noise,* a defect that makes your picture look grainy. See Chapter 7 for tips on dealing with this and other exposure problems.

 ✔ **Flash:** If the flash fires but your picture is still too dark, move closer to the subject. The built-in flash has a range of only about 16 feet.

In Scene Intelligent Auto mode, you can set the flash to the Red-Eye Reduction mode (the control lives on Shooting Menu 1). Chapter 2 provides the full story.

 ✔ **Autofocusing:** If the camera can't establish focus, you may be too close to your subject. Additionally, some scenes simply confuse autofocusing systems — water, highly reflective objects, and subjects behind fences are some problematic subjects. Just switch to manual focusing and set focus yourself as outlined in Chapter 1.

 ✔ **Color:** Color decisions are also handled for you automatically. Normally, the camera's color brain does a good job of rendering the scene, but if you want to tweak color, you're out of luck.

The results you get from Scene Intelligent Auto and Flash Off vary depending on the available light and how well the camera detects whether you're trying to shoot a portrait, a landscape, an action shot, or whatever. The bottom line is that both modes take a one-size-fits-all approach that may not take best advantage of your camera's capabilities. If you want to more consistently take great pictures instead of good ones, explore the exposure, focus, and color information found in Part III so that you can abandon this exposure mode in favor of ones that put more photographic decisions in your hands. At the very least, step up to one of the scene modes, detailed next, or Creative Auto, covered in the last section of this chapter.

Taking Advantage of Scene Modes

In Scene Intelligent Auto and Flash Off modes, the camera tries to figure out what type of picture you want to take by assessing what it sees through the lens. If you don't want to rely on the camera to make that judgment, your camera offers five Image Zone modes, more commonly known as *scene modes* because they're designed to capture specific scenes using traditional picture "recipes." For example, most people prefer portraits that have softly focused backgrounds. So in Portrait mode, the camera selects settings that can produce that type of background. And action shots typically show the subject frozen in time, so that's the route the camera takes when you select Sports mode.

Scene modes also apply color, exposure, contrast, and sharpness adjustments to the picture according to the traditional characteristics of the scene type. Landscape mode produces more vibrant colors, especially in the blue-green range, for example.

The next section provides an overview of using scene modes; following that, you can find details about the individual modes.

Trying out the scene modes

To select a scene mode, turn the Mode dial to the icon that represents the type of picture you want to take: Portrait, Landscape, Close-up, Sports, or Night Portrait. I labeled the five modes in Figure 3-6. After you select a scene mode, the Shooting Settings screen displays information similar to what you see in Figure 3-7. As with Scene Intelligent Auto, described in the preceding section, the camera's selected exposure settings appear briefly on the left side of the screen and then disappear, leaving only information about the ISO setting, as shown in Figure 3-7. (Chapter 7 details ISO and the other exposure settings.)

Using the Quick Control screen, you can adjust the following settings:

Portrait | Close-up | Night Portrait

Landscape   Sports

Figure 3-6: These five icons represent automatic exposure modes geared to specific types of scenes.

✔ **Shoot by Ambience:** This option enables you to play with image colors and request a darker or brighter exposure on your next shot. The section "Shoot by Ambience," later in this chapter, explains your choices.

✔ **Shoot by Lighting or Scene Type:** This option manipulates color only and is primarily designed to eliminate odd color casts that can occur when you shoot in some types of lighting. Check out "Shoot by Lighting or Scene Type," also later in this chapter, for details.

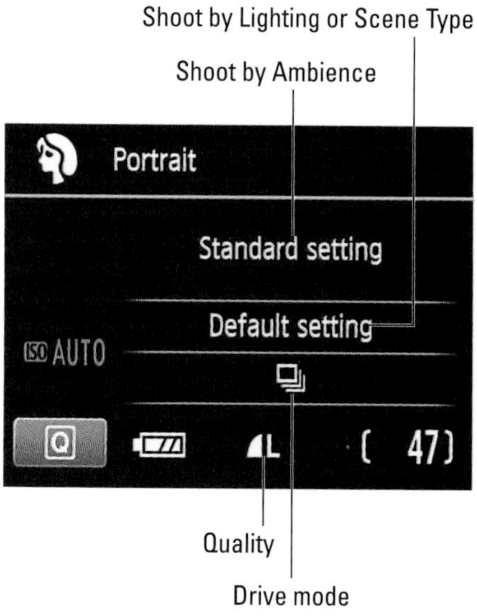

✔ **Drive mode:** Close-up, Landscape, and Night Portrait modes set the Drive mode to Single (one shot per each shutter-button press) by default; Portrait and Sports modes use the Continuous Drive mode. (The camera records a burst of images as long as you hold down the shutter button.) All five modes enable you to switch to Self-Timer: 10 Sec/Remote Control or Self-Timer: Continuous modes, however. See Chapter 2 for details on the Drive mode options.

Shoot by Lighting or Scene Type

Shoot by Ambience

Portrait

Standard setting

Default setting

Quality

Drive mode

Figure 3-7: You can adjust these options in the scene modes.

You can adjust the Quality setting (resolution and file type) as well, but only via Shooting Menu 1. Chapter 2 explains the impact of that setting; if you're unsure of which option to choose, stick with the default (Large/Normal). The symbol on the Shooting Settings screen should look like the one shown in Figure 3-7.

As for the actual picture-taking process, everything works pretty much as outlined in the steps provided earlier in the first section of this chapter. You do need to be aware of a few variations on the theme, which I spell out in the upcoming sections detailing each scene mode.

Portrait mode

Portrait mode is designed to produce the classic portraiture look featured in Figure 3-8: a sharply focused subject against a blurred background. In photography lingo, this picture has a *short depth of field.*

Figure 3-8: Portrait setting produces a softly focused background.

One way to control depth of field is to adjust an exposure control called *aperture,* or *f-stop setting,* so Portrait mode attempts to use an f-stop setting that produces a short depth of field. But the range of f-stops available to the camera depends on the lens and the lighting conditions, so one picture taken in Portrait mode may look very different from another. Additionally, the amount of background blurring depends on a couple other factors, all covered in Chapter 8. In other words, your mileage may vary.

Along with favoring an f-stop that produces a shorter depth of field, Portrait mode results in a slightly less sharp image overall, the idea being to keep skin texture nice and soft. Colors are also adjusted subtly to enhance skin tones. A few other Portrait mode facts to note:

✓ **Drive mode:** Contrary to what you may expect, Drive mode is set to Continuous, which means that the camera records a series of images in rapid succession as long as you hold down the shutter button. This technique can come in handy if your portrait subject can't be counted on to remain still for very long — a toddler or pet, for example.

Should you want to include yourself in the portrait, switch the Drive mode setting to either the 10-second/remote control or continuous self-timer option. See Chapter 2 for Drive mode details.

✔ **Flash:** The built-in flash pops up and fires if the camera deems extra lighting is needed. For outdoor portraits, this can pose a problem. A flash generally improves outdoor portraits, and if the ambient light is very bright, the camera doesn't give you access to the flash. You must switch to Creative Auto mode or one of the advanced exposure modes to take control of flash firing. (See Chapter 7 for the full story on flash photography.)

If the camera does pop up the flash, however, you can choose to enable or disable Red-Eye Reduction flash, which I explain in Chapter 2. Change the setting via Shooting Menu 1.

✔ **Autofocusing:** Portrait mode employs the One-Shot AF (autofocus) mode. This is one of three AF modes available on your camera, all detailed in Chapter 8. In One-Shot mode, the camera locks focus when you press the shutter button halfway. Typically, the camera locks focus on the closest object that falls under one of the nine autofocus points.

If your subject moves out of the selected autofocus point, the camera doesn't adjust focus to compensate, as it does if it senses a moving object when you shoot in Scene Intelligent Auto or Flash Off mode.

Landscape mode

Landscape mode, designed for capturing scenic vistas, city skylines, and other large-scale subjects, produces a large depth of field. As a result, objects both close to the camera and at a distance appear sharply focused, as shown in Figure 3-9.

Like Portrait mode, Landscape mode achieves the greater depth of field by manipulating the aperture (f-stop) setting. Consequently, the extent to which the camera can succeed in keeping everything in sharp focus depends on your lens and on the available light. To fully understand this issue and other factors that affect depth of field, see Chapters 7 and 8.

Whereas Portrait mode tweaks the image to produce soft, flattering skin tones, Landscape mode results in sharper, more contrasty, photos. Color saturation is increased as well, and blues and greens appear especially bold.

Figure 3-9: Landscape mode produces a large zone of sharp focus.

The other critical shooting settings are as follows:

- ✔ **Drive mode:** The default setting is Single, which records one image for each press of the shutter button. As with the other scene modes, you can switch to the Self-Timer: 10 Sec/Remote Control or Self-Timer: Continuous drive mode.

- ✔ **Flash:** The built-in flash is disabled, which is typically no big deal. Because of its limited range — about 16 feet — the built-in flash is of little use when shooting most landscapes, anyway. But for some still-life shots, such as of a statue at close range, a flash may prove helpful. Again, try switching to Creative Auto mode, detailed later in this chapter if you want to use flash.

- ✔ **Autofocusing:** As with Portrait mode, Landscape mode uses One-Shot autofocusing; focus locks when you press the shutter button halfway. Focus usually is set on the nearest object that falls under one of the nine autofocus points.

Close-up mode

 Switching to Close-up mode doesn't enable you to focus at a closer distance to your subject than normal as it does on some non-SLR cameras. The close-focusing capabilities of your camera depend entirely on the lens you use. (Your lens manual should specify the minimum focusing distance.)

Choosing Close-up mode does tell the camera to try to select an aperture (f-stop) setting that results in a short depth of field, which blurs background objects so that they don't compete for attention with your main subject. I took this creative approach to capture the orchid in Figure 3-10, for example. As with Portrait mode, though, how much the background blurs varies depending on a number of factors, all detailed in Chapters 7 and 8.

Figure 3-10: Close-up mode also produces short depth of field.

As far as overall image colors, sharpness, and contrast, the camera doesn't play with those characteristics as it does in Portrait and Landscape modes. So in that regard, Close-up mode is the same as Scene Intelligent Auto and Flash Off modes.

Other settings that apply to Close-up mode:

- **Drive mode:** The Drive mode is set to Single, so you record one photo each time you fully press the shutter button. However, you can switch to the 10-Sec/Remote Control or Continuous Self-Timer options if you choose. (Don't know how those work? Chapter 2 explains.)

- **Flash:** Flash is set to Auto, so the camera decides whether the picture needs the extra pop of light from the built-in flash. For times when the camera enables the flash, you can enable Red-Eye Reduction mode on Shooting Menu 1.

- **Autofocusing:** The AF mode is set to One-Shot mode; again, that simply means that when you press the shutter button halfway, the camera locks focus, usually on the nearest object that falls under one of the nine auto-focus points. If you have trouble focusing, first make sure that you're not *too* close up: Remember, every lens has a minimum close-focusing distance. Then just use manual focusing if the camera has trouble locking on your subject in autofocus mode.

See Chapter 8 for more details about AF modes and other focusing issues. Chapter 9 offers additional tips on close-up photography.

Sports mode

Sports mode results in a number of settings that can help you photograph moving subjects, such as the soccer player in Figure 3-11. First, the camera selects a fast shutter speed, which is needed to "stop motion." *Shutter speed* is an exposure control that you can explore in Chapter 7.

Colors, sharpness, and contrast are all standard in Sports mode, with none of the adjustments that occur in Portrait and Landscape mode. Other settings to note include the following:

Figure 3-11: To capture moving subjects and minimize blur, try Sports mode.

✔ **Drive mode:** To enable rapid-fire image capture, the Drive mode is set to Continuous. This mode enables you to record multiple frames with a single press of the shutter button. You also have the option of switching to either Self-Timer: 10 Sec/Remote Control, which results in a single image being captured with each shutter-button press, or Self-Timer: Continuous, which lets you set the camera to record from 2 to 10 shots with each shutter release. See Chapter 2 for the lowdown on those options.

✔ **Flash:** Flash is disabled, which can be a problem in low-light situations, but it also enables you to shoot successive images more quickly because the flash needs a brief period to recycle between shots. In addition, disabling the flash permits a faster shutter speed; when the flash is on, the maximum shutter speed is 1/200 second. (See Chapter 7 for details about flash and shutter speeds.)

✔ **Autofocusing:** The AF mode is set to AI Servo, which is designed for focusing on moving subjects. When you press the shutter button halfway, the camera establishes focus on whatever is under the center focus point. But if the subject moves, the camera attempts to refocus up to the moment you take the picture.

For this feature to work correctly, you must adjust framing so that your subject remains within one of the autofocus points.

The other critical thing to understand about Sports mode is that whether the camera can select a shutter speed fast enough to stop motion depends on the available light and the speed of the subject itself. In dim lighting, a subject that's moving at a rapid pace may appear blurry even when photographed in Sports mode. And the camera may need to increase light sensitivity by boosting the ISO setting, which has the unhappy side effect of creating *noise,* a defect that looks like grains of sand.

To fully understand shutter speed and ISO, visit Chapter 7. See Chapter 8 for focusing help, and for more tips on action photography, check out Chapter 9.

Night Portrait mode

As its name implies, Night Portrait mode is designed to deliver a better-looking portrait at night (or in any dimly lit environment). Night Portrait does so by combining flash with a slow shutter speed. That slow shutter speed produces a longer exposure time, which enables the camera to rely more on ambient light and less on the flash to expose the picture. The result is a brighter background and softer, more even lighting.

Slow shutter speed issues are covered in detail in Chapter 7; Chapter 9 has some additional nighttime photography tips. For now, the important thing to know is that the slower shutter speed means that you probably need a tripod. If you try to handhold the camera, you run the risk of moving the camera during the long exposure, resulting in a blurry image. Enabling the Image Stabilizer (IS) feature of your lens (if available) can help, but for night-time shooting, even using that may not permit successful handheld shooting. Your subjects also must stay perfectly still during the exposure, which can also be a challenge.

Night Portrait mode also differs from regular Portrait mode in that it renders the scene in the same way as Scene Intelligent Auto in terms of colors, contrast, and sharpness. So shots taken in Night Portrait mode typically display sharper, bolder colors than those taken in Portrait mode.

Other Night Portrait settings to note:

- ✔ **Drive mode:** The default setting is Single, but you also can switch to the 10-Sec/Remote Control or Continuous Self-Timer options. Check out Chapter 2 for details.

- ✔ **Flash:** Flash is enabled when the camera thinks more light is needed — which, assuming that you're actually shooting at night, should be most of the time. You can set the flash to Red-Eye Reduction mode (Shooting Menu 1) if you prefer. See the section "Using Red-Eye Reduction flash," in Chapter 2, for help.

- ✔ **Autofocusing:** The AF mode is set to One-Shot, which locks focus when you press and hold the shutter button halfway down.

Modifying scene mode results

With the Scene Intelligent Auto and Flash Off modes, what you see on the playback monitor is what you get — you can't modify the camera settings to get different results on the next shot. But with the scene modes, you can play around a little with image color, sharpness, contrast, and exposure through the Shoot by Ambience and Shoot by Lighting or Scene Type features.

Key words here: play around *a little*. These features don't give you anywhere near the level of control as the advanced exposure modes (P, Tv, Av, M, and A-DEP) or even as much as Creative Auto mode, explained at the end of this chapter. But they do offer an easy way to start exploring your creative possibilities and begin thinking about how *you* want to record a scene.

My only beef with these two features is that they aren't presented in the most user-friendly fashion, especially for the novice photographer — heck, even for the advanced photographer. For starters, the feature names don't give you a lot of information about what you can accomplish by using them. And the names of the default settings — shown on the Shooting Settings screen in Figure 3-12 — are Standard and Default. Well, that's helpful, huh? Then again, if it weren't for confusing stuff like this, you might not need my input, so I probably shouldn't complain.

At any rate, here's a quick explanation of each feature:

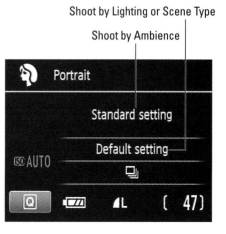

Figure 3-12: These settings enable you to adjust picture color, contrast, sharpness, and exposure when shooting in the scene modes.

- **Shoot by Ambience:** With this option, you can affect the color, exposure, contrast, and sharpness of your pictures. This option is available in all the scene modes, as well as in Creative Auto mode, explained later in this chapter.

- **Shoot by Lighting or Scene Type:** This option has to do with picture colors only: It's designed to remove unwanted color casts that can occur if the camera can't properly compensate for the color of the light source (for example, the warm red glow of candlelight may cause skin colors to look too red).

In the Night Portrait scene mode, this second option is off limits, as it is in Creative Auto mode.

The next two sections give you a better idea of what you can accomplish with these options; following that, you can find step-by-step instructions for using them on your next shot.

Taking a look at the Shoot by Ambience options

In Chapter 8, I introduce the Picture Style feature, which enables you to choose how the camera "processes" your original picture data when you use one of the JPEG Quality settings. (Chapter 2 explains JPEG.) You can choose the Landscape Picture Style for bold, sharp colors, for example, or select Portrait to give skin a warm, soft look. (Yes, the camera offers Landscape and Portrait exposure modes and Landscape and Portrait Picture Styles. Don't get me started.)

You can control Picture Styles only in the advanced exposure modes, however — that option is off limits in the other modes. But as compensation, the scene modes and Creative Auto mode give you Shoot by Ambience, which lets you accomplish results similar to those that you could achieve by using Picture Styles. You also get two Shoot by Ambience settings that enable you to achieve exposure adjustments similar to what you can produce with Exposure Compensation, another feature that's available only in the advanced exposure modes.

Don't waste time wondering why Canon doesn't just let you access those features in the first place — it'll only drive you as crazy as me. Just have fun playing with the Shoot by Ambience settings, which work as follows:

- **Standard:** Consider this the "off" setting. When you select this option, the camera makes no adjustment to the characteristics normally produced by your selected scene mode.
- **Vivid:** Increases contrast, color saturation, and sharpness.
- **Soft:** Creates the appearance of slightly softer focus.
- **Warm:** Warms (adds a reddish-orange color cast) and softens.
- **Intense:** Boosts contrast and saturation (color intensity) even more than the Vivid setting.
- **Cool:** Adds a cool (blue) color cast.
- **Brighter:** Lightens the photo.
- **Darker:** Darkens the photo.
- **Monochrome:** Creates a black-and-white photo, with an optional color tint.

All adjustments are applied *in addition* to whatever adjustments occur by virtue of your selected scene mode. For example, Landscape mode already produces slightly sharper, more vivid colors than normal. If you add the Vivid Shoot by Ambience option, you amp things up another notch.

In addition, you can control the amount of the adjustment through a related setting, Effect (another less-than-clear feature name, if you ask me). You can choose from three Effect levels — Low, Standard, and Strong. (Would "Medium" have been so wrong? Sigh.) In the case of the Monochrome setting, the Effect setting enables you to switch from a black-and-white image to a monochrome image with a warm (orange) or cool (blue) tint.

As a quick example of the color effects you can create, Figure 3-13 shows the same subject taken at four different Shoot by Ambience settings. I took all pictures in the Landscape scene mode. For the three variations — Vivid,

Warm, and Intense — I applied the maximum level of adjustment, setting the Effect option to Strong.

Standard

Vivid

Warm

Intense

Figure 3-13: To create these Shoot by Ambience variations, I used the maximum amount of adjustment for the Vivid, Warm, and Intense settings.

Although the color effects are entertaining, I think you'll get more use out of the Brighter and Darker settings, as they give you a way to overrule the camera's exposure decisions — which, as illustrated by the left image in Figure 3-14, can be less than optimal when you shoot a light subject against a dark background, or vice versa. In all the exposure modes covered in this chapter, the camera chooses exposure settings based on the entire frame, which can lead to an under- or overexposed subject. The exposure of the background in the water lily image was fine, for example, but the flower was overexposed. So I set the Shoot by Ambience option to Darker, set the Effect option to Standard (that's medium, to us normal folk), and shot the flower again.

Standard   Darker

Figure 3-14: If the initial exposure leaves your subject too bright, choose the Darker setting and reshoot.

Because the Shoot by Lighting or Scene Type feature also affects image colors, it's a good idea to consider both options together. So the next section explains this second "Shoot by" feature; following that, I provide step-by-step instructions for enabling both options.

Eliminating color casts with Shoot by Lighting or Scene Type

This option might be better named "Eliminate Color Cast" because that's what it's designed to do: remove unwanted color casts that can occur when the camera makes a *white balance* misstep.

Chapter 8 explains white balancing fully, but in short, it has to do with the fact that every light source emits its own color cast — candlelight, a warm hue; flash, a slightly cool hue, and so on. The camera's White Balance setting is the mechanism that compensates for the color of the light so that colors in the scene are rendered accurately.

Normally, the camera uses automatic white balancing in the scene modes (and in the other modes covered in this chapter), and things turn out just fine. But if a scene is lit by different types of light, each throwing their own color bias into the mix, the camera sometimes gets confused, and colors may be out of whack. The left image in Figure 3-15 has an example — a white-balance error caused the scene to be too yellow. The image on the right shows the correct image colors.

Figure 3-15: If your photo has a color cast (left), you may be able to use the Shoot by Lighting or Scene Type option to eliminate it (right).

In the advanced exposure modes, you deal with color casts by changing the White Balance setting; again, Chapter 8 shows you how. You can't access the White Balance setting in the scene modes, but in all scene modes except Night Portrait, you can use the Shoot by Lighting or Scene Type option to tell the camera to balance colors for a specific light source.

You can choose from the following settings:

- **Default:** Colors are balanced for the light source automatically.
- **Daylight:** For bright sunlight.
- **Shade:** For subjects in shade.
- **Cloudy:** For shooting under overcast skies.
- **Tungsten Light:** For incandescent and tungsten bulbs; not available for Landscape scene mode.
- **Fluorescent Light:** For subjects lit by fluorescents (although this may not be suitable for some compact-fluorescent lights — try tungsten if you get bad results). Also not available for Landscape scene mode.
- **Sunset:** Helps capture brilliant sunset colors, especially when you're shooting into the sun. (P.S.: Don't aim the lens directly at the sun or look through the viewfinder directly into the sun. You can damage the camera and hurt your eyes.)

Don't worry if you don't know which setting will produce the correct colors — as explained in the next section, you can use the Live View feature on your camera to preview the effect of each setting.

Adjusting (and previewing) the "Shoot by" settings

As the examples in Figures 3-14 through 3-16 illustrate, the two "Shoot by" options together determine your final photo colors and exposure. So being able to preview the possible combinations of settings without having to take a bunch of shots to experiment would be great, yes?

Well, luckily, you can enjoy that advantage in Live View mode — the feature that enables you to compose pictures using the monitor instead of the viewfinder. As you vary the Shoot by Ambience and Shoot by Lighting or Scene Type settings, the Live View display updates to show you how the subject will be rendered. (Note that the Live View preview isn't always 100% accurate, especially in terms of image brightness, but it's fairly close.)

For reasons that I spell out in Chapter 4, I (and Canon, for that matter) recommend that you use the viewfinder for normal, still photography. So in the following steps, which explain how to select the "Shoot by" settings, I show you how to choose and preview the effects using Live View and then switch back to the viewfinder before actually taking the picture.

1. **Press the Live View button to shift to Live View mode.**

   The viewfinder goes dark, and the scene in front of the lens appears on the monitor. Use the monitor to compose the shot.

2. **Press the Quick Control button and then use the cross keys to highlight the Shoot by Ambience option, as shown on the left in Figure 3-16.**

   In Live View mode, the settings appear superimposed on the subject, as shown in the figure. By default, the Standard setting is selected for the Shoot by Ambience option.

Shoot by Ambience   Effect (strength)

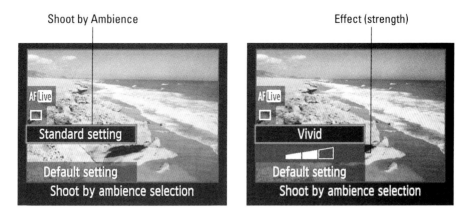

Figure 3-16: After highlighting the Shoot by Ambience option (left), rotate the Main dial to change the setting and display the Effect setting.

3. **Rotate the Main dial to change the setting.**

   As soon as you shift out of Standard mode, you see the impact of the newly selected ambience setting on the scene, as shown on the right in Figure 3-16. In addition, the Effect setting, which determines the level at which the adjustment is applied, becomes available.

4. **Highlight the Effect setting and rotate the Main dial to set the level of the adjustment.**

   You can choose from Low (one notch on the little gauge), Standard (medium impact, represented by two notches), or Strong (three notches). For the record, all the variations shown in Figure 3-13 were taken using the Strong setting; in Figure 3-14, however, I set the Darker adjustment to the Standard setting.

5. **Highlight the Shoot by Lighting or Scene Type option, as shown on the left in Figure 3-17.**

6. **Rotate the Main dial to cycle through the settings.**

Shoot by Lighting/Scene Type

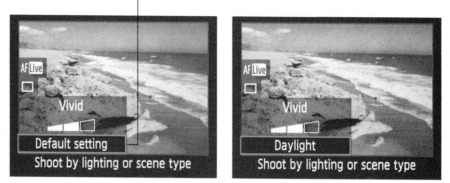

Figure 3-17: Here I used the Shoot by Lighting or Scene Type option to add, instead of remove, a warm color cast.

This setting, as I explain in the preceding section, is designed to remove unwanted color casts from a scene. But there's nothing preventing you from using the option to *add* a slight cast to the scene if your heart so desires. You may like the effect of making your subject look a little warmer or cooler, and again, you can see the results of each setting on the camera monitor. For example, the screen on the right in Figure 3-17 shows the result of changing the setting to the Daylight setting. In this case, colors got warmer, but what impact any setting has on your subject depends on the actual lighting conditions.

7. **When you're happy with the results of the two options, press the Live View button to exit Live View mode.**

   The monitor goes dark, and you can once again see your subject through the viewfinder. The Shoot by Ambience and Shoot by Lighting or Scene Type settings you dialed in remain in force until you change the Mode dial or turn the camera off.

8. **Take the picture.**

If you already know what settings you want to use, you can get the job done more quickly by staying out of Live View mode and just using the Quick Control screen to dial in both options. Follow these steps:

1. **Display the Shooting Settings screen.**

   Just give the shutter button a quick half-press and then release it.

 2. **Press the Quick Control button.**

3. **Use the cross keys to highlight the Shoot by Ambience setting, as shown on the left in Figure 3-18.**

Shoot by Ambience setting

Effect (amount) setting

Figure 3-18: After highlighting this option, rotate the Main dial to cycle through the different Shoot by Ambience settings.

4. Rotate the Main dial to cycle through the available options.

If you prefer to see all the Shoot by Ambience options at once, you can press Set instead or rotate the Main dial to cycle through them one by one. You then see a menu listing all the settings; highlight your choice and press Set to return to the Quick Control screen.

Either way, after you choose a setting other than Standard, the Effect option becomes available, as shown on the right in Figure 3-18.

5. To set the adjustment amount, highlight the Effect option, as shown in Figure 3-19, and rotate the Main dial.

Or you can press the right/left cross keys.

6. Highlight the Shoot by Lighting or Scene Type option, as shown in Figure 3-20.

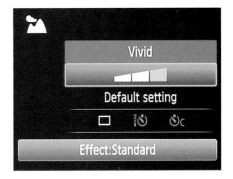

Figure 3-19: To adjust the impact of the adjustment, highlight the Effect option and then rotate the Main dial.

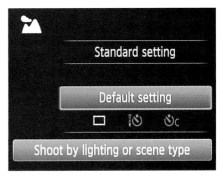

Figure 3-20: If you photo displays a color cast, try changing this setting.

7. **Rotate the Main dial to adjust the setting.**

8. **Press the Quick Control button again to exit the display.**

    Or just press the shutter button halfway and release it. Either way, you're ready to start shooting.

Gaining More Control with Creative Auto

When you use the scene modes, described in the preceding few sections, the camera selects settings that render your subject using the traditional "look" for the scene — blurry backgrounds for Portrait mode, greater depth of field and bold colors for Landscapes, and so on. You then can modify the colors and exposure somewhat by using the Shoot by Ambience and Shoot by Lighting or Scene Type options, but all in all, you're fairly limited as to the overall look of your pictures.

Creative Auto mode enables you to take a bit more control. As its name implies, this mode is still mostly automatic, but if you check the monitor after taking a shot and don't like the results, you can make the following adjustments for your next shot:

- ✔ Enable or disable the flash.
- ✔ Adjust color, sharpness, contrast, and exposure through the Shoot by Ambience option, as explained in the preceding few sections.
- ✔ Soften or sharpen the apparent focus of the picture background.

What about the Shoot by Lighting or Scene Type option that's available in the scene modes? Sorry, that dog won't hunt in Creative Auto mode. But remember that using that option typically isn't necessary: It's designed to fix white-balancing issues, and in Creative Auto mode, the camera uses automatic white balancing, which works well for the majority of shooting situations.

Here's how to use Creative Auto mode:

1. **Set the Mode dial on top of the camera to the CA setting.**

    The Creative Auto version of the Shooting Settings screen appears on the monitor, as shown in Figure 3-21. (If you don't see the screen, press the Disp button or press the shutter button halfway and then release it.) Just as in the other automatic modes, the camera displays its selected exposure settings for a few seconds, as shown in the figure. To find out more about those settings, visit Chapter 7.

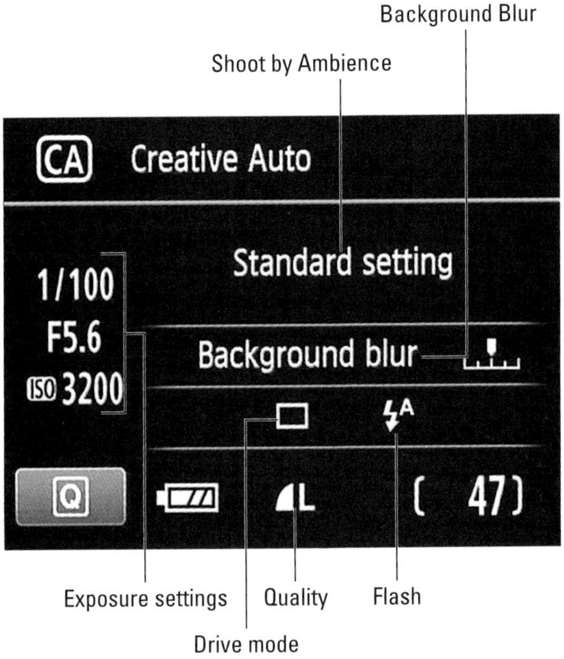

Background Blur

Shoot by Ambience

CA Creative Auto

1/100
F5.6
ISO 3200

Standard setting

Background blur

Q 🔋 ▲L (47)

Exposure settings | Quality   Flash
Drive mode

Figure 3-21: In Creative Auto mode, the Shooting Settings screen displays this information.

2. To adjust the Drive Mode, Flash, and Shoot by Ambience settings, press the Quick Control button.

One of the settings becomes highlighted, and a text label appears at the bottom of the screen to remind you what the highlighted setting does. In Figure 3-22, for example, the Shoot by Ambience setting is highlighted.

3. Use the cross keys to move the highlight over the setting you want to adjust.

4. Adjust the highlighted setting.

See the upcoming list for details about each setting.

For the Drive and Flash options, you can't simply rotate the Main dial to adjust the setting. Instead, press Set to access a screen containing the settings. Select your choice and press Set again to return to the Quick Control screen.

5. **After selecting all the options you want to use, exit the Quick Control screen by pressing the shutter button halfway and releasing. (Or press the Quick Control button again.)**

   The monitor returns to the normal Shooting Settings display.

6. **To adjust the Quality setting, use Shooting Menu 1.**

   As with the other exposure modes discussed in this chapter, you can't change that setting via the Quick Control screen in Creative Auto mode.

Figure 3-22: Use the Quick Control screen to adjust the Drive mode, Flash, and Shoot by Ambience settings.

7. **Frame, focus, and shoot.**

   From this point on, everything works as outlined for the Scene Intelligent Auto mode, explained in the first section of this chapter.

The settings you choose remain in effect from shot to shot. If you turn the camera off or switch to a different exposure mode, though, the settings return to their defaults. (The default settings are shown in Figure 3-21.)

Now for the promised explanations of how the Creative Auto options work:

- **Shoot by Ambience:** This setting enables you to alter how the camera processes the photo, enabling you to tweak color, contrast, and exposure slightly. The earlier section "Taking a look at the Shoot by Ambience options" explains this feature.

- **Background Blur:** This feature gives you some control over depth of field. That term, again, refers to the distance over which focus remains sharp. Consider the images in Figure 3-23, for example. In both shots, I set focus on the flag. But the left image features a long depth of field, so both the flag and the tractor in the background are sharp. The right image has a very shallow, or short, depth of field, so the tractor is blurry.

Unfortunately, this feature doesn't play nice with the flash. If you set the flash mode to On, the Background Blur bar becomes dimmed and out of your reach when the flash pops up. Ditto if you set the flash mode to Auto and the camera sees a need for flash.

Assuming that the flash doesn't get in your way, press the Quick Control button to shift to the Quick Control screen, highlight the setting, and then use the Main dial to move the little indicator on the bar to the left to shorten depth of field, which makes distant objects appear blurrier. Shift the indicator to the right to make distant objects appear sharper.

f/22 (large depth of field)   f/2.8 (short depth of field)

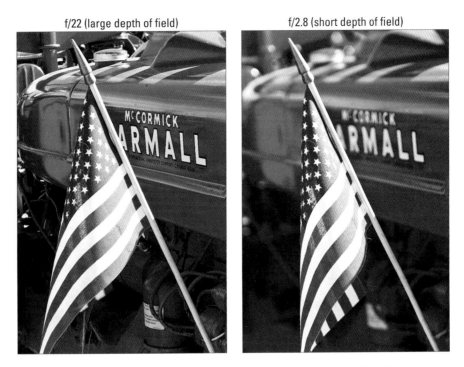

Figure 3-23: You can choose to make background objects appear sharp (left) or blurry (right).

The camera creates this shift in depth of field by adjusting the aperture setting (f-stop), which is an exposure control you can explore in Chapter 7. A lower f-stop number produces a more shallow depth of field, for a blurrier background, as shown on the right in Figure 3-23; a higher f-stop setting produces a greater depth of field, for a sharper background, as shown on the left. Additionally, because aperture also plays a critical role in exposure, the range of f-stops the camera can choose — and, therefore, the extent of focus shift you can achieve with this setting — depends on the available light. The camera gives priority to getting a good exposure, assuming that you'd prefer a well-exposed photo to one that has the background blur you want but is too dark or too light. Understand, too, that when the aperture changes, the camera also must change the shutter speed, ISO (light sensitivity setting), or both to maintain a good exposure.

At slow shutter speeds, moving objects appear blurry, regardless of your depth of field. But even for still subjects, a slow shutter speed creates the risk that camera shake during the exposure will blur the image. A blinking shutter speed value in the viewfinder or Shooting Settings display alerts you to a potentially risky shutter speed; put your camera on a tripod to avoid the risk of camera shake. Figure 3-24 shows you where to find the shutter speed and f-stop settings in the Shooting Settings display.

To find out more about depth of field, aperture, shutter speed, ISO, and exposure, see Chapters 7 and 8. In the meantime, note these easy ways to tweak depth of field beyond using the Background Blur slider:

- *For blurrier backgrounds,* move the subject farther from the background, get closer to the subject, and zoom in to a tighter angle of view, if you use a zoom lens.

- *For sharper backgrounds,* do the opposite of the above.

✔ **Drive mode:** You can choose from four Drive mode options: Single, Continuous, Self-Timer: 10 Sec/Remote Control, and Self-Timer: Continuous. Remember that you can access the settings by pressing the left cross key as well as by using the Quick Control screen. Chapter 2 details all the Drive modes.

✔ **Flash:** You can choose from three flash settings, which are represented on the Shooting Settings screen by the icons in the margin:

- *Auto:* The camera fires the flash automatically if it thinks extra light is needed to expose the picture.

- *On:* The flash fires regardless of the ambient light.

- *Off:* The flash doesn't fire.

For the Auto and On settings, you can use the Red-Eye Reduction flash feature, found on Shooting Menu 1. See Chapter 2 for more information about flash photography.

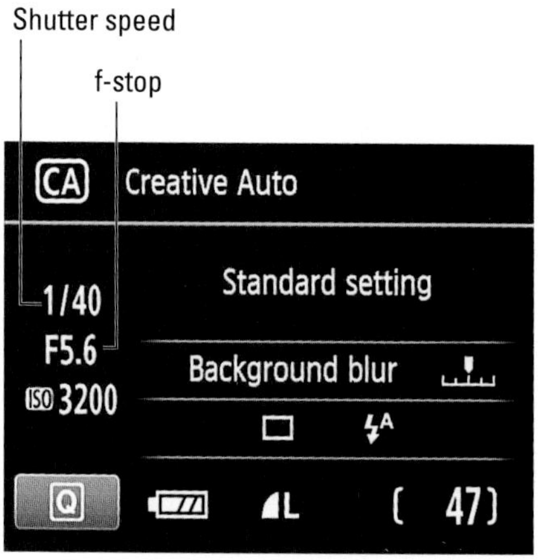

Shutter speed

f-stop

| CA | Creative Auto |

1/40
F5.6
ISO 3200

Standard setting

Background blur

Figure 3-24: A blinking shutter speed value warns you of a shutter speed; use a tripod to avoid camera shake that can blur the photo.

Keep in mind that even though Creative Auto offers more points of control than the other exposure modes explored in this chapter, you still don't get anywhere near the level of flexibility you enjoy in the advanced exposure modes. For example, you can decide whether you want the flash to fire in Creative Auto mode, but you can't adjust flash power or change the way the camera calculates the flash exposure, as you can in the P, Tv, Av, M, and A-DEP modes. That said, if you're just not ready to dive into the more advanced exposure modes covered in Chapters 7 and 8, Creative Auto gives you the best chance of taking the picture as you envision it in your mind's eye.

4

Exploring Live View Shooting and Movie Making

*L*ike many newer dSLR cameras, the T3i/600D offers *Live View,* a feature that enables you to use the monitor instead of the viewfinder to compose photos. Turning on Live View is also the first step in recording a movie; using the viewfinder isn't possible when you shoot movies.

In many respects, shooting in Live View mode is no different from using the viewfinder. But a few aspects, such as focusing, are quite different. So the first part of this chapter provides an overview of the Live View process and also clues you in on some precautions to take to avoid damaging the camera when using the feature. Following that, you can find details on taking still photos in Live View mode and shooting, viewing, and editing movies.

Getting Started with Live View

The basics of taking advantage of Live View are pretty simple:

✓ **Enabling Live View for still photography:** Before you can use Live View for still photography, you must enable the Live View Shooting function. Where you find the option depends on the current exposure mode:

• *Scene Intelligent Auto, Flash Off, Creative Auto, and the scene modes:* Look for the option on Shooting Menu 2, as shown on the left in Figure 4-1.

• *P, Tv, Av, M, and A-DEP:* The setting lives on Shooting Menu 4, as shown on the right.

Notice, too, that the menu for the advanced exposure modes contains options not found on the one presented when you use the other exposure modes — as with viewfinder photography, you have access to all Live View options only when you use those advanced modes.

✓ **Switching to Live View:** This time, the process depends on whether you want to shoot photographs or record movies:

• *Still photography:* Set the Mode dial to one of the still photography settings and then press the Live View button, labeled on the left in Figure 4-2.

• *Movie shooting:* Just set the Mode dial to the Movie position, as shown on the right in Figure 4-2.

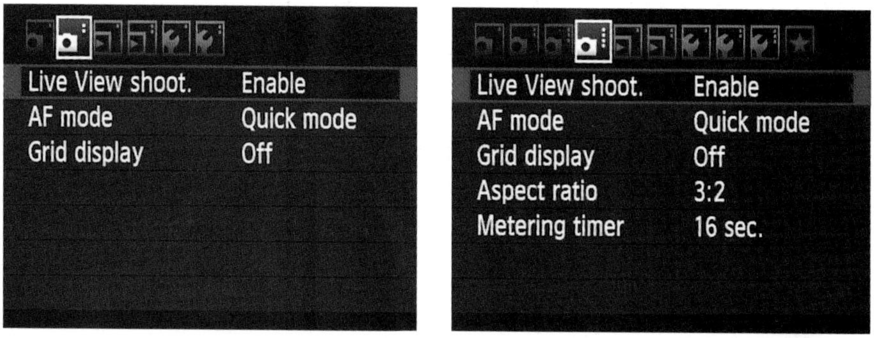

Figure 4-1: Enable Live View either on Shooting Menu 2 (left) or 4 (right), depending on your exposure mode.

Live View button   Movie mode

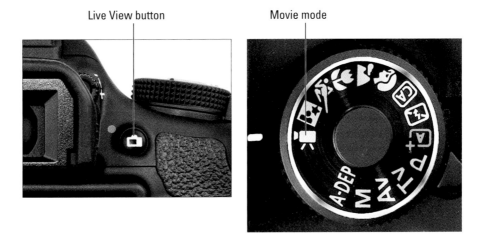

Figure 4-2: For still photography, press the Live View button to engage Live View; for movies, just set the Mode dial to Movie.

As soon as you take either step, you hear a clicking sound as the internal mirror that normally sends the image from the lens to the viewfinder flips up. Then the scene in front of the lens appears on the monitor, and you no longer can see anything in the viewfinder. Instead of the normal Shooting Settings screen, you see the Live View version, with symbols representing certain camera settings over the live image, as shown in Figure 4-3. Don't panic if your screen doesn't show the same data — you can customize this display, as outlined later in this chapter, by pressing the Info button. The onscreen data also depends on whether you're shooting movies or stills.

Figure 4-3: In Live View mode, the Shooting Settings data and some other picture information is superimposed over the live preview.

- **Shooting photos:** Most steps are the same as for viewfinder photography — frame, focus, and press the shutter button — although a few advanced shooting options are disabled. Focusing methods, however, are quite different. See the upcoming sections "Exploring Your Focusing Options" and "Shooting Still Pictures in Live View Mode" for details.

You can adjust picture-taking settings via the menus or, in some cases, by using the Quick Control screen, as you normally do. See the afore-mentioned sections for the complete scoop on how to access the avail-able Live View photography options.

✔ **Recording movies:** After setting the Mode dial to Movie, press the Live View button to start and stop recording. Your focusing options are the same as for still photography in Live View mode. But you also encounter lots of movie-specific settings that affect video quality, sound recording, and the like. See "Customizing Movie Recording Settings," in the latter part of this chapter, for details.

✔ **Viewing photos and movies while in Live View mode:** Just press the Playback button to look at your images and movies. To switch back to Live View shooting, give the Playback button another press or give the shutter button a half-press and then release it. Check out the end of this chapter to discover some special options available for movie playback; see Chapter 5 for details on reviewing still pictures.

✔ **Exiting Live View mode:** Press the Live View button or, if the Mode dial is set to Movie, select any other exposure mode.

As you may have guessed from the fact that I devoted a whole chapter to the topic of Live View and movie recording, these points comprise just the start of the story, however. The next two sections provide some additional general information that applies to both still photography and movie recording; later sections get into the nitty-gritty.

Live View safety tips

Whether your goal is a still image or a movie, be aware of the following tips and warnings any time you enable Live View:

✔ **Cover the viewfinder to prevent light from seeping into the camera and affecting exposure.** The camera ships with a little cover designed just for this purpose. In fact, it's conveniently attached to the camera strap. To install it, first remove the rubber eyecup that surrounds the viewfinder by sliding it up and out of the groove that holds it in place. Then slide the cover down into the groove and over the viewfinder, as shown in Figure 4-4. (Orient the cover so that the *Canon* label faces the viewfinder.)

✔ **Using Live View for an extended period can harm your pictures and the camera.** When you work in Live View mode, the camera's innards heat up more than usual, and that extra heat can create the right elec-tronic conditions for *noise*, a defect that gives your pictures a speckled look. Chapter 7 contains an illustration of this defect, which also is caused by long exposure times and high ISO Sensitivity settings.

Perhaps more critically, the increased temperatures can damage the camera. The symbol shown in the margin appears on the monitor to warn you when the camera is getting too hot. Initially, the symbol is white. If you continue shooting and the temperature continues to increase, the symbol turns red and blinks, alerting you that the camera soon will shut off automatically. In extremely warm environments, you may not be able to use Live View mode for very long before the system shuts down.

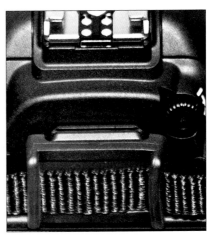

Figure 4-4: Use the rubber cover on the camera strap to prevent light from seeping through the viewfinder and messing up exposure metering.

✒ **Aiming the lens at the sun or other bright lights also can damage the camera.** Of course, you can cause problems doing this even during normal shooting, but the possibilities increase when you use Live View. You not only can harm the camera's internal components but also the monitor.

✒ **Live View puts additional strain on the camera battery.** The monitor is a big consumer of battery juice, so keep an eye on the battery level icon to avoid running out of power at a critical moment.

✒ **The risk of camera shake during handheld shots is increased.** When you use the viewfinder, you can help steady the camera by bracing it against your face. But with Live View, you have to hold the camera away from your body to view the monitor, making it harder to keep the camera absolutely still. As Chapter 7 explains, any camera movement during the exposure can blur the shot, so using a tripod is the best course of action for Live View photography. If you do handhold the camera, enabling Image Stabilization can help compensate for a bit of camera shake; Chapter 1 discusses this feature in more detail.

Because of these complications, I don't use Live View for still photography very often. Rather, I think of it as a special-purpose tool geared to situations where framing with the viewfinder is cumbersome. I find Live View most helpful for still-life, tabletop photography, especially in cases that require a lot of careful arrangement of the scene.

For example, I have a shooting table that's about waist high. Normally, I put my camera on a tripod, come up with an initial layout of the objects I want to photograph, set up my lights, and then check the scene through the viewfinder. Then there's a period of refining the object placement, the lighting, and so on. If I'm shooting from a high angle, requiring the camera to be positioned above the table and pointing downward, I have to stand on my tiptoes or get a stepladder to check things out through the viewfinder between each compositional or lighting change. At lower angles, where the camera is tabletop height or below, I have to either bend over or kneel to look through the viewfinder, causing no end of later aches and pains to back and knees. With Live View, I can alleviate much of that bothersome routine (and pain) because I can adjust the articulating monitor so that I can see how things look no matter what the camera position.

Customizing the Live View display

You can choose from a few different Live View display options, each of which adds different types of information to the screen. Here's a quick look at your decorating possibilities:

- **Press Info to change the type of data that appears on the display.** You can choose from four basic styles; press the Info button repeatedly to cycle from one style to the next. Figure 4-5 shows the screen as it appears in each of the four styles for still photography. In Movie mode, the type of data displayed changes to show you movie-recording options instead of some of the still-photography settings, and the upper-right display shown in Figure 4-5 is not available. Later sections in this chapter explain exactly what information you can glean from each symbol shown on the screen.

    The chart in the upper-right corner of the top-right screen in Figure 4-5 is a *Brightness histogram,* which is a tool you can use to gauge whether your current settings will produce a good exposure — again, though, only for the still photography exposure modes. See the discussion on interpreting a Brightness histogram in Chapter 5 to find out how to make sense of what you see. But note that when you use flash, the histogram is dimmed; the histogram can't display accurate information because the final exposure will include light from the flash and not just the ambient lighting. The histogram also is disabled if you set the shutter speed to Bulb, an option available only in the M (manual) exposure mode. Chapter 7 has details on bulb shooting.

- **Display a grid:** When you're doing the kind of work for which Live View is best suited, such as taking product shots or capturing other still-life subjects, the exact placement of objects in the frame is often important. To assist careful composition, the camera can display a grid on the monitor, as illustrated in Figure 4-6.

Figure 4-5: Press the Info button to cycle through the four Live View display styles.

Where you turn the grid on depends on your exposure mode:

- *P, Tv, Av, M and A-DEP modes:* Shooting Menu 4 (see the left screen in Figure 4-7)

- *Other still-photography modes:* Shooting Menu 2 (the right screen in Figure 4-7)

- *Movie mode:* Movie Menu 2 (see Figure 4-24 in the Movie Menu 2 section found later in this chapter)

Figure 4-6: The grid is helpful for checking the alignment of objects in the scene.

Either way, you can choose from two grid styles: Grid 1 gives you loosely spaced gridlines, as shown in Figure 4-6; Grid 2 offers a more tightly spaced grid.

P, Tv, Av, M, and A-DEP

Live View shoot.	Enable
AF mode	Live mode
Grid display	Off
Aspect ratio	3:2
Metering timer	1 min.

Other still-photography modes

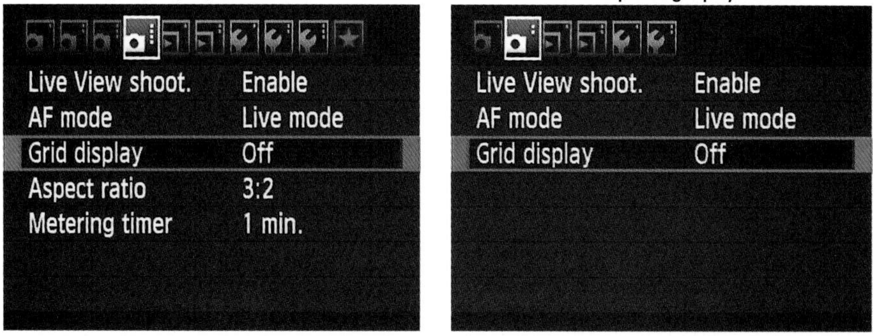

Live View shoot.	Enable
AF mode	Live mode
Grid display	Off

Figure 4-7: For still photography, adjust the grid display and metering timer through these menus.

✔ **Metering Timer:** By default, exposure information such as f-stop and shutter speed disappears from the display after 16 seconds if you don't press any camera buttons. If you want the exposure data to remain visible for a longer period, you can adjust the shutdown time, but only if you shoot in the following exposure modes:

- *P, Tv, Av, M, or A-DEP exposure modes:* Look for the Metering Timer option on Shooting Menu 4.

- *Movie mode:* The option lives on Movie Menu 2.

You can set the timer to values ranging from 4 seconds to 30 minutes. Just keep in mind that the metering mechanism uses battery power, so the shorter the cutoff time, the better.

✔ **Viewing the display on a TV:** You can send the Live View video signal to a television via a standard A/V cable (supplied in the camera box) or an HDMI cable (must be purchased separately). This option comes in especially handy for shooting portraits, for example, enabling you to see the details of your subject's face more clearly. Chapter 5 provides help with connecting the camera to a TV.

In addition, you can connect the camera to your computer with the supplied USB cable and then use the Canon EOS Utility software (also provided in your camera box) to operate the camera remotely. You can even see the Live View preview on your computer monitor. See the software manual, provided on one of the two CDs in the camera box, for more information.

Exploring Your Focusing Options

As with viewfinder photography, you can opt for autofocusing or manual focusing during Live View shooting, assuming that your lens supports both. Focusing during Live View shooting involves some different tools than you use for viewfinder photography, though, so the following sections guide you through both your manual and automatic focusing options.

Manual focusing

Manual focusing is the easiest of the Live View focusing options — and in most cases, it's faster, too. Simply set the lens switch to the MF position if you're using the kit lens or a similarly featured lens. Then twist the lens focusing ring to bring the scene into focus.

I find that most people who shy away from manual focusing do so because they don't trust their eyes to judge focus. And admittedly, the Live View display isn't as sharp as the viewfinder display, so it's not always easy to tell if you focused perfectly. But thanks to a feature that enables you to magnify the Live View preview, you can feel more confident in your manual focusing skills. Here's how it works:

1. **Set the lens to the manual focusing position and engage Live View.**

   You see a large rectangle in the center of the screen. This rectangle is the *magnification frame.*

2. **Rotate the lens focusing ring to set approximate focus.**

3. **Use the cross keys to move the frame over your subject.**

   For example, I moved the frame over the garnish in the soup bowl in the screen shown on the left in Figure 4-8. Remember, what other data appears on the screen depends on the Live View display style; press the Info button to display more or less data. (The magnification frame appears in all cases.)

4. **Press the AF Point Selection button to magnify the display.**

   Note that the button has a blue label that shows a magnifying glass with a plus sign — the universal symbol for zoom in. (During playback, you press the same button to magnify the playback display.)

   Your first press of the button displays a view that's magnified five times, as shown on the right in Figure 4-8. Press again for a ten-times magnification. The current magnification level appears on the right side of the screen, as shown in the figure. If needed, press the cross keys to reposition the magnification frame — the little white box inside the big rectangle under the magnification value indicates the area of the frame that is currently visible.

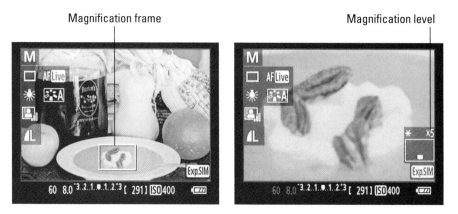

Figure 4-8: Move the magnification frame over your subject (left) and then press the AF Point Selection button to shift to a 5x magnification (right).

5. Adjust focus if needed.

6. When you're satisfied with focus, press the AF Point Selection button again to return to the normal display magnification.

Pretty cool, yes? Now you have no reason to fear manual focusing.

A couple tips on using the magnification feature:

✔ Because you use the cross keys to reposition the magnification frame in Live View, they don't serve their normal purpose — to provide quick access to the White Balance, AF mode, Picture Style, and Drive mode settings. Instead, you change those settings via the Quick Control screen. See the upcoming section "Viewing and adjusting picture settings" for help.

✔ Press the Erase button to quickly shift the magnification frame back to the center of the screen. You don't want your cross-key-pushing finger to get worn out, after all.

✔ Even in manual focusing mode, the Live View display mode shown in Figure 4-8 includes a symbol representing the current autofocusing (AF) mode (Quick, Live, or Live with Face Detection). Ignore the symbol — it's irrelevant when you focus manually. The next section explains more about the autofocus options.

✔ Magnification is available only in Live View mode. But there's no reason you can't set initial focus in viewfinder mode, switch to Live View to check focus, and then shift back out of Live View mode to take the picture. Just make sure you don't change the camera position along the way, or the focusing distance may vary.

Reviewing the three autofocus modes

For autofocusing, the AF (autofocus) mode setting determines the focusing method, as it does for viewfinder shooting. But the AF mode options for Live View autofocus work differently from the normal ones, which I cover in Chapter 8. For Live View, you have the following choices, represented by the icons you see in the margins:

AF QUICK ✒ **Quick mode:** In this mode, the camera uses the same nine-point autofocusing system as it does for viewfinder photography. As its name implies, Quick mode offers the fastest autofocusing of the three Live View AF options. The downside to Quick mode is that it blanks out the Live View display temporarily as it sets focus, which can be a little disconcerting if you're not expecting it to happen.

AF Live ✒ **Live mode:** This is the default AF mode in Live View. Instead of presenting you with nine AF points, the camera displays a single focusing rectangle, which you position over your subject before focusing. Although simpler to use, this mode uses a slower type of autofocusing than the normal, through-the-viewfinder focusing system.

AF ⎍̈ ✒ **Live mode with Face Detection:** This mode works the same as Live mode, but the camera automatically locks focus on a face in the scene if it can find one. When the conditions are just right in terms of lighting, composition, and phase of the moon, this setup works fairly well. However, a number of issues can trip it up. For example, the camera may mistakenly focus on an object that has a similar shape, color, and contrast to a face. It also doesn't work if the face isn't just the right size with respect to the background, is tilted at an angle, is too bright or dark, or partly obscured. And, like regular Live mode autofocus, it's slower than normal (viewfinder) autofocusing.

An icon representing the current AF mode appears in the upper-left corner of the Live View display. To change the setting, you can't press the AF button (right cross key) as you can during viewfinder shooting. Instead, use either of these methods:

 ✒ **Quick Control screen:** This option is fastest. Press the Quick Control button and then highlight the icon that represents the focusing method, as shown in Figure 4-9. Then rotate the Main dial to change the setting. Or select the icon, press Set to display a screen containing all three options, highlight your favorite, and press Set again.

Don't see any AF icons? Press Info to cycle through the various Live View display modes until one appears. What other data shows up depends both on the display mode and your exposure mode; the screens in Figure 4-9 show the monitor as it appears in the M (manual exposure) mode and with all data but the histogram displayed.

✔ **Menus:** You can also head to the menus to change the setting, but as with the other Live View options, which menu you need depends on which exposure mode you're using:

- *P, Tv, Av, M, and A-DEP:* Shooting Menu 4

- *Scene Intelligent Auto, Flash Off, Creative Auto, and scene modes:* Shooting Menu 2

- *Movie:* Movie Menu 1

AF mode

Live mode

Figure 4-9: In Quick Control mode, highlight the AF icon and then rotate the Main dial to change the setting.

Your chosen Live View AF mode remains in force until you change it, even if you turn the camera off, change exposure modes, or do some viewfinder shooting before your next Live View session.

The following sections provide you with step-by-step instructions for focusing in each AF mode.

Quick mode autofocusing

As its name implies, Quick mode offers the fastest autofocusing during Live View or movie shooting. It also is the most similar to the autofocusing system used for regular viewfinder photography, based on the same nine-point focusing grid. So I present this AF mode first, even though it's not the default setting.

1. **Set the lens switch to the AF position.**

   Or if you use a lens other than the kit lens, select whichever switch position enables autofocusing.

2. **Engage the Live View or Movie display.**

   - *For Live View:* Press the Live View button, shown in the margin.

   - *For Movie recording:* Turn the Mode dial to the little movie-camera icon, and the live preview appears without further ado.

3. **Press the Quick Control button, highlight the Autofocus mode icon, and rotate the Main dial to set the mode to Quick.**

   Rectangles representing the nine autofocus points appear in the center of the screen, as shown in Figure 4-10.

If you're shooting in the Scene Intelligent Auto, Flash Off, Creative Auto, or a scene mode (Portrait, Landscape, and so on), the camera automatically selects which of the nine points to use when focusing, just as it does when you shoot using the viewfinder in those exposure modes. Typically, focus is established on the closest object to the lens. Skip to Step 5 to continue the focusing dance.

For the other exposure modes, continue to Step 4.

Figure 4-10: In Quick AF mode, the small rectangles represent autofocus points.

4. **If you're using Movie, P, Tv, Av, M, or A-DEP, set the AF Point Selection mode.**

This option tells the camera which of the autofocus points you want it to consider when it sets focus. You have two choices:

- *Automatic:* All nine autofocus points are active, and the camera decides which one to use when setting the focus distance — again, usually selecting the closest object as the focus target.

- *Manual:* You select which of the nine focusing points you want the camera to use.

Press the up cross key to highlight the autofocus points, as shown in Figure 4-11. (If the camera shifts out of Quick Control mode before you get to this point, just press the Quick Control button, highlight the AF mode icon again, and then press up.) When all nine points are highlighted (see the left side of Figure 4-11), automatic focus-point selection is in force. The label at the bottom of the screen reminds you of that fact. Rotate the Main dial to shift to manual point selection; continue rotating the dial until the point you want to use is highlighted. In the right screen in Figure 4-11, for example, the center point is active.

If you already explored Chapter 8, which details autofocusing options for viewfinder photography, you may be familiar with the AF Point Selection option. But note that in Live View mode, you can't adjust the setting by pressing the AF Point Selection button (top-right corner on the back of the camera) as you can during viewfinder shooting. In Live View mode, that button magnifies the display so you can check focus, as outlined in the preceding discussion of manual focusing. Nor can you press the Set button to quickly select the center focus point as you can during viewfinder photography.

Figure 4-11: After choosing Quick AF mode, press the up cross key to activate the focus points; then rotate the Main dial to choose automatic or manual focus-point selection.

5. Press the shutter button halfway and release it to exit the Quick Control display.

Now you see an additional large rectangle along with your single selected point or with all nine points, if you opted for automatic focus-point selection. The rectangle is the magnification frame detailed in the aforementioned section related to manual focusing. You can use the magnification feature with Quick mode autofocusing, but it's pretty cumbersome; see the tips following these steps for details.

6. Frame your shot so that your subject falls under the selected autofocus point(s).

If you're shooting in one of the fully automatic exposure modes or if you're using an advanced exposure mode and set the camera to automatic focus-point selection (all nine points are active), just make sure that one of the small rectangles falls over your subject. Framing the subject under the center focus point typically enables the autofocus system to do its best work.

Note that in Sports mode, the camera doesn't base focus automatically on the center point as it does for viewfinder photography. And continuous autofocusing isn't possible in Live View mode, either.

7. Press and hold the shutter button halfway down to focus.

As soon as you press the button, the monitor turns black and the autofocusing mechanism kicks into gear. (It may sound as though the camera took the picture, but don't worry — that isn't actually happening.) Keep pressing the button until the camera beeps and the Live View display reappears. The beep signals you that focus is set; one or more of the focus points appears green to tell you which areas of the frame are in focus. If the camera can't find a focusing target, the focus point turns orange and blinks. Try using manual focusing instead.

Unless you're using manual exposure, the autoexposure system fires up and establishes exposure settings along with focus when you press the shutter button halfway.

After focus is established, press the shutter button all the way to take your picture. Or to start recording a movie, release the shutter button and then press the Live View button. (Focus will remain set at the point you just established.) Press the Live View button again to end the recording. Later sections provide details about setting other picture-taking and movie-recording options.

Okay, now for the promised tip regarding using the magnifying feature described in the earlier discussion on manual focusing. Magnifying the display to check focus *is* possible in the Quick autofocus mode, but it requires some concentration and finger dexterity. Here's the method I recommend: Before you press the shutter button halfway to establish focus (Step 7), move the magnifying frame over your subject. After you set focus, keep pressing the shutter button halfway as you press the AF Point Selection button to magnify the display. If focus looks good, keep pressing the shutter button halfway to maintain focus as you press the AF Point Selection button to return to the nonmagnified view. Then press the shutter button the rest of the way to take the picture. (I *told* you it was cumbersome.) If focus doesn't look right in the magnified view, you can release the shutter button and then press it halfway again to reset focus without changing the magnification level. In fact, you can even take the picture in the magnified view — just remember that the actual picture will contain the entire scene in front of the lens, not just the magnified portion that's visible in the monitor.

Live mode autofocusing

Live mode autofocusing enables you to set focus without temporarily losing the monitor preview as you do with Quick mode. Additionally, instead of selecting from nine autofocus points, you simply move a single focus point over your subject. In short, this autofocusing method is probably more intuitive to use than Quick mode.

On the significant downside, however, Live mode autofocusing is noticeably slower than Quick mode, and the camera may have more trouble locking focus than in Quick mode. (The difference is caused by the autofocusing system that the camera employs.) Because of its sluggishness, Live mode autofocus is best suited for shooting static subjects, such as landscapes, portraits, or still lifes. If you're shooting someone who is running all over the place, you're going to have an impossible time focusing and getting a good shot using Live mode.

To try it out for yourself, first set the lens switch to the AF position and fire up the Live View display. Then follow these steps:

1. **Set the AF mode to Live.**

   The fastest option is to press the Quick Control button, highlight the autofocus option (see the left screen in Figure 4-12) and then rotate the Main dial to cycle through the three AF settings. To exit the Quick Control screen, press the Quick Control button again or press the shutter button halfway and release it.

   A large rectangle appears in the center of the frame, as shown on the right in Figure 4-12. This rectangle is the Live mode version of an autofocus point.

2. **Use the cross keys to move the rectangle over the area on which you want to focus.**

   To quickly reset the box to the center of the screen, press the Erase button, located on the back-right side of the camera.

3. **Press and hold the shutter button halfway down to focus.**

   The camera attempts to establish focus and also sets exposure, if you're using any exposure mode but M (manual). When focus is set, the focus point turns green and you hear a beep. If the camera can't establish focus, the focus point turns orange. The fastest fix is to switch to manual focusing.

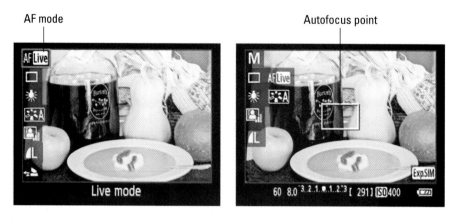

Figure 4-12: Use the cross keys to move the autofocus point over your subject.

Focus remains locked as long as you hold the shutter button halfway down. Press the button the rest of the way to take the picture. Or for movie recording, you can release the shutter button and then press the Live View button to start and stop recording. (Focus remains locked as long as you don't press the shutter button again.)

You can press the AF Point Selection button to magnify the view and check focus, just as in Quick autofocus mode. Use the same technique described at the end of the preceding section; the only difference is that you don't have to move the magnification rectangle over your subject — the focusing rectangle and the magnification rectangle are one and the same in Live mode.

Using Live mode with Face Detection AF

Designed for portrait shooting, this AF mode tells the camera to find and lock on faces in the scene. If the camera is successful in detecting a face, it automatically places a focusing frame over the face and sets focus at that spot.

After you set the AF mode to Face Detection — using the Quick Control display is the fastest option — the camera goes to work tracking down possible faces in the scene. If it finds one, you see a small focusing frame over the person, as shown on the right in Figure 4-13. If the camera detects more than one face, little triangles appear on the left and right side of the focusing frame, as in the figure. That's your cue to use the right or the left cross key to move the frame over the person who is most likely to yell at you if not perfectly focused.

Face Detection focusing frame

Figure 4-13: Face Detection mode tries to pick out a face on which to set focus.

If you don't see the little box, the camera can't detect any faces and will set focus based on the center of the screen. You can switch to one of the other AF modes or use manual focusing if that solution doesn't work for you.

To focus on the face within the focus frame, press and hold the shutter button halfway. As usual, you hear a beep and see the focus frame turn green when focus is established. If the autofocus system can't find a focus point, the frame turns orange.

Continue pressing the shutter button the rest of the way to take the picture. Or if you're shooting movies, let up on the shutter button — the focus distance will remain locked — and then press the Live View button to start and stop recording.

In this autofocus mode, you can't magnify the display to check focus as you can in the other two modes.

Shooting Still Pictures in Live View Mode

After sorting out the focusing options, the rest of the steps involved in taking a picture in Live View mode are essentially the same as for viewfinder photography. However, a few differences occur, so the next section explains how you view and choose picture settings in Live View mode. Following that, I provide a step-by-step summary that walks you through the process of actually taking a picture in Live View mode. (Finally, you say!)

Viewing and adjusting picture settings

When Live View is enabled, you can set the display to reveal many of the same picture settings that normally appear on the Shooting Settings screen — and then some. Figure 4-14 labels all the components that appear when you shoot in the P, Tv, Av, M, or A-DEP modes and display the maximum shooting data, for example. Press the Info button to switch from that display to one of the three other display styles. In the fully automatic modes and Creative Auto mode, options that you can't control disappear from the screen.

Here's an explanation of all the stuff you see in the figure:

   ✔ **A symbol representing the current exposure mode appears in the top-left corner.** For example, in Figure 4-14, the exposure mode is set to Av (aperture-priority autoexposure).

✔ **Data along the bottom of the screen is similar to data you normally see in the viewfinder display.** With the exception of the shots-remaining value and the battery level status, these settings relate to exposure issues you can explore in Chapter 7. Note that the flash status icon appears only when the flash is enabled.

If you turn on Highlight Tone Priority, a D+ symbol appears to the left of the battery status symbol. And if you enable AE (autoexposure) lock, an asterisk appears near the flash status symbol.

You see the meter only in the advanced exposure modes. In the M exposure mode, the meter indicates whether the camera thinks your chosen exposure settings are on target. In the other advanced modes, it indicates whether any exposure compensation is applied.

You can change the Exposure Compensation setting via Shooting Menu 2 or by pressing the Exposure Compensation button and rotating the Main dial. Again, Chapter 7 provides the full story on the meter and the Exposure Compensation feature.

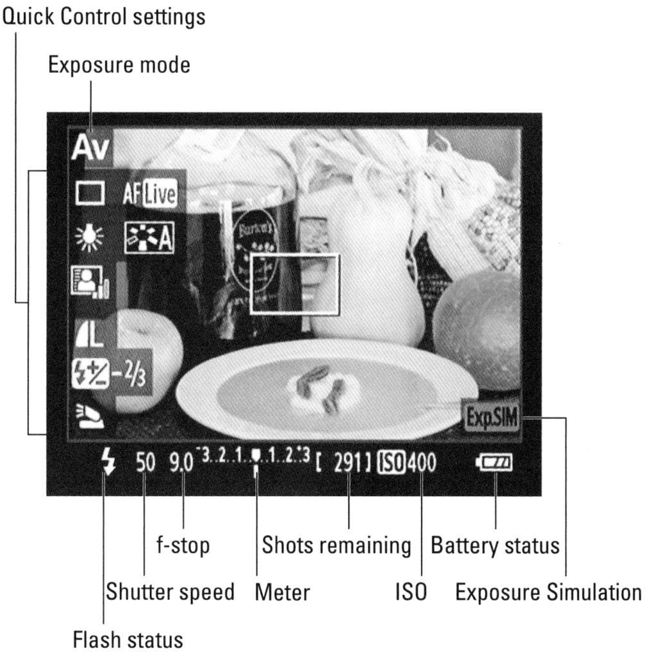

Figure 4-14: Symbols representing the current picture settings appear on the Live View display.

✔ **Settings adjustable via the Quick Control display appear on the left side of the screen.** The settings you can adjust in the advanced exposure modes are labeled in Figure 4-15. A quick intro to these options:

Auto Lighting Optimizer

White Balance

Drive mode   AF mode

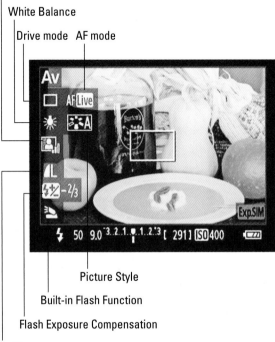

Picture Style

Built-in Flash Function

Flash Exposure Compensation

Quality

Figure 4-15: You can use the Quick Control screen to modify these settings.

- *Drive mode:* The icon you see in the figure represents Single Drive mode, in which you capture one image for each press of the shutter button. See Chapter 2 for information about other Drive modes.

- *AF mode:* The AF mode symbol appears regardless of whether you set your lens to manual or autofocus. The symbol tells you which of the three possible Autofocus options is selected (Live, Live with Face Detection, or Quick).

- *White Balance:* This setting determines how the camera compensates for the color of the light source that's illuminating your subject. The symbol in Figure 4-15 represents the Tungsten setting, for example. To see what icons for other settings look like and find out what white balance does in the first place, visit Chapter 8. (By default, the setting is Auto White Balance, represented by the symbol AWB.)

- *Picture Style:* Chapter 8 details Picture Styles, which affect picture color, contrast, and sharpness. The symbol you see in Figure 4-15 represents the Auto style.

- *Auto Lighting Optimizer:* Check out Chapter 7 for help understanding this feature, which aims to accomplish what its name implies: optimize exposure to produce better image contrast. By default, the Standard setting is used; the symbol shown in Figure 4-15 represents that setting.

- *Quality:* This icon tells you the selected Quality setting, which Chapter 2 explains. The symbol shown in the figure represents the Large/Fine Quality setting.

- *Flash Exposure Compensation:* This setting enables you to adjust flash power, as explained in Chapter 7. The symbol in Figure 4-15 shows that I used a Flash Exposure Compensation of –0.7 (–2/3 stop).

- *Built-in Flash Function:* Another of the flash features covered in Chapter 7, this one determines whether the flash fires normally or is used to control off-camera flash units. For normal operation, the icon should look like the one in Figure 4-15.

To adjust a setting, press the Quick Control button. The setting icons then rearrange themselves into a single column, as shown on the left in Figure 4-16. Press the up and down cross keys to highlight an icon and then rotate the Main dial to change the setting. A text label displays the current setting at the bottom of the screen. Alternatively, you can press Set after highlighting an option to view a screen containing all settings. Select your choice and press Set to return to the Quick Control screen.

Figure 4-16: When you adjust some settings, such as White Balance, the preview updates to show you the impact of the change.

As you adjust some settings, the Live View preview updates to show you the results. For example, the left screen in Figure 4-16 shows the scene colors as they appeared when I set the White Balance option to Auto. Usually, that setting works fine, but in this case, mixed lighting gave the camera some trouble. Because my main lights for this shoot used tungsten bulbs, I set the White Balance option to Tungsten. Voilà — no yellow color cast, as shown on the right. In the scene modes, the preview also shows the result of adjustments you make to the Shoot by Ambience and Shoot by Lighting or Scene Type settings. (See Chapter 3 for help with both features.)

Symbols you might see in the lower-right corner indicate the following:

- *AEB:* This symbol appears when you enable automatic exposure bracketing (AEB), an exposure tool covered in Chapter 7. You see an *FEB* symbol if you enable flash exposure bracketing, a function possible only when you shoot with a compatible Canon Speedlite external flash. See the flash unit's manual for help with this option.

- *Exp.SIM:* This symbol, which stands for *Exposure Simulation,* indicates whether the image brightness you see on the monitor is simulating the actual exposure you will record. If the symbol blinks or is dimmed, the camera can't provide an accurate exposure preview, which can occur if the ambient light is either very bright or very dim. Exposure Simulation is also disabled when you use flash in Live View mode.

✔ **Aspect Ratio:** By default, the T3i/600D takes photos with a traditional 3:2 *aspect ratio* (the relationship of a photo's width to its height). But in Live View mode, you can choose a different aspect ratio if you shoot in the P, Tv, Av, M, or A-DEP exposure modes. You can select the following aspect ratios from Shooting Menu 4, as shown in Figure 4-17:

- *3:2:* The standard aspect ratio and the same as 35mm film (as well as a 4 x 6-inch print)

- *4:3:* The same aspect ratio as older televisions and computer monitors

- *16:9:* Uses the same aspect ratio as most new TVs and monitors

- *1:1:* Produces square photos

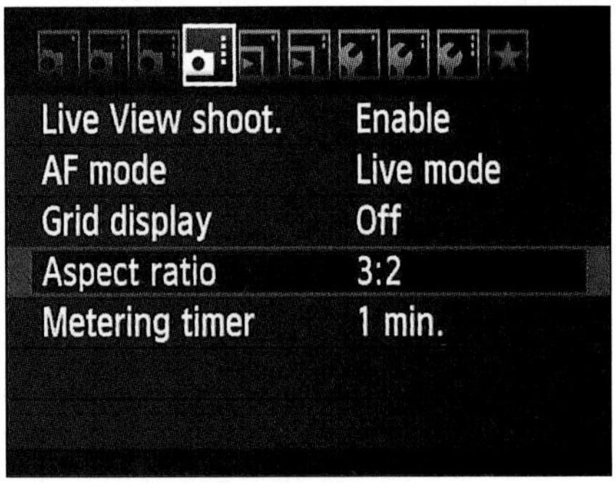

Live View shoot.	Enable
AF mode	Live mode
Grid display	Off
Aspect ratio	3:2
Metering timer	1 min.

Figure 4-17: When you use Live View in the advanced exposure modes, you can change the picture aspect ratio.

How many pixels your image contains depends on the aspect ratio; at the 3:2 setting, you get the full complement of pixels delivered by your chosen Quality setting. (Chapter 2 explains that setting.) Note, too, that if you set the Quality option to record JPEG pictures, the camera creates the different aspect ratios by cropping a 3:2 original — and the cropped data can't be recovered. Raw photos, although they appear cropped on the camera monitor, actually retain all the original data, which means you can change your mind about the aspect ratio later, when you process your Raw files. (Read about that subject in Chapter 6.)

At any setting except 3:2, the Live View display shows crop lines to indicate the area of the frame that will be captured at the chosen aspect ratio. For example, the crop lines in Figure 4-18 represent the 16:9 aspect ratio.

Aspect ratio framing boundary

Figure 4-18: At aspect ratios other than 3:2, crop lines indicate the area of the frame that will be included in the photo.

As far as adjusting camera settings, remember these additional rules of the Live View road:

- ✔ **The cross keys don't access their usual settings.** For example, pressing the up cross key doesn't take you to the White Balance options as it normally does. Instead, the cross keys move the autofocus point or the magnification frame, depending on your focusing mode. So to change the White Balance, AF mode, Picture Style, and Drive mode, use the Quick Control screen or the menus.

- ✔ **The AF Point Selection button also doesn't function as it does for viewfinder photography.** The AF Point Selection button magnifies the display, as explained in the earlier section "Manual focusing." You can select a different AF Selection Point setting only in the Quick AF mode; see the section discussing that feature for how-to's.

- ✔ **ISO button:** This one works as it usually does. Press the ISO button to display a screen showing all the available ISO settings. Select the setting you want to use and press Set. Remember, though, that you can control ISO only in the P, Tv, Av, M, and A-DEP exposure modes. See Chapter 7 for help.

✔ **The following settings are either disabled or limited:**

- *Flash:* Flash Exposure Lock (covered in Chapter 7) is disabled. Additionally, non-Canon flash units don't work in Live View mode. And here's one more quirk: When you take a flash shot in Live View mode, the camera's shutter sound leads you to believe that two shots have been recorded; in reality, though, only one photo is captured.

- *Continuous shooting:* You can use Continuous Drive mode (introduced in Chapter 2), but the camera uses the exposure settings chosen for the first frame for all images. And as with flash shots, you hear two shutter sounds for the first frame in the continuous sequence.

- *A-DEP exposure mode:* When Live View is enabled, A-DEP exposure mode loses its automatic depth-of-field calculation feature and operates just like P exposure mode. Chapter 7 explains both exposure modes.

- *Metering mode:* You cannot use center-weighted average, partial, or spot exposure metering; the camera always uses evaluative metering in Live View mode. In short, that means that exposure is always based on the entire frame rather than just a portion of the frame. Chapter 7 explains metering modes.

- *Mirror Lock-Up and Set button functions:* You can't use mirror lock-up in Live View mode. Also, if you select the Custom Function option that enables you to use the Set button to turn the monitor on and off, that feature doesn't work in Live View mode. Chapter 11 has more information about both features.

Taking a shot in Live View mode

After you digest all the whys and wherefores of the Live View autofocus options and other details about this shooting feature, follow these steps to take a picture.

1. **Turn the Mode dial (on top of the camera) to select an exposure mode.**

   Remember, the exposure mode determines what picture settings you can control. Chapter 3 introduces you to the fully automatic modes and Creative Auto mode; Chapter 7 provides help with the advanced modes (P, Tv, Av, M, and A-DEP).

2. **Set the Enable Live View menu option to Enable.**

   Look for the Enable Live View option on Shooting Menu 4 if you set the Mode dial to one of the advanced exposure modes; otherwise, find the option on Shooting Menu 2.

3. **Set the lens switch to your desired focusing method.**

Move the switch to AF for autofocusing and MF for manual focusing.

4. **For handheld shots, also enable Image Stabilization by setting the Stabilizer switch to On.**

5. **Press the Live View button to switch to Live View mode.**

The viewfinder pulls the blanket over its head and goes to sleep, and the scene in front of the lens appears on the monitor. What data you see superimposed on top of the scene depends on your display mode; press Info to cycle through the four available display options. (See "Customizing the Live View display," earlier in this chapter, for a look at all your choices.)

6. **Review and adjust picture settings.**

The preceding section outlines the main options available to you. Note that exposure compensation adjustments aren't always reflected by the monitor brightness. When you increase or decrease exposure using this feature, available only in the P, Tv, Av, M, and A-DEP modes, the image on the monitor becomes brighter or darker only up to shifts of +/– EV 3.0, even though you can select values as high as +5.0 and as low as –5.0. See Chapter 7 to get a primer on exposure compensation.

7. **If you're autofocusing, position the focus point(s) over your subject, following the guidelines for your selected AF mode.**

I spell out the details in earlier sections of this chapter, but here's a lightning-quick recap:

AF QUICK
- *Quick mode:* In P, Tv, Av, M, and A-DEP modes, press the Quick Control button, highlight the AF mode symbol, and then press the up cross key to activate the cluster of nine autofocus points. Then rotate the Main dial to cycle from Automatic Point selection (the camera chooses the point, usually focusing on the closest object) or to a specific point (focus is established just on the object under that point).

AF Live
- *Live mode:* Use the cross keys to move the focus point over your subject.

AF ᵕ
- *Live mode with Face Detection:* If the camera detects a face, it displays a box over it. You can press the left and right cross keys to select another face in a group shot. No face-detect box? Then just use the cross keys to move the normal focus point over the subject.

8. **Set focus.**

   Use these techniques, depending on your focusing settings:

   - *Autofocusing:* Press and hold the shutter button halfway down.
     - *Manual focusing:* Twist the focusing ring on the lens. Be sure that the viewfinder is adjusted to your eyesight so that you can accurately gauge focus. (Chapter 1 has instructions.) Remember that you can press the AF Point Selection button to magnify the view and check focus, as outlined earlier in this chapter.

9. **Press the shutter button fully to take the shot.**

   You see your just-captured image on the monitor for a few seconds before the Live View preview returns.

10. **To exit the Live View preview, press the Live View button.**

    You see the standard Shooting Settings screen. You can then return to framing your images through the viewfinder.

Recording Your First Movie

By shifting the T3i/600D to Movie mode, you can record high-definition video, with or without sound. Although you lose one important feature of a "real" video camera — continuous autofocus tracking — you gain the ability to use any of your favorite lenses to capture your subject. So if you own a long telephoto lens, for example, you can record your child's piano recital performance without getting so close that you make the young virtuoso nervous (or, more likely, embarrassed). And when the whole school orchestra performs, you can put on a wide-angle lens to include everyone from the last marimba player to the bass player in the shot.

The camera records movies in the MOV format, a popular file format for storing digital video. Movie filenames begin with the characters MVI_. You can play MOV files on your computer with most movie-playback programs. If you want to view your movies on a TV, you can connect the camera to the TV, as explained in Chapter 5. Or if you have the necessary computer software, you can convert the MOV file to a format that a standard DVD player can recognize and then burn the converted file to a DVD. You also can edit your movie in a program that can work with MOV files.

Recording a movie using the default camera settings is a cinch:

1. **To use an external microphone, plug the mic into the port under the little rubber cover on the left side of the camera, as shown on the left in Figure 4-19.**

   Otherwise, sound is recorded via the internal microphone, positioned in the location shown on the right in the figure. Be careful not to cover up the little microphone holes with your finger, and remember that anything you say during the recording likely will be picked up by the mic.

External microphone jack   Internal microphone

Figure 4-19: You can record sound using the internal microphone (right) or attach an external mic (left).

2. **Set the Mode dial to the little movie camera symbol, as shown in Figure 4-20.**

   The viewfinder shuts off, and the live preview appears on the monitor. You also see various data onscreen, as shown on the left in Figure 4-21. The next section explains what each bit of information means. For now, the one critical detail to note is the available recording time, which depends on how much free space exists on your memory card.

Figure 4-20: To access movie recording options, set the Mode dial to the movie camera icon.

Available recording time   Elapsed recording time   Recording symbol

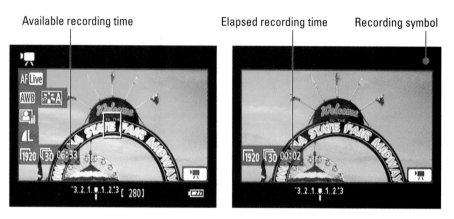

Figure 4-21: The display shows how many minutes of video will fit on your memory card (left) and, after you begin recording, elapsed recording time (right).

3. Focus.

You can use any of the focusing options outlined in the earlier part of this chapter: manual focus or autofocusing in Live, Quick, or Live with Face Detection mode.

If you expect your subject to move a lot during the recording, using manual focus is usually the best option. You can reset autofocus after you begin recording, but you may see the camera "hunt" for a new focus point and even hear the sounds of the focusing motor in the video if you record audio using the built-in microphone. To make life a little easier, use a tripod so that you have a free hand to manipulate the focus ring on the lens.

4. To start recording, press the Live View button.

Most of the shooting data disappears from the screen, and a red "recording" symbol appears, as shown on the right in Figure 4-21. Now, instead of showing you the length of the recording that will fit on your memory card, the display shows the elapsed recording time.

Depending on the memory card you use, the camera may have trouble moving movie data to the card quickly enough to keep pace with the speed of the recording. A little vertical bar on the right side of the screen, technically named the Data Transfer Alert, shows you how much movie data the camera has in its *buffer* — a temporary data storage tank — awaiting transfer to the memory card. If the indicator level reaches the top, the camera stops recording new data so that it can finish sending existing data to the card. You can try reducing the Movie Recording Size setting, explained later in this chapter, to improve the transfer speed. If the recording progress indicator keeps hitting the limit, buy a faster memory card. Canon recommends cards with a speed-class rating of 6 or higher. (Chapter 1 explains more about memory cards.)

Regardless of your memory card speed, a movie file can't exceed 4GB in size. At the default recording settings, that means you can record 11 minutes of video at a time. The upcoming section "Resolution, frame rate, and digital zoom" explains this limitation.

5. **To stop recording, press the Live View button again.**

At the default settings, your movie is recorded using the following settings:

- ✔ Full HD video quality (1920 x 1080p, or pixels) at 30 frames per second (fps)
- ✔ Audio recording enabled
- ✔ Automatic exposure
- ✔ Automatic white balancing
- ✔ Auto Lighting Optimizer applied at the Standard setting
- ✔ Auto Picture Style

But of course, you didn't buy this book so that you could remain trapped in the camera's default behaviors. So the upcoming sections explain all your recording options, which range from fairly simply to fairly not.

Customizing Movie Recording Settings

After you set the Mode dial to Movie, you can monitor the most critical recording settings via the Shooting Settings screen, shown in its cinematic incarnation in Figure 4-22. If you don't see the same type of data on your monitor, press the Info button to cycle through different display styles. In Movie mode, you can access the same display options as for regular Live View shooting, with the exception of the one that adds the histogram.

The following list offers some other insights into a few of the screen symbols; upcoming sections provide more details about recording settings.

- ✔ **The shots-remaining and Quality settings relate only to still shots you capture during a recording session.** See the later section "Snapping a still photo during movie recording" for help with this feature.

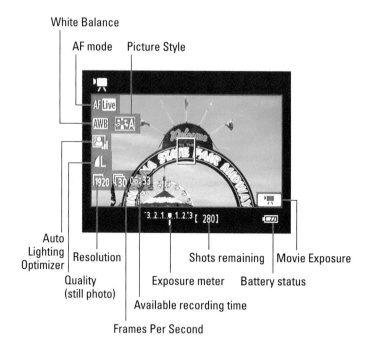

White Balance

AF mode   Picture Style

Auto
Lighting   Resolution   Shots remaining   Movie Exposure
Optimizer
Quality   Exposure meter   Battery status
(still photo)
Available recording time

Frames Per Second

Figure 4-22: To view the maximum amount of shooting data,
press the Info button to cycle to this display.

✔ **By default, the camera controls the aperture, shutter speed, and ISO for you.** These exposure settings apply to both your movie and any still shots you capture. But you can switch to manual exposure control for movies through Movie Menu 1, as outlined in the next section. When manual exposure control is enabled, a little M appears next to the Movie Exposure icon in the lower-right corner of the display.

✔ **With autoexposure, the exposure meter indicates the amount of Exposure Compensation.** Exposure Compensation enables you to request that the camera adjust the brightness of your next recording or still shot. If the little white bar under the meter is at the center position, as shown in Figure 4-22, no compensation has been applied. See the later section "Movie Menu 3" for help with this setting.

✔ **You can press the AE Lock button to disable automatic exposure adjustment at any time.** When you use autoexposure, the camera adjusts exposure during the recording as needed. If you prefer to use the same settings throughout the recording — or to lock in the current settings during the recording — you can use AE (autoexposure) Lock.

Just press the AE Lock button (its label appears in the margin). A little asterisk appears in the lower-left corner of the screen, to the left of the exposure meter.

To cancel AE Lock during recording, press the AF Point Selection button.

✔ **Autofocus options:** Again, you can use either manual focusing or one of the three available Live View autofocusing options. As with Live View still photography, you see a symbol representing the currently selected AF mode even if you set the lens to the MF position for manual focusing.

To adjust recording options, you can go two routes:

✔ **Movie Menus 1, 2, and 3:** When you set the Mode dial to Movie, you also access three menus of options, which I detail in the next several sections.

✔ **Quick Control screen:** You can also adjust some recording options via the Quick Control screen. The icons running down the left side of the screen represent these settings. Most are the same as for Live View still photography: AF mode, Picture Style, White Balance, Auto Lighting Optimizer, and Quality (again, the latter affects only still pictures that you shoot during a recording). You also can change the Movie Recording Size, which affects resolution (frame size) and frames per second (fps) and enable or disable digital zoom (not shown in Figure 4-22).

Movie Menu 1

Start customizing your production with the options on Movie Menu 1, shown in Figure 4-23:

✔ **Movie Exposure:** This setting controls whether the camera handles exposure for you — the default setting — or you adjust exposure by setting the aperture (f-stop), shutter speed, and ISO. If you're an expert on exposure and want to handle those chores, set this option to Manual. You then use the same techniques to adjust exposure settings as you do when controlling exposure manually for still photography: Rotate the Main dial to change

Figure 4-23: Set the Mode dial to Movie to access the Movie menus.

shutter speed; press and hold the Exposure Compensation button while rotating the dial to adjust f-stop; and press the ISO button to access the ISO settings.

Canon suggests that you stick with shutter speeds in the range of 1/30 second to 1/125 second. At faster shutter speeds, the subject's movement may not appear smooth during playback.

✔ **AF Mode:** This option does the same thing as the AF mode option available via the Quick Control screen. Select one of the three autofocus methods: Live, Live with Face Detection, and Quick mode.

✔ **AF w/Shutter Button During Movie:** If you enable this option, you can press the shutter button halfway to reset autofocus during movie recording. But understand that doing so can be distracting during playback — the image can drift in and out of focus — and the sound of the lens focusing mechanism might be recorded if you use the internal microphone. In other words, it's best not to use this option if you can avoid it.

✔ **Shutter/AE Lock Button:** This setting enables you to mess with the normal functions of the shutter button and the AE Lock button. Don't. Or at least read the information in Chapter 11 about how the various settings affect your picture taking and movie making.

✔ **Remote Control:** If you want to use the optional Remote Controller RC-6 to start and stop recording, change this setting to Enable. Be sure to set the controller's release-mode switch to the 2 position. If you instead set it to the immediate shooting position (indicated with a circle), pressing the controller button records a still photo rather than controlling movie recording.

✔ **Highlight Tone Priority:** By default, this setting is turned off, as it is for still photography. Leave the feature turned off until you explore the details in Chapter 7. If you do turn on Highlight Tone Priority, the Auto Lighting Optimizer feature is automatically disabled.

Movie Menu 2

Movie Menu 2, shown in Figure 4-24, includes the following settings:

✔ **Movie Recording Size:** This option determines movie resolution (frame size, in pixels), frames per second (fps), and frame aspect ratio. It also enables you to access a feature called *digital zoom*. This setting is a little complex, so see the next section if you don't know what options to choose.

✔ **Sound Recording:** Here's where you control whether and how the audio track is recorded. This topic, too, gets its own section; skim ahead to "Audio recording options" for details.

✔ **Metering Timer:** This option is the one that adjusts the auto shutoff timing of the exposure meter, as explained in the earlier section "Customizing the Live View display." By default, the meter shuts down and disappears from the display after 16 seconds.

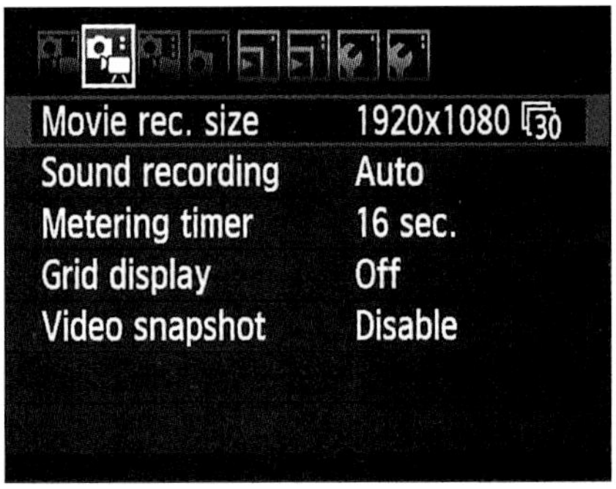

Movie rec. size	1920x1080 ⒭₃₀
Sound recording	Auto
Metering timer	16 sec.
Grid display	Off
Video snapshot	Disable

Figure 4-24: Options controlling video quality and sound recording reside on Movie Menu 2.

✔ **Grid Display:** This option also is a display customization option. Choose Grid 1 for a loosely spaced grid; choose Grid 2 for a more tightly spaced grid. For no grid, leave the option set to Off, the default. See Figure 4-6 for a look at the grid.

✔ **Video Snapshot:** This feature enables you to create multiple brief movie clips — each no more than 8 seconds in length — and then combine the clips into one movie. See the section "Creating video snapshots" to try it out. Turn the feature off for normal movie recording.

Resolution, frame rate, and digital zoom

When you select the Movie Recording Size option on Movie Menu 2 and press Set, you see the somewhat obtuse screen shown in Figure 4-25. The screen actually enables you to control two different options: You set the movie resolution and frame rate together through the Movie Rec Size portion of the screen. Then, if you select certain size options, you can turn digital zoom on or off through the setting at the bottom of the screen. (The little symbols to the right of each option name remind you how to change each one; use the Main dial to select the recording size, and press the right/left arrow keys to enable or disable digital zoom.)

More about digital zoom momentarily. First, consider resolution and frame rate. You get the following choices:

✔ 1920 x 1080 pixels, 30 fps (16:9 aspect ratio)

✔ 1920 x 1080 pixels, 24 fps (16:9)

✔ 1280 x 1080 pixels, 60 fps (16:9)

✔ 640 x 480 pixels, 30 fps (3:4)

The frame rate options depend on the Video System option on Setup Menu 3, which sets the camera to one of two video standards, NTSC or PAL. NTSC is the standard in North America; PAL is used in Europe, China, Japan, and many other countries. If you choose NTSC, you see the recording options shown in Figure 4-25 and in the preceding list. If you select PAL, you can choose frame rates of 25, 30, and 50 instead of 24, 30, and 60.

Here's a bit more information to help you choose the best resolution and frame rate combo:

Resolution/frame rate   Available recording time

Digital zoom setting

Figure 4-25: After you choose a resolution setting, the screen updates to show the length of the movie that will fit on your memory card.

- *For high-definition (HD) video, choose 1920 x 1080 (Full HD) or 1280 x 1080 (Standard HD).* The 640 x 480 setting gives you standard definition (SD) video (what you see on your TV if you don't own an HD set and spring for HD programming).

- *Higher resolution means larger data files.* And of course, the larger the file, the more space it eats up on your memory card. An 11-minute movie shot at either of the HD settings consumes about 4GB of space, while you can store 46 minutes of footage in that same 4GB closet if you use the SD setting.

- *Resolution helps determine the maximum length of your movie.* The maximum file size for a movie is 4GB, regardless of the capacity of your memory card. So again, at the HD settings, your maximum movie length is 11 minutes. At the SD settings, however, the maximum movie length is just shy of 30 minutes, even though you can fit more minutes of recording in the 4GB file size limit. (Don't yell at me — I don't set the limits, I just report them.)

  Either way, when the maximum recording time is up, the camera automatically stops recording. You can always start a new recording, however, and you can join the segments in a movie-editing program later, if you want.

- *Frame rate affects playback quality.* Higher frame rates transfer to smoother playback, especially for fast-moving subjects. But the frame rate also influences the crispness of the picture. To give you some reference, 30 fps is the NTSC standard for television-quality video, and 24 fps is the motion picture standard. Movies shot at 60 fps tend to appear very sharp and detailed — a look that some people like and others find too harsh. It's hard to explain the difference in words, so experiment to see which look you prefer. The uber-high frame rate is also good for maintaining video quality if you edit your video to create slow-motion effects. Additionally, if you want to "grab" a still frame from a video to use as a photograph, 60 frames per second gives you more frames from which to choose.

✒ *If you select one of the Full HD settings, you can enable digital zoom.* This feature works similar to the digital zoom feature found on some point-and-shoot cameras: It magnifies the area at the center of the frame and crops out the rest, creating the appearance that you zoomed in on your subject with a real zoom lens. For example, the left image in Figure 4-26 shows the fair scene after I enabled digital zoom, which results in an initial 3x magnification.

By holding down the Disp button and pressing the AF Point Selection button, you can zoom to an increased magnification, going as high as 10x, as shown on the right in the figure. An indicator on the right side of the screen shows you the current magnification. (When you first enable digital zoom, a text message at the top of the screen appears briefly to remind you to press Disp in conjunction with the AF Point Selection button to zoom in.)

To zoom out, press the AE Lock button (magnifying glass with the minus sign). To exit the zoomed view altogether, you must disable digital zoom via the Movie Recording Size option.

Digital zoom magnification level

Figure 4-26: Enabling digital zoom magnifies the center of the frame, with possible magnifications ranging from 3x (left) to 10x (right).

You also can adjust the resolution, frame rate, and digital zoom settings via the Quick Control screen. After pressing the Quick Control button, highlight the setting, as shown in Figure 4-27. Then rotate the Main dial to cycle through all the settings. For resolution/frame rate options that allow digital zoom, you're presented with settings that enable and disable the feature.

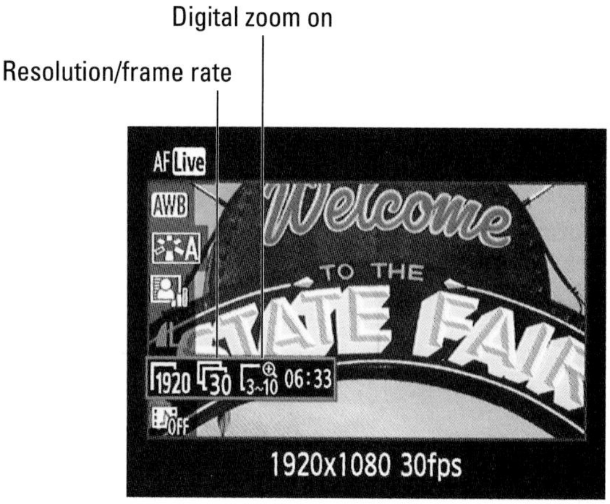

Digital zoom on

Resolution/frame rate

1920x1080 30fps

Figure 4-27: You also can access the setting via the Quick Control screen.

Audio recording options

The Sound Recording option on Movie Menu 2, shown on the left in Figure 4-28, offers three types of audio control, as shown on the right in the figure. The settings apply whether you use the internal microphone or attach an external one.

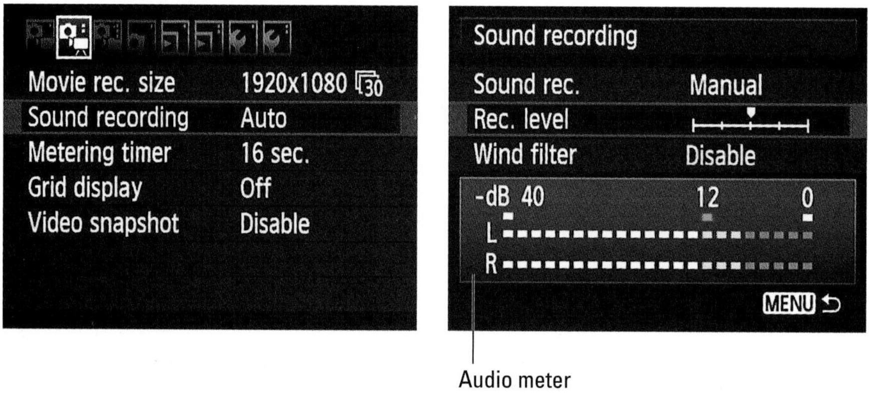

Movie rec. size	1920x1080 🔲30
Sound recording	Auto
Metering timer	16 sec.
Grid display	Off
Video snapshot	Disable

Sound recording

Sound rec.	Manual
Rec. level	
Wind filter	Disable

-dB 40   12   0

L

R

MENU ↰

Audio meter

Figure 4-28: The sound meter at the bottom of the screen offers guidance if you choose to set audio recording levels manually.

The audio controls work as follows:

✏ *Sound Rec.:* At the default setting, Auto, sound is recorded, with the camera automatically adjusting recording volume. If you're an audio expert and want to control recording levels yourself, choose Manual. To record a silent movie, choose Disable.

✏ *Rec. Level:* If you choose the Manual sound recording option, select this option, as shown on the right in Figure 4-28, and then press the right and left cross keys to adjust recording volume. To guide you, a volume-level meter appears at the bottom of the screen, as shown in the figure.

Audio levels are measured in decibels (dB). Levels on the volume meter range from –40 (very, very soft) to 0 (as much as can be measured digitally without running out of room).

For best results, adjust the recording level until the sound peaks consistently in the –12 range, as shown in Figure 4-28. The indicators on the meter turn yellow in this range, which is good. (The extra space beyond that level, called *headroom,* gives you both a good signal and a comfortable margin of error.) If the sound is too loud, the volume indicators will peak at 0 and appear red — a warning that the audio may sound distorted.

✏ *Wind Filter:* Ever seen a newscaster out in the field, carrying a microphone that looks like it's covered with a big piece of foam? That foam thing is a wind filter. It's designed to lessen the sounds that the wind makes when it hits the microphone.

You can enable a digital version of the same thing via the Wind Filter menu option. Essentially, the filter works by reducing the volume of noises that are similar to those made by wind. The problem is that some noises *not* made by wind can also be muffled when the filter is enabled. So when you're indoors or shooting on a still day, keep this option set to Disable. If you use an external microphone, try using a real wind filter instead of this digital alternative.

Movie Menu 3

Through Movie Menu 3, shown in Figure 4-29, you can access some of the same advanced exposure and color options that are available when you shoot still pictures in the P, Tv, Av, M, or A-DEP exposure modes. Specifically, you can adjust the following settings:

✏ **Exposure Compensation:** If you use automatic exposure for your movie recordings, you can apply Exposure Compensation just as you can for still photographs. Select a higher setting for a brighter picture; lower the value for a darker image. See Chapter 7 for more information on Exposure Compensation.

For a faster way to adjust this setting, press and hold the Exposure Compensation button as you rotate the Main dial.

Either way, the indicator on the exposure meter updates to show you the amount of compensation being applied, as shown in Figure 4-30. Move the indicator to the right for a brighter exposure; move it left to darken the scene. For example, in Figure 4-30, the indicator shows that a +1.0 adjustment is in effect, producing a one-stop increase in exposure.

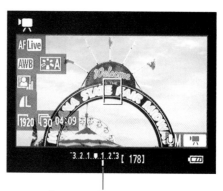

Figure 4-29: These options work just as they do for still photography.

- **Auto Lighting Optimizer:** This feature also works just as it does for still photos, as explained in Chapter 7. It's enabled by default; until you have time to dig into the pros and cons of changing the setting, let it be.

- **Custom White Balance:** As with stills, you can customize the white balance to match the lighting used for your movie. Chapter 8 explains the steps involved in using this feature.

- **Picture Style:** By default, movies are recorded using the Auto Picture Style, the same one used for still photographs by default. Changing the Picture Style enables you to tweak color, contrast, and sharpness. For a black-and-white movie, choose the Monochrome setting. Chapter 8 provides complete details about Picture Styles.

Exposure Compensation amount

Figure 4-30: The meter tells you how much Exposure Compensation is in effect.

The last three settings also can be changed via the Quick Control screen. Refer to Figure 4-22 to see the icons that represent each setting.

Other Fun Movie Mode Tricks

As if the oodles of movie recording options weren't enough, the T3i/600D offers a couple additional Movie mode features: You can snap a still photo during a recording or create a video *snapshot* — a series of short clips that can later be stitched together into a single movie.

Snapping a still photo during movie recording

You can interrupt your recording to take a still photo without exiting Movie mode. Just press the shutter button as usual to take the shot. The camera records the still photo as a regular image file, using the same Picture Style, White Balance, and Auto Lighting Optimizer settings you chose for your movie. The Quality setting determines the picture resolution and file format, as outlined in Chapter 2.

There are a few drawbacks to capturing a still photo during a recording:

- If you're shooting a movie at one of the two highest size settings, which capture a movie in the 16:9 aspect ratio, the area included in your still photo is different from what's in the movie shots. All still photos have an aspect ratio of 3:2, so you gain some image area at the top and bottom and lose it from the sides. If the movie size is set to 640 x 480, your still photo still has a 3:2 aspect ratio.

- You can't use flash.

- Perhaps most importantly, your movie will contain a still frame at the point you took the photo; the frame lasts about one second. Ouch. If you're savvy with a video editor, you can edit each still photo out of the video, but if you shoot 50 stills in 5 minutes of video, editing is going to take a while.

Creating video snapshots

Although the name of this feature makes it sound like you use it to take still photos, it's actually designed for capturing short video clips that you stitch into a single recording, called a *video album* in Canon nomenclature. One fun way to use this feature is to shoot one snapshot with digital zoom turned off to show the entire view of a scene and then record additional snapshots with the zoom turned on, to get several close-up views.

A few pertinent facts before I show you the steps involved in using the feature:

- ✔ Each clip can be a maximum of 8 seconds in length. You also can record 2- and 4-second clips.
- ✔ All clips in an album must be the same length.
- ✔ You need to record all snapshots you want to include in an album before you take any still photos or record a regular movie.
- ✔ When you finish recording your snapshots, the camera automatically creates an album to hold them. The snapshots appear in the order they were shot; you can't rearrange the clips. Nor can you add additional clips after you switch back to regular movie or still photography.

Okay, so those restrictions are pretty limiting, but what the heck — it's a fun diversion anyway. So try it out:

1. Set the Mode dial to Movie and then locate the Video Snapshot feature on the Quick Control screen or Movie Menu 2.

When the feature is disabled, as it is by default, the icon representing the setting doesn't appear on the Shooting Settings screen. But after you press the Quick Control button, you can use the cross keys to scroll down to access the option, as shown on the left in Figure 4-31.

You also find the option on Movie Menu 2, as shown on the right in the figure.

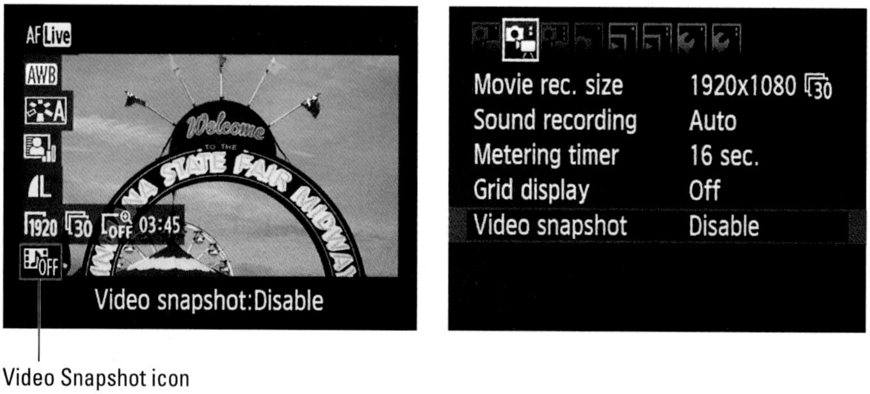

Movie rec. size	1920x1080
Sound recording	Auto
Metering timer	16 sec.
Grid display	Off
Video snapshot	Disable

Video snapshot:Disable

Video Snapshot icon

Figure 4-31: Use the Video Snapshot feature to record and combine multiple short movie clips.

2. Choose the length of the snapshots you want to record and press Set.

If you're using the Quick Control screen, just rotate the Main dial to adjust the snapshot length. On the menu, highlight the Video Snapshot option and press Set to access a screen showing all three settings (2, 4, and 8 seconds). Select your choice and press Set to return to the live preview.

The bottom of the display now includes a horizontal blue progress bar.

3. Press the Live View button to start the recording.

Now you see a screen similar to the one in Figure 4-32. The progress bar starts to shrink as the camera ticks off the seconds of your recording. When you reach the maximum clip length, recording stops automatically. The monitor temporarily shuts off, and then you see the last frame of the clip along with the options shown in Figure 4-33.

4. Tell the camera what to do with the clip.

Press the right/left cross keys to choose from these options, represented by the icons labeled in Figure 4-33:

- Create a new album and use the recording as the first snapshot in the album.

- Play the clip.

- Trash the clip. Don't like what you see in the playback? Choose this option to delete it.

Elapsed time

Progress bar

Figure 4-32: As you record a clip, the progress bar indicates how much shooting time remains.

Save as album   Delete snapshot

Play snapshot

Figure 4-33: After recording a clip, you can save it to a new album or an existing album.

If you choose to play the clip, you see the controls labeled in Figure 4-34 at the bottom of the screen. Use the cross keys to highlight a control and press Set to "press" it.

5. **To start recording the next clip, press the Live View button.**

6. **When that clip is recorded, choose one of the options shown in Figure 4-35.**

This time, you get the same three options described in Step 6. But you also can choose to create an entirely new album for this clip by selecting the icon labeled in Figure 4-35. (You can't add the clip to albums you created during another video snapshot recording session.)

7. **To stop capturing snapshots, turn off Video Snapshot via the Quick Control screen or Movie Menu 2.**

You can then shoot regular movies again or set the Mode dial to one of the still photography modes.

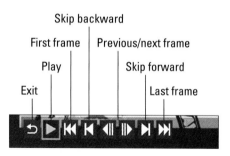

Figure 4-34: Highlight a playback control and press Set to "push" the selected "button."

Figure 4-35: You can choose to add the second clip to the album you just created or start another new album.

Playing Movies and Snapshot Albums

Chapter 5 explains how to connect your camera to a television set for big-screen movie playback. To view movies on the camera monitor, follow these steps:

1. **Press the Playback button and then locate the movie file.**

When reviewing pictures in full-frame view, you can spot a movie file by looking for the little movie camera icon in the upper-left corner of the screen, as shown on the left in Figure 4-36. Video snapshot albums are marked with the symbol shown on the right in the figure.

Movie symbol   Video Snapshot symbol

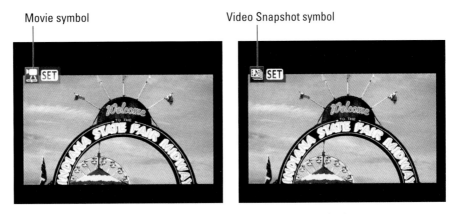

Figure 4-36: These two symbols indicate a regular movie (left) and a video snapshot album (right).

If you see thumbnails instead of a full movie frame on the screen, use the cross keys to highlight the movie or snapshot album with a yellow box. Then press Set to display the file in the full-frame view. You can't play movies or albums in thumbnail view (officially named Index view and detailed fully in Chapter 5.)

2. **Press the Set button.**

You see a strip of playback controls at the bottom of the screen. The controls vary depending on whether you're viewing a movie or video snapshot. Figure 4-37 shows the playback controls. The controls are a little different for snapshots in "official" play-back mode than they are when you're in the process of record-ing snapshots. In addition, you get a little scissors icon, which enables you to edit your movies. (See the next section for details.)

The playback controls disap-pear after a few seconds; you can bring them back by pressing any cross key.

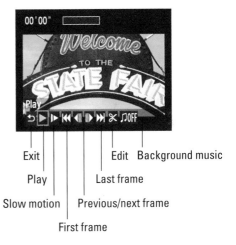

Exit   Edit Background music

Play   Last frame

Slow motion Previous/next frame

First frame

Figure 4-37: If the playback controls disappear, just press any cross key to redisplay them.

3. **Use the cross keys to highlight the Play button and then press Set.**

   The control strip disappears, and your movie begins playing.

   You can pause playback by pressing Set.

4. **To adjust the volume, rotate the Main dial.**

   On your playback screen, you should see a little white wheel and a volume display bar at the right end of the control strip. (It's not possible to capture those controls in the screen grabs for this book.) The wheel icon reminds you to use the Main dial to adjust volume. Rotating the dial controls only the camera speaker's volume; if you connect the camera to a TV, control the volume on the TV instead.

A few other pertinent facts about movie sound:

- ✔ If you recorded a movie without sound, you can enable the Background Music option to play a sound file. In order to use this feature, you must install the Canon EOS Utility found on the software provided with your camera and then use the program to copy music files to your camera memory card. The EOS Utility program offers all the details you need to know to copy music files to the card.

- ✔ Playback Menu 2 contains a Bass Boost option that, when enabled, amps up the volume of low-pitched sounds. Unfortunately, the resulting audio can sometimes sound a little distorted; disable the feature if it offends your ears.

Editing Movies

Although never intended as a substitute for computer-based video editing software, the T3i/600D Edit feature makes it delightfully easy to remove unwanted parts from the beginning or end of a movie — right on your camera. If you read that previous sentence carefully, you might be asking, "What if I want to cut that bad section in the middle of my movie, where I aimed the camera at my feet?" Well, that's why we have computers. This onboard editing is handy but basic, so don't expect miracles.

Here are the simple steps for trimming the start of a movie:

1. **Follow the steps in the preceding section to display the initial movie playback screen.**

2. **Use the cross keys to highlight the Edit icon (it looks like a pair of scissors; see Figure 4-37) and press Set to enter the Editing screen.**

   Figure 4-38 shows the screen.

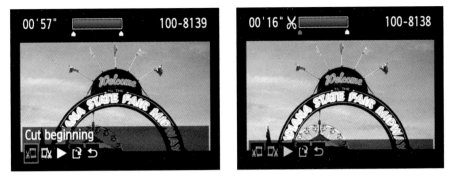

Figure 4-38: From the playback screen, highlight the scissors icon and press Set to get to these editing functions.

3. **Select the Cut Beginning icon.**

4. **Press Set.**

   The bar at the top of the screen becomes active, and a little pair of scissors appears at the left end, as shown on the right in Figure 4-38. The bar indicates the current frame length of the movie.

5. **Press and hold the right cross key to advance frame by frame to the last frame you want to cut.**

   As you advance through the movie, the little blue triangle indicates the position of the frame within the entire movie, as shown on the left in Figure 4-39.

6. **Press Set to display the screen shown on the right in Figure 4-39.**

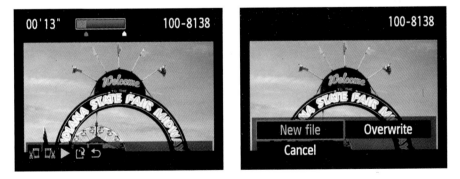

Figure 4-39: Choose New File to avoid overwriting the original movie with the edited version.

7. **To save the trimmed movie as a separate file from your original, choose New File.**

   It's *much* safer to save the edited version as a new file. That way, if you ever decide that you did a lousy job (you edited out the cake cutting at your sister's wedding, for instance), you'll have your original movie on the memory card to save the day. But if you know you never want the original back, you can choose Overwrite instead.

8. **Press Set.**

To trim the end of a movie, follow the same process, but choose Cut End in Step 3.

Part II
Working with Picture Files

In this part . . .

*Y*ou have a memory card full of pictures. Now what?

Turn to the two chapters in this part, that's what. The first chapter explains how to review, rate, and delete pictures from your memory card. In addition, you can find out how to connect your camera to your TV so that you can display your masterpieces on the big screen instead of just on the camera monitor.

When you're ready to move those pictures from your camera to your computer, the second chapter shows you how. Information on processing Raw (CR2) files, printing pictures, and preparing photos for online sharing also await in this part.

5

Picture Playback

*W*ithout question, one of the best things about digital photography is being able to view pictures right after you shoot them. No more guessing whether you got the shot you want or need to try again; no more wasting money on developing and printing pictures that stink. But seeing your pictures is just the start of the things you can do when you switch your camera to playback mode. You also can review the settings you used to take the picture, display graphics that alert you to exposure problems, and add file markers that protect the picture from accidental erasure. This chapter tells you how to use all these playback features and more.

Disabling and Adjusting Image Review

After you take a picture, it automatically appears briefly on the camera monitor. By default, the instant-review period lasts just two seconds. You can customize this behavior via the Image Review option on Shooting Menu 1, as shown in Figure 5-1.

After you highlight Image Review and press Set, you can select from the following options:

- **Select a specific review period:** Pick 2, 4, or 8 seconds.

- **Off:** Disables automatic instant review. Turning off the monitor saves battery power, so keep this option in mind if the battery is running low. You can still view pictures by pressing the Playback button. See the next section for details.

- **Hold:** Displays the current image until you press the shutter button halfway to return to shooting or the camera automatically shuts off to save power. See the Chapter 1 section about Setup Menu 1 to find out about the auto shutdown feature.

Quality	▲L
Beep	Enable
Release shutter without card	
Image review	2 sec.
Peripheral illumin. correct.	
Red–eye reduc.	Disable
Flash control	

Figure 5-1: Use this option to control the timing of instant picture review.

Viewing Pictures in Playback Mode

To switch your camera to Playback mode and view the images on your memory card, just press the Playback button, labeled in Figure 5-2.

You may see your photo only, as in Figure 5-2, or see a little or a lot of shooting data along with the image. Press the Info button to change how much data appears — you can choose from four display styles, as outlined in the section "Viewing Picture Data," later in this chapter. You can also display multiple images at a time; the next section tells all.

To scroll through your pictures, press the right or left cross key. To return to shooting, either press the Playback button again or give the shutter button a quick half-press and release it.

Figure 5-2, like the rest of the illustrations in this chapter, assumes that you're viewing a still photo and not a movie or video snapshot. Playback differs for movies and video snapshots, so check out Chapter 4 for details on viewing those files.

Viewing multiple images at a time

To quickly review and compare several photos, press the AE Lock button — labeled "Press to reduce size/display thumbnails" in Figure 5-2. The camera shifts to Index display mode, and you see either four or nine image thumbnails, as shown in Figure 5-3. Press once to display four thumbnails at a time; press again to display nine thumbnails.

Press to change information display   Press to magnify photo

Press to reduce size/display thumbnails

Playback button

Erase button

Figure 5-2: The default Playback mode displays one picture at a time, with minimal picture data.

Selected photo

Figure 5-3: You can view four or nine thumbnails at a time.

Note the little blue checkerboard and magnifying glass icons under the button. Blue labels are reminders that the button serves a function in Playback mode. In this case, the checkerboard indicates the Index function, and the minus sign in the magnifying glass tells you that pressing the button reduces the size of the thumbnail image.

Remember these factoids about Index display mode:

- **Select a photo.** For some playback operations, you start by selecting a photo. A highlight box surrounds the currently selected photo; for example, in Figure 5-3, the upper-right photo is selected. To select a different image, press the cross keys to move the highlight box over it.

- **Scroll to the next screen of thumbnails.** You can simply press the cross keys to scroll the screen, but to shift from screen to screen more quickly, rotate the Main dial.

- **Reduce the number of thumbnails.** Press the AF Point Selection button, labeled *Press to magnify photo* in Figure 5-2. This button also has a blue magnifying glass icon, this time with a plus sign in the center to indicate that pressing it enlarges the thumbnail size. Press once to switch from nine thumbnails to four; press again to switch from four thumbnails to singe-image view, filling the screen with the selected image.

For a quicker way to shift from Index view to full-frame view, select a photo and then press Set.

Using the Quick Control screen during playback

During playback, you can access a handful of playback functions via the Quick Control screen. Here's how it works:

1. **Press the Quick Control button.**

   If you were viewing pictures in Index mode, the camera shifts temporarily to full-frame playback. Then a strip of icons appears on the left side of the screen, as shown in Figure 5-4. The labels in the figure show you what feature each icon represents.

2. **Use the up and down arrows to highlight one of the icons.**

   The name of the selected feature appears at the bottom of the screen, along with symbols that represent the available settings for that option. For example, in Figure 5-4, the Protect Images feature is selected.

You can read more about rotating, rating, protecting, and jumping through images in other sections of this chapter. See Chapter 11 for a look at the Creative Filters, and visit Chapter 6 for information about the Resize feature.

3. **Use the left and right cross keys to select the setting you want to use.**

4. **Press the Quick Control button again to return to image playback.**

Jumping through images

If your memory card contains scads of images, here's a trick you'll love: By using the Jump feature, you can rotate the Main dial to leapfrog through images rather than press the right or left cross key a bazillion times to get to the picture you want to see. You also can search for the first image shot on a specific date, tell the camera to display only movies or only still shots, or display images with a specific rating. (See the upcoming section "Rating Photos" for details on that feature.)

Rate

Rotate

Protect

Jump method

Resize

Apply Creative Filters

Figure 5-4: You can control these playback features via the Quick Control screen.

You can choose from the following jumping options:

- ✓ **1 Image:** This option, in effect, disables jumping, restricting you to browsing pictures one at a time. So what's the point? You can use this setting to scroll pictures using the Main dial as well as pressing the right/left cross keys.

- ✓ **10 Images:** Select this option to advance 10 images at a time.

- ✓ **100 Images:** Select this option to advance 100 images at a time.

- ✓ **Date:** If your card contains images shot on different dates, you can jump between dates with this option. For example, if you're looking at the first of 30 pictures taken on June 1, you can jump past all others from that day to the first image taken on, say, June 5.

✔ **Folder:** If you create custom folders on your memory card — an option outlined in Chapter 11 — this option jumps you from the current folder to the first photo in a different folder.

✔ **Movies:** Does your memory card contain both still photos and movies? If you want to view only the movie files, select this option. Then you can rotate the Main dial to jump from one movie to the next without seeing any still photos.

✔ **Stills:** This one is the opposite of the Movies option: Your movie files are hidden from view when you use the Main dial to scroll photos. You scroll one picture at a time, just as when you use the 1 Image option.

✔ **Image Rating:** If you've set ratings for one or more photos on the memory card, you can use this Jump mode to view all rated photos or only those with a specific rating.

Use one of these two methods to specify which type of jumping you want to do:

✔ **Quick Control screen:** Press the Quick Control screen and use the up/ down cross keys to highlight the Jump option, as shown on the left in Figure 5-5. Use the left/right cross keys to change the setting and then press the Quick Control button again. If you select the Image Rating mode, as I did in Figure 5-5, the current star rating appears with the option. Use the Main dial to select a rating (number of stars).

✔ **Playback Menu 2:** Highlight Image Jump, as shown on the right in Figure 5-5, and press Set to display a screen showing the Jump settings. Select your choice and press Set again; then press Playback to return to Playback mode. As with the Quick Control screen, be sure to specify a star rating if you select the Rating Jump mode.

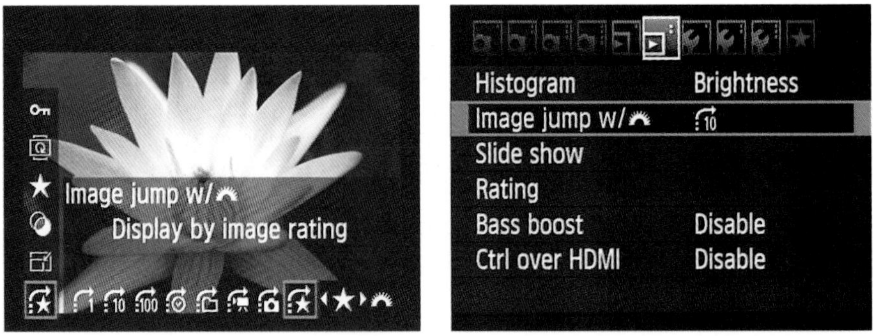

Figure 5-5: You can specify a Jump mode by using the Quick Control screen or Playback Menu 2.

After selecting a Jump mode, take the following steps to jump through your photos during playback:

1. **Set the camera to display a single photo.**

   You can use jumping only when viewing a single photo at a time. To leave Index mode, just press Set.

2. **Rotate the Main dial.**

   The camera jumps to the next image. The number of images you advance, and whether you see movies as well as still photos, depends on the Jump mode you select.

   If you select any Jump setting except 1 Image, a *jump bar* appears for a few seconds at the bottom of the monitor, as shown in Figure 5-6, indicating the current Jump setting. For the Rating Jump mode, you also see the number of stars you specified — in Figure 5-6, for example, the four tiny stars above the jump bar indicate that I asked the camera to show me only four-star photos.

Figure 5-6: Rotate the Main dial to start jumping through pictures.

3. **To exit Jump mode, press the right or left cross key.**

   Now you're back to regular Playback mode, in which each press of the right or left cross key advances to the next picture.

Rotating pictures

When you take a picture, the camera can record the image *orientation:* that is, whether you held the camera horizontally or on its side to shoot vertically. This bit of data is simply added into the picture file. Then when you view the picture, the camera reads the data and rotates the image so that it appears upright in the monitor, as shown on the left in Figure 5-7, instead of on its side, as shown on the right. The image is also rotated automatically when you view it in the Canon photo software that shipped with your camera (as well as in some other programs that can read the rotation data).

Figure 5-7: Display a vertically oriented picture upright (left) or sideways (right).

Official photo lingo uses the term *portrait orientation* to refer to vertically oriented pictures and *landscape orientation* to refer to horizontally oriented pictures. The terms stem from the traditional way that people and places are captured in painting and photographs — portraits, vertically; landscapes, horizontally.

By default, the camera tags the photo with the orientation data and rotates the image automatically both on the camera and on your computer screen. But you have other choices, as follows:

✔ **Disable or adjust automatic rotation:** Select Auto Rotate on Setup Menu 1, as shown on the left in Figure 5-8. Then choose from these options, listed in the order they appear on the menu:

- *On, camera and computer:* This option is the default.

- *On, computer only:* Pictures are tagged with orientation data but rotated only on your computer monitor.

- *Off:* New pictures aren't tagged with the orientation data, and existing photos aren't rotated during playback on the camera, even if they are tagged.

✔ **Rotate pictures during playback:** If you stick with the default Auto Rotate setting, you can rotate pictures during playback via the Quick Control screen. Highlight the Rotate option, labeled in the right screen in Figure 5-9, and then press the right or left cross keys to select one of the three orientation icons at the bottom of the screen. Press the Quick Control button a second time to exit the Quick Control screen.

If the Auto Rotate menu option is set to Off or computer-rotation only, the Quick Control technique only adds the rotation data to the image file — your picture doesn't rotate on the camera monitor. However, you can still rotate pictures for on-camera display via the Rotate option on Playback Menu 1, shown on the right in the figure.

Choose the menu option and Press Set to display your photos. In Index display mode, use the cross keys to select the image that needs rotating. In full-frame display, just scroll to the photo. Either way, press Set once to rotate the image 90 degrees; press again to rotate 180 degrees from the first press (270 total degrees); press once more to return to 0 degrees, or back where you started. Press Playback to return to viewing pictures. The photo remains in its rotated orientation only if the Auto Rotate option is set to the default.

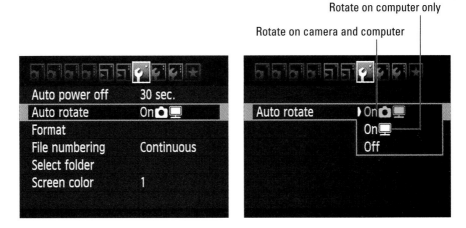

Figure 5-8: Go to Setup Menu 1 to disable or adjust automatic image rotation.

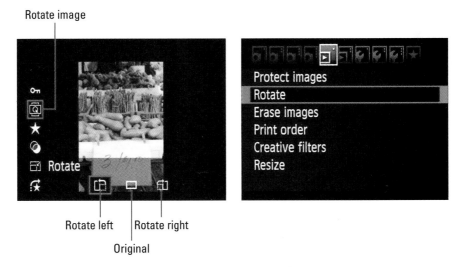

Figure 5-9: The fastest way to rotate individual images is to use the Quick Control screen.

These steps apply only to still photos; you can't rotate movies during play-back. See Chapter 4 for more about movie playback.

Zooming in for a closer view

During playback, you can magnify a photo to inspect small details, as shown in Figure 5-10. As with image rotating, zooming works only for still photos and only when you're displaying photos one at a time, though. So if you're viewing pictures in Index display mode, press Set to return to full-frame view. Then use these techniques to adjust the image magnification:

Magnified image area

Figure 5-10: After displaying your photo in full-frame view (left), press the AF Point Selection button to zoom in for a closer view (right).

✓ **Zoom in.** Press and hold the AF Point Selection button until you reach the magnification you want. You can enlarge the image up to ten times its normal display size.

Again, note the blue magnifying glass label under the button — the plus sign reminds you that you use the button to magnify the view.

✓ **View another part of the picture.** Whenever the image is magnified, a little thumbnail representing the entire image appears in the lower-right corner of the monitor, as shown in the right image in Figure 5-10. The white box indicates the area of the image that's visible. Press the cross keys to scroll the display to see another portion of the image.

✓ **View more images at the same magnification.** Here's an especially neat trick: While the display is zoomed, you can rotate the Main dial to display the same area of the next photo at the same magnification. For example, if you shot a group portrait several times, you can easily check each one for shut-eye problems.

▱ **Zoom out.** To zoom out to a reduced magnification, press the AE Lock button. (Note that the magnifying glass label contains a minus sign, for zoom out.) Continue holding down the button until you reach the magnification you want.

▱ **Return to full-frame view when zoomed in.** When you're ready to exit the magnified view, you don't need to keep pressing the AE Lock button until you zoom out all the way. Instead, press the Playback button, which quickly returns you to full-frame view.

Viewing Picture Data

When you review photos, you can press the Info button to change the type and amount of shooting data that appear with the photo in the monitor. Choose from the following four display styles, shown in Figure 5-11:

▱ **No Information:** True to its name, this display option shows just your picture, with no shooting or file data.

▱ **Basic Information:** What's this? Two settings with clear-cut names? Holy cannoli, pretty soon you won't need me at all. Well, at least check out the next section, which explains the basic data that appears in this display mode.

▱ **Shooting Information:** This mode gives you a slew of tiny symbols and numbers, all representing various shooting settings, plus a histogram (the graph in the upper-right corner of the screen). If you need help deciphering all the data, it's presented two sections from here. If not, I'd like to hire you to sort out the chicken-scratch notes I made to myself over the course of the last year to remind myself how to handle certain numbers during tax season.

▱ **Histogram:** This mode gives you a Brightness histogram plus an RGB histogram. Head to "Understanding Histogram display mode," later in this chapter, to find out what wisdom you can glean from these little graphs.

A couple of notes before you start exploring each display mode: First, when you view images on your camera monitor, some data is actually overlaid on the image instead of appearing above the photo, as it does in the figures in this book. The difference is due to the process used to capture the camera screens for publication. Don't worry about it — the data itself is the same; only the positioning varies.

Also, if you shot your picture using Scene Intelligent Auto, Flash Off, Creative Auto, or a scene mode, you see less data in Shooting Information and Histogram display modes than appears in Figure 5-11. You get the full complement of data only if you took the picture in P, Tv, Av, M, or A-DEP modes.

Figure 5-11: Press the Info button to change the amount of picture data displayed with your photo.

Basic Information display data

In Basic Information mode, you see the following bits of information (labeled in Figure 5-12):

✔ **Shutter speed, f-stop (aperture), and Exposure Compensation setting:** Chapter 7 explains these exposure settings, the last of which appears in the display only if you enabled it when you took the shot.

✓ **Protected status:** A little key icon appears if you used the Protect feature to prevent your photo from being erased when you use the normal picture-deleting feature. You can find out how to protect photos later in this chapter. The key doesn't appear for unprotected images.

✓ **Rating:** If you rated the photo, you can see how many stars you assigned it. For example, I gave the picture in Figure 5-12 four stars. See the section "Rating Photos" for details about image ratings.

✓ **Folder number and last four digits of file number:** See Chapter 1 for information about how the camera assigns folder and file numbers. And visit Chapter 11 for details on how you can create custom folders if you're into that sort of organizational control.

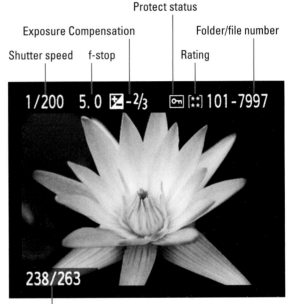

Protect status

Exposure Compensation

Folder/file number

Shutter speed   f-stop   Rating

1/200 5.0 ⊠-²⁄₃   🔒 [∷] 101-7997

238/263

Frame number/total frames

Figure 5-12: You can view basic exposure and file data in this display mode.

✓ **Frame number/total frames:** Displayed in the bottom-left corner of the screen, this pair of values shows you the current image number and the total number of images on the memory card. For example, in Figure 5-12, you see picture 238 of 263.

Shooting Information display mode

In Shooting Information display mode, the camera presents a thumbnail of your image along with scads of shooting data. You also see a *Brightness histogram* — the chart-like thingy on the top-right side of the screen. You can get schooled in the art of reading histograms in the next section. (Remember, just press the Info button to cycle through the other display modes to this one.)

How much data you see, though, depends on the exposure mode you used to take the picture, as illustrated in Figure 5-13. The screen on the left shows the data dump that occurs when you shoot in the advanced exposure modes, where you can control all the settings indicated on the playback screen. When you shoot in the other exposure modes, you get a far-less detailed playback screen. For example, the right screen in Figure 5-13 shows the data that appears for a picture taken in Close-up mode. Here, you can view the Shoot by Ambience and Shoot by Lighting and Scene Type settings you used, but not all the individual exposure and color settings that appear for pictures shot in the advanced exposure modes.

Brightness histogram

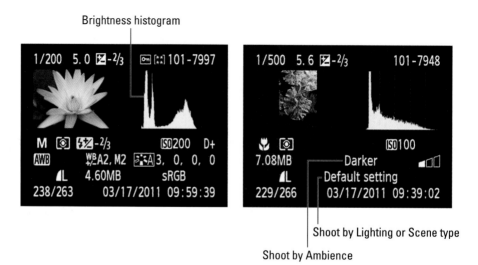

Shoot by Lighting or Scene type

Shoot by Ambience

Figure 5-13: How much data appears depends on which exposure mode you used to shoot the picture.

I'm going to go out on a limb here and assume that if you're interested in the Shooting Information display mode, you're shooting in the advanced exposure modes, so the rest of this section concentrates on that level of playback data. To that end, it helps to break the display shown on the left in Figure 5-13 into five rows of information: the row along the top of the screen and the four rows that appear under the image thumbnail and histogram. Here's what appears in the five rows:

🖊 **Row 1 data:** You see the same data that appears in the Basic Information display mode explained in the preceding section, including the f-stop and shutter speed.

What are these blinking spots?

When you view photos in the Shooting Information or Histogram display modes, you may notice some areas of the photo thumbnail blinking black and white. Those blinking spots indicate pixels that are completely white. Depending on the number and location of the "blinkies," you may or may not want to adjust exposure settings and retake the photo. For example, if someone's face contains the blinking spots, you should take steps to correct the problem. But if the blinking occurs in, say, a bright window behind the subject, and the subject looks fine, you may choose to simply ignore it.

   ✓ **Row 2 data:** This row contains the exposure settings labeled in Figure 5-14. You can find details about all of them in Chapter 7.

Flash Exposure Compensation

ISO

Metering mode

Highlight Tone Priority

Exposure mode

Figure 5-14: This row contains additional exposure information.

Note that in Figures 5-14 to 5-16, I show all possible shooting data for the purpose of illustration. If a data item doesn't appear on your monitor, it simply means that the feature wasn't enabled when you captured the photo.

   ✓ **Row 3 data:** Information on this row of the display, labeled in Figure 5-15, relates to color settings that you can explore in Chapter 8.

White Balance Correction

Picture Style

White Balance

Figure 5-15: Look to this row for details about advanced color settings.

✔ **Row 4 data:** Figure 5-16 labels the data found in this row. See Chapter 2 for help understanding the Quality setting and file size; Chapter 8 explains the Color Space option.

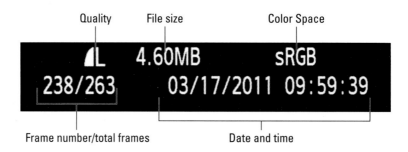

Figure 5-16: The bottom two rows of the display offer this data.

✔ **Row 5 data:** Wrapping up the smorgasbord of shooting data, the bottom row of the playback screen holds the information labeled along the bottom of Figure 5-16. If you use Eye-Fi memory cards, you also see a small icon depicting the card's wireless connection status. See Chapter 1 for more information about Eye-Fi cards and setting the current date and time.

Understanding Histogram display mode

A variation of the Shooting Information display, the Histogram display offers the data you see in Figure 5-17. Again, you see an image thumbnail, but some of the detailed color and exposure information that you see in Shooting Information display is left out, making room for an additional histogram, called an RGB histogram. Again, remember that this figure shows you the play-back screen for pictures taken in the advanced exposure modes; in the other exposure modes, you see slightly different data, but you still get two histograms.

The next two sections explain what information you can gain from both types of histograms.

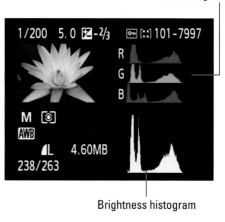

Figure 5-17: Histogram display mode replaces some shooting data with an RGB histogram.

Interpreting a Brightness histogram

One of the most difficult photo problems to correct in a photo-editing program is known as *blown highlights,* or *clipped highlights* in others. In plain English, both terms mean that *highlights* — the brightest areas of the image — are so overexposed that areas that should include a variety of light shades are instead totally white. For example, in a cloud image, pixels that should be light to very light gray become white because of overexposure, resulting in a loss of detail in those clouds.

In Shooting Information and Histogram display modes, areas that fall into this category blink in the image thumbnail. This warning is a helpful feature because simply viewing the image on the camera monitor isn't always a reliable way to gauge exposure. The relative brightness of the monitor and the ambient light in which you view it affect the appearance of the image onscreen.

The *Brightness histogram,* found in both display modes, offers another analysis of image exposure. This little graph, featured in Figure 5-18, indicates the distribution of shadows, highlights, and *midtones* (areas of medium brightness) in an image. Photographers use the term *tonal range* to describe this aspect of their pictures.

The horizontal axis of the graph represents the possible picture brightness values, from black, which has a value of 0, to white, which has a value of 255. And the vertical axis shows you how many pixels fall at a particular brightness value. A spike indicates a heavy concentration of pixels. For example, in Figure 5-18, which shows the histogram for the water lily image you see in Figure 5-17, the histogram indicates a broad range of brightness values but with very few at either end of the brightness spectrum.

Black (0)   White (255)

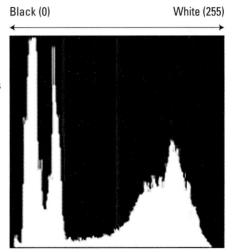

Figure 5-18: The Brightness histogram indicates the tonal range of an image.

Keep in mind that there is no "perfect" histogram that you should try to duplicate. Instead, interpret the histogram with respect to the amount of shadows, highlights, and midtones that make up your subject. For example, don't expect to see lots of shadow pixels in a photo of a white polar bear standing amid a snowy landscape. Pay attention, however, if you see a very high concentration of pixels at the far right or left end of the histogram, which can indicate a seriously overexposed or underexposed image, respectively.

In Figure 5-18, the lack of white pixels may seem odd for the water lily photo —
after all, the petals contain a lot of light tones. But when taking this picture,
I purposely underexposed the image just a hair to avoid the possibility of
blowing out the highlights. So in this case, the histogram offered reassurance
that I hadn't overshot the exposure, which can be difficult to determine from
just looking at the image itself.

Reading an RGB histogram

When you view images in Histogram
display mode, you see two histograms: the Brightness histogram
(covered in the preceding section)
and an RGB histogram, shown in
Figure 5-19.

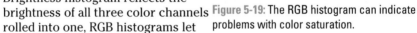
Less Saturated ← → More Saturated

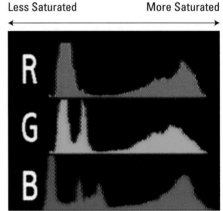

To make sense of an RGB histogram, you first need to know that
digital images are known as *RGB
images* because they're created
from three primary colors of light:
red, green, and blue. Whereas the
Brightness histogram reflects the
brightness of all three color channels
rolled into one, RGB histograms let
you view the values for each individual channel.

Figure 5-19: The RGB histogram can indicate
problems with color saturation.

When you look at the brightness data for a single channel, though, you glean
information about *color saturation* rather than image brightness. I don't have
space in this book to provide a full lesson in RGB color theory, but the short
story is that when you mix red, green, and blue light, and each component is
at maximum brightness, you create white. Zero brightness in all three channels creates black. If you have maximum red and no blue or green, though,
you have fully saturated red. If you mix two channels at maximum brightness,
you also create full saturation. For example, maximum red and blue produce
fully saturated magenta. And, wherever colors are fully saturated, you can
lose picture detail. For example, a rose petal that should have a range of
tones from medium to dark red may instead be a flat blob of dark red.

The upshot is that if all the pixels for one or two channels are slammed to the
right end of the histogram, you may be losing picture detail because of overly
saturated colors. If all three channels show a heavy pixel population at the
right end of the histogram, you may have blown highlights — again, because
the maximum levels of red, green, and blue create white. Either way, you may
want to adjust the exposure settings and try again.

A savvy RGB histogram reader can also spot color balance issues by looking at the pixel values. But frankly, color balance problems are fairly easy to notice just by looking at the image on the camera monitor.

If you're a fan of RGB histograms, however, you may be interested in another possibility: You can swap the standard Brightness histogram that appears in Shooting Information playback mode with the RGB histogram. Just set the Histogram option on Playback Menu 2 to RGB instead of Brightness.

For information about manipulating color, see Chapter 8.

Deleting Photos

When you spot a clunker during your picture review, you can erase it from your memory card in a few ways, as outlined in the next three sections.

Erasing single images

To delete photos one at a time, just display the photo (in single image view) or select it (in Index view). Then press the Erase button. The words *Cancel* and *Erase* appear at the bottom of the screen, as shown in Figure 5-20. Press the right cross key to highlight Erase and press Set to zap that photo into digital oblivion.

Figure 5-20: Highlight Erase and press Set to delete the current image.

Erasing all images

To erase all images on the memory card — with the exception of those you locked by using the Protect feature discussed later in this chapter — take the following steps:

1. **Display Playback Menu 1 and highlight Erase Images, as shown on the left in Figure 5-21.**

2. **Press the Set button to display the screen on the right in Figure 5-21.**

3. **Highlight All Images on Card and press Set.**

   After you press Set, a confirmation screen asks whether you really want to delete all your pictures.

4. **Select OK and press Set to go ahead and dump the photos.**

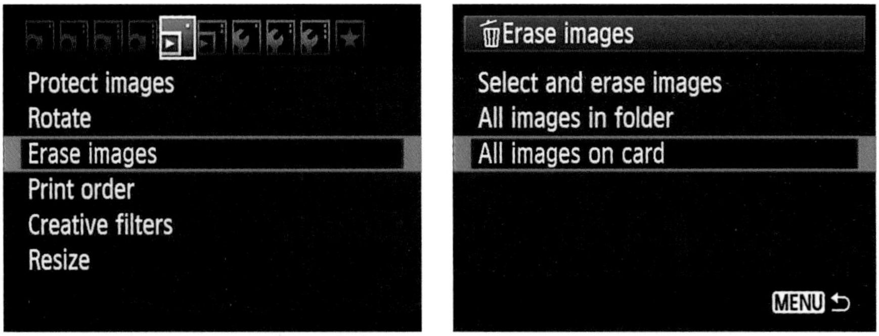

Figure 5-21: Use the Erase option on Playback Menu 1 to delete multiple images quickly.

 If your card contains multiple folders, you can limit the card-wide image dump to just the images in a specific folder. Take these same steps but choose All Images in Folder in Step 3. Then press Set to display a list of folders, highlight the folder you want to empty, and press Set again to display the normal confirmation screen. Select OK and press Set to wrap up. (See Chapter 11 to find out how to create folders in addition to the ones the camera creates by default.)

Erasing selected images

To erase more than a few but not all images on your memory card, save time and trouble by using this alternative to deleting photos one by one:

1. **On Playback Menu 1, highlight Erase Images and press Set.**

   You see the main Erase Images screen, shown in Figure 5-22.

2. **Highlight Select and Erase Images and press the Set button.**

   You see the current image in the monitor. At the top of the screen, a little check box appears, as shown on the left in Figure 5-23.

Figure 5-22: You can delete multiple selected images at once.

Erase tag

Number of images tagged

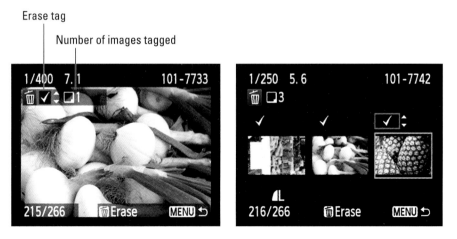

Figure 5-23: Press the up or down cross keys to tag images you want to delete.

3. Press the up or down cross key to put a check mark in the box and tag the image for deletion.

If you change your mind, press up or down again to remove the check mark.

4. Press the right or left cross key to view the next image.

5. Keep repeating Steps 3 and 4 until you mark all images you want to trash.

If you don't need to inspect each image closely, you can display up to three thumbnails per screen. (Refer to the image on the right in Figure 5-23.) Just press the AE Lock button to shift into this display. Again, use the up or down cross keys to tag photos for deletion, and use the right and left cross keys to advance through images.

To return to full-frame view, press the AF Point Selection button.

6. After tagging all the photos you want to delete, press the Erase button.

You see a confirmation screen asking whether you really want to get rid of the selected images.

7. Highlight OK and press Set.

The selected images are deleted, and you return to the Erase Images menu.

8. Press Menu to return to Playback Menu 1.

Or to continue shooting, press the shutter button halfway and release it.

Protecting Photos

You can protect pictures from accidental erasure by giving them protected status. After you take this step, the camera doesn't allow you to delete a picture from your memory card, whether you press the Erase button or use the Erase Images option on Playback Menu 1.

I also use the protection feature when I want to keep a handful of pictures on the card but delete the rest. Instead of using the Erase Selected Images option, which requires that you tag each photo you want to delete, I protect the handful I want to preserve. Then I use the Erase All Images option to dump the rest — the protected photos are left intact.

Although the Erase functions don't touch protected pictures, formatting your memory card *does* erase them. For more about formatting, see the Chapter 1 discussion related to memory cards.

Also note that when you download protected files to your computer, they show up as read-only files, meaning that the photo can't be altered. To remove the read-only status in Canon ZoomBrowser EX, the free Windows-based software that ships with your camera, click the image thumbnail and choose File⇨Protect. This command toggles image protection on and off. In ImageBrowser, the Mac version of the Canon software, set the thumbnail display to List Mode and click the photo thumbnail. Then choose File⇨Get Info and click the Lock box to toggle file protection on and off. See Chapter 6 for help with using these programs.

Anyway, protecting a picture on the camera is easy. You can use either of the techniques outlined in the next two sections.

Protecting a single photo

To apply protection to just one or two photos, the Quick Control screen offers the fastest option. Display the photo you want to protect in full-frame view. Or in Index view, select the photo by moving the highlight box over it. Then press the Quick Control button and highlight the Protect symbol, labeled in Figure 5-24. Select Enable, and a little key symbol appears at the top of the frame, as shown in the figure. Press the Quick Control button again to exit the Quick Control display.

Protect images

Protected symbol

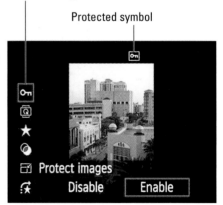

Figure 5-24: You can use the Quick Control screen to protect the current photo.

If you later want to remove the protected status, follow the same steps but choose Disable on the Quick Control screen.

Protecting multiple photos

When you want to apply protected status — or remove it — from more than a couple photos, going through Playback Menu 1 is faster than using the Quick Control screen. Take these steps:

1. **Display Playback Menu 1 and choose Protect Images, as shown on the left in Figure 5-25.**

2. **Press Set to display the options shown on the right in Figure 5-25.**

   Now you get the following options:

   - *Select Images:* This option enables you to choose the photos you want to protect.

   - *All Images in Folder:* Protects all the photos in a folder. Unless your memory card contains multiple folders, this option protects all your pictures. If you do have multiple folders, you can select a folder in the next step.

   - *Unprotect All Images in Folder:* This does the opposite, in case you downloaded those images and no longer need them protected.

   - *All Images on Card:* This is a handy option to protect all existing photos on the card.

   - *Unprotect All Images on Card:* Removes protected status from all pictures on the card.

3. **Highlight your choice and press Set.**

   What happens now depends on which option you chose:

   - *Select Images:* An image appears on the monitor, along with a little key icon and the word Set in the upper-left corner of the screen as shown in Figure 5-26. Press the left or right cross key to scroll through your pictures to the first image you want to protect. Then press Set to "lock" the picture. A key icon appears with the data at the top of the screen, as shown in the right image of Figure 5-26. After you finish protecting photos, press Menu to exit the protection screens.

   - *All Images in Folder* or *Unprotect All Images in Folder:* You see a screen where you can select a specific folder. Highlight that folder, press Set, and then press Menu to return to Playback Menu 1.

   - *All Images on Card* or *Unprotect All Images on Card:* Nothing more to do if you chose this option in Step 2. Just press the Menu button to return to Playback Menu 1.

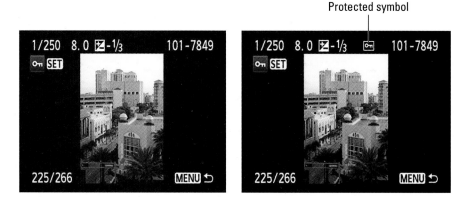

Figure 5-25: To protect more than a couple images, use the menu option instead.

Protected symbol

Figure 5-26: The key icon indicates that the picture is protected.

To remove protection from individual pictures while the memory card is still in the camera, follow these same steps, choosing Select Images in Step 2. When you display the locked picture, just press Set to turn off the protection. The little key icon disappears from the top of the screen to let you know that the picture is no longer protected.

Rating Photos

Many image browsers provide a tool that you can use to assign a rating to a picture: five stars for your best shots, one star for those you wish you could reshoot, and so on. But you don't have to wait until you make it to your computer, because your camera offers the same feature. If you later view your pictures in the Canon image software, as detailed in the next chapter, you can see the ratings you assigned and even sort pictures according to rating.

You assign a rating to a photo either via the Quick Control screen or Playback Menu 2. For rating just a photo or two, either works fine, but for rating a batch of photos, using the menu is fastest. Here's how the two options work:

✔ **Quick Control screen:** Display your photo in full-screen view or, in Index view, select it by moving the highlight box over it. Then press the Quick Control button and highlight the Rating icon, as shown in Figure 5-27. Press the right or left cross key to highlight the number of stars you want to give the photo and then press the Quick Control button to return to the normal playback screen. You must exit the Quick Control screen before rating a second photo — there's no way to advance to another image while the Quick Control screen is active.

Rating option   Assigned rating

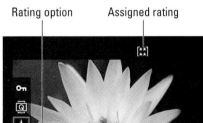

Figure 5-27: You can rate photos via the Quick Control screen.

✔ **Playback Menu 2:** Choose Rating, as shown in Figure 5-28, and press Set. You then see the screen shown on the left in Figure 5-29. Above the image, you get a control box for setting the rating of the current picture — just press the up or down cross keys to give the photo anything from one to five stars. The values next to the control box indicate how many other photos on the card have been assigned each of the ratings. For example, in the figure, the numbers tell me that I have two four-star photos and two three-star images.

Figure 5-28: Rating photos is a great organizational tool.

You can press the AE Lock button to display three thumbnails at a time, as shown on the right in Figure 5-29. Use the right/left cross keys to highlight a thumbnail; its rating appears in the box right above the thumbnails. A value of Off simply means you haven't rated the photo yet.

To go back to the one-image display, press the AF Point Selection button.

After rating your photos, press Menu to return to the Playback menu.

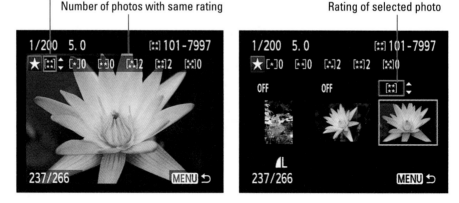

Figure 5-29: Press up or down to change the photo rating.

Presenting a Slide Show

Many photo-editing and cataloging programs offer a tool for creating digital slide shows that can be viewed on a computer or (if copied to DVD) on a DVD player. But if you want a simple slide show — that is, one that just displays all the photos and movies on the camera memory card one by one — you don't need a computer or any photo software. You can create and run the slide show right on your camera. You can even add some transition effects and background music if you choose. And by connecting your camera to a TV, as outlined in the next section, you can display your best images to the whole roomful of people.

To create and run the slide show, follow these steps:

1. **Display Playback Menu 2 and highlight Slide Show, as shown on the left in Figure 5-30.**

2. **Press Set.**

   You see the screen shown on the right in Figure 5-30. The thumbnail shows the first image to appear in the slide show.

   Also on this screen, you see the total number of images slated for inclusion in the show. On your first trip to this menu screen, all images on the card are selected for the show.

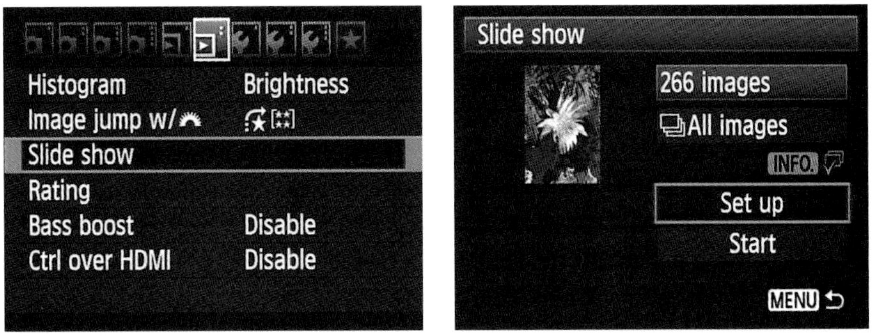

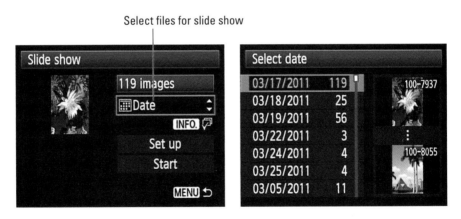

Figure 5-30: Choose Slide Show and then use the options to customize a few aspects of the playback.

3. Highlight the Select Files option (labeled in Figure 5-31) and press Set.

The option box becomes active, as shown in the figure, enabling you to specify which images or movies you want to include in the show. In the figure, the option is set to select photos by date.

Select files for slide show

Figure 5-31: Use this option to specify which photos or movies you want to include in the show.

4. Press the up or down cross keys to choose one of the following settings:

- *All Images:* Choose this setting to include all files, regardless of whether they're still photos or movies.

- *Date:* Select this option to play only pictures or movies taken on a single date. As soon as you select the option, the little Info label underneath the option box turns white, clueing you in to the fact that you can press the Info button to display a screen listing all the shooting dates on the memory card, as shown on the right in Figure 5-31. Again, press the up or down cross keys to select a date and then press Set to exit the date list.

- *Folder:* This option includes still photos and movies in the selected folder. Again, press Info to display a list of folders and highlight the one you want to use, and then press Set to exit the folder list. Chapter 11 shows you how to create custom folders.

- *Movies:* Select this option to include only movies and video snapshots in your show.

- *Stills:* Select this option to include only still photos.

- *Rating:* This option enables you to select the photos and movies you want to see based on their ratings. Press Info to display a screen where you can specify the rating and see how many photos you assigned that rating. After selecting the rating, press Set to exit the rating screen.

5. **Press Set.**

6. **Highlight Set Up, as shown on the left in Figure 5-32, and then press Set.**

   You cruise to the screen shown on the right in the figure, which offers the following slide show options:

   - *Display Time:* This option determines how long each still photo appears on the screen. You can choose timing settings ranging from 1 to 20 seconds. Movies, however, are always played in their entirety.

   - *Repeat:* Set this option to Enable if you want the show to play over and over until you decide you've had enough. Choose Disable to play the show only once.

   - *Transition Effect:* You can enable one of three different transition effects. With Slide In, photos push their way onto the screen from the left. With Fade 1, photos fade in as if placed atop the previous slide; with Fade 2, one slide fades to black and then the next slide fades into view. Choose Off if you don't want any effects between slides.

   - *Background Music:* By using the EOS Utility software that ships with your camera, you can transfer music files to the camera memory card and then use the files as audio tracks for your slide show. In fact, Canon even supplies five sample music files. If you're interested in this feature, the EOS Utility user manual (found on another disc that ships with the camera) provides the step-by-step instructions. Remember, though, that music files can be large, so make sure your camera memory card has room for them.

If you do copy music to the card, set the Background Music option to on; then press Set to choose the music file you want to use.

When background music is enabled, the setting of the Bass Boost option on Playback Menu 2 affects audio playback, just as it does for movies and video snapshots. If the audio sounds scratchy, turn Bass Boost off.

Figure 5-32: Use these four options to specify your playback preferences.

7. **After selecting your playback options, press Menu to return to the main Slide Show screen.**

Refer to the screen on the left in Figure 5-32.

8. **Highlight Start and press Set.**

Your slide show begins playing.

During the show, you can do the following to control the display:

- ✓ **Pause playback:** Press the Set button. While the show is paused, you can press the right or left cross key to view the next or previous photo. Press Set again to restart playback.

- ✓ **Change the information display style:** Press the Info button. (See the earlier section "Viewing Picture Data" for details about the available display styles.)

- ✓ **Adjust sound volume:** Rotate the Main dial.

- ✓ **Exit the slide show:** Press the Menu button twice to return to Playback Menu 1. Or press the Playback button to return to normal photo playback.

Viewing Your Photos on a Television

Your camera is equipped with a feature that allows you to play your pictures and movies on a television screen. In fact, you have three playback options:

- **Regular video playback:** Haven't made the leap yet to HDTV? No worries: You can set the camera to send a regular standard-definition audio and video signal to the TV. For this option, no added cable investment is needed because the cable you need is included with the camera. It's the one that has three plugs (one yellow, one red, and one white) at one end.

- **HDTV playback:** If you have a high-definition television, you can set the camera to high-def playback. However, you need to purchase an HDMI cable to connect the camera and television; the Canon part number you need is HDMI cable HTC-100. Do *not* use the HDMI port with anything other than the HDMI HTC-100 cable or a quality equivalent.

- **For HDMI CEC TV sets:** If your television is compatible with HDMI CEC, your Rebel T3i/600D enables you to use the TV's remote control to rule your playback operations. You can put the camera on the coffee table and sit back with your normal remote in hand to entertain family and friends with your genius. To make this operation work, you must enable it on Playback Menu 1, as shown in Figure 5-33.

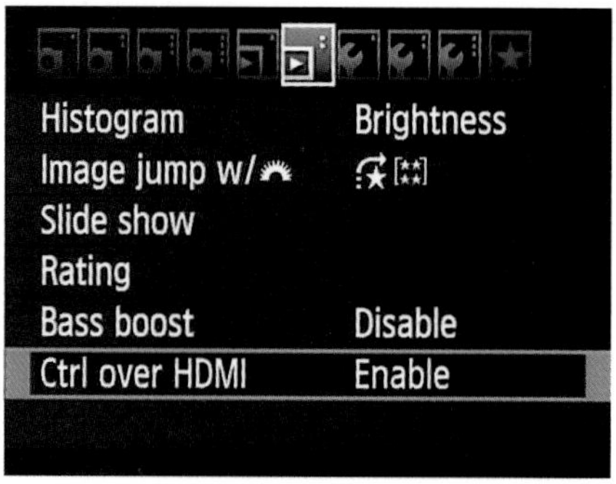

Histogram	Brightness
Image jump w/	
Slide show	
Rating	
Bass boost	Disable
Ctrl over HDMI	Enable

Figure 5-33: To use your HDTV's remote to control playback, enable this option.

Before you begin connecting your camera to your TV, you may need to adjust one camera setting, Video System, which is found on Setup Menu 2. You have just two options: NTSC and PAL. Select the video mode used by your part of the world. (In the United States, Canada, and Mexico, NTSC is the standard.) The camera should have shipped from the factory with the right setting selected, but it never hurts to double-check.

With the right cable in hand and the camera turned off, open the little rubber door that covers the video-out ports — it's the door closest to the back of the camera — as shown in Figure 5-34. The camera has two *ports* (connection slots): one for a standard audio/video (A/V) signal and one for the HDMI signal. The A/V port is the same one you use to connect the camera via USB for picture download, as explained in Chapter 6.

The smaller plug on the A/V cable attaches to the camera. For A/V playback, your cable has three plugs at the other end: Put the yellow one into your TV's video jack and the red and white ones into your TV's stereo audio jacks. For HDMI playback, a single plug goes to the TV.

At this point, I need to point you to your specific TV manual to find out exactly which of its jacks to use to connect your camera. You also need to consult your manual to find out which channel to select for playback of signals from auxiliary input devices.

After you sort out that issue, turn on your camera to send the signal to the TV set. If you don't have the latest and greatest HDMI CEC capability (or lost your remote), you can control playback using the same camera controls as you normally do to view pictures on your camera monitor. You can also run a slide show by following the steps outlined in the preceding section.

A/V port

HDMI port

Figure 5-33: You can connect your camera to a television, VCR, or DVD player.

6

Downloading, Printing, and Sharing Your Photos

For many novice digital photographers, the task of moving pictures from camera to computer — *downloading* — is one of the more confusing aspects of the art form. Unfortunately, providing you with detailed downloading instructions is impossible because the steps vary widely depending on which computer software you use to do the job.

To give you as much help as possible, however, this chapter starts with a quick review of photo software, in case you aren't happy with your current solution. Following that, you can find general information about downloading images, converting pictures that you shoot in the Raw format to a standard format, and preparing your pictures for print and e-mail.

Choosing the Right Photo Software

Programs for downloading, archiving, and editing digital photos abound, ranging from entry-level software designed for beginners to high-end options geared to professionals. The good news is that if you don't need serious photo-editing capabilities, you can find free programs (including two from Canon) that should provide all the basic tools you require. The next section takes a look at the Canon programs along with a couple other freebies; following that, I offer some advice on a few programs to consider when the free options don't meet your needs.

Four free photo programs

If you don't plan on doing a lot of retouching or other manipulation of your photos and simply want a tool for downloading, organizing, printing, and sharing photos online, one of the following free programs may be a good solution:

- ✓ **Canon ZoomBrowser EX (Windows) and ImageBrowser (Mac):** The CD that comes with your camera includes a number of Canon software tools, including this one, which goes by different names depending on whether you use a Windows or Macintosh computer. It's a pretty capable image organizer and even offers a few basic photo-editing features, which Chapter 10 shows you how to use. Figure 6-1 shows the Windows version of the program; the Mac version looks a little different but contains the same major ingredients.

    This program also includes wizards that assist you with printing and e-mailing photos. And through the Canon Image Gateway feature, you can access Canon's own online album site, which offers you 2GB of free file-storage space. You can share movies as well as still photos, and there's even a tool for posting pictures from your album to a blog. The only requirement is that you register your camera with Canon; a tool for doing that appears when you install the Canon software or access the album site for the first time. (Registering your equipment is always a good idea anyway; the company then can send you notices of any firmware upgrades, software updates, and the like.)

- ✓ **Canon Digital Photo Professional:** Designed for more advanced users, this Canon product (see Figure 6-2) offers a higher level of control over certain photo functions. But its most important difference from ZoomBrowser EX/ImageBrowser is that it offers a tool to convert photos that you shoot in the Raw (CR2) format into a standard format (JPEG or TIFF). The upcoming section "Processing Raw (CR2) Files" shows you how to make the conversions using the program.

- ✓ **Apple iPhoto:** Most Mac users are very familiar with this photo browser, built in to the Mac operating system. Apple provides some great tutorials on using iPhoto at its website (www.apple.com) to help you get started if you're new to the program.

- ✓ **Windows Photo Gallery:** Some versions of Microsoft Windows also offer a free photo downloader and browser. In Windows 7 and Vista, the tool is Windows Photo Gallery.

Click to hide/display shooting information   Metadata

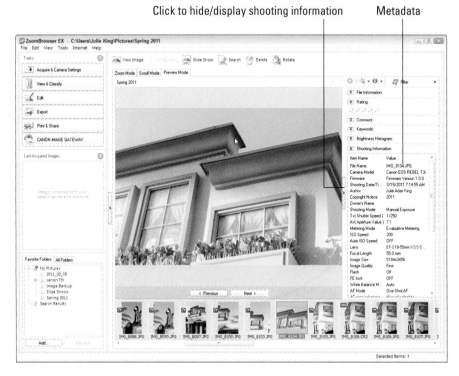

Figure 6-1: Canon ZoomBrowser EX (called ImageBrowser on a Macintosh computer) provides easy-to-use photo viewing and organizing tools.

After you download your photos, you can view camera *metadata* — the data that records the camera settings you used to take the picture. If you use one of the Canon programs, display the metadata as follows:

✔ *ZoomBrowser EX/ImageBrowser:* Choose View➪Preview Mode to set the window to Preview mode, the display mode used in Figure 6-1. The metadata panel then appears on the right side of the screen as a collection of expandable information groups. If you don't see the panel in Windows, click the little hide/display control, labeled in the figure. Or, on a Mac, choose View➪View Settings➪Information Display Panel.

✔ *Canon Digital Photo Professional:* Choose File➪Info to display the shooting information. In this case, the information appears in a separate window, as shown on the right in Figure 6-2.

Many other photo programs also can display camera metadata but sometimes can't display data that's very camera specific, such as the Picture Style. Every camera manufacturer records metadata differently, so it's a little difficult for software companies to keep up with each new model.

Figure 6-2: Canon Digital Photo Professional offers more advanced features, including a tool for converting Raw files to a standard picture format.

Four advanced photo-editing programs

Any of the programs mentioned in the preceding section can handle simple photo downloading and organizing tasks and even a few minor photo repairs. But if you're interested in serious photo retouching or digital imaging artistry, you need to step up to a full-fledged photo-editing program.

As with software in the free category, you have many choices. The following list describes a few that are most widely known:

- **Adobe Photoshop Elements (www.adobe.com, about $100):** Elements has been the best-selling consumer-level photo-editing program for some time, and for good reason. With a full complement of retouching tools, onscreen guidance for beginners, and an assortment of templates for creating photo projects such as scrapbooks, Elements offers all the features that most consumers need.

- **Apple Aperture (www.apple.com, about $200):** Aperture is geared more to shooters who need to organize and process lots of images but typically do only light retouching work — wedding photographers and school portrait photographers, for example.

✔ **Adobe Photoshop Lightroom (www.adobe.com, about $300):**
Lightroom is the Adobe counterpart to Aperture. In its latest version, it offers some fairly powerful retouching tools as well. Many pro photographers rely on this program or Aperture for all their photo organizing and Raw processing work.

✔ **Adobe Photoshop (www.adobe.com, about $700):** This program is for serious image editors only, not just because of its price but because it doesn't provide the type of onscreen help that you get with an entry-level editor, such as Elements. As you can see from Figure 6-3, which shows the Photoshop editing window, this isn't a program for the easily intimidated. Photoshop also doesn't include the creative templates and other photo-crafting tools that you find in Elements. What you get instead are the industry's most powerful, sophisticated retouching tools, including tools for producing HDR (high dynamic range) and 3D images.

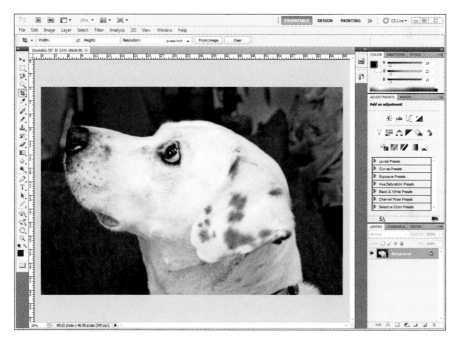

Figure 6-3: Adobe Photoshop is geared toward pros and serious photo-editing enthusiasts.

Not sure which tool you need, if any? Good news: You can download 30-day free trials of all these programs from the manufacturers' websites.

Sending Pictures to the Computer

Whatever photo software you choose, you can take the following approaches to downloading images to your computer:

- ✔ **Connect the camera to the computer via a USB cable.** The USB cable you need is supplied in the camera box.

- ✔ **Use a memory card reader.** With a card reader, you simply pop the memory card out of your camera and into the card reader instead of hooking the camera to the computer. Many computers and printers now have card readers, and you also can buy standalone readers for under $30. *Note:* If you use the new SDHC (Secure Digital High-Capacity) or SDXC (Secure Digital Extended-Capacity) cards, the reader must specifically support that type.

- ✔ **Invest in Eye-Fi memory cards and transfer images via a wireless network.** You can find out more about these special memory cards, and how to set up the card to connect with your computer, at the manufacturer's website, www.eye.fi. Your computer must be connected to a wireless network for the transfer technology to work.

For most people, I recommend a card reader. Sending pictures directly from the camera, whether via cable or wirelessly, requires that the camera be turned on during the entire download process, wasting battery power. Additionally, not all devices can use Eye-Fi memory cards, meaning that you're spending money on cards that may have limited use beyond serving as storage on your camera. Card readers, on the other hand, can accept cards from any device that uses SD cards, which are fast becoming the standard storage medium for portable devices.

That said, I include information about cable transfer in the next section in case you don't have a card reader. To use a card reader, skip ahead to "Starting the transfer process," in this chapter.

Connecting your camera and computer

You need to follow a specific set of steps when connecting the camera to your computer. Otherwise, you can damage the camera or the memory card. Also note that for the process to work smoothly, Canon suggests that your computer run one of the following operating systems:

- ✔ Windows 7, Vista, or XP with Service Pack 3
- ✔ Mac OS X 10.5 and higher

If you use another OS (operating system), check the support pages on the Canon website (www.canon.com) for the latest news about updates to system compatibility. You can always simply transfer images with a card reader, too.

With that preamble out of the way, these steps show you how to get your camera to talk to your computer:

1. **Assess the level of the camera battery and recharge it if it's low.**

   Running out of battery power during the transfer process can cause problems, including lost picture data.

   Alternatively, if you have an AC adapter, use it to power the camera during picture transfers.

2. **If your computer isn't already on, turn it on and give it time to finish its normal startup routine.**

3. **Make sure that the camera is turned off.**

4. **Insert the smaller of the two plugs on the USB cable into the A/V Out/ Digital port on the side of the camera.**

   This port is hidden behind the little rubber door that's just around the corner from the left side of the monitor, as shown in Figure 6-4.

5. **Plug the other end of the cable into the computer's USB port.**

   Plug the cable into a port that's built in to the computer, as opposed to one that's on your keyboard or part of an external USB hub. Those accessory-type connections can sometimes foul up the transfer process.

6. **Turn on the camera.**

   What happens next depends on what software you choose to use to download photos. As for the camera itself, it doesn't give you any indications that it's in transfer mode, aside from a brief flicker of the card access lamp. If you try to focus or take a photo, the word "Busy" appears in the viewfinder.

   For details about the next step in the downloading routine, move on to the next section.

Connect USB cable here

Figure 6-4: Connect the smaller end of the USB cable here to download pictures.

Starting the transfer process

After you connect the camera to the computer (be sure to carefully follow the steps in the preceding section) or insert a memory card into the card reader, your next step depends, again, on the software installed on your computer and on the OS it runs.

Here are the most common possibilities and how to move forward:

- **On a Windows-based computer, a Windows dialog box appears, asking you what program you want to use to view or transfer the files.** The design of the window varies depending on what version of Windows you use and how you set your system preferences, but you should be offered a choice of programs to use to transfer and view the pictures. If you installed the Canon software, one or more of those programs should appear in the list. To proceed, just click the transfer program you want to use. (I show you how to use the Canon tools in the next section.)

- **An installed photo program automatically displays a photo download wizard.** For example, if you installed the Canon software, the EOS Utility window or MemoryCard Utility window may leap to the forefront. Or, if you installed another program, such as Photoshop Elements, its down-loader may pop up instead.

  Usually, the downloader that appears is associated with the software you most recently installed. Each new program you add to your system tries to wrestle away control over your image downloads from the previous program.

  If you don't want a program's auto downloader to launch whenever you insert a memory card or connect your camera, you should be able to turn off that feature. Check the software manual to find out how to disable the auto launch.

- **Nothing happens.** Don't panic; assuming that your card reader or camera is properly connected, all is probably well. Someone — maybe even you — simply may have disabled all automatic downloaders on your system. Just launch your photo software and then transfer your pictures using whichever command starts that process.

  You can also use Windows Explorer or the Mac Finder to simply drag and drop files from your memory card to your computer's hard drive. The process is exactly the same as when you move any other file from a CD or DVD or another storage device onto your hard drive.

Downloading images with Canon tools

The next two sections explain how to download pictures to your computer using two tools provided on the software CD that shipped with your camera: Canon EOS Utility and MemoryCard Utility. Both actually are components of Canon ZoomBrower EX (Windows) and ImageBrowser (Mac).

Using EOS Utility to transfer images from your camera

Follow these steps to transfer images directly from your camera to the computer using the Canon EOS Utility software:

1. **Connect your camera (turned off) to the computer.**

   See the first part of this chapter for specifics.

2. **Turn on the camera.**

   After a few moments, the EOS Utility window should appear automatically. If it doesn't, launch the program as you would any other on your system. Figure 6-5 shows the Windows version of the screen; the Mac version looks much the same.

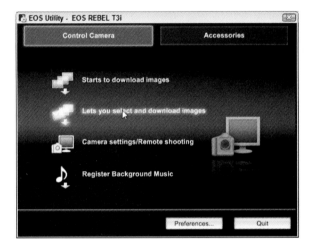

Figure 6-5: EOS Utility is designed for sending pictures from the camera to the computer.

3. **Click the Lets You Select and Download Images option, as shown in the figure.**

   Using this option, you can specify which pictures you want to download from the camera. After you click the option, you see a browser window that looks similar to the one in Figure 6-6, with thumbnails of the images on your memory card. The figure shows the Windows version, but the Mac version contains the same components. Click the magnifying glass icons in the lower-right corner of the window to enlarge or reduce the thumbnail size.

4. **Select the images you want to copy to the computer.**

   Each thumbnail contains a check box in its lower-left corner. To select an image for downloading, click the box to put a check mark in it.

Selected for download   Select menu

Figure 6-6: Select the thumbnails of the images you want to transfer.

For a quick way to select all images, press Ctrl+A (Windows) or ⌘+A (Mac). You also can open the Select drop-down list, labeled in the figure, where you find options that automatically select different categories of photos — for example, all protected photos or all photos that have a five-star rating.

5. **Click the Download button at the bottom of the window.**

   A screen appears that tells you where the program wants to store your downloaded pictures. Figure 6-7 shows the Windows version of this notice; the Mac version contains the same options.

By default, pictures are stored in the Pictures or My Pictures folder in Windows (depending on the version of Windows you use) and in the Pictures folder on a Mac. You can put images anywhere you like; however, most photo-editing programs look first for photos in those folders, so sticking with this universally accepted setup makes some sense.

6. **Verify or change the storage location for your pictures.**

   If you want to put the pictures in a location different from the one the program suggests, click the Destination Folder button and then select the storage location and folder name you prefer.

Figure 6-7: You can specify where you want to store the photos.

7. **Click OK to begin the download.**

   A progress window appears, showing you the status of the download.

8. **When the download is complete, turn off the camera.**

   You can safely remove the cable connecting it to the computer.

That's the basic process, but you need to know a couple of fine points:

- ✔ **Setting download preferences:** While the camera is still connected and turned on, you can click the Preferences button at the bottom of the EOS Utility browser to open the Preferences dialog box, where you can specify many aspects of the transfer process.

- ✔ **Auto-launching the other Canon programs:** After the download is complete, the EOS Utility may automatically launch Canon Digital Photo Professional or ZoomBrowser EX (Windows) or ImageBrowser (Mac) so that you can immediately start working with your pictures. (You must have installed the programs for this to occur.)

   If you want to change the program that's launched, visit the Linked Software panel of the EOS Utility's Preferences dialog box. You then can select the program you want to use or choose None to disable auto-launch altogether.

- ✔ **Closing the EOS Utility:** The utility browser window doesn't close automatically after the download is complete. You must return to it and click the Quit button in the lower-right corner to shut it down.

Using MemoryCard Utility for card-to-computer transfers

To transfer images from a memory card reader, you can use the Canon MemoryCard Utility that comes with the Windows and Mac versions of ZoomBrowser EX and ImageBrowser. To try it out, take these steps:

1. **Put your card in the card reader.**

   If all the planets are aligned — if the Canon software was the last photo software you installed and another program doesn't try to handle the job for you — the MemoryCard Utility window, shown in Figure 6-8, appears. The figure shows the Windows version of the window; the Mac version is identical except that the top of the window refers to ImageBrowser, which is the Mac version of ZoomBrowser EX.

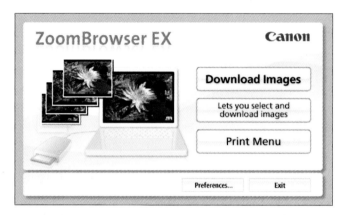

Figure 6-8: Use MemoryCard Utility to transfer pictures via a card reader.

   If the window doesn't appear, you can access it this way:

   • *Windows:* Open the ZoomBrowser EX MemoryCard Utility program, using the steps you usually take to start a program.

   • *Mac:* Start the program Canon Camera Window. The program should detect your memory card and display the MemoryCard Utility window.

2. **Click the Lets You Select and Download Images option.**

   You then see the browser window shown in Figure 6-9. Again, the figure features the Windows version of the browser window; the Mac version contains the same basic components but follows conventional Mac design rules. Either way, thumbnails of the images on your memory card are displayed in the window.

3. **Select the images you want to download.**

   • *To select the first photo:* Click its thumbnail.

   • *To select additional pictures:* Ctrl+click (Windows) or ⌘+click (Mac) their thumbnails.

- *To quickly select all images:* Press Ctrl+A in Windows or ⌘+A on a Mac.

You also can use the Select drop-down menu to access a number of other selection options — select only protected photos, for example, or only new photos (pictures that you haven't yet downloaded). On a Mac, the drop-down list is named Select Image and is located at the bottom of the program window instead of at the location labeled in Figure 6-9.

4. **Click the Image Download button.**

In Windows, the button is near the upper-left corner of the browser window. On a Mac, it's in the lower-left corner (and for whatever reason, is named Download Images instead of Image Download).

Select menu

Figure 6-9: Select images to download from the browser window.

Either way, a new window opens to show you where the downloader wants to put your files and the name it plans to assign the storage folder, as shown in Figure 6-10.

If you're not happy with the program's choices, click the Change Settings button to open a dialog box where you can select a different storage location. In the same dialog box, you can also choose to have the files renamed when they're copied. Click OK to close the Change Settings dialog box when you finish.

5. **Click the Starts Download button.**

   Your files start making their way to your computer. When the download is finished, the MemoryCard Utility window closes and either ZoomBrowser EX (Windows) or ImageBrowser (Mac) appears, displaying the downloaded files.

Figure 6-10: Tell the software where you want it to store the downloaded photos via this dialog box.

Processing Raw (CR2) Files

Chapter 2 introduces you to the Raw file format, which enables you to capture images as raw data. Although you can print Raw files immediately if you use the Canon software, you can't take them to a photo lab for printing, share them online, or edit them in your photo software until you process them using a raw converter tool. You can do the job using Digital Photo Professional, the Canon software that shipped with your camera.

After downloading photos to your computer, follow these steps:

1. **Open Digital Photo Professional, click the thumbnail of the image you want to process, and choose View⇨Edit in Edit Image Window.**

   Your photo appears inside an editing window, as shown in Figure 6-11. The exact appearance of the window may vary depending on your program settings. If you don't see the Tool palette on the right side of the window, choose View⇨Tool Palette to display it. (Other View menu options enable you to customize the window display.)

2. **Adjust the image using controls in the Tool palette.**

   The Tool palette offers three tabs full of controls for adjusting photos. You can find complete details in the program's Help system, but here are some tips for using a couple of the critical options:

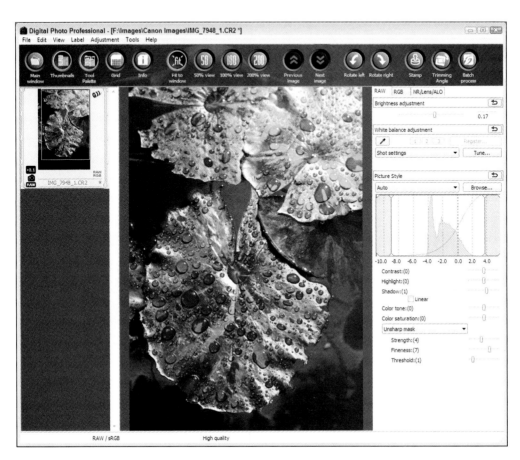

Figure 6-11: You can convert Raw images using Digital Photo Professional.

- *Raw tab:* On this tab, shown in Figure 6-11, you find controls for tweaking exposure, white balance, color, and sharpness. For white balance, you can choose a specific setting, as shown in the figure (in this case, the current White Balance value is Shot Settings, which means the camera setting is preserved), or click the little eyedropper and then click an area of the image that should be white, black, or gray to remove any color cast. Using the Picture Style option, you can apply one of the camera's Picture Style options to the photo.

If you captured the picture in Live View and set the aspect ratio to anything other than 3:2, you see a thumbnail image at the bottom of the Raw tab (not shown in the figure). Remember, Raw images are captured using the 3:2 aspect ratio and then the Raw processing function crops the original to the aspect ratio you chose. Within the thumbnail, you see a crop rectangle indicating the area of the photo that will be retained in the processed image. You can drag inside the box to reposition the crop rectangle over a different part of the frame if needed.

- *RGB tab:* From this tab, you adjust exposure further by using Tone Curve adjustment, a tool that may be familiar to you if you've done any advanced photo editing. You can make additional color and sharpness adjustments here as well, but make those changes using the controls on the Raw tab instead. (The RGB tab options are provided primarily for manipulating JPEG and TIFF photos and not for Raw conversion.)

- *NR/Lens/ALO tab:* On this tab, shown in Figure 6-12, you find controls for softening image noise and correcting certain lens distortion problems. You can even apply Peripheral Illumination Correction and the Auto Lighting Optimizer effects here instead of using the in-camera corrections. Click the Tune button to access the lens correction options.

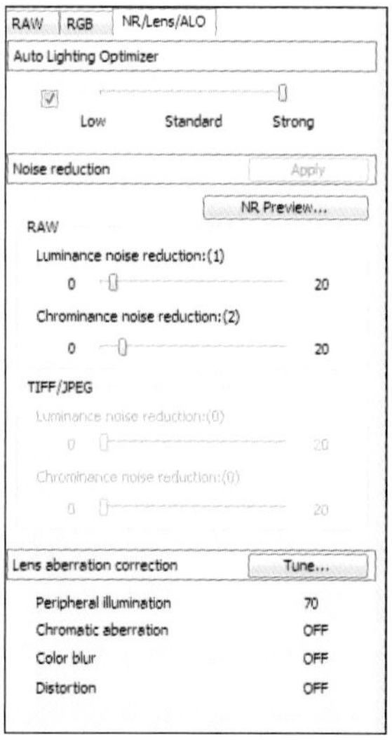

Figure 6-12: Apply Peripheral Illumination Correction from here as well as in the camera.

REMEMBER

At any time, you can revert the image to the original settings by choosing Adjustment⇨Revert to Shot Settings.

3. Choose File⇨Convert and Save.

You see the standard file-saving dialog box with a few additional controls, as shown in Figure 6-13. The figure features the Windows version of the dialog box, but the critical controls are the same no matter what type of computer you use.

4. Set the save options.

Here's the rundown of the critical options:

- *Save as type:* Choose Exif-TIFF (8bit). This option saves your image in the TIFF file format, which preserves all image data. Don't choose the JPEG format; doing so is destructive to the photo because of the lossy compression that's applied. (Chapter 2 explains JPEG compression.)

TECHNICAL STUFF

A *bit* is a unit of computer data; the more bits you have, the more colors your image can contain. Many photo-editing programs can't open 16-bit files, or else they limit you to a few editing tools, so stick with the standard, 8-bit image option unless you know that your software can handle the higher bit depth. If you prefer 16-bit files, you can select TIFF 16bit as the file type.

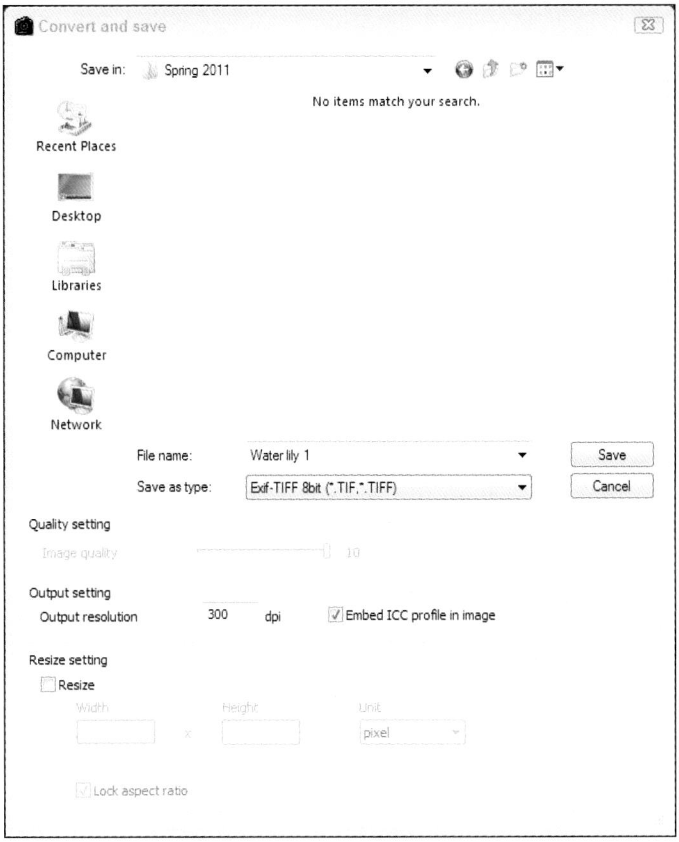

Figure 6-13: Always save processed files to TIFF format.

- *Output Resolution:* This option *does not* adjust the pixel count of an image, as you might imagine. It only sets the default output resolution to be used if you send the photo to a printer. Most photo-editing programs enable you to adjust this value before printing. The Canon software does not, however, so if you plan to print from the browser, set this value to 300.

- *Embed ICC Profile in Image:* On your camera, you can shoot in either the sRGB or Adobe RGB color space; Chapter 8 has details on color space. Select this check box when saving your processed Raw file to include the color space data in the file. If you then open the photo in a program that supports color profiles, the colors are rendered more accurately. (*ICC* refers to the International Color Consortium, the group that created color-space standards.)

• *Resize*: Clear this check box so that your processed file contains all its original pixels.

5. **Enter a filename, select the folder and browse where you want to store the image, and then click Save.**

   A progress box appears, letting you know that the conversion and file saving is going forward. Click the Exit button (Windows) or the Terminate button (Mac) to close the progress box when the process is complete.

6. **Close the Edit window to return to the browser.**

7. **Close Digital Photo Professional.**

   You see a dialog box that tells you that your Raw file was edited and asks whether you want to save the changes.

8. **Click Yes to store your raw-processing "recipe" with the Raw file.**

   The Raw settings you used are then kept with the original image so that you can create additional copies of the Raw file easily without having to make all your adjustments again.

Again, these steps give you only a basic overview of the process. If you regularly shoot in the Raw format, take the time to explore the Digital Photo Professional Help system so that you can take advantage of its other features.

Planning for Perfect Prints

Images from your T3i/600D can produce dynamic prints, and getting those prints made is easy and economical, thanks to an abundance of digital printing services in stores and online. For home printing, today's printers are better and less expensive than ever, too.

That said, getting the best prints from your picture files requires a little bit of knowledge and prep work on your part, regardless of whether you decide to do the job yourself or use a retail lab. To that end, the next three sections offer tips to help you avoid the most common causes of printing problems.

Check the pixel count before you print

Resolution — the number of pixels in your digital image — plays a huge role in how large you can print your photos and still maintain good picture quality. You can get the complete story on resolution in Chapter 2, but here's a quick recap as it relates to printing:

✔ **Choose the right resolution before you shoot.** On your camera, you set picture resolution via the Quality option, found on Shooting Menu 1, or via the Quick Control display.

You must select the Quality option *before* you capture an image, which means that you need some idea of the ultimate print size before you shoot. When you do the resolution math, remember to consider any cropping you plan to do.

✔ **Aim for a minimum of 200 pixels per inch (ppi).** You'll get a wide range of recommendations on this issue, even among professionals. In general, if you aim for a resolution in the neighborhood of 200 ppi, you should be pleased with your results. If you want a 4 x 6–inch print, for example, you need at least 800 x 1200 pixels.

Depending on your printer, you may get even better results at a slightly lower resolution. On the other hand, some printers do their best work when fed 300 ppi, and a few request 360 ppi as the optimum resolution. However, using a resolution higher than that typically doesn't produce any better prints.

Unfortunately, because most printer manuals don't bother to tell you what image resolution produces the best results, finding the right pixel level is a matter of experimentation. Don't confuse *ppi* with the manual's statements related to the printer's dpi. *Dots per inch (dpi)* refers to the number of dots of color the printer can lay down per inch; many printers use multiple dots to reproduce one image pixel.

If you're printing photos at a retail kiosk or at an online site, the software you use to order prints should determine the resolution of your files and then suggest appropriate print sizes. If you're printing on a home printer, though, you need to be the resolution cop.

What do you do if you find that you don't have enough pixels for the print size you have in mind? Well, if you can't compromise on print size, you have the following two choices:

✔ **Keep the existing pixel count and accept lowered photo quality.** In this case, the pixels simply get bigger to fill the requested print size. When pixels grow too large, they produce a defect known as *pixelation:* The picture starts to appear jagged, or stair-stepped, along curved or oblique lines. Or at worst, your eye can make out the individual pixels and your photo begins to look more like a mosaic than, well, like a photograph.

✔ **Add more pixels and accept lowered photo quality.** In some photo programs, you can use a process called *resampling* to add pixels to an existing image. Some other photo programs even resample the photo automatically for you, depending on the print settings you choose.

Although adding pixels might sound like a good option, it actually doesn't help in the long run. You're asking the software to make up photo information out of thin air, and the resulting image usually looks worse than the original. You don't see pixelation, but details turn muddy, giving the image a blurry, poorly rendered appearance.

Just to hammer home the point and show you the impact of resolution picture quality, Figures 6-14 and 6-15 show you the same image as it appears at 300 ppi (the resolution required by the publisher of this book), at 50 ppi, and then resampled from 50 ppi to 300 ppi. As you can see, there's just no way around the rule: If you want the best-quality prints, you need the right pixel count from the get-go.

300 ppi   50 ppi

Figure 6-14: A high-quality print depends on a high-resolution original.

Allow for different print proportions

Unlike many digital cameras, yours produces images that have a 3:2 aspect ratio: Images are 3 units wide by 2 units tall — just like 35mm film — which means that they translate perfectly to the standard 4-x-6-inch print size. (Most compact digital cameras produce 4:3 images, which means that the pictures must be cropped to fit a 4-x-6-inch piece of paper.)

If you want to print an original image at other standard sizes — 5 x 7, 8 x 10, 11 x 14, and so on — you need to crop the photo to match those proportions. (Chapter 10 shows you how to do it using the Canon software.) Alternatively, you can reduce the photo size slightly and leave an empty margin along the edges of the print as needed.

50 ppi resampled to 300 ppi

Figure 6-15: Adding pixels in a photo editor doesn't rescue a low-resolution original.

As a point of reference, both images in Figure 6-16 are original, 3:2 images. The blue outlines indicate how much of the original can fit within a 5-x-7-inch frame and an 8-x-10-inch frame, respectively.

To allow yourself some printing flexibility, leave at least a little margin of background around your subject when you shoot, as I did when shooting the photo in Figure 6-16. That way, you don't clip off the edges of the subject, no matter what print size you choose. (Some people refer to this margin padding as *head room,* especially when describing portrait composition.)

Get print and monitor colors in sync

Ah, your photo colors look perfect on your computer monitor, but when you print the picture, the image is too red or too green or has another nasty color tint. This problem, which is probably the most prevalent printing issue, can occur because of any or all of the following factors:

✔ **Your monitor needs to be calibrated.** If the monitor isn't accurately calibrated, chances are that it's not displaying an accurate rendition of image colors and exposure. To ensure that your monitor is displaying photos on a neutral canvas, you can start with a software-based *calibration utility,* which is just a small program that guides you through the process of adjusting your monitor. The program displays various color swatches and other graphics and then asks you to provide feedback about the colors you see onscreen.

If you use a Mac, its operating system (OS) offers a built-in calibration utility, the Display Calibrator Assistant; Windows 7 offers a similar tool: Display Color Calibration. You also can find free calibration software for both Mac and Windows systems online; just enter the term *free monitor calibration software* into your favorite search engine.

Software-based tools, though, depend on your eyes to make decisions during the calibration process. For a more reliable calibration, you may want to invest in a hardware solution, such as the Pantone huey PRO ($99, www.pantone.com) or the Datacolor Spyder3Express ($89, www. datacolor.com). These products use a device known as a *colorimeter* to accurately measure display colors.

Whichever route you take, the calibration process produces a monitor *profile,* which is simply a data file that tells your computer how to adjust the display to compensate for any monitor color casts or brightness and contrast issues. Your Windows or Mac operating system loads this file automatically when you start your computer. Your only responsibility is to perform the calibration every month or so because monitor colors drift over time.

✔ **One of your printer cartridges is empty or clogged.** If your prints look great one day but are way off the next, the number-one suspect is an empty ink cartridge or a clogged print nozzle or head. Check your manual to find out how to perform the necessary maintenance to keep the nozzles or print heads in good shape.

If black-and-white prints have a color tint, a logical assumption is that your black ink cartridge is to blame, if your printer has one. The truth is that images from a printer that doesn't use multiple black or gray cartridges always have a slight color tint because to create gray, the printer has to mix yellow, magenta, and cyan in perfectly equal amounts, which is difficult for a typical inkjet printer to pull off. If your black-and-white prints have a strong color tint, however, a color cartridge might be empty, and replacing it may help somewhat. Long story short: Unless your printer is marketed for producing good black-and-white prints, you'll probably save yourself some grief by simply having your black-and-whites printed at a retail lab.

5 x 7 frame area   8 x 10 frame area

Figure 6-16: Composing shots with a little head room enables you to crop to different frame sizes.

When you buy replacement ink, by the way, keep in mind that third-party brands (although perhaps cheaper) may not deliver the same performance as cartridges from your printer manufacturer. A lot of science goes into getting ink formulas to mesh with the printer's ink-delivery system, and the printer manufacturer obviously knows most about that delivery system.

✔ **You chose the wrong paper setting in your printer software.** When you set up a print job, be sure to select the right setting from the paper type option: glossy or matte, for example. This setting affects the way the printer lays down ink on the paper.

✔ **Your photo paper is low quality.** Sad but true: Cheap, store-brand photo papers usually don't render colors as well as the higher-priced, name-brand papers. For best results, try papers from your printer manufacturer; again, those papers are engineered to provide top performance with the printer's specific inks and ink-delivery system.

DPOF, PictBridge, and computerless printing

The T3i/600D offers two features that enable you to print directly from your camera or a memory card, assuming that your printer offers the required options.

With DPOF (*dee-pof*), which is short for Digital Print Order Format, you select pictures from your memory card to print and then specify how many copies you want of each image. Then, if your photo printer has a compatible memory-card slot and supports DPOF, you pop the memory card into that slot, and the printer reads your "print order" and outputs just the requested prints. You use the printer's own controls to set paper size, print orientation, and other print settings.

A second direct-printing feature, PictBridge, works a little differently. If you have a PictBridge-enabled photo printer, you can connect the camera to the printer by using the USB cable supplied with your camera. A PictBridge interface appears on the camera monitor, and you use the camera controls to select the pictures you want to print as well as specify other print options, such as page size.

If you're interested in exploring either printing feature, your camera manual provides details.

Some paper manufacturers, especially those that sell fine-art papers, offer downloadable *printer profiles*, which are simply little bits of software that tell your printer how to manage color for the paper. Refer to the manufacturer's website for information on how to install and use the profiles. And note that a profile mismatch can also cause incorrect colors in your prints, including the color tint in black-and-white prints alluded to earlier.

✔ **Your printer and photo software are fighting over color management duties.** Some photo programs offer *color management* tools, which enable you to control how colors are handled as an image passes from camera to monitor to printer. Most printer software also offers color management features. The problem is, if you enable color management controls in both your photo software and printer software, you can create conflicts that lead to wacky colors. Check your photo software and printer manuals for color management options and ways to turn them on and off.

Even if all the aforementioned issues are resolved, however, don't expect perfect color matching between printer and monitor. Printers simply can't reproduce the entire spectrum of colors that a monitor can display. In addition, monitor colors always appear brighter because they are, after all, generated with light.

Finally, be sure to evaluate print colors and monitor colors in the same ambient light — daylight, office light, whatever — because that light source has its own influence on the colors you see. Also allow your prints to dry for 15 minutes or so before you make any final judgments.

Preparing Pictures for Online Sharing

How many times have you received an e-mail message that looks like the one in Figure 6-17? Some well-meaning friend or relative sent you a digital photo that's so large you can't view the whole thing on your monitor.

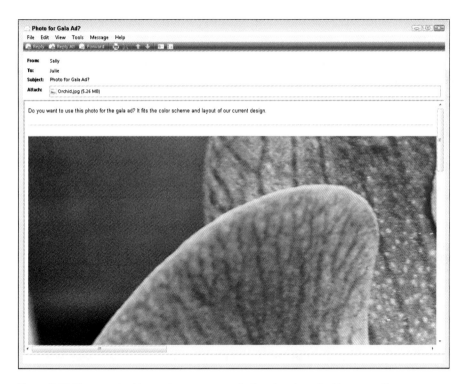

Figure 6-17: The attached image has too many pixels to be viewed without scrolling.

The problem is that computer monitors can display only a limited number of pixels. The exact number depends on the monitor's resolution setting and the capabilities of the computer's video card, but suffice it to say that the average photo from one of today's digital cameras has a pixel count in excess of what the monitor can handle.

Thankfully, the newest e-mail programs incorporate features that automatically shrink the photo display to a viewable size. In Windows Live Mail, for example, photos arrive with a thumbnail link to a slide show viewer that can handle even gargantuan images. But that still doesn't change the fact that a large photo file means longer downloading times and, if recipients choose to hold onto the picture, a big storage hit on their hard drives.

Sending a high-resolution photo *is* the thing to do if you want the recipient to be able to generate a good print. But it's polite practice to ask people if they *want* to print 11 x 14 glossies of your new puppy before you send them a dozen 18-megapixel shots.

For simple onscreen viewing, I suggest limiting photos to about 800 pixels across and 600 pixels down. That ensures that people who use an e-mail program that doesn't offer the latest photo-viewing tools can see your entire picture without scrolling, as in Figure 6-18. The image in the figure measures 720 x 480 pixels.

Figure 6-18: At 720 x 480 pixels, the entire photo is visible even when the e-mail window consumes some of the screen real estate.

At the lowest Quality setting on your camera, S3, pictures contain the same pixel count as my example photo — 720 x 480 pixels. But recording your originals at that tiny size isn't a good idea because if you want to print the photo, you won't have enough pixels to produce a good result. Instead, shoot your originals at a resolution appropriate for print and then create a low-res copy of the picture for e-mail sharing or for other online uses, such as posting to Facebook. (Posting only low-res photos to Facebook and online photo-sharing sites also helps dissuade would-be photo thieves looking for free images for use in their company's brochures and other print materials.)

In addition to resizing high-resolution images, also check their file types; if the photos are in the Raw or TIFF format, you need to create a JPEG copy for online use. Web browsers and e-mail programs can't display Raw or TIFF files.

You have a couple ways to tackle both bits of photo prep. You can use the built-in Resize feature on the camera, which creates a small JPEG copy of your original image. The next section shows you how. Unfortunately, that option is off the table if you captured the photo using the Raw format. For Raw files as well as TIFF files, follow the steps in the last section of the chapter, which shows you how to use the free Canon software to resize the picture and save it in the JPEG format.

Creating small copies in the camera

With the Resize feature on Playback Menu 1, you can make a small copy of any photo on your memory card, as long as you didn't capture it using the Raw file format. Pictures captured using the S3 Quality setting are also exempt from resizing — at 740 x 480 pixels, they're already the smallest images the camera can create.

You can create your small copy in two ways:

✔ **Playback Menu 1:** Select Resize, as shown on the left in Figure 6-19, and press Set. You see a photo along with a Resize icon in the upper-left corner, as shown on the right in Figure 6-19. Other data may appear according to the playback display style; as always, press Info to cycle through the four display modes. The camera also briefly displays a message telling you that only pictures that are compatible with the Resize feature are viewable.

Use the cross keys to scroll to the picture you want to resize and then press Set. You see display size options available for the photo, as shown on the left in Figure 6-20. Which sizes appear depends on the size of the original photo; you're offered only sizes that produce a smaller picture. The text label above the options indicates the file size and pixel count of the selected setting.

Highlight a setting and press Set to display a confirmation screen. Highlight OK and press Set again. The camera creates your low-res copy and displays a text message similar to the one shown on the right in Figure 6-20. The first three numbers indicate the folder number where the copy is stored (102, in the figure), and the last four numbers represent the last four numbers of the image filename. Be sure to note the filename of the small copy so that you can tell it apart from its high-pixel sibling later.

Figure 6-19: Choose the Resize command to make a low-resolution copy of an existing image.

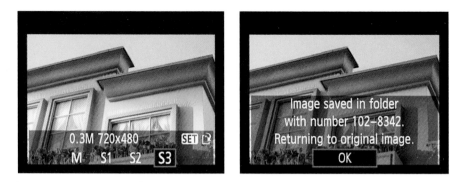

Figure 6-20: The camera displays the folder number and last four digits of the filename of the low-resolution copy.

Highlight OK and press Set one more time to wrap up.

✓ **Quick Control screen:** After putting the camera in playback mode, display the photo you want to resize, press the Quick Control button, and then highlight the Resize icon, as shown in Figure 6-21. Use the right/left cross keys to select a size and then press Set. From that point, things work the same as just described.

Figure 6-21: You also can resize photos from the Quick Control screen during playback.

Creating web-friendly copies using the Canon software

You can't use the in-camera Resize feature for photos shot using the Raw format. No worries — just download the picture and create your web-friendly copy using the free Canon software. I also prefer this method to using the in-camera option when I need to make small copies of multiple photos because I don't have to fill up my memory card with a bunch of extra copies and then waste time downloading all of them. You can use this method for Raw, JPEG, and TIFF originals. And for Raw and TIFF pictures, you can resize the photo and save a copy in the web-friendly JPEG format at the same time.

Click this way:

1. **For Raw files, follow the steps outlined earlier in this chapter to convert the photo to the TIFF format.**

   You use Canon Digital Photo Professional to do the conversion. After you finish the process, close that program and return to ZoomBrowser (Windows) or ImageBrowser (Mac).

   Given that you need to make a JPEG copy of a TIFF file for online sharing, why not just save converted Raw files as JPEG images at the processing stage? Because JPEG is a destructive format that eliminates image data as a trade-off for producing smaller file sizes, you want to create the original Raw conversion in the TIFF format, which retains top image quality. Chapter 2 explains more about the pros and cons of JPEG.

2. **In the image browser, click the thumbnail of the photo you want to e-mail.**

   The photo can be in JPEG or TIFF format.

3. Choose File⇨Export⇨Export Still Images (Windows) or File⇨Export Image (Mac).

In Windows, you next see a window that contains the file-saving options, shown in Figure 6-22. On a Mac, you see the Write a Still Image box instead; click Edit and Save Image and then click the Next button to get to the file-saving options. They're arranged a little differently on the Mac than shown in Figure 6-22, but the basic controls are the same.

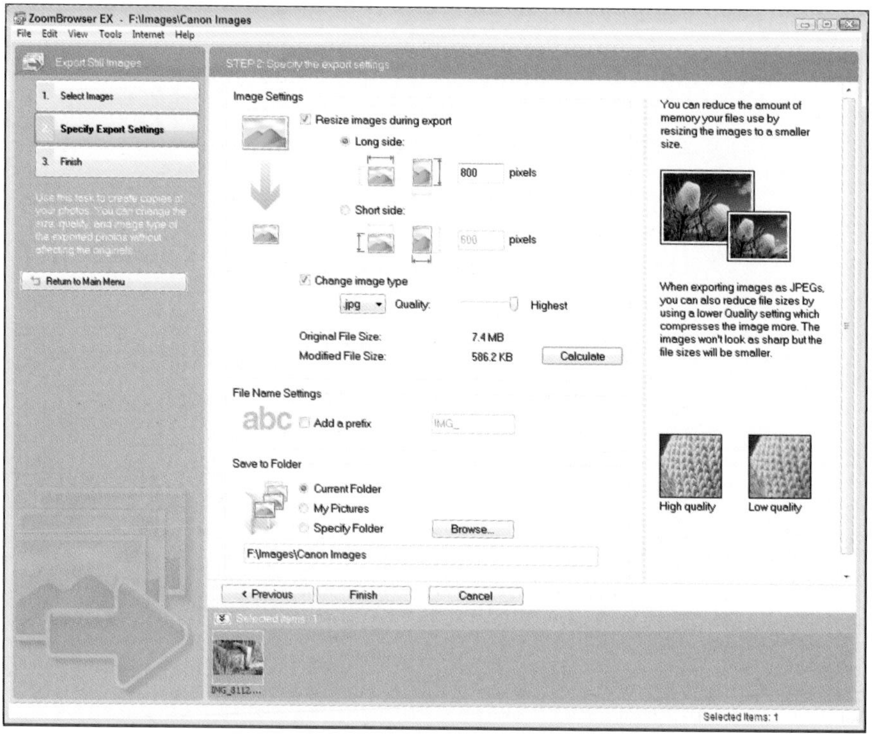

Figure 6-22: Use the Export command to create a JPEG copy of a TIFF photo.

4. Set the image size.

To keep the original pixel count, deselect the Resize Images during Export check box (Windows) or Resize the Image box (Mac). If you want to resample the image (trim the pixel count), select the box, as shown in the figure. Then select Long Side (Windows) or Specify the Length Dimension (Mac) and type a value in the neighboring box. The value you enter determines the number of pixels the image contains along its longest side. The program automatically sets the pixel count of the shortest side to retain the original image proportions.

For e-mail images, setting the long side of the image to 800 pixels or fewer ensures that the recipient can view the entire image without scrolling the e-mail window. If you're posting to an online photo-sharing site, check the site guidelines about picture dimensions. Some sites enable you to upload high-resolution photos so that people who view them can order prints. Usually, the main photo page contains small thumbnails that people can click to view the larger version of the images.

5. Select the Change Image Type check box.

For JPEG originals, you aren't going to really change the file type, but you must check the box anyway so that you can access an important file-saving option used later, in Step 7.

6. Select the JPEG format from the drop-down list under the check box.

This setting should already be selected for you if your original is a JPEG file.

7. Use the Quality (Windows) or Image Quality (Mac) slider to set the image quality.

At the highest Quality setting, the program applies the least amount of *JPEG compression,* which is the process that reduces file sizes by dumping image data. For the best image quality, set the slider to either Highest or High. (The file size is already small because of the reduced pixel count.)

By clicking the Calculate button, you can see the approximate file size of your JPEG copy, which is determined by the dimensions (pixel count) and quality level you choose. If you're sending the photo to someone who's forced to still use a dialup Internet connection, you may want to notch down the quality level a bit so that the picture can download faster.

8. Specify a filename.

You have two options:

- *Accept the program's filename.* If you deselect the Add a Prefix check box (Windows) or the Rename the File box (Mac), the program gives your JPEG copy the same name as the original — for example, IMG_7813.TIF becomes IMG_7813.JPG. For JPEG photos, the program tags a number to the end of the filename so that you don't overwrite your original file. IMG_7813.jpg becomes IMG_7813_2.jpg, for example.

- *Create a new filename.* You also can assign a new filename to your e-mail–sized copy. First, select the Add a Prefix check box (Windows) or the Rename the File box (Mac). Then type the text in the adjacent text box. Note that the program automatically appends the numbers 0001 to whatever text you enter. For example, if you type **Web** in the box, the filename of your JPEG copy is Web0001.jpg.

9. **Choose the folder where you want to store the JPEG file.**

   • *Windows:* Specify the folder by using the Save to Folder option. Click Current Folder to put the copy in the same folder as the original. Click Pictures (or My Pictures, depending on the version of Windows you use) to put the copy in that folder instead, or click Browse to select another folder.

   Depending on the size of the program window, you may need to scroll the window display to be able to see the Save to Folder option.

   • *Mac:* On a Mac, the current folder destination appears at the bottom of the dialog box; click the Browse button to select a different storage bin.

10. **Click Finish to save the copy.**

    The program displays an alert telling you that some shooting information may not be retained in the new photo file. Don't sweat it — you still have your original with all the shooting data if you need it. Click OK and move forward.

If you need to prepare a photograph for use on a web page, you can use these same steps. Just ask the website designer which dimensions to use in Step 4. Also find out whether the site has a maximum file size limit and, if so, adjust the quality level in Step 7 until you fit the picture file within those guidelines. (Click the Calculate button after each adjustment to see the new file size.)

Part III
Taking Creative Control

In this part . . .

*A*s nice as it is to rely on the point-and-shoot exposure modes and let the camera handle all decisions for you, I encourage you to also explore the advanced exposure modes (P, Tv, Av, M, and A-DEP). In these modes, you control settings that affect exposure, focus, and color, which is key to capturing an image as you see it in your mind's eye. And don't think that you have to be a genius or spend years to be successful — adding just a few simple techniques to your photographic repertoire can make a huge difference in how happy you are with the pictures you take.

The first two chapters in this part explain everything you need to know to do just that, providing some necessary photography fundamentals and details about using the advanced exposure modes. Following that, Chapter 9 helps you draw together all the information presented earlier in this book, summarizing the best camera settings and other tactics to use when capturing portraits, action shots, landscapes, and close-up shots.

7

Getting Creative with Exposure and Lighting

*B*y using the simple exposure modes I cover in Chapter 3, you can take good pictures with your Rebel T3i/600D. But to fully exploit your camera's capabilities — and, more importantly, to exploit *your* creative capabilities — you need to explore your camera's five advanced exposure modes, represented on the Mode dial by the letters P, Tv, Av, M, and A-DEP.

This chapter explains everything you need to know to start taking advantage of these five modes. First, you get an introduction to three critical exposure controls: aperture, shutter speed, and ISO. Adjusting these settings enables you to not only fine-tune image exposure but also affect other aspects of your image, such as *depth of field* (the zone of sharp focus) and motion blur. In addition, this chapter explains other advanced exposure features, such as exposure compensation and metering modes, and discusses the flash options available to you in the advanced exposure modes. (For movie-recording exposure information, see Chapter 4.)

Kicking Your Camera into Advanced Gear

With your camera in Creative Auto mode, covered in Chapter 3, you can affect picture brightness and depth of field to some extent by using the Shoot by Ambience and Background Blur features. The scene modes let you request a slightly brighter or darker exposure via the Shoot by Ambience setting, but that's pretty much it. So if you're really concerned with these picture characteristics — and you should be — set the Mode dial to one of its five advanced exposure modes, highlighted in Figure 7-1: P, Tv, Av, M, or A-DEP.

Using these five modes lets you manipulate two critical exposure controls, *aperture* and *shutter speed*. That's not a huge deal in terms of exposure — the camera typically gets that part of the picture right in the fully automatic modes. But changing the aperture setting also affects the distance over which focus is maintained *(depth of field)*, and shutter speed determines whether movement of the subject or camera creates blur. The next part of the chapter explains the details; for now, just understand that having input over these two settings provides you with a whole range of creative options that you don't enjoy in the fully automatic modes.

Advanced exposure modes

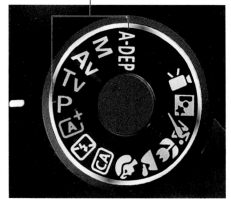

Figure 7-1: To fully control exposure and other picture properties, choose one of these exposure modes.

Each of the five advanced modes offers a different level of control over aperture and shutter speed, as follows:

- **P (programmed autoexposure):** The camera selects both the aperture and shutter speed for you, but you can choose from different combinations of the two.

- **Tv (shutter-priority autoexposure):** You select a shutter speed, and the camera chooses the aperture setting that produces a good exposure.

  Why *Tv?* Well, shutter speed controls exposure time; *Tv* stands for *t*ime *v*alue.

- **Av (aperture-priority autoexposure):** The opposite of shutter-priority autoexposure, this mode asks you to select the aperture setting — thus *Av,* for *a*perture *v*alue. The camera then selects the appropriate shutter speed to properly expose the picture.

✓ **A-DEP (auto depth of field):** In A-DEP mode, the camera assesses the distance between the lens and major objects in the frame and tries to choose an aperture setting that keeps all those objects within the zone of sharp focus. Then the camera sets the appropriate shutter speed for the aperture it selected.

Although this mode enables you to tell the camera that extending the depth of field to cover everything in the frame is your goal, there's no guarantee that the camera will select the aperture setting you have in mind. In addition, when you use flash or enable Live View shooting, you lose the automatic depth-of-field feature, and A-DEP mode works just like P mode — but without giving you the benefit of being able to select from different combinations of aperture and shutter speed. So if you want to control depth of field but still enjoy autoexposure, you're better off with Av mode.

✓ **M (manual exposure):** In this mode, you specify both shutter speed and aperture. Although that prospect may sound intimidating, it's actually the fastest and least complicated way to dial in exactly the exposure settings you want to use. And even in M mode, the camera assists you by displaying a meter that tells you whether your exposure settings are on target.

A quick reminder about a point that is often misunderstood: Setting the Mode dial to M has *no effect* on whether autofocusing or manual focusing is enabled. To choose your focusing method, use the switch on the lens. You can focus manually or use autofocus no matter what your exposure mode.

Again, these modes won't make much sense to you if you aren't schooled in the basics of exposure. To that end, the next several sections provide a quick lesson in this critical photography subject.

Introducing the Exposure Trio: Aperture, Shutter Speed, and ISO

Any photograph, whether taken with a film or digital camera, is created by focusing light through a lens onto a light-sensitive recording medium. In a film camera, the film negative serves as the medium; in a digital camera, it's the image sensor, which is an array of light-responsive computer chips.

Between the lens and the sensor are two barriers, the *aperture* and *shutter,* which together control how much light makes its way to the sensor. The actual design and arrangement of the aperture, shutter, and sensor vary depending on the camera, but Figure 7-2 offers an illustration of the basic concept.

The aperture and shutter, along with a third feature, ISO, determine exposure — what most of us would describe as picture brightness. This three-part exposure formula works as follows:

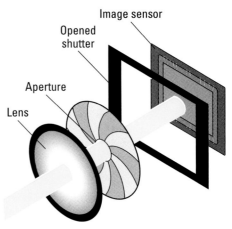

Figure 7-2: The aperture size and shutter speed determine how much light strikes the image sensor.

- ✐ **Aperture (controls amount of light):** The *aperture* is an adjustable hole in a diaphragm set inside the lens. By changing the size of the aperture, you control the size of the light beam that can enter the camera. Aperture settings are stated as *f-stop numbers,* or simply *f-stops,* and are expressed with the letter *f* followed by a number: f/2, f/5.6, f/16, and so on. The lower the f-stop number, the larger the aperture, as illustrated in Figure 7-3.

  The range of possible f-stops depends on your lens and, with most lenses, on the zoom position (focal length) of the lens. For the kit lens sold with the Rebel T3i/600D, you can select apertures from f/3.5 to f/22 when zoomed all the way out to the shortest focal length (18mm). When you zoom in to the maximum focal length (55mm), the aperture range is from f/5.6 to f/36. (See Chapter 8 for a discussion of focal lengths.)

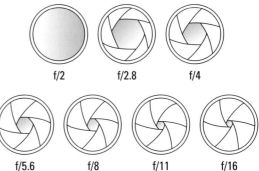

Figure 7-3: The smaller the f-stop number, the larger the aperture.

- ✐ **Shutter speed (controls duration of light):** Set behind the aperture, the shutter works something like, er, the shutters on a window. When you aren't taking pictures, the camera's shutter stays closed, preventing light from striking the image sensor. When you press the shutter button, the shutter opens briefly to allow light that passes through the aperture to hit the image sensor. The exception to this scenario is when you compose in Live View mode — the shutter remains open so that your image can form on the sensor and be displayed on the camera's LCD. In fact, when you press the shutter release in Live View mode, you hear several clicks as the shutter first closes and then reopens for the actual exposure.

The length of time that the shutter is open is the *shutter speed* and is measured in seconds: 1/60 second, 1/250 second, 2 seconds, and so on. Shutter speeds on the Rebel T3i/600D range from 30 seconds to 1/4000 second when you shoot without flash. If you want a shutter speed longer than 30 seconds, manual exposure mode also provides the *bulb* exposure feature. At this setting, the shutter stays open indefinitely as long as you press the shutter button.

If you use the built-in flash, the fastest available shutter speed is 1/200 second; the slowest ranges from 1/60 second to 30 seconds, depending on the exposure mode. See the section "Understanding your camera's approach to flash," later in this chapter, for details.

✐ **ISO (controls light sensitivity):** ISO, which is a digital function rather than a mechanical structure on the camera, enables you to adjust how responsive the image sensor is to light. The term *ISO* is a holdover from film days, when an international standards organization rated each film stock according to light sensitivity: ISO 100, ISO 200, ISO 400, ISO 800, and so on. A higher ISO rating means greater light sensitivity.

On a digital camera, the sensor itself doesn't actually get more or less sensitive when you change the ISO — rather, the light "signal" that hits the sensor is either amplified or dampened through electronics wizardry, sort of like how raising the volume on a radio boosts the audio signal. But the upshot is the same as changing to a more light-reactive film stock: A higher ISO means that less light is needed to produce the image, enabling you to use a smaller aperture, faster shutter speed, or both. (In other words, from now on, don't worry about the technicalities and just remember that ISO equals light sensitivity.)

On your camera, you can select ISO settings ranging from 100 to a whopping 12800 when you shoot in the advanced exposure modes. (You're restricted to an ISO range of 200 to 6400, however, if you enable the Highlight Tone Priority function, which you can explore later in this chapter.) For the fully automatic modes, you have no control over ISO; the camera chooses a setting ranging from ISO 100 to 3200 automatically. (Highlight Tone Priority isn't available in those modes.)

Distilled to its essence, the image-exposure formula is this simple:

✐ Aperture and shutter speed together determine the quantity of light that strikes the image sensor.

✐ ISO determines how much the sensor reacts to that light.

The tricky part of the equation is that aperture, shutter speed, and ISO settings affect your pictures in ways that go *beyond* exposure. You need to be aware of these side effects, explained in the next section, to determine which combination of the three exposure settings will work best for your picture.

Understanding exposure-setting side effects

You can create the same exposure with different combinations of aperture, shutter speed, and ISO, which Figure 7-4 illustrates. Although the figure shows only two variations of settings, your choices are pretty much endless — you're limited only by the aperture range the lens allows and the shutter speeds and ISO settings the camera offers.

f/13, 1/25 second, ISO 200　　　　　f/5.6, 1/125 second, ISO 200

Figure 7-4: Aperture and shutter speed affect depth of field and motion blur.

But the settings you select impact your image beyond mere exposure, as follows:

 ↙ Aperture affects *depth of field,* or the zone of sharp focus.

 ↙ Shutter speed determines whether moving objects appear blurry or sharply focused.

 ↙ ISO affects the amount of image *noise,* which is a defect that looks like tiny specks of sand.

The next three sections explore these exposure side effects in detail.

Aperture and depth of field

The aperture setting, or f-stop, affects *depth of field,* or the distance over which sharp focus is maintained. I introduce this concept in Chapter 3, but here's a quick recap: With a shallow depth of field, your subject appears more sharply focused than faraway objects; with a large depth of field, the sharp-focus zone spreads over a greater distance.

When you reduce the aperture size — "stop down the aperture," in photo lingo — by choosing a higher f-stop number, you increase depth of field. For example, notice that the background in the left image in Figure 7-4, taken at f/13, appears sharper than the right image, taken at f/5.6.

Aperture is just one contributor to depth of field, however. The camera-to-subject distance and the focal length of your lens also play a role in this characteristic of your photos. Depth of field is reduced as you move closer to the subject or increase the focal length of the lens (moving from a wide-angle lens to a telephoto lens, for example.) See Chapter 8 for the complete story on how these three factors combine to determine depth of field.

TIP

Putting the f (stop) in focus

One way to remember the relationship between f-stop and depth of field, or the distance over which focus remains sharp, is simply to think of the f as *focus:* The higher the f-stop number, the larger the zone of sharp *focus.*

Please *don't* share this tip with photography elites, who will roll their eyes and inform you that the f in *f-stop* most certainly does *not* stand for focus but, rather, for the ratio between aperture size and lens focal length — as if *that's* helpful to know if you aren't an optical engineer. (Chapter 8 explains focal length, which *is* helpful to know.)

Shutter speed and motion blur

At a slow shutter speed, moving objects appear blurry, whereas a fast shutter speed captures motion cleanly. Compare the water motion in the photos in Figure 7-4, for example. At a shutter speed of 1/25 second (left photo), the water blurs, giving it a misty look. At 1/125 second (right photo), the splashing water appears more sharply focused. The shutter speed you need in order to freeze action depends on the speed of your subject.

If your picture suffers from overall image blur, like you see in Figure 7-5, where even stationary objects appear out of focus, the camera moved during the exposure — which is always a danger when you handhold the camera at slow shutter speeds. The longer the exposure time, the longer you have to hold the camera still to avoid the blur caused by camera shake.

How slow is too slow? It depends on your physical capabilities and your lens. For reasons that are too technical to get into, camera shake affects your picture more when you shoot with a lens that has a long focal length. For example, you may be able to use a much slower shutter speed when you shoot with a lens that has a maximum focal length of 55mm, like the kit lens, than if you switch to a 200mm telephoto lens. The best idea is to do your own tests to see where your handholding limit lies. Check out Chapter 6 to find out how to see each picture's shutter speed when you view your test images.

f/29, 1/5 second, ISO 200

Figure 7-5: Slow shutter speeds increase the risk of allover blur caused by camera shake.

To avoid the issue altogether, use a tripod or otherwise steady the camera. If you need to handhold (and face it — no one can carry a tripod *all* the time), improve your odds of capturing a sharp photo by turning on image stabilization, if your lens offers it. (On the kit lens, turn the Stabilizer switch on the side of the lens to On.) See Chapter 8 for tips on solving other focus problems and Chapter 9 for more help with action photography.

ISO and image noise

As ISO increases, making the image sensor more reactive to light, you increase the risk of *noise.* Noise looks like sprinkles of sand and is similar in appearance to film *grain,* a defect that often mars pictures taken with high ISO film. Figure 7-6 offers an example.

Figure 7-6: Caused by a very high ISO or long exposure time, noise becomes more visible as you enlarge the image.

Ideally, then, you should always use the lowest ISO setting on your camera to ensure top image quality. But sometimes, the lighting conditions don't permit you to do so. Take my rose image as an example. On my first attempt, taken at ISO 100, f/6.3, and 1/40 second, the flower was slightly blurry, as shown on the left in Figure 7-7. I was using a tripod, so camera shake wasn't the problem. But a very slight breeze was moving the flower just enough that 1/40 second wasn't fast enough to freeze the action. My aperture already was at the maximum opening the lens offered, so the only way to be able to use a faster shutter speed was to raise the ISO. By increasing the ISO to 200, I was able to use a shutter speed of 1/80 second, which captured the flower cleanly, as shown on the right.

ISO 100, f/6.3, 1/40 second   ISO 200, F/6.3, 1/80 second

Figure 7-7: Raising the ISO enabled me to bump the shutter speed up enough to permit a blur-free handheld shot.

Fortunately, you don't encounter serious noise on the T3i/600D until you really crank up the ISO. In fact, you may even be able to get away with a fairly high ISO if you keep your print or display size small. Some people probably wouldn't even notice the noise in the left image in Figure 7-6 unless they were looking for it, for example. But as with other image defects, noise becomes more apparent as you enlarge the photo, as shown on the right in that same figure. Noise is also easier to spot in shadow areas of your picture and in large areas of solid color.

How much noise is acceptable, and, therefore, how high an ISO is safe, is a personal choice. Even a little noise isn't acceptable for pictures that require the highest quality, such as images for a product catalog or a travel shot that you want to blow up to poster size.

It's also important to know that a high ISO isn't the only cause of noise: A long exposure time (slow shutter speed) can also produce the defect. So how high you can raise the ISO before the image gets ugly varies depending on shutter speed. I can pretty much guarantee, though, that your pictures will exhibit visible noise at the camera's highest ISO setting, 12800. In fact, that's why Canon doesn't make that setting available until you enable it via a menu option, ISO Expansion. It's a way to let you know that you should use that setting only if the light is so bad that you have no other way to get the shot. If you do need the maximum ISO, see the section "Controlling ISO" to find out how to enable the 12800 setting.

Doing the exposure balancing act

When you change any of the three exposure settings — aperture, shutter speed, or ISO — one or both of the others must also shift to maintain the same image brightness.

Say you're shooting a soccer game and you notice that although the overall exposure looks great, the players appear slightly blurry at the current shutter speed. If you raise the shutter speed, you have to compensate with either a larger aperture, to allow in more light during the shorter exposure, or a higher ISO setting, to make the camera more sensitive to the light. Which way should you go? Well, it depends on whether you prefer the shorter depth of field that comes with a larger aperture or the increased risk of noise that accompanies a higher ISO. Of course, you can also adjust both settings if you choose to get the exposure results you need.

All photographers have their own approaches to finding the right combination of aperture, shutter speed, and ISO, and you'll no doubt develop your own system when you become more practiced at using the advanced exposure modes. In the meantime, here are some handy recommendations:

- ✔ Use the lowest possible ISO setting unless the lighting conditions are so poor that you can't use the aperture and shutter speed you want without raising the ISO.

- ✔ If your subject is moving (or might move, as with a squiggly toddler or an excited dog), give shutter speed the next highest priority in your exposure decision. Choose a fast shutter speed to ensure a blur-free photo or, on the flip side, select a slow shutter speed to intentionally blur that moving object, an effect that can create a heightened sense of motion. When shooting waterfalls, for example, consider using a slow shutter speed to give the water that blurry, romantic look.

- ✔ For images of nonmoving subjects, make aperture a priority over shutter speed, setting the aperture according to the depth of field you have in mind. For portraits, for example, try using a wide-open aperture (a low f-stop number) to create a short depth of field and a nice, soft background for your subject.

Be careful not to go too shallow with depth of field when shooting a group portrait, though — unless all the subjects are the same distance from the camera, some may be outside the zone of sharp focus. A short depth of field also makes action shots more difficult because you have to be absolutely spot on with focus. With a larger depth of field, the subject can move a greater distance toward or away from you before leaving the sharp-focus area, giving you a bit of a focusing safety net.

Keeping all this information straight is a little overwhelming at first, but the more you work with your camera, the more the whole exposure equation will make sense to you. You can find tips in Chapter 9 for choosing exposure settings for specific types of pictures; keep moving through this chapter for details on how to monitor and adjust aperture, shutter speed, and ISO settings.

Monitoring Exposure Settings

When you press the shutter button halfway, the current f-stop, shutter speed, and ISO speed appear in the viewfinder display, as shown in Figure 7-8. Or if you're looking at the Shooting Settings display, the settings appear as shown in Figure 7-9. In Live View mode, the exposure data appears at the bottom of the monitor and takes a form similar to what you see in the viewfinder. (See Chapter 4 for details about this and other Live View exposure issues.)

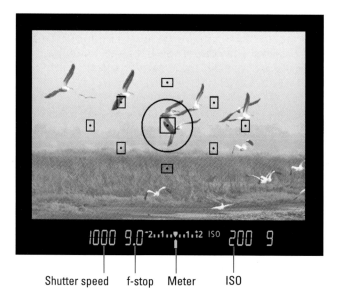

Shutter speed   f-stop   Meter   ISO

Figure 7-8: The shutter speed, f-stop, and ISO speed appear in the viewfinder.

In the viewfinder and on the monitor in Live View mode, shutter speeds are presented as whole numbers, even if the shutter speed is set to a fraction of a second. For example, for a shutter speed of 1/1000 second, you see just the number 1000 in the display. (Refer to Figure 7-8.) When the shutter speed slows to 1 second or more, you see quote marks after the number in both displays — 1" indicates a shutter speed of 1 second, 4" means 4 seconds, and so on.

The viewfinder, Shooting Settings display, and Live View display also offer an *exposure meter,* labeled in Figures 7-8 and 7-9. This little graphic serves two different purposes, depending on which of the advanced exposure modes you're using:

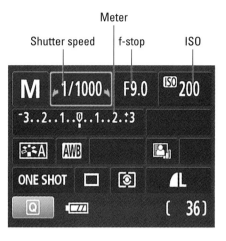

Figure 7-9: You also can view the settings in the Shooting Settings display.

✔ **In manual exposure (M) mode, the meter acts in its traditional role, which is to indicate whether your settings will properly expose the image.** Figure 7-10 gives you three examples. When the *exposure indicator* (the bar under the meter) aligns with the center point of the meter, as shown in the middle example, the current settings will produce a proper exposure. If the indicator moves to the left of center, toward the minus side of the scale, as in the left example in the figure, the camera is alerting you that the image will be underexposed. If the indicator moves to the right of center, as in the right example, the image will be overexposed. The farther the indicator moves toward the plus or minus sign, the greater the potential exposure problem.

Keep in mind that the information reported by the meter is dependent on the *metering mode,* which determines what part of the frame the camera uses to calculate exposure. You can choose from four metering modes, as covered in the next section. But regardless of metering mode, consider the meter a guide, not a dictator — the beauty of manual exposure is that *you* decide how dark or bright an exposure you want, not the camera.

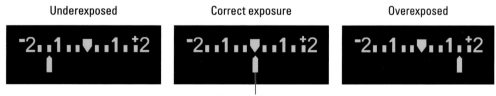

Figure 7-10: In manual exposure (M) mode, the meter indicates whether exposure settings are on target.

✔ **In the other modes (P, Tv, Av, and A-DEP), the meter displays the current Exposure Compensation setting.** Remember, in those modes the camera sets either the shutter speed or aperture, or both, to produce a good exposure — again, depending on the current metering mode. Because you don't need the meter to tell you whether exposure is okay, the meter instead indicates whether you enabled *Exposure Compensation,* a feature that forces a brighter or darker exposure than the camera thinks is appropriate. (Look for details later in this chapter.) When the exposure indicator is at 0, no compensation is being applied. If the indicator is to the right of 0, you applied compensation to produce a brighter image; when the indicator is to the left, you asked for a darker photo.

In some lighting situations, the camera *can't* select settings that produce an optimal exposure in the P, Tv, Av, or A-DEP mode, however. Because the meter indicates the Exposure Compensation amount in those modes, the camera alerts you to exposure issues as follows:

✔ **Av mode (aperture-priority autoexposure):** The shutter speed value blinks to let you know that the camera can't select a shutter speed that will produce a good exposure at the aperture you selected. Choose a different f-stop or adjust the ISO.

✔ **Tv mode (shutter-priority autoexposure):** The aperture value blinks to tell you that the camera can't open or stop down the aperture enough to expose the image at your selected shutter speed. Your options are to change the shutter speed or ISO.

✔ **P mode (programmed autoexposure):** In P mode, both the aperture and shutter speed values blink if the camera can't select a combination that will properly expose the image. Your only recourse is to either adjust the lighting or change the ISO setting.

✔ **A-DEP mode (auto depth of field):** Either the aperture or the shutter speed value may blink. If the shutter speed value blinks 30" (for 30 seconds) or 4000 (for 1/4000 second), the light is too dark or too bright, respectively, for the camera to expose the image properly at any combination of aperture and shutter speed. To compensate for dim lighting, you can raise the ISO or add flash. In too-bright light, lower the ISO if possible — otherwise, find a way to shade or relocate the subject.

If the aperture setting blinks, the exposure will be okay but the f-stop won't produce the depth of field needed to keep everything in the frame in sharp focus. (See Chapter 8 for complete details on depth of field and A-DEP mode.)

Choosing an Exposure Metering Mode

The *metering mode* determines which part of the frame the camera analyzes to calculate the proper exposure. The Rebel T3i/600D offers four metering modes, described in the following list and represented in the Shooting Settings display by the icons you see in the margin. However, you can access all four modes only in the advanced exposure modes (P, Tv, Av, M, and A-DEP) and only during regular, through-the-viewfinder shooting. In Live View mode, as well as in the fully automatic exposure modes, you're restricted to the first of the four modes, Evaluative metering.

- **Evaluative metering:** The camera analyzes the entire frame and then selects exposure settings designed to produce a balanced exposure.

- **Partial metering:** The camera bases exposure only on the light that falls in the center 9 percent of the frame. The left image in Figure 7-11 provides a rough approximation of the area that factors into the exposure equation.

- **Spot metering:** This mode works like Partial metering but uses a smaller region of the frame to calculate exposure. For Spot metering, exposure is based on just the center 4 percent of the frame, as indicated by the illustration on the right in Figure 7-11.

- **Center-Weighted Average metering:** The camera bases exposure on the entire frame but puts extra emphasis — or *weight* — on the center.

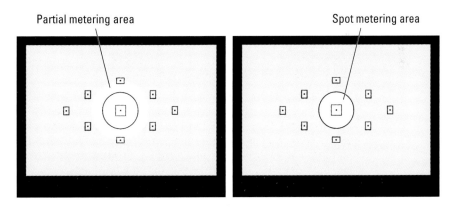

Figure 7-11: The spotlights indicate the metered area for Partial metering and Spot metering.

One other important difference to note: With Spot, Partial, and Center-weighted metering, exposure is adjusted up to the time you actually take the picture. If you want to lock in the current exposure settings, you can do so by using AE (autoexposure) Lock, explained later in this chapter. With Evaluative metering, exposure is locked when you press the shutter button halfway except when you use Live View or A-DEP exposure modes, in which case exposure is adjusted continually and you must use AE Lock to lock the current settings.

In most cases, Evaluative metering does a good job of calculating exposure. But it can get thrown off when a dark subject is set against a bright background or vice versa. For example, in the left image in Figure 7-12, the amount of bright background caused the camera to select exposure settings that underexposed the statue, which was the point of interest for the photo. Switching to Partial metering properly exposed the statue. (Spot metering would produce a similar result for this particular subject.)

Evaluative   Partial

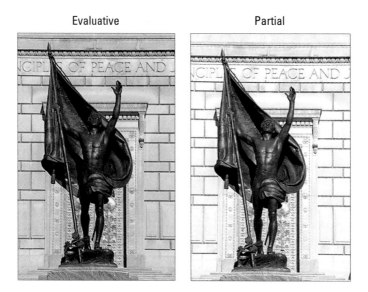

Figure 7-12: In Evaluative mode, the camera underexposed the statue; switching to Partial metering produced a better result.

 Of course, if the background is very bright and the subject is very dark, the exposure that does the best job on the subject typically overexposes the background. You may be able to reclaim some lost highlights by turning on Highlight Tone Priority, a Custom Function explored later in this chapter.

Use either of these two options to change the metering mode:

    ✔ **Quick Control screen:** After displaying the screen, highlight the option shown on the left in Figure 7-13. The selected setting appears in the label at the bottom of the screen. Rotate the Main dial to cycle through the four modes or press Set to display a list of all four modes, as shown on the right in the figure. If you take the second route, use the cross keys or Main dial to highlight the icon for the mode you want to use and then press Set to lock in your decision.

 ✓ **Shooting Menu 2:** You also can find the metering mode option at the menu address shown in Figure 7-14.

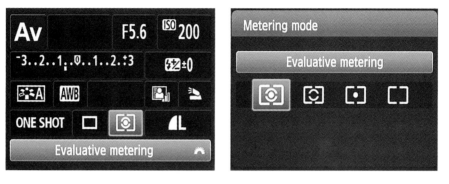

Figure 7-13: You can quickly adjust the Metering mode from the Quick Control screen.

In theory, the best practice is to check the metering mode before each shot and choose the mode that best matches your exposure goals. But in practice, it's a pain, not just in terms of having to adjust yet one more setting but also in terms of having to *remember* to adjust one more setting. So until you're comfortable with all the other controls on your camera, just stick with Evaluative metering. It produces good results in most situations, and after all, you can see in the monitor whether you like your results and, if not, adjust exposure settings and reshoot. This option makes the whole metering mode issue a lot less critical than it is when you shoot with film.

Figure 7-14: You also can access the Metering mode from Shooting Menu 2.

Setting ISO, f-stop, and Shutter Speed

If you want to control ISO, aperture (f-stop), or shutter speed, set the camera to one of the five advanced exposure modes: P, Tv, Av, M, or A-DEP. Then check out the next several sections to find the exact steps to follow in each of these modes.

Controlling ISO

To recap the ISO information presented at the start of this chapter, your camera's ISO setting controls how sensitive the image sensor is to light. At a camera's higher ISO values, you need less light to expose an image correctly.

Remember the downside to raising ISO, however: The higher the ISO, the greater the possibility of noisy images. Refer to Figure 7-6 for a reminder of what that defect looks like.

In Scene Intelligent Auto, Creative Auto, Flash Off, and the scene modes (Portrait, Landscape, and so on), the camera controls ISO. But in the advanced exposure modes, you have the following ISO choices:

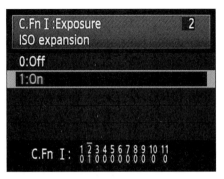

Figure 7-15: Using Custom Function 2, you can push the available ISO range to 12800.

✔ **Select a specific ISO setting.** Normally, you can choose ISO 100, 200, 400, 800, 1600, 3200, or 6400. But you can push ISO up one notch, to ISO 12800, if you're okay with the added noise that results.

To expand the ISO range, go to Setup Menu 3, highlight Custom Functions, and press Set. Press the right or left cross key to display Custom Function 2, as shown in Figure 7-15. (The function number appears in the top-right corner of the screen.) Press Set to activate the menu options, highlight On, and press Set again. Now when you adjust ISO, an H (for High) appears as a possible setting; select that setting for ISO 12800.

One complication to note: If you enable Highlight Tone Priority, an exposure feature covered later in this chapter, you lose the option of using ISO 100 as well as the expanded ISO setting (H, 12800).

✔ **Let the camera choose (Auto ISO).** You can ask the camera to adjust ISO for you if you prefer. And you can specify the highest ISO setting that you want the camera to use, up to ISO 6400. (ISO 12800 isn't an option, even if you enable ISO Expansion.) Set the top ISO limit via the ISO Auto setting on Shooting Menu 3, as shown in Figure 7-16.

Figure 7-16: This setting enables you to specify the maximum ISO setting the camera can use in Auto ISO mode.

I like to use Auto ISO when the light is changing fast or my subject is moving from light to dark areas quickly. In these situations, Auto ISO can save the day, giving you properly exposed images without any ISO futzing on your part.

You can view the current ISO setting in the upper-right corner of the Shooting Settings screen, as shown on the left in Figure 7-17. You can also monitor the ISO in the viewfinder display. (Refer to Figure 7-8.) During Live View shooting, the setting appears at the bottom of the screen unless you choose the display mode that hides all the shooting data. (See Chapter 4 for details on the Live View display.)

ISO

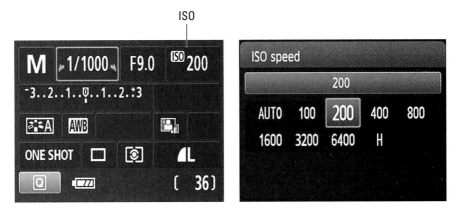

Figure 7-17: Press the ISO button on top of the camera to access the ISO setting.

To adjust the setting, you have two options:

- ✔ **Press the ISO button (on top of the camera).** You then see the screen shown on the right in Figure 7-17. Highlight your choice and press Set.

 ✔ **Use the Quick Control screen.** After displaying the Shooting Settings screen, press the Quick Control button to shift to Quick Control mode and then highlight the ISO setting. Then either rotate the Main dial to cycle through the available ISO settings or press Set to display the same screen you see on the right in Figure 7-17. If you take the second approach, highlight your ISO setting and press Set again.

 In Auto ISO mode, the Shooting Settings display and Live View display initially show Auto as the ISO value, as you would expect. But when you press the shutter button halfway, which initiates exposure metering, the value changes to show you the ISO setting the camera has selected. You also see the selected value rather than Auto in the viewfinder. *Note:* When you view shooting data during playback, you may see a value reported that isn't on the list of "official" ISO settings — ISO 320, for example. This happens because in Auto mode, the camera can select values all along the available ISO range, whereas if you select a specific ISO setting, you're restricted to specific notches within the range.

Adjusting aperture and shutter speed

You can adjust aperture and shutter speed only in P, Tv, Av, and M exposure modes. To see the current exposure settings, press the shutter button halfway. The following actions then take place:

✔ The exposure meter comes to life. If autofocus is enabled, focus is also established at this point.

✔ The aperture and shutter speed appear in the viewfinder or the Shooting Settings display, if you have it enabled. In Live View mode, the settings appear under the image preview on the monitor, assuming that you're using a display mode that reveals shooting data. (Press the Info button to cycle through the available Live View display modes.)

✔ In manual exposure (M) mode, the exposure meter lets you know whether the current settings will expose the image properly. In the other modes, the camera indicates an exposure problem by flashing the shutter speed or the f-stop value. (See the section "Monitoring Exposure Settings," earlier in this chapter, for details.)

Dampening noise

Noise, the digital defect that gives your pictures a speckled look (refer to Figure 7-6), can occur for two reasons: a long exposure time and a high ISO setting.

The Rebel T3i/600D offers two noise-removal filters, one to address each cause of noise. Both filters are provided through Custom Functions, which means that you can control whether and how they're applied only in the advanced exposure modes.

To control Long Exposure Noise Reduction, visit Setup Menu 3, select Custom Functions, press Set, and then use the right or left cross key to select Custom Function 4, as shown in the left figure. Press Set to access the options, highlight your choice, and then press Set again. The three settings work as follows:

✔ *Off:* No noise reduction is applied. This setting is the default.

✔ *Auto:* Noise reduction is applied when you use a shutter speed of 1 second or longer, but only if the camera detects the type of noise that's caused by long exposures.

✔ *On:* Noise reduction is always applied at exposures of 1 second or longer. (*Note:* Canon suggests that this setting may result in more noise than either Off or Auto when the ISO setting is 1600 or higher.)

For high ISO noise removal, move to Custom Function 5. This filter offers four settings, as shown in the right figure:

↙ *Standard:* The default setting

↙ *Low:* Applies a little noise removal

↙ *Strong:* Goes after noise in a more dramatic way

↙ *Disable:* Turns off the filter

Although noise reduction is a useful concept in theory, both filters have a few disadvantages. First, they're applied after you take the picture, when the camera processes the image data and records it to your memory card, which slows your shooting speed. In fact, using the Strong setting for High ISO noise removal reduces the maximum frame rate (shots per second) that you can click off.

Second, High ISO noise-reduction filters work primarily by applying a slight blur to the image. Don't expect this process to eliminate noise entirely, and expect some resulting image softness. You may be able to get better results by using the blur tools or noise-removal filters found in many photo editors because then you can blur just the parts of the image where noise is most noticeable — usually in areas of flat color or little detail, such as skies.

Long Exposure Noise Reduction is a different beast and can usually do a better job of reducing noise than you can with extra software on your computer. The only downside to using Long Exposure Noise Reduction is that it doubles the processing time for each exposure — longer than one second — that you shoot. Say that you make a 30-second exposure at night. After the shutter closes at the end of the exposure, the camera takes a *second* 30-second exposure to measure the noise by itself, and then subtracts that noise from your *real* exposure.

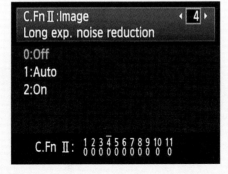

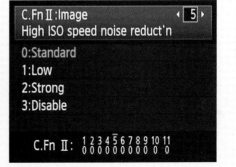

The technique you use to change the exposure settings depends on the exposure mode, as outlined in the following list:

↙ **P (programmed auto):** In this mode, the camera initially displays its recommended combination of aperture and shutter speed. To select a different combination, rotate the Main dial.

↙ **Tv (shutter-priority autoexposure):** Rotate the Main dial. When you change the shutter speed, the camera automatically adjusts the aperture as needed to maintain the proper exposure.

Changing the aperture also changes depth of field. So even though you're working in shutter-priority mode, keep an eye on the f-stop, too, if depth of field is important to your photo. *Note:* In extreme lighting conditions, the camera may not be able to adjust the aperture enough to produce a good exposure at the current shutter speed — again, possible aperture settings depend on your lens. So you may need to compromise on shutter speed (or, in dim lighting, raise the ISO).

✔ **Av (aperture-priority autoexposure):** Rotate the Main dial. As you change the f-stop, the camera automatically adjusts the shutter speed to maintain the exposure.

If you're handholding the camera, be careful that the shutter speed doesn't drop so low when you stop down the aperture that you run the risk of camera shake. If your scene contains moving objects, make sure that when you dial in your preferred f-stop, the shutter speed that the camera selects is fast enough to stop action (or slow enough to blur it, if that's your creative goal).

✔ **M (manual exposure):** In this mode, you select both aperture and shutter speed, like so:

Av
±

- *To adjust shutter speed:* Rotate the Main dial.

- *To adjust aperture:* Press and hold the Exposure Compensation button, shown in Figure 7-18, while you rotate the Main dial. (See the *Av* label next to the Exposure Compensation button? That's your clue to the aperture-related function of the button — *Av* stands for *aperture value.*) Don't let up on the button when you rotate the Main dial — if you do, you instead adjust the shutter speed. And remember that you need to press the button only in Manual mode; in Av mode, simply rotating the Main dial gets the job done.

In M, Tv, and Av modes, the setting that's available for adjustment appears in the Shooting Settings display in purple, with little arrows at each side. Your camera manual refers to this display as the Main dial pointer, and it's provided as a reminder that you use the Main dial to change the setting. For example, in M mode, the shutter speed appears purple until you hold down the Exposure Compensation button, at which point the marker shifts to the aperture (f-stop) value, as shown in Figure 7-18.

You also can use the Quick Control method of adjusting the settings in the M, Tv, and Av modes. This trick is especially helpful for M mode because you can adjust the f-stop setting without having to remember what button to push to do the job. Try it out: After displaying the Shooting Settings screen, press the Quick Control button to shift to Quick Control mode and then use the cross keys to highlight the setting you want to change. For example, in Figure 7-19, the aperture setting is highlighted, and a text label offers a helpful reminder with the name of the option at the bottom of the screen. Now, rotate the Main dial to adjust the setting, press the shutter button halfway, and release it to exit Quick Control mode.

Exposure Compensation button

Figure 7-18: To set the aperture in M mode, press the Exposure Compensation button while you rotate the Main dial.

Keep in mind that when you use P, Tv, Av, and A-DEP modes, the settings that the camera selects are based on what it thinks is the proper exposure. If you don't agree with the camera, you have two options. Switch to manual exposure (M) mode and simply dial in the aperture and shutter speed that deliver the exposure you want, or if you want to stay in P, Tv, Av, or A-DEP mode, you can tweak the autoexposure settings by using Exposure Compensation, one of the exposure-correction tools described in the next section.

Figure 7-19: You can also use the Quick Control screen to adjust aperture and shutter speed in the M, Tv, and Av exposure modes.

Sorting through Your Camera's Exposure-Correction Tools

In addition to the normal controls over aperture, shutter speed, and ISO, your Rebel offers a collection of tools that enable you to solve tricky exposure problems. The next four sections give you the lowdown on these features.

Overriding autoexposure results with Exposure Compensation

When you set your camera to the P, Tv, Av, or A-DEP exposure modes, you can enjoy the benefits of autoexposure support but retain some control over the final exposure. If you think that the image the camera produced is too dark or too light, you can use a feature known as *Exposure Compensation,* which is sometimes also called *EV Compensation.* (The *EV* stands for *exposure value.*)

Whatever you call it, this feature enables you to tell the camera to produce a darker or lighter exposure than what its autoexposure mechanism thinks is appropriate. Best of all, this feature is probably one of the easiest on the camera to understand. Here's all there is to it:

- Exposure compensation is stated in EV values, as in +2.0 EV. Possible values range from +5.0 EV to –5.0 EV.

- Each full number on the EV scale represents an exposure shift of one *full stop.* In plain English, it means that if you change the Exposure Compensation setting from EV 0.0 to EV –1.0, the camera adjusts either the aperture or the shutter speed to allow half as much light into the camera as it would get at the current setting. If you instead raise the value to EV +1.0, the settings are adjusted to double the light.

- A setting of EV 0.0 results in no exposure adjustment.

- For a brighter image, you raise the EV value. The higher you go, the brighter the image becomes.

- For a darker image, you lower the EV value. The picture becomes progressively darker with each step down the EV scale.

Exposure compensation is especially helpful when your subject is much lighter or darker than an average scene. For example, take a look at the first image in Figure 7-20. Because of the very bright sky, the camera chose an exposure that made the tree too dark. Setting the Exposure Compensation value to EV +1.0 resulted in a properly exposed image.

Sometimes you can cope with situations like this one by changing the Metering mode setting, as discussed earlier in this chapter. The images in Figure 7-20 were metered in Evaluative mode, for example, which meters exposure over the entire frame. Switching to Partial or Spot metering probably wouldn't have helped in this case because the center of the frame was bright. In any case, I find it easier to simply adjust Exposure Compensation than to experiment with metering modes.

You can take several different roads to applying exposure compensation. However, note that the option you choose controls whether you can apply compensation values greater than +/–2.0. In most cases, the 2-stop range is more than enough; a setting beyond that is typically useful only for creating HDR (high dynamic range) images, which you can explore in a later sidebar in this chapter.

EV 0.0   EV +1.0

Figure 7-20: For a brighter exposure than the autoexposure mechanism chooses, dial in a positive Exposure Compensation value.

To stay within the normal 2-stop range, take one of these two routes:

✔ **Exposure Compensation button:** The fastest option is to press and hold the Exposure Compensation button (shown in the margin) while rotating the Main dial. Note the little plus/minus sign on the button label — that's your reminder that you use the button to raise or lower the Exposure Compensation amount. (The Av label, as explained in the preceding section, refers to the button's role in adjusting aperture when you shoot in M exposure mode.)

If the Shooting Settings screen is displayed, the meter becomes active while the button is pressed, as shown in Figure 7-21. Remember, in any of the advanced exposure modes but M, the meter indicates the Exposure Compensation amount. As you rotate the dial, the little notch under the meter moves to show the current Exposure Compensation value. For example, in Figure 7-21, the amount of adjustment is +1.0. The viewfinder meter also displays the amount of adjustment.

✔ **Quick Control screen:** After shifting to the Quick Control screen, highlight the exposure meter and rotate the Main dial to move the exposure indicator left or right along the meter.

To access the entire five-stop range of exposure compensation, pick one of these two paths instead:

✔ **Shooting Menu 2:** Visit this menu and select Expo. Comp/AEB, as shown on the left in Figure 7-22; press Set to display the screen shown on the right. Notice that the meter in this screen gives you access to the full five stops (+/–5.0) of compensation.

Exposure Compensation amount

Figure 7-21: In any advanced exposure mode but M, the meter indicates the amount of Exposure Compensation adjustment.

Be aware that this screen has a double purpose: You use it to enable automatic exposure bracketing (AEB) as well as exposure compensation. To apply exposure compensation, you must use the left and right cross keys to move the exposure indicator. Note the little right/left triangles near the +5 side of the meter and the +/– sign on the far right — those represent the Exposure Compensation feature. If you rotate the Main dial, represented by the curved notch under the little triangles, you adjust the AEB setting instead. Press Set to lock in the amount of exposure compensation and exit the screen.

✔ **Quick Control screen:** After highlighting the meter, press Set to display the same screen shown on the right in Figure 7-22. Again, be sure to use the right/left cross keys to change the setting and press Set to lock in your selected setting.

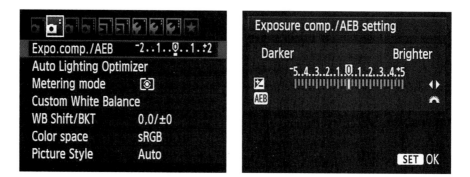

Figure 7-22: When adjusting Exposure Compensation via this screen, you can access the entire five-stop range of adjustment.

When you dial in an adjustment of greater than two stops, the notch under the viewfinder meter disappears and is replaced by a little triangle at one end of the meter — at the right end for a positive Exposure Compensation value and at the left for a negative value. You have to revisit the screen shown on the right in Figure 7-22 to determine exactly how far past two stops you went when setting the Exposure Compensation amount.

How the camera arrives at the brighter or darker image you request depends on the exposure mode:

- ✔ In Av (aperture-priority) mode, the camera adjusts the shutter speed but leaves your selected f-stop in force. Be sure to check the resulting shutter speed to make sure that it isn't so slow that camera shake or blur from moving objects is problematic.

- ✔ In Tv (shutter-priority) mode, the opposite occurs: The camera opens or stops down the aperture, leaving your selected shutter speed alone.

- ✔ In P (programmed autoexposure) and A-DEP modes, the camera decides whether to adjust aperture, shutter speed, or both to accommodate the Exposure Compensation setting.

These explanations assume that you have a specific ISO setting selected rather than Auto ISO. If you do use Auto ISO, the camera may adjust that value instead.

Keep in mind, too, that the camera can adjust the aperture only so much, according to the aperture range of your lens. The range of shutter speeds is limited by the camera. So if you reach the end of those ranges, you have to compromise on either shutter speed or aperture or adjust ISO.

A final, and critical, point about exposure compensation: When you power off the camera, it doesn't return you to a neutral setting (EV 0.0). The setting you last used remains in force for the P, Tv, Av, and A-DEP exposure modes until you change it.

Improving high-contrast shots with Highlight Tone Priority

When a scene contains both very dark and very bright areas, achieving a good exposure can be difficult. If you choose exposure settings that render the shadows properly, the highlights are often overexposed, as in the left image in Figure 7-23. Although the dark lamppost in the foreground looks fine, the white building behind it has become so bright that all detail has been lost. The same thing occurred in the highlight areas of the green church steeple.

Highlight Tone Priority off　　　　　　Highlight Tone Priority on

Figure 7-23: The Highlight Tone Priority feature can help prevent overexposed highlights.

Your camera offers an option that can help produce a better image in this situation — Highlight Tone Priority — which was used to produce the second image in Figure 7-23. The difference is subtle, but if you look at that white building and steeple, you can see that the effect does make a difference. Now the windows in the building are at least visible, the steeple has regained some of its color, and the sky, too, has a bit more blue.

This feature is turned off by default, which may seem like an odd choice after looking at the improvement it made to the scene in Figure 7-23. What gives? The answer is that in order to do its thing, Highlight Tone Priority needs to play with a few other camera settings, as follows:

✔ **The ISO range is reduced to ISO 200–6400.** The camera needs the more limited range in order to favor the image highlights. (The whys and wherefores aren't important.) Losing the highest ISO is no big deal — the noise level at that setting can make your photo unattractive anyway. But in bright light, you may miss the option of lowering the ISO to 100 because you may be forced to use a smaller aperture or a faster shutter speed than you like.

✔ **Auto Lighting Optimizer is disabled.** This feature, which attempts to improve image contrast, is incompatible with Highlight Tone Priority. So read the next section, which explains Auto Lighting Optimizer, to determine which of the two exposure tweaks you want to use.

Exposure stops: How many do you want to see?

In photography, the term *stop* refers to an increment of exposure. To increase exposure by one stop means to adjust the aperture or shutter speed to allow twice as much light into the camera as the current settings permit. To reduce exposure a stop, you use settings that allow half as much light. Doubling or halving the ISO value also adjusts exposure by one stop.

By default, all the major exposure-related settings on the T3i/600D are based on one-third stop adjustments. For example, when you adjust the Exposure Compensation value, a feature that enables you to request a brighter or darker picture than the camera's autoexposure system thinks is correct, you can choose settings of EV 0.0 (no adjustment), +0.3, +0.7, and +1.0 (a full stop of adjustment).

If you prefer, you can tell the camera to present exposure adjustments in half-stop increments so that you don't have to cycle through as many settings each time you want to make a change. Make your preferences known by selecting Custom Functions on Setup Menu 3, as shown in the left figure here, and then bringing up Custom Function 1, as shown on the right. (Use the right/left cross keys to scroll through the available Custom Functions.) Press Set and then press the up or down cross key to change the setting. Press Set again to lock in the new setting.

Note that when you use the 1/2-stop setting, the meter appears slightly different in the Shooting Settings display and Live View display than you see it in this book. (Only one intermediate notch appears between each number on the meter instead of the usual two.) The viewfinder meter doesn't change, but the exposure indicator bar appears as a double line if you set the Exposure Compensation value to a half-step value (+0.5, +1.5, and so on).

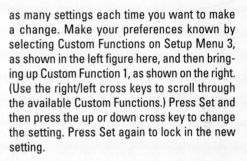

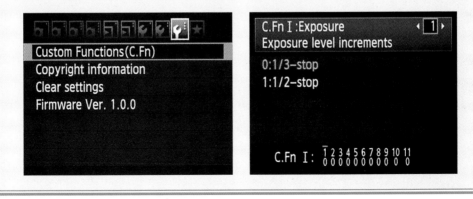

Additionally, you can wind up with slightly more noise in the shadows of your photo when you use Highlight Tone Priority. If none of those drawbacks are a concern and you want to enable the feature, follow these steps:

1. **Set the camera Mode dial to one of the advanced exposure modes.**

   You can take advantage of the Highlight Tone Priority feature only in the P, Tv, Av, M, and A-DEP modes.

2. **Display Setup Menu 3.**

3. **Highlight Custom Functions, as shown on the left in Figure 7-24, and press Set.**

   You're taken to command central for accessing custom functions.

4. **Press the right or left cross key as needed to display Custom Function 6.**

   Look for the Custom Function number in the upper-right corner of the screen.

5. **Press Set and then press the up or down cross key to highlight the Enable option, shown on the right in Figure 7-24.**

6. **Press Set.**

   Highlight Tone Priority is now enabled and remains on until you visit the Custom Functions playground again to turn it off.

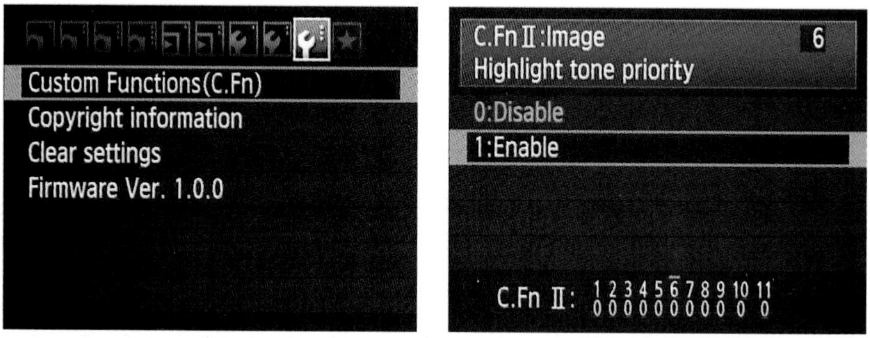

Figure 7-24: Enable Highlight Tone Priority from Custom Function 6 on Setup Menu 3.

As a reminder that Highlight Tone Priority is enabled, a D+ symbol appears near the ISO value in the Shooting Settings display, as shown in Figure 7-25. The same symbol appears with the ISO setting in the viewfinder and in the shooting data that appears onscreen in Live View mode and Playback mode. (See Chapter 5 to find out more about picture playback.) Notice that the symbol that represents Auto Lighting Optimizer is dimmed because that feature is now disabled.

Experimenting with Auto Lighting Optimizer

When you select a Quality setting that results in a JPEG image file — that is, any setting other than Raw — the camera tries to enhance your photo while it's processing the picture. Unlike Highlight Tone Priority, which concentrates on preserving highlight detail only, Auto Lighting Optimizer adjusts both shadows and highlights to improve the final image tonality (range of darks to lights). In other words, it's a contrast adjustment.

Highlight Tone Priority

Auto Lighting Optimizer

Figure 7-25: These symbols indicate that Highlight Tone Priority is enabled and Auto Lighting Optimizer is disabled.

In the fully automatic exposure modes as well as in Creative Auto, you have no control over how much adjustment is made. But in the other five exposure modes — P, Tv, Av, M, and A-DEP — you can decide whether to enable Auto Lighting Optimizer. You also can request a stronger or lighter application of the effect than the default setting. Figure 7-26 offers an example of the type of impact of each Auto Lighting Optimizer setting.

Given the level of improvement that the Auto Lighting Optimizer correction made to this photo, you may be thinking that you'd be crazy to ever disable the feature. But it's important to note a few points:

✐ The level of shift that occurs between each Auto Lighting Optimization setting varies dramatically depending on the subject. This particular example shows a fairly noticeable difference between the Strong and Off settings. But you don't always see this much impact from the filter. Even in this example, it's difficult to detect much difference between Off and Low.

✐ Although the filter improved this particular scene, at times you may not find it beneficial. For example, maybe you're purposely trying to shoot a backlit subject in silhouette or produce a low-contrast image. Either way, you don't want the camera to insert its opinions on the exposure or contrast you're trying to achieve.

✐ Because the filter is applied after you capture the photo, while the camera is writing the data to the memory card, it can slow your shooting rate.

✐ In some lighting conditions, Auto Lighting Optimizer can produce an increase in image noise.

The corrective action taken by Auto Lighting Optimization can make some other exposure-adjustment features less effective. So turn it off if you don't see the results you expect when you're using the following features:

- Exposure compensation, discussed earlier in this chapter
- Flash compensation, discussed later in this chapter
- Automatic exposure bracketing, also discussed later in this chapter

Off

Low

Standard

Strong

Figure 7-26: For this image, Auto Lighting Optimizer brought more life to the shot by increasing contrast.

By default, the camera applies the Auto Lighting Optimizer feature at the Standard level. If you want to experiment with other settings, you can do so via Shooting Menu 2 or the Quick Control screen, as illustrated in Figure 7-27. Notice the little vertical bars that appear as part of the setting icon — the number of bars tells you how much adjustment is being applied. Two bars, as in Figure 7-27, represent the Standard setting; three bars, Strong, and one bar, Low. The bars are replaced by the word *Off* when the feature is disabled.

If you're not sure what level of Auto Lighting Optimization might work best or you're concerned about the other drawbacks of enabling the filter, consider shooting the picture in the Raw file format. For Raw pictures, the camera applies no post-capture tweaking, regardless of whether this filter or any other one is enabled. Then, by using Canon Digital Photo Professional, the software provided free with the camera, you can apply the Auto Lighting Optimizer effect when you convert your Raw images to a standard file format. (See Chapter 6 for details about processing Raw files.)

Figure 7-27: Adjust the Auto Lighting Optimizer setting from Shooting Menu 2 or the Quick Control display.

Correcting lens vignetting with Peripheral Illumination Correction

Because of some optical science principles that are too boring to explore, some lenses produce pictures that appear darker around the edges of the frame than in the center, even when the lighting is consistent throughout. This phenomenon goes by several names, but the two heard most often are *vignetting* and *light fall-off.* How much vignetting occurs depends on the lens, your aperture setting, and the lens focal length. (Chapter 8 explains focal length.)

To help compensate for vignetting, the Rebel T3i/600D offers Peripheral Illumination Correction, which adjusts image brightness around the edges of the frame. Figure 7-28 shows an example. In the left image, just a slight amount of light fall-off occurs at the corners, most noticeably at the top of the image. The right image shows the same scene with Peripheral Illumination Correction enabled.

Now, this "before" example hardly exhibits serious vignetting — it's likely that most people wouldn't even notice if it weren't shown next to the "after" example. And frankly, you're not likely to notice significant vignetting with the 18–55mm kit lens bundled with the camera, either. But if your lens suffers from stronger vignetting, it's worth trying Peripheral Illumination Correction.

Peripheral Illumination Correction off   Peripheral Illumination Correction on

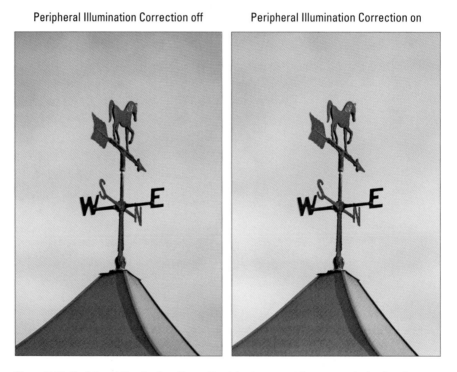

Figure 7-28: Peripheral Illumination Correction tries to correct the corner darkening that can occur with some lenses.

The adjustment is available in all your camera's exposure modes. But a few factoids need spelling out:

✐ **The correction is available only for photos captured in the JPEG file format.** For Raw photos, you can choose to apply the correction and vary its strength if you use Canon Digital Photo Professional to process your Raw images. Chapter 6 talks more about Raw processing.

✓ **For the camera to apply the proper correction, data about the specific lens must be included in the camera's *firmware* (internal software).** You can determine whether your lens is supported by opening Shooting Menu 1 and selecting Peripheral Illumination Correction, as shown on the left in Figure 7-29. Press Set to display the right screen in the figure. If the screen reports that correction data is available, as in the figure, the feature is enabled by default.

If your lens isn't supported, you may be able to add its information to the camera; Canon calls this step *registering your lens.* You do this by cabling the camera to your computer and then using some tools included with the free EOS Utility software, also provided with your camera. I must refer you to the software manual for help on this bit of business because of the limited number of words that can fit in these pages. (The manuals for all the software are located on one of the two CDs that ship in the camera box.)

✓ **For non-Canon lenses, Canon recommends disabling Peripheral Illumination Correction even if correction data is available.** To turn off the feature, select the Disable setting. (Refer to the screen shown on the right in Figure 7-29.) You can still apply the correction in Digital Photo Professional when you shoot in the Raw format.

✓ **In some circumstances, the correction may produce increased noise at the corners of the photo.** This problem occurs because exposure adjustment can make noise more apparent. Also, at high ISO settings, the camera applies the filter at a lesser strength — presumably to avoid adding even more noise to the picture. (See the first part of this chapter for an understanding of noise and its relationship to ISO.)

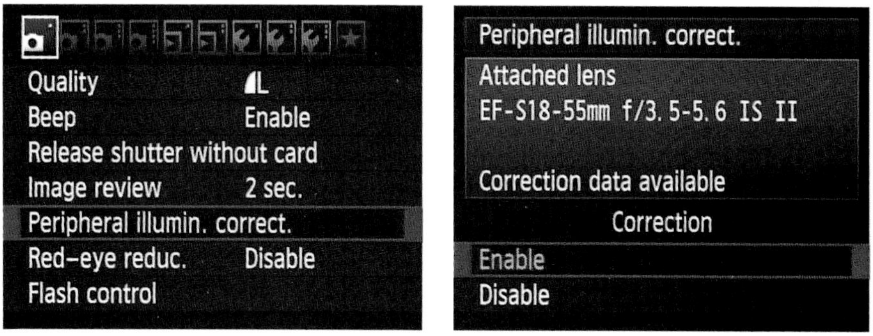

Quality	▲L
Beep	Enable
Release shutter without card	
Image review	2 sec.
Peripheral illumin. correct.	
Red–eye reduc.	Disable
Flash control	

Peripheral illumin. correct.

Attached lens
EF-S18-55mm f/3. 5-5. 6 IS II

Correction data available

Correction

Enable
Disable

Figure 7-29: If the camera has information about your lens, you can enable the feature.

Locking Autoexposure Settings

When you combine Spot, Partial, or Center-weighted metering with the P, Tv, or Av exposure modes, your camera continually meters the light and adjusts the exposure settings until the moment you press the shutter button fully to shoot the picture. The same thing happens with Evaluative metering if you use the A-DEP exposure mode or Live View.

For most situations, this approach works great, resulting in the right settings for the light that's striking your subject when you capture the image. But on occasion, you may want to lock in a certain combination of exposure settings. For example, perhaps you want your subject to appear at the far edge of the frame. If you were to use the normal shooting technique, you would place the subject under a focus point, press the shutter button halfway to lock focus and set the initial exposure, and then reframe to your desired composition to take the shot. The problem is that exposure is then recalculated based on the new framing, which can leave your subject under- or overexposed.

The easiest way to lock in exposure settings is to switch to M (manual exposure) mode and use the same f-stop, shutter speed, and ISO settings for each shot. In manual exposure mode, the camera never overrides your exposure decisions; they're locked until you change them.

But if you prefer to use autoexposure, you can lock the current exposure settings by pressing the AE (autoexposure) Lock button while holding the shutter button halfway down.

Exposure remains locked for four seconds, even if you release the AE Lock button and the shutter button. To remind you that AE Lock is in force, the camera displays a little asterisk in the viewfinder. If you need to relock exposure, just press the AE Lock button again.

Note: If your goal is to use the same exposure settings for multiple shots, you must keep the AE Lock button pressed during the entire series of pictures. Every time you let up on the button and press it again, you lock exposure anew based on the light that's in the frame.

One other critical point to remember about using AE Lock: The camera establishes and locks exposure differently depending on the metering mode, the focusing mode (automatic or manual), and on an autofocusing setting called AF Point Selection mode. (Chapter 8 explains this option thoroughly.) Here's the scoop:

✔ **Evaluative metering and automatic AF Point Selection:** Exposure is locked on the focusing point that achieved focus.

✔ **Evaluative metering and manual AF Point Selection:** Exposure is locked on the selected autofocus point.

✔ **All other metering modes:** Exposure is based on the center autofocus point, regardless of the AF Point Selection mode.

✔ **Manual focusing:** Exposure is based on the center autofocus point.

Again, if this focusing lingo sounded like gibberish, check out Chapter 8 to get a full explanation.

By combining autoexposure lock with Spot metering, you can ensure a good exposure for photographs in which you want your subject to be off-center, and that subject is significantly darker or lighter than the background. Imagine, for example, a dark statue set against a light blue sky. First, select Spot metering so that the camera considers only the object located in the center of the frame. Frame the scene initially so that your statue is located in the center of the viewfinder. Press and hold the shutter button halfway to establish focus and then lock exposure by pressing the AE Lock button. Now reframe the shot to your desired composition and take the picture. (See Chapter 8 for details on selecting an autofocus point.)

These bits of advice assume that you haven't altered the function of the AE Lock button, which you can do via a Custom Function. You can swap the tasks of the shutter button and AE Lock button, for example, so that pressing the shutter button halfway locks exposure and pressing the AE Lock button locks focus. Chapter 11 offers details on the relevant Custom Function.

Bracketing Exposures Automatically

Many photographers use a strategy called *bracketing* to ensure that at least one shot of a subject is properly exposed. They shoot the same subject multiple times, slightly varying the exposure settings for each image.

To make bracketing easy, your camera offers *automatic exposure bracketing* (AEB). When you enable this feature, your only job is to press the shutter button to record the shots; the camera automatically adjusts the exposure settings between each image.

Aside from cover-your, uh, "bases" shooting, bracketing is useful for *HDR imaging.* HDR stands for *high dynamic range,* with dynamic range referring to the spectrum of brightness values in a photograph. The idea behind HDR is to capture the same shot multiple times, using different exposure settings for each image. You then use special imaging software, called *tone mapping software,* to combine the exposures in a way that uses specific brightness values from each shot. By using this process, you get a shot that contains more detail in both the highlights and shadows than a camera could ever record in a single image. Figure 7-30 shows an example. The first two images show you the brightest and darkest exposures; the bottom image shows the HDR composite.

Figure 7-30: Using HDR software tools, I merged the brightest and darkest exposures (top) along with several intermediate exposures, to produce the composite image (bottom).

When applied to its extreme limits, HDR produces images that have something of a graphic-novel look. My example is pretty tame; some people might not even realize that any digital trickery has been involved. To me, it has the look of a hand-tinted photo.

Whether you're interested in automatic exposure bracketing for HDR or just want to give yourself an exposure safety net, keep these points in mind:

- **Exposure mode:** AEB is available only in the P, Tv, Av, M, and A-DEP exposure modes.

- **Flash:** AEB isn't available when you use flash. You can still bracket your shots — you just have to change the exposure settings between frames yourself.

- **Bracketing amount:** You can request an exposure change of up to two stops from the auto bracketing system.

- **Exposure Compensation:** You can combine AEB with Exposure Compensation if you want. The camera simply applies the compensation amount when it calculates the exposure for the three bracketed images.

- **Auto Lighting Optimizer:** Because that feature is designed to automatically adjust images that are underexposed or lacking in contrast, it can render AEB ineffective. So it's best to disable the feature when bracketing. See the section "Experimenting with Auto Lighting Optimizer," earlier in this chapter, for information on where to find and turn off the feature.

The next two sections explain how to set up the camera for automatic bracketing and how to actually record a series of bracketed shots.

Turning auto bracketing on and off

With that preamble out of the way, the following steps show you how to turn on automatic exposure bracketing via Shooting Menu 2. (More about another option for enabling the feature momentarily.)

1. **Display Shooting Menu 2 and highlight Expo. Comp./AEB, as shown on the left in Figure 7-31.**

Figure 7-31: Automatic exposure bracketing records your image at three exposure settings.

2. Press Set.

You see a screen like the one shown on the right in Figure 7-31. This is the same dual-natured screen that appears when you apply exposure compensation, as explained earlier in this chapter. In M mode, exposure compensation isn't relevant — if you want a darker or brighter image, you just adjust the f-stop, shutter speed, or ISO. So the Exposure Compensation controls are dimmed on the AEB/Exp. Comp screen, as shown in the figure, if the Mode dial is set to M.

3. Rotate the Main dial to establish the amount of exposure change you want between images.

What you see onscreen after you rotate the dial depends on your exposure mode.

- *M mode:* The screen changes to look similar to the one on the left in Figure 7-32, with only the AEB setting active. On the little meter, each whole number represents one stop of exposure shift. The little red lines under the meter show you the amount of shift that will occur in your bracketed series of shots. For example, the settings in Figure 7-32 represent the maximum two stops of adjustment. No matter what the settings, the first image is captured at the actual exposure settings; the second, at settings that produce a darker image; and the third, at settings that produce a brighter photo.

- *P, Tv, Av, or A-DEP modes:* For these modes, both the Exposure Compensation and AEB features are enabled. And the meter expands, as shown on the right in Figure 7-32, to represent the total 7-stop adjustment you can make in bracketed shots if you also enable the maximum amount of Exposure Compensation. (The meter expands after you rotate the Main dial; otherwise, it just shows the 5-stop range for Exposure Compensation.)

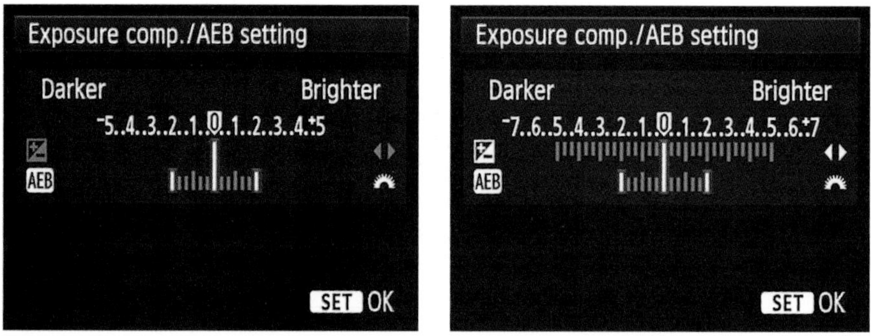

Figure 7-32: The bracketing control appears different in M mode (left) than in the other advanced exposure modes (right).

Where does the 7-stop thing come from? Well, you're still limited to adjusting exposure a total of two stops between bracketed shots, but if you turn on Exposure Compensation and set that value to +5.0 and then set the bracketed amount to +2.0, your brightest shot in the bracketed series is captured at +7.0. Your darkest shot is captured at +3.0.

Keep rotating the dial until you get the exposure indicators to reflect the amount of adjustment you want between each bracketed shot. (If you want to adjust the Exposure Compensation setting, press the right/left cross keys.)

4. **Press Set.**

   AEB is now enabled. To remind you of that fact, the exposure meter in the Shooting Settings display and on Shooting Menu 2 shows the three exposure indicators to represent the exposure shift you established in Step 3, as shown in Figure 7-33. You see the same markers on the viewfinder meter.

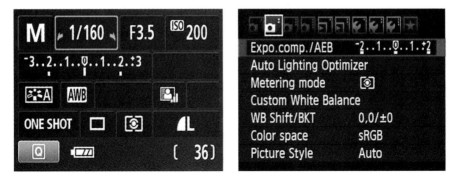

Figure 7-33: The three bars under the meter remind you that automatic exposure bracketing is enabled.

If you prefer, you can also enable AEB through the Quick Control screen. With the Shooting Settings screen displayed, press the Quick Control button and then use the cross keys to highlight the exposure meter. Press Set again to display a screen that works just like the one you get through the menus. Again, rotate the Main dial to set the bracketing amount and then press Set to wrap things up.

To turn off auto exposure bracketing, just revisit Shooting Menu 2 or the Quick Control screen and use the Main dial to change the AEB setting back to 0, so that you see only one meter indicator instead of three.

AEB is also turned off when you power down the camera, enable the flash, replace the camera battery, or replace the memory card. You also can't use the feature in manual exposure (M) mode if you set the shutter speed to the Bulb option. (At that setting, the camera keeps the shutter open as long as you press the shutter button.)

Shooting a bracketed series

After you enable auto bracketing, the way you record your trio of bracketed exposures depends on whether you set the Drive mode to Single or Continuous. Drive mode, which is described in Chapter 2, determines whether the camera records a single image or multiple images with each press of the shutter button. (Press the left cross key to access the screen that enables you to change this setting.)

✔ **AEB in Single mode:** You take each exposure separately, pressing the shutter button fully three times to record your trio of images.

If you forget which exposure you're taking, look at the exposure meter. After you press the shutter button halfway to lock focus, the meter shows just a single indicator bar instead of three. If the bar is at 0, you're ready to take the first capture. If it's to the left of 0, you're on capture two, which creates the darker exposure. If it's to the right of 0, you're on capture three, which produces the brightest image. This assumes that you haven't also applied exposure compensation, in which case the starting point is at a notch other than zero. (And yes, all these possible combinations make my head spin, too.)

✔ **AEB in Continuous mode:** The camera records all three exposures with one press of the shutter button. To record another series, release and then press the shutter button again. In other words, when AEB is turned on, the camera doesn't keep recording images until you release the shutter button as it normally does in Continuous mode — you can take only three images with one press of the shutter button.

✔ **Self-Timer/Remote modes:** All three exposures are recorded with a single press of the shutter button, as with Continuous mode.

Using Flash in Advanced Exposure Modes

Sometimes, no amount of fiddling with aperture, shutter speed, and ISO produces a bright enough exposure — in which case you simply have to add more light. The built-in flash on your camera offers the most convenient solution.

Chapter 2 offers a primer in flash basics, but here's a quick recap:

- In Scene Intelligent Auto and the scene modes, the camera decides when flash is needed.

- In Creative Auto mode, you can either let the camera retain flash control (auto flash) or set the flash to always fire or never fire. You make the selection via the Quick Control screen.

- The advanced exposure modes leave flash decisions entirely up to you. There's no automatic flash mode that lets you hand the reins over to the camera. Instead, when you want to use the built-in flash, just press the Flash button on the left side of the camera. The flash pops up and fires on your next shot. To turn off the flash, just press down on the flash assembly to close it.

- For normal flash operation in the advanced modes, set the Built-in Flash Function to Normal. The fastest way to adjust the setting is via the Quick Control screen. I labeled the icon that represents the Normal setting in Figure 7-34. (You don't see the icon until you raise the flash.)

Built-in Flash Function setting

Figure 7-34: Set the Built-in Flash Function to Normal for regular flash photography.

- You can set the flash to Red-Eye Reduction mode in all the exposure modes that allow flash. Just display Shooting Menu 1 and turn the Red-Eye option on or off. When you take a picture with the feature enabled, the camera lights the Red-Eye Reduction lamp on the front of the camera for a brief time before the flash goes off in an effort to constrict the subject's pupils and thereby lessen the chances of red-eye. See Chapter 2 for a few more pointers about using this feature.

- When you use the built-in flash, the fastest shutter speed possible is 1/200 second. The limitation is needed for the camera to synchronize the timing of the flash with the opening and closing of the shutter. So fast-action photography and the built-in flash really aren't compatible. (If you use some compatible external flash units, you can access the entire range of shutter speeds.)

- Pay careful attention to your results when you use the built-in flash with a telephoto lens that is very long. You may find that the flash casts an unwanted shadow when it strikes the lens. For best results, try switching to an external flash head.

Getting more help with flash

In order to keep this book from being exorbitantly large (and expensive), I can cover only the basics of flash photography. But I can point you toward a couple of my favorite resources for delving more deeply into the subject:

✔ Canon's website (www.canon.com) offers some great tutorials on flash photography (as well as other subjects). Look for the Digital Learning Center links to resources related to Canon Speedlite flash technology.

✔ A website completely dedicated to flash photography, www.strobist.com, enables you to learn from and share with other photographers.

✔ You can find many good books detailing the art of flash photography — and trust me,

when you're working with the harsh and narrowly focused light that a flash emits, it *is* an art to produce great pictures. A seasoned portrait photographer, for example, knows where to place and modify the light to produce soft, beautiful images that look as though no artificial light at all was used. That's why wedding pictures taken by a professional photographer look so nice and the snapshots taken by most wedding guests look so, um, not. (That's also why a good wedding photographer costs money.)

✔ Chapter 9 of this book offers additional flash and lighting tips related to portraits and other specific types of photographs.

The next section goes into a little background detail about how the camera calculates the flash power that's needed to expose the image. This stuff is a little technical, but it will help you to better understand how to get the results you want because the flash performance varies depending on the exposure mode.

Following that discussion, the rest of the chapter covers advanced flash features.

Understanding your camera's approach to flash

When you use flash, your camera automatically calculates the flash power needed to illuminate the subject. This process is sometimes referred to as *flash metering.* Your Rebel T3i/600D uses a flash-metering system that Canon calls E-TTL II. The *E* stands for *evaluative, TTL* stands for *through the lens,* and *II* refers to the fact that this system is an update to the first version of the system.

It isn't important that you remember what the initials stand for or even the flash system's official name. What is helpful to keep in mind is how the system is designed to work.

First, you need to know that a flash can be used in two basic ways: as the primary light source or as a *fill flash*. When flash is the primary light source, both the subject and background are lit by the flash. In dim lighting, this typically results in a brightly lit subject and a dark background, as shown on the left in Figure 7-35. This assumes that the background is far enough from the subject that it's beyond the reach of the flash, of course.

Flash as primary light source   Fill flash

Figure 7-35: Fill flash produces brighter backgrounds.

With fill flash, the background is exposed primarily by ambient light, and the flash adds a little extra illumination to the subject. Fill flash typically produces brighter backgrounds and, often, softer lighting of the subject because not as much flash power is needed. The downside is that if the ambient light is dim, as in this nighttime example, you need a slow shutter speed to properly expose the image, and both the camera and the subject must remain still to avoid blurring. The shutter speed for the fill-flash image, shown on the right in Figure 7-35, was 1/30 second. Fortunately, I had a tripod, and the deer was happy to stay perfectly still as long as I needed.

Neither flash approach is necessarily right or wrong. Whether you want a dark background depends on the scene and your artistic interpretation. If you want to diminish the background, you may prefer the darker background you get when you use flash as your primary light source. But if the background is important to the context of the shot, allowing the camera to absorb more ambient light and adding just a small bit of fill flash may be more to your liking.

So how does this little flash lesson relate to your camera? Well, the exposure mode you use (P, Tv, Av, M, or A-DEP) determines whether the flash operates as a fill flash or as the primary light source. The exposure mode also controls the extent to which the camera adjusts the aperture and shutter speed in response to the ambient light in the scene.

In all modes, the camera analyzes the light both in the background and on the subject. Then it calculates the exposure and flash output as follows:

✓ **P:** In this mode, the shutter speed is automatically set between 1/60 and 1/200 second. If the ambient light is sufficient, the flash output is geared to providing fill-flash lighting. Otherwise, the flash is determined to be the primary light source, and the output is adjusted accordingly. In the latter event, the image background may be dark, as in the left example in Figure 7-35, depending on its distance from the flash.

✓ **Tv:** In this mode, the flash defaults to fill-flash behavior. After you select a shutter speed, the camera determines the proper aperture to expose the background with ambient light. Then it sets the flash power to provide fill-flash lighting to the subject.

You can select a shutter speed between 30 seconds and 1/200 second. If the aperture (f-stop) setting blinks, the camera can't expose the background properly at the shutter speed you selected. You can adjust either the shutter speed or ISO to correct the problem.

✓ **Av:** Again, the flash is designed to serve as fill-flash lighting. After you set the f-stop, the camera selects the shutter speed needed to expose the background using only ambient light. The flash power is then geared to fill in shadows on the subject.

Depending on the ambient light and your selected f-stop, the camera sets the shutter speed at anywhere from 30 seconds to 1/200 second. So be sure to note the shutter speed before you shoot — at slow shutter speeds, you may need a tripod to avoid camera shake. Your subject also must remain still to avoid blurring.

If you want to avoid the possibility of a slow shutter altogether, you can: Display Setup Menu 3, select Custom Functions, and press Set. Then select Custom Function 3, as shown in Figure 7-36. At the default setting, the camera operates as just described. If you instead select the second option, the camera sticks with a shutter-speed range of 1/60 to 1/200 second. And with the third option, the shutter speed is always set to 1/200 second when you use flash.

The latter two options both ensure that you can handhold the camera without blur, but obviously, in dim lighting, it can result in a dark background because the camera doesn't have time to soak up much ambient light. At the 1/200 to 1/60 setting, the backgrounds are usually brighter than the 1/200 fixed setting, of course, because the camera at least has the latitude to slow the shutter to 1/60 second.

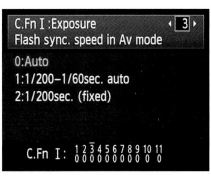

Figure 7-36: You can limit the camera to a fast shutter when using Av mode with flash.

✔ **M:** In this mode, the shutter speed, aperture, and ISO setting you select determine how brightly the background will be exposed. The camera takes care of illuminating the subject with fill flash. The maximum shutter speed you can select is 1/200 second; the slowest normal shutter speed is 30 seconds.

You also can set the shutter speed to the Bulb setting — which keeps the shutter open as long as you keep the shutter button pressed, however. In Bulb mode, the flash fires at the beginning of the exposure if the Shutter Sync setting is set to the 1st Curtain setting; with the 2nd Curtain setting, the flash fires at the beginning of the exposure and again at the end. See the upcoming section "Exploring more flash options" for details about the Shutter Sync setting.

✔ **A-DEP:** You can use flash in this mode, but doing so disables the automatic depth-of-field feature. The flash and exposure systems then operate as described for P mode. However, you can't choose from multiple combinations of aperture and shutter speed as you can in that mode; you're stuck with the combination that the camera selects.

If the flash output in any mode isn't to your liking, you can adjust it by using flash exposure compensation, explained a little later in this chapter. Also check out the upcoming section "Locking the flash exposure" for another trick to manipulate flash results. In any autoexposure mode, you can also use exposure compensation, discussed earlier, to tweak the ambient exposure — that is, the brightness of your background. So you have multiple points of control: exposure compensation to manipulate the background brightness, and flash compensation and flash exposure lock to adjust the flash output.

Again, these guidelines apply to the camera's built-in-flash. If you use certain Canon external flash units, you not only have more flash control but can also select a faster shutter speed than the built-in flash permits.

Using flash outdoors

Although most people think of flash as a tool for nighttime and low-light photography, adding a bit of light from the built-in flash can improve close-ups
and portraits that you shoot outdoors during the day. After all, your main
light source — the sun — is overhead, so although the top of the subject may
be adequately lit, the front typically needs some additional illumination. And
if your subject is in the shade, getting no direct light, using flash is even more
critical. For example, the two photos in Figure 7-37 show you the same scene,
captured with and without fill flash. The fruit stand was shaded by an awning,
so even though it was a bright, cloudless day, I popped up the built-in flash to
bring just a smidge more light to the scene and produce a better result.

Without flash   With flash

Figure 7-37: Flash often improves daytime pictures outdoors.

You do need to be aware of a couple issues that can arise when you supple-
ment the sun with the built-in flash:

  ✓ **You may need to make a White Balance adjustment.** Adding flash may
    result in colors that are slightly warmer (more yellow/red), as in the flash
    example here, or cooler (bluish) because the camera's white balancing

system can get tripped up by mixed light sources. If you don't appreciate the shift in colors, see Chapter 8 to find out how to make a white balance adjustment to solve the problem.

↙ **You may need to stop down the aperture or lower ISO to avoid over-exposing the photo.** The top shutter speed for the built-in flash, 1/200 second, may not be fast enough to produce a good exposure in very bright light when you use a wide-open aperture, even if you use the lowest possible ISO setting. If you want both flash *and* the short depth of field that comes with an open aperture, you can place a neutral density filter over your lens. This accessory reduces the light that comes through the lens without affecting colors. In addition, some Canon external flash units enable you to access the entire range of shutter speeds on the camera.

↙ **Don't bother using the built-in flash for landscapes.** Unless your subject is within about 16 feet, it's going to be outside the effective range of the built-in flash.

Adjusting flash power with Flash Exposure Compensation

When you shoot with your built-in flash, the camera attempts to adjust the flash output as needed to produce a good exposure in the current lighting conditions. On some occasions, you may find that you want a little more or less light than the camera thinks is appropriate.

You can adjust the flash output by using the feature called *Flash Exposure Compensation.* Similar to exposure compensation, discussed earlier in this chapter, flash exposure compensation affects the output level of the flash unit, whereas exposure compensation affects the brightness of the background in your flash photos. As with exposure compensation, flash exposure compensation is stated in terms of EV *(exposure value)* numbers. A setting of 0.0 indicates no flash adjustment; you can increase the flash power to +2.0 or decrease it to –2.0.

Figure 7-38 shows an example of the benefit of this feature — again, available only when you shoot in the advanced exposure modes. The first image shows you a flash-free shot. Clearly, a little more light was needed, but at normal flash power, the flash was too strong, blowing out the highlights in some areas, as shown in the middle image. Reducing the flash power to EV –1.3, resulted in a softer flash that straddled the line perfectly between no flash and too much flash.

As for boosting the flash output, well, you may find it necessary on some occasions, but don't expect the built-in flash to work miracles even at a Flash Exposure Compensation of +2.0. Any built-in flash has a limited range — about 16 feet, in the case of the one on the T3i/600D — so the light simply can't reach faraway objects.

No flash   Flash EV 0.0   Flash EV –1.3

Figure 7-38: When normal flash output is too strong, lower the Flash Exposure Compensation value.

Whichever direction you want to go with flash power, you have two ways to do so:

- ✓ **Quick Control screen:** This path is by far the easiest way to travel. After shifting to the Quick Control display, highlight the Flash Exposure Compensation value, as shown on the right in Figure 7-39. Rotate the Main dial to raise or lower the amount of flash adjustment. Or if you need more help, press Set to display a screen that contains a little meter along with a text note that tells you that if you use an external flash, any compensation you dial in via the flash itself overrides the on-camera setting. You can use the Main dial or cross keys to adjust the flash power on this screen; press Set when you finish.

  When flash compensation is in effect, the value appears in the Shooting Settings screen, as shown on the right in Figure 7-39. You see the same plus/minus flash symbol in the viewfinder and Live View display, although in both cases without the actual Flash Exposure Compensation value. If you change the Flash Exposure Compensation value to zero, the flash-power icon disappears from all the displays.

- ✓ **Shooting Menu 2:** The menu route to flash power is a little more tedious. Display Shooting Menu 1, select Flash Control, and press Set. You then see the left screen in Figure 7-40. Highlight Built-in Flash Func. Setting and press Set to display the right screen. Now highlight Flash Exp. Comp. and press Set again. The little flash power meter becomes activated, and you can then use the right or left cross keys to adjust the setting. Press Set when you finish. (In other words, learn the Quick Control method and save yourself a bunch of button presses!)

Flash Exposure Compensation amount

Figure 7-39: The quickest way to adjust flash power is via the Quick Control screen.

Figure 7-40: You can also change flash power by using the menus, but it's a tedious task.

You also have the option of customizing the Set button to whisk you directly to the Flash Exposure Compensation setting. (Chapter 11 shows you how.)

As with exposure compensation, any flash-power adjustment you make remains in force until you reset the control, even if you turn off the camera. So be sure to check the setting before using your flash. Additionally, the Auto Lighting Optimizer feature, covered earlier in this chapter, can interfere with the effect produced by flash exposure compensation, so you might want to disable it.

Locking the flash exposure

You might never notice it, but when you press the shutter button to take a picture with flash enabled, the camera emits a brief *preflash* before the actual flash. This preflash is used to determine the proper flash power needed to expose the image.

Occasionally, the information that the camera collects from the preflash can be off-target because of the assumptions the system makes about what area of the frame is likely to contain your subject. To address this problem, your camera has a feature called *Flash Exposure Lock,* or FE Lock. This tool enables you to set the flash power based on only the center of the frame.

Unfortunately, FE Lock isn't available in Live View mode. If you want to use this feature, you must abandon Live View and use the viewfinder to frame your images.

Follow these steps to use FE Lock:

1. **Frame your photo so that your subject falls under the center autofocus point.**

   You want your subject smack in the middle of the frame. You can reframe the shot after locking the flash exposure, if you want.

2. **Press the shutter button halfway.**

   The camera meters the light in the scene. If you're using autofocusing, focus is set on your subject, and the green focus confirmation dot appears in the viewfinder. (If focus is set on another spot in the frame, see Chapter 8 to find out how to select the center autofocus point.) You can now lift your finger off the shutter button, if you want.

3. **While the subject is still under the center autofocus point, press and release the AE Lock button.**

   You can see the button in the margin here. The camera emits the pre-flash, and the letters FEL display for a second in the viewfinder. (FEL stands for *flash exposure lock.*) You also see the asterisk symbol — the one that appears above the AE Lock button on the camera body — next to the flash icon in the viewfinder. (Of course, the flash must be in the open position for this to work.)

4. **If needed, reestablish focus on your subject.**

   In autofocus mode, press and hold the shutter button halfway. (Take this step only if you released the shutter button after Step 2.) In manual focus mode, twist the focusing ring on the lens to establish focus.

5. **Reframe the image to the composition you want.**

   While you do, keep the shutter button pressed halfway to maintain focus if you're using autofocusing.

6. **Press the shutter button the rest of the way to take the picture.**

   The image is captured using the flash output setting you established in Step 3.

Flash exposure lock is also helpful when you're shooting portraits. The pre-flash sometimes causes people to blink, which means that with normal flash shooting, in which the actual flash and exposure occur immediately after the preflash, their eyes are closed at the exact moment of the exposure. With flash exposure lock, you can fire the preflash and then wait a second or two for the subject's eyes to recover before you take the actual picture.

Better yet, the flash exposure setting remains in force for about 16 seconds, meaning that you can shoot a series of images using the same flash setting without firing another preflash at all.

Exploring more flash options

When you set the Mode dial to P, Tv, Av, M, or A-DEP, Shooting Menu 1 offers a Flash Control option. Using this menu item, you can adjust flash power, as explained a couple of sections earlier (although using the Quick Control screen is easier). The Flash Control option also enables you to customize a few other aspects of the built-in flash as well as control an external flash head.

To explore your options, highlight Flash Control, as shown on the left in Figure 7-41, and press Set. You then see the screen shown on the right in the figure. Here's the rundown of the available options:

Quality	◢L
Beep	Enable
Release shutter without card	
Image review	2 sec.
Peripheral illumin. correct.	
Red-eye reduc.	Disable
Flash control	

Flash control	
Flash firing	Enable
E–TTL II meter.	Evaluative
Built–in flash func. setting	
External flash func. setting	
External flash C.Fn setting	
Clear ext. flash C.Fn set.	

Figure 7-41: You can customize additional flash options via Setup Menu 1.

> ✓ **Flash Firing:** Normally, this option is set to Enable. If you want to dis-able the flash, you can choose Disable instead. However, you don't have to take this step in most cases — just close the pop-up flash head on top of the camera if you don't want to use flash.
>
> What's the point of this option, then? Well, if you use autofocusing in dim lighting, the camera may need some help finding its target. To that end, it sometimes emits an *AF-assist beam* from the flash head — the

beam is a series of rapid pulses of light. If you want the benefit of the AF-assist beam but you don't want the flash to fire, you can disable flash firing. Remember that you have to pop up the flash unit to expose the lamp that emits the beam. You also can take advantage of this option when you attach an external flash head.

✓ **E-TTL II Metering:** This option enables you to switch from the default flash metering approach, called Evaluative. In this mode, the camera operates as described in the earlier section, "Understanding your camera's approach to flash." That is, it exposes the background using ambient light when possible and then sets the flash power to serve as fill light on the subject.

If you instead select the Average option, the flash is used as the primary light source, meaning that the flash power is set to expose the entire scene without relying on ambient light. Typically, this results in a more powerful (and possibly harsh) flash lighting and dark backgrounds.

✓ **Built-in Flash Function Setting:** If you highlight this option and press Set, you display the screen shown in Figure 7-42.

But which options are adjustable depends on whether you set the first option, Built-in Flash, to Normal Firing, as in the figure, or to one of the two settings that set the built-in flash to trigger off-camera flash units. See the sidebar "Using one flash to control others" for details on that possibility.

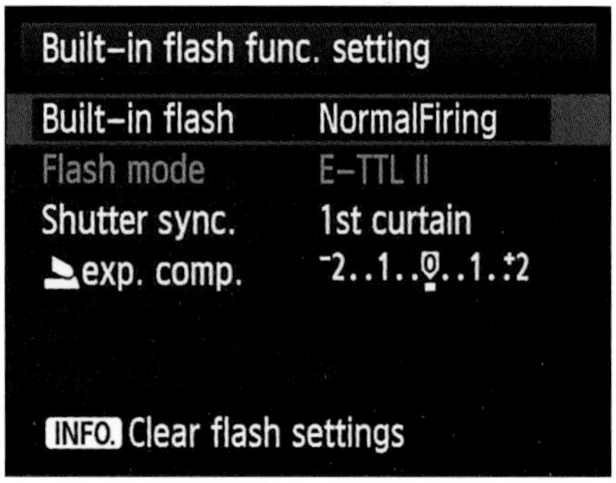

Figure 7-42: These advanced flash options affect only the built-in flash.

The other options available for normal flash operation work like so:

- *Shutter Sync:* By default, the flash fires at the beginning of the exposure. This flash timing, known as *1st curtain sync,* is the best choice for most subjects. However, if you use a very slow shutter speed and you're photographing a moving object, 1st curtain sync causes the blur that results from the motion to appear in front of the object, which doesn't make much visual sense.

  To solve this problem, you can change the Shutter Sync option to *2nd curtain sync,* also known as *rear-curtain sync.* In this flash mode, the motion trails appear behind the moving object. The flash fires twice in this mode: once when you press the shutter button and again at the end of the exposure.

- *Flash Exposure Compensation:* This setting adjusts the power of the built-in flash; again, see the earlier section "Adjusting flash power with Flash Exposure Compensation" for details.

✔ **External Flash controls:** The last three options on the Flash Control list (refer to the right screen in Figure 7-41) relate to external flash heads; they don't affect the performance of the built-in flash. However, they apply only to Canon EX-series Speedlites that enable you to control the flash through the camera. If you own such a flash, refer to the flash manual for details.

Using one flash to control others

If you're ready to try some multiple-light shooting, you can use your built-in flash as a *master* to wirelessly trigger off-camera flash units, which are called *slaves.* (I know, but don't write me any nasty letters — I'm here to tell you what the current terminology is, no matter how politically insensitive.) You can even set the power of the external units through the camera's flash options and specify whether you want the built-in flash to simply trigger the other flash heads or add its own flash power to the scene.

Using a master/slave flash setup can provide you with great added lighting flexibility without requiring you to spend lots of money (although you certainly can) or carrying around lots of bulky, traditional lighting equipment. In fact, I rely on this lighting option to shoot most of my product and still-life shots, using the on-board flash to trigger two off-camera flashes.

In order to use this camera function, your external flash units must support wireless control, of course. You can find a list of compatible Canon flash products that fit the bill in the camera manual. You also have to change the Built-in Flash Function option to one of the two wireless modes, as shown in the figures here.

With the Easy Wireless option, the camera handles most of the flash-firing settings for you, although you do have to take a couple simple setup steps. To really control the lighting, choose the Custom Wireless setting instead. It enables you to adjust the output of each flash unit separately to fine-tune the way your subject is lit.

Your camera manual offers complete details on setting up the camera and your flash units for wireless operation. Also visit the Canon website (www.canon.com) and look for the Digital Learning Center tutorials about using Canon Speedlite flash heads.

Built-in flash func. setting	
Built-in flash	NormalFiring
Flash mode	E-TTL II
Shutter sync.	1st curtain
▲exp. comp.	⁻2..1..0̲..1..⁺2
INFO. Clear flash settings	

Built-in flash func. setting	
Built-in flash	▶NormalFiring
	EasyWireless
	CustWireless
INFO. Clear flash settings	

You can probably discern from these descriptions that most of these features are designed for photographers schooled in flash photography who want to mess around with advanced flash options. If that doesn't describe you, don't worry about it. The default settings selected by Canon will serve you well in most every situation — the exception is flash exposure compensation, which you can just as easily adjust via the Quick Control screen instead of digging through the menus.

Manipulating Focus and Color

*T*o many people, the word *focus* has just one interpretation when applied to a photograph: Either the subject is in focus or it's blurry. But an artful photographer knows that there's more to focus than simply getting a sharp image of a subject. You also need to consider *depth of field,* or the distance over which objects remain sharply focused. This chapter explains all the ways to control depth of field and also discusses how to use your Rebel's advanced autofocus options.

In addition, this chapter dives into the topic of color, explaining such concepts as *White Balance* (a feature that compensates for the varying color casts created by different light sources), and *color space* (an option that determines the spectrum of colors your camera can capture).

Reviewing Focus Basics

Chapters 1, 3, and 7 touch on various focus issues. But just in case you're not reading this book from front to back, the following steps provide a recap of the basic process of focusing.

These steps relate only to regular, still photography — you can find details on autofocusing in Live View mode and Movie mode in Chapter 4.

1. **If you haven't already done so, adjust the viewfinder to your eyesight.**

   Chapter 1 explains how to take this critical step.

2. **Set the focusing switch on the lens to manual or automatic focusing.**

   To focus manually, set the switch to the MF position. For autofocusing, set the switch to the AF position, as in Figure 8-1. (These directions are specific to the kit lens sold with the Rebel T3i/600D, shown in the figure. If you use another lens, the switch may look or operate differently, so check the product manual.)

3. **For handheld shooting, turn on Image Stabilization.**

   For sharper handheld shots, set the Stabilizer switch on the kit lens to On. (Refer to Figure 8-1.) If you use another lens that offers image stabilization (it may go by a different name, depending on the manufacturer), check the lens manual to find out how to turn on the feature.

   For tripod-mounted shooting with a non-Canon lens, the manufacturer may suggest turning off stabilization, so again, check the lens manual. You don't need to turn off the feature for most Canon IS lenses, but you can save battery power by doing so.

   Figure 8-1: Select AF for autofocus or MF for manual focus.

4. **Set focus:**

   • *To autofocus:* In Sports mode, frame your subject under the center focus point and press the shutter button halfway to focus. You hear a series of beeps, indicating that the camera is adjusting focus as needed to track the subject's movement up to the time you take the shot.

   In the advanced exposure modes as well as Portrait, Landscape, Close-up, and Night Portrait mode, frame your subject so that it appears under one of the nine autofocus points. Then press and hold the shutter button halfway. The focus lamp in the viewfinder lights, one or more of the focus points turns red, as shown in Figure 8-2, and you hear a tiny beep. A red dot indicates that the area under the focus points is in focus. Focus is locked as long as you hold down the shutter button halfway.

Focus point

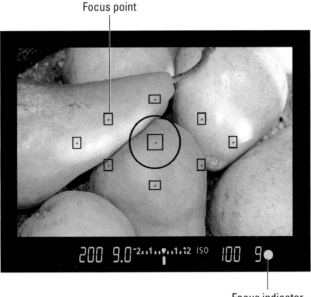

Focus indicator

Figure 8-2: The viewfinder offers these focusing aids.

The same thing happens in Scene Intelligent Auto, Creative Auto, and Flash Off modes unless the camera senses motion in front of the lens, in which case it adjusts focus as needed to track the moving subject, as it does in Sports mode.

For the P, Tv, Av, M, and A-DEP exposure modes, you can vary this autofocusing behavior; see the next section for how-to's. In all modes, you can silence the focus beep by setting the Beep option on Shooting Menu 1 to disable.

• *For manual focus:* Twist the focusing ring on the lens.

Even in the camera's manual mode, you can confirm focus by pressing the shutter button halfway. The autofocus point or points that achieved focus flash for a second or two, the viewfinder's focus lamp lights up, and you hear the focus-achieved beep.

Never twist the lens focusing ring on the kit lens without first setting the lens switch to the MF position. You can damage the lens by doing so! If you use another lens, check the lens manual for advice. Some lenses enable you to set focus initially using autofocus and then fine-tune focus by twisting the focusing ring without officially setting the lens to manual-focusing mode.

Shutter speed and blurry photos

A poorly focused photo isn't always related to the issues discussed in this chapter. Any movement of the camera or subject can also cause blur. Both problems are related to shutter speed, an exposure control I cover in Chapter 7. Be sure to also visit Chapter 9, which provides additional tips for capturing moving objects without blur.

Adjusting Autofocus Performance

In the point-and-shoot photography modes that I cover in Chapter 3, you can't adjust the camera's autofocusing behavior. You're stuck with the choices the camera makes for each exposure mode. (The individual descriptions of the modes in Chapter 3 tell you what to expect.)

But in the advanced exposure modes, you can tweak autofocusing behavior through the following two controls:

- **AF (autofocus) mode:** This option determines whether the camera locks focus when you press the shutter button halfway or continues to adjust focus from the time you press the shutter button halfway to the time you press the button the rest of the way to take the shot.

- **AF Point Selection:** This setting determines which autofocus points the camera uses to establish the focusing distance. At the default setting, all nine points are in play, and the camera typically focuses on the closest object. But you can choose to base focus on a single point that you select instead. The exception is when you set the exposure mode to A-DEP; that mode always uses all nine points in order to perform its automatic depth-of-field calculation. (See "Using A-DEP mode," later in this chapter, for more information.)

Although letting the camera handle these decisions for you certainly takes some of the work out of autofocusing, you can get more reliable focusing results — especially with difficult-to-focus subjects — by taking control of the AF mode and AF Point Selection settings yourself. The next few sections explain both options in more detail.

One note before you dig in: Information in this chapter assumes that you haven't changed the default functions of camera buttons (such as the AE Lock button and the shutter button). I detail those customization options in Chapter 11, but leave the buttons at their default settings until you're fully acquainted with the camera — otherwise, instructions here (and those you find in the camera manual) aren't going to work. Also note that the settings and techniques described here relate to normal, through-the-viewfinder photography. Autofocusing works differently in Live View mode; Chapter 4 covers that topic as well as all other Live View and movie-making information.

AF Selection Point: One focus point or many?

When you shoot in Sports mode, the camera bases focus on the center focus point. In the other fully automatic exposure modes (Scene Intelligent Auto, Portrait, Landscape, and so on) as well as in Creative Auto and A-DEP mode, the camera's autofocusing system looks at all nine autofocus points when trying to establish focus. Typically, the camera sets focus on the point that falls over the object closest to the lens. If these focusing decisions don't suit your needs, you have two options:

✔ Focus manually.

✔ Set the camera to P, Tv, Av, or M exposure mode. In these modes, you can tell the camera to base focus on a specific auto-focus point.

Again, manual focusing is a simple matter of setting the switch on the lens to the MF position and then twisting the focusing ring on the lens. To use autofocusing and specify an autofocus point, take these steps.

1. **Set the Mode dial to P, Tv, Av, or M.**

2. **Press and release the AF Point Selection button, highlighted in Figure 8-3.**

   When you do, you see the AF Point Selection screen on the monitor. From this screen, you can choose one of two modes:

AF Point Selection button

Figure 8-3: Press and release the AF Point Selection button to select an autofocus point.

Automatic AF Point Selection, in which all focus points are considered, or Manual AF Point Selection, in which you choose a single focus point.

In Automatic AF Point Selection mode, all autofocus points appear in color, as shown in Figure 8-4. In Manual AF Point Selection mode, only one point is selected and appears in color, as shown in Figure 8-5. In the figure, the center AF point is selected.

You can check the current mode by looking through the view-finder, too. When you press and release the AF Point Selection button, all nine autofocus points turn red in the viewfinder if you're in Automatic AF Point Selection mode. A single point turns red if you're in Manual AF Point Selection mode.

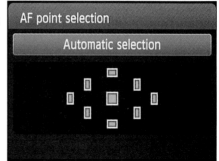

Figure 8-4: In Automatic mode, all nine autofocus points are active.

3. **To choose a single autofocus point, set the camera to Manual AF Point Selection mode.**

   You can shift from Automatic AF Point Selection mode to Manual mode in two ways:

   - *Rotate the Main dial.* This option is easiest when you're looking through the viewfinder.

   - *Press the Set button.* Pressing the button toggles the camera between Automatic AF Point Selection and Manual AF Point Selection with the center point activated.

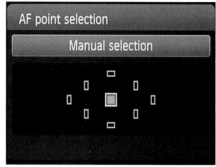

Figure 8-5: You also can base autofocus on a single point; here, the center point is selected.

4. **Specify which AF Point you want to use.**

   You can either rotate the Main dial or press the cross keys to select a point. When all autofocus points again turn red, you've cycled back to automatic AF Point Selection mode. Rotate the dial or press a cross key to switch back to single-point selection.

That's all there is to it. After you select the autofocus point, just frame your shot so that your subject falls under that point and then press the shutter button halfway to focus.

Changing the AF (autofocus) mode

Your camera offers three different autofocusing schemes, which you select through the AF mode control. The three choices work like so:

- **One Shot:** In this mode, which is geared to shooting stationary subjects, the camera locks focus when you press the shutter button halfway. Focus remains locked as long as you hold the shutter button at that halfway position. This autofocus setting is always used for Portrait, Landscape, Night Portrait, and Close-up modes.

- **AI Servo:** In this mode (the *AI* stands for *artificial intelligence,* if you care), the camera adjusts focus continually as needed from when you press the shutter button halfway to the time you take the picture. This mode is designed to make focusing on moving subjects easier, and it's the one the camera uses when you shoot in Sports exposure mode.

  For AI Servo to work properly, you must reframe as needed to keep your subject under the active autofocus point if you're working in Manual AF Point Selection mode. If the camera is set to Automatic AF Point Selection, the camera initially bases focus on the center focus point. If the subject moves away from the point, focus should still be okay as long as you keep the subject within the area covered by one of the other nine autofocus points. (The preceding section explains these two modes.)

  In either case, the green focus dot in the viewfinder blinks rapidly if the camera isn't tracking focus successfully. If all is going well, the focus dot doesn't light up, nor do you hear the beep that normally sounds when focus is achieved. (You can hear the autofocus motor whirring a little when the camera adjusts focus.)

- **AI Focus:** This mode automatically switches the camera from One Shot to AI Servo as needed. When you first press the shutter button halfway, focus is locked on the active autofocus point (or points), as usual in One Shot mode. But if the subject moves, the camera shifts into AI Servo mode and adjusts focus as it thinks is warranted. AI Focus is the only setting available when you shoot in the Scene Intelligent Auto, Flash Off, and Creative Auto modes.

I prefer not to use AI Focus because I don't want to rely on the camera to figure out whether I'm interested in a moving or stationary subject. So I stick with One Shot for stationary subjects and AI Servo for focusing on moving subjects.

One way to remember which mode is which: For still subjects, you only need *one shot* at setting focus. For moving subjects, think of a tennis or volleyball player *serving* the ball — so AI *Servo* for action shots.

You can set the AF mode in two ways:

✓ **AF mode button (right cross key):** Your fastest move is to press this button, labeled in Figure 8-6. It takes you directly to the screen shown on the monitor in the figure. Select a setting and press Set.

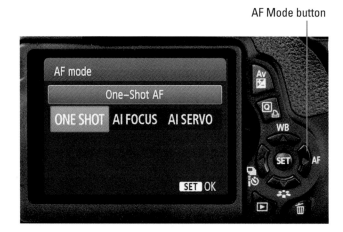

Figure 8-6: The fastest way to access the AF mode setting is to press the right cross key.

✓ **Quick Control screen:** Display the Shooting Settings screen. (Just press the shutter button halfway and release it.) Then press the Quick Control button and use the cross keys to highlight the icon shown in Figure 8-7. The selected AF mode setting appears at the bottom of the screen. Rotate the Main dial to cycle through the three mode options.

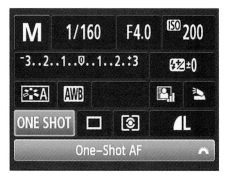

Figure 8-7: But you also can adjust the setting via the Quick Control screen.

If you prefer, you can press Set after highlighting the AF mode icon to display the screen shown in Figure 8-6, where all the mode choices appear. Then use the cross keys or Main dial to highlight your choice and press Set again.

Choosing the right autofocus combo

You'll get the best autofocus results if you pair your chosen AF mode with the most appropriate AF Point Selection mode, because the two settings work in tandem. Here are the combinations that I suggest for the maximum autofocus control:

- **For still subjects: One Shot and Manual AF Point Selection.** You then select a specific focus point, and the camera locks focus on that point at the time you press the shutter button halfway. Focus remains locked on your subject even if you reframe the shot after you press the button halfway.

- **For moving subjects: AI Servo and Automatic AF Point Selection.** You begin by framing your subject so that it's under the center focus point — remember, when you combine AI Servo with Automatic AF Point Selection, the camera chooses the center point to establish the initial focusing distance when you press the shutter button halfway. But the camera adjusts focus as needed if your subject moves within the frame before you take the shot. All you need to do is reframe as needed to keep your subject within the boundaries of the autofocus points.

Keeping these two combos in mind should greatly improve your autofocusing accuracy. But please don't forget that in some situations, no combination will enable speedy or correct autofocusing. For example, if you try to focus on a very reflective subject, the camera may hunt and hunt for an autofocus point forever. And if you try to focus on a subject behind a fence, the autofocus system may continually insist on focusing on the fence instead of your subject. In such scenarios, don't waste time monkeying with the autofocus settings — just switch to manual focusing and twist the focusing ring on the lens to focus.

Manipulating Depth of Field

Getting familiar with the concept of depth of field is one of the biggest steps you can take to becoming a more artful photographer. *Depth of field* simply refers to the distance over which objects in a photograph appear sharply focused. Chapters 3 and 7 provide an introduction to depth of field, but here's a quick summary just to hammer home the lesson:

✔ **With a shallow (small) depth of field:** Only your subject and objects very close to it appear sharp. Objects at a distance from the subject appear blurry.

✔ **With a large depth of field:** The zone of sharp focus extends to include distant objects.

Which arrangement works best depends entirely on your creative vision and your subject. In portraits, for example, a classic technique is to use a shallow depth of field, as in Figure 8-8. This approach increases emphasis on the subject while diminishing the impact of the background. But for the photo shown in Figure 8-9, the goal was to give the historical marker, the lighthouse, and the cottage equal weight in the scene, so settings that produced a large depth of field were used to keep them all in focus.

Shallow depth of field

Figure 8-8: A shallow depth of field blurs the background and draws added attention to the subject.

Note, though, that with a shallow depth of field, which part of the scene appears blurry depends on the spot at which you establish focus. In the lighthouse scene, for example, had settings that produced a short depth of field been used and focus set on the lighthouse, both the historical marker in the foreground and the cottage in the background might be outside the zone of sharp focus.

So how do you adjust depth of field? You have these three points of control:

✔ **Aperture setting (f-stop):** The aperture is one of three exposure settings, all explained fully in Chapter 7. Depth of field increases as you stop down the aperture (by choosing a higher f-stop number). For shallow depth of field, open the aperture (by choosing a lower f-stop number).

Figure 8-10 offers an example. Notice that the trees in the background are much more softly focused in the f/5.6 example than in the f/11 version. Of course, changing the aperture requires adjusting the shutter speed or ISO to maintain the equivalent exposure; for these images, shutter speed was adjusted.

✔ **Lens focal length:** In lay terms, *focal length,* which is measured in millimeters, determines what the lens "sees." As you increase focal length (use a "longer" lens, in photography-speak) the angle of view narrows, objects appear larger in the frame, and — the important point in this discussion — depth of field decreases. Additionally, the spatial relationship of objects changes as you adjust focal length.

For example, Figure 8-11 compares the same scene shot at focal lengths of 138mm and 255mm. An f/22 aperture was used for both examples.

Whether you have any focal-length flexibility depends on your lens: If you have a zoom lens, you can adjust the focal length by zooming in or out. (The Rebel T3i/600D kit lens, for example, offers a focal-length range of 18mm to 55mm.) If your lens offers only a single focal length — a *prime* lens in photo-speak — scratch this means of manipulating depth of field (unless you want to change to a different prime lens, of course).

Large depth of field

Figure 8-9: A large depth of field keeps both near and far subjects in sharp focus.

f/5.6, 1/1000 second   f/11, 1/200 second

Figure 8-10: Raising the f-stop value increases depth of field.

For more technical details about focal length and your camera, see the later sidebar "Fun facts about focal length."

✔ **Camera-to-subject distance:** When you move the lens closer to your subject, depth of field decreases. This statement assumes that you don't zoom in or out to reframe the picture, thereby changing the focal length. If you do, depth of field is affected by both the camera position and focal length.

138mm, f/22   255mm, f/22

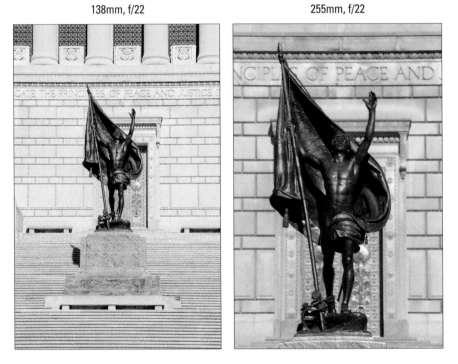

Figure 8-11: Using a longer focal length also reduces depth of field.

The extent to which background focus shifts as you adjust depth of field also is affected by the distance between the subject and the background. For increased background blurring, move the subject farther away from the background.

Together, these three factors determine the maximum and minimum depth of field you can achieve, as illustrated by Figure 8-12 and summed up in the following list:

✓ **To produce the shallowest depth of field:** Open the aperture as wide as possible (select the lowest f-stop number), zoom in to the maximum focal length of your lens, and move as close as possible to your subject.

✓ **To produce maximum depth of field:** Stop down the aperture to the highest possible f-stop setting, zoom out to the shortest focal length your lens offers, and move farther from your subject.

Greater depth of field:
Select higher f-stop
Decrease focal length (zoom out)
Move farther from subject

Shorter depth of field:
Select lower f-stop
Increase focal length (zoom in)
Move closer to subject

Figure 8-12: Aperture, focal length, and your shooting distance determine depth of field.

Here are a few additional tips and tricks related to depth of field:

✓ **Aperture-priority autoexposure (Av) mode:** When depth of field is a primary concern, try using aperture-priority autoexposure (Av). In this mode, detailed fully in Chapter 7, you set the f-stop, and then the camera selects the appropriate shutter speed to produce a good exposure. The range of aperture settings you can access depends on your lens.

✓ **Creative Auto mode:** Creative Auto mode also gives you some control over depth of field. In that mode, you can use the Background Blur slider to request a greater or smaller depth of field, as outlined in Chapter 3.

✓ **Scene modes:** Some of the scene modes are also designed with depth of field in mind. Portrait and Close-up modes produce shortened depth of field; Landscape mode produces a greater depth of field. You can't adjust aperture in these modes, however, so you're limited to the setting the camera chooses. And in certain lighting conditions, the camera may not be able to choose an aperture that produces the depth of field you expect from the selected mode.

✔ **A-DEP mode:** The Rebel T3i/600D also offers the special A-DEP mode, which stands for *automatic depth of field.* In this mode, the camera selects the aperture setting that it thinks will keep all objects in the frame within the zone of sharp focus. You can read more about this mode in the next section.

✔ **Depth of field preview:** Not sure which aperture setting you need to produce the depth of field you want? Good news: Your camera offers *depth of field preview,* which enables you to see in advance how the aperture affects the focus zone. See the later section "Checking depth of field" for details on how to use this feature.

✔ **Shutter speed:** If you adjust aperture to affect depth of field, be sure to always keep an eye on shutter speed as well. To maintain the same exposure, shutter speed must change in tandem with aperture, and you may encounter a situation where the shutter speed is too slow to permit handholding a camera. Lenses that offer optical image stabilization enable most people to handhold the camera at slower shutter speeds than nonstabilized lenses, but double-check your results. You can also consider raising the ISO setting to make the image sensor more reactive to light, but remember that higher ISO settings can produce noise. (Chapter 7 has details.)

Using A-DEP mode

In addition to the four advanced exposure modes found on most digital SLR cameras, your Rebel T3i/600D offers a fifth mode, A-DEP, as shown in Figure 8-13. The initials stand for *automatic depth of field.*

This mode is designed to assist you in producing photos that have a depth of field sufficient to keep all objects in the frame in sharp focus. The camera accomplishes this by analyzing the lens-to-subject distance for all those objects and then selecting the aperture that results in the appropriate depth of field. After choosing the aperture, the camera then selects the necessary shutter speed to properly expose the image at the selected f-stop.

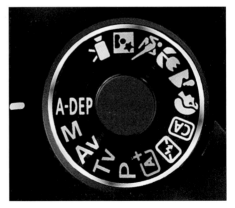

Figure 8-13: A-DEP stands for automatic depth of field.

Fun facts about focal length

Every lens can be characterized by its *focal length,* or in the case of a zoom lens, the range of focal lengths it offers. Measured in millimeters, focal length determines the camera's angle of view, the apparent size and distance of objects in the scene, and depth of field. According to photography tradition, a focal length of about 50mm is a "normal" lens. Most point-and-shoot cameras feature this focal length, which is a medium-range lens that works well for the type of snapshots that users of those kinds of cameras are likely to shoot.

A lens with a focal length less than 35mm is typically known as a *wide angle* lens because at that focal length, the camera has a wide angle of view and produces a long depth of field, making it good for landscape photography. A short focal length also has the effect of making objects seem smaller and farther away. At the other end of the spectrum, a lens with a focal length longer than about 80mm is considered a *telephoto* lens (often referred to as a *long lens*). With a long lens, angle of view narrows, depth of field decreases, and faraway subjects appear closer and larger, which is ideal for wildlife and sports photographers.

Note, however, that the focal lengths stated here and elsewhere in the book are so-called "35mm equivalent" focal lengths. Here's the deal: For reasons that aren't really important, when you put a standard lens on most digital cameras, including your Rebel T3i/600D, the available frame area is reduced, as if you took a picture on a camera that uses 35mm film (the kind you've probably been using for years) and then cropped it.

This so-called *crop factor* (sometimes called the *magnification factor*) varies depending on the digital camera, which is why the photo industry adopted the 35mm-equivalent measuring stick as a standard. With your camera, the cropping factor is roughly 1.6. So the 18–55mm kit lens sold with the Rebel T3i/600D, for example, captures the approximate area you would get from a 29–88mm lens on a 35mm film camera. In the following figure, for example, the red outline indicates the image area that results from the 1.6 crop factor.

Note that although the area the lens can capture changes when you move a lens from a 35mm film camera to a digital body, depth of field isn't affected, nor are the spatial relationships between objects in the frame. So when lens shopping, you gauge those two characteristics of the lens by looking at the stated focal length — no digital-to-film conversion math is required.

A-DEP mode isn't a surefire bet, however, and it has some restrictions that may make it unsuitable for your subject. Here's what you need to know:

- **In very dim lighting, the shutter speed the camera selects may be too slow to allow you to handhold the camera without risking camera shake.** Check the shutter speed in the viewfinder after you press the shutter button halfway to meter and focus the image.

- **If the aperture value blinks in the viewfinder, the camera can't set the f-stop so that you get both a good exposure and the depth of field necessary to keep all objects in the frame in sharp focus.** In this situation, the camera assumes that your primary goal is a good exposure and adjusts the aperture as needed based on the available light.

- **If the shutter speed blinks in the viewfinder, the light is either too bright or too dim for the camera to properly expose the image at any combination of aperture and shutter speed.** In bright light, you can lower the ISO, if it isn't already at 100, or reposition or shade your subject. In dim lighting, raise the ISO or add artificial light.

- **You can use flash with A-DEP mode, but the minute you turn on the flash, the camera no longer does its automatic depth of field calculation.** The same thing occurs if you switch to Live View shooting. In either case, the camera simply presents you with a fixed combination of aperture and shutter speed that will properly expose the image. The depth of field may or may not be what you want.

Given these limitations, my recommendation is that as soon as you fully understand the impact of aperture on depth of field, politely decline the option of using A-DEP mode and work in aperture-priority autoexposure mode (Av) instead. Then you can simply match the f-stop to the depth of field you have in mind, without giving up the option of using flash or Live View shooting.

Checking depth of field

When you look through your viewfinder and press the shutter button halfway, you can see only a partial indication of the depth of field that your current camera settings will produce. You can see the effect of focal length and the camera-to-subject distance, but because the aperture doesn't actually stop-down to your selected f-stop until you take the picture, the viewfinder doesn't show you how that setting will affect depth of field.

By using the Depth-of-Field Preview button on your camera, however, you can do just that when you shoot in the advanced exposure modes. Almost hidden away on the front of your camera, the button is labeled in Figure 8-14.

To use this feature, just press and hold the shutter button halfway and then press and hold the Depth-of-Field Preview button with the other hand. Depending on the selected f-stop, the scene in the viewfinder may then get darker. Or in Live View mode, the same thing happens in the monitor preview. Either way, this effect doesn't mean that your picture will be darker; it's just a function of how the preview works.

Note that the preview doesn't engage in P, Tv, Av, or A-DEP mode if the aperture and shutter speed aren't adequate to expose the image properly. You have to solve the exposure issue before you can use the preview.

Depth-of-Field Preview button

Figure 8-14: Press this button to see how the aperture setting will affect depth of field.

Controlling Color

Compared with understanding some aspects of digital photography — resolution, aperture, shutter speed, and depth of field, for example — making sense of your camera's color options is easy-breezy. First, color problems aren't all that common, and when they are, they're usually simple to fix with a quick shift of your camera's White Balance control. Second, getting a grip on color requires learning only a couple of new terms, an unusual state of affairs for an endeavor that often seems more like high-tech science than art.

The rest of this chapter explains the White Balance control, plus a couple of other options that enable you to fine-tune the way your camera renders colors. For information on how to alter colors of existing pictures by using the software that shipped with your camera, see Chapter 10.

Correcting colors with white balance

Every light source emits a particular color cast. The old-fashioned fluorescent lights found in most public restrooms, for example, put out a bluish-green light, which is why our reflections in the mirrors in those restrooms always look so sickly. And if you think that your beloved looks especially attractive by candlelight, you aren't imagining things: Candlelight casts a warm, yellow-red glow that's flattering to the skin.

Science-y types measure the color of light, officially known as *color temperature,* on the Kelvin scale, which is named after its creator. You can see an illustration of the Kelvin scale in Figure 8-15.

When photographers talk about "warm light" and "cool light," though, they aren't referring to the position on the Kelvin scale — or at least not in the way we usually think of temperatures, with a higher number meaning hotter. Instead, the terms describe the visual appearance of the light. Warm light, produced by candles and incandescent lights, falls in the red-yellow spectrum you see at the bottom of the Kelvin scale in Figure 8-15; cool light, in the blue-green spectrum, appears at the top of the scale.

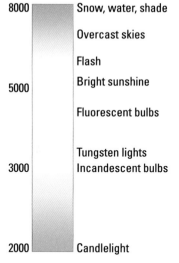

Figure 8-15: Each light source emits a specific color.

At any rate, most of us don't notice these fluctuating colors of light because our eyes automatically compensate for them. Except in extreme lighting conditions, a white tablecloth appears white to us no matter whether we view it by candlelight, fluorescent light, or regular house lights.

Similarly, a digital camera compensates for different colors of light through a feature known as *white balancing.* Simply put, white balancing neutralizes light so that whites are always white, which in turn ensures that other colors are rendered accurately. If the camera senses warm light, it shifts colors slightly to the cool side of the color spectrum; in cool light, the camera shifts colors in the opposite direction.

The good news is that your camera's Automatic White Balance setting, which carries the label AWB, tackles this process remarkably well in most situations. In some lighting conditions, though, the AWB adjustment doesn't quite do the trick, resulting in an unwanted color cast like the one you see in the left image in Figure 8-16.

Serious AWB problems most often occur when your subject is lit by a variety of light sources. For example, I shot the figurine in Figure 8-16 under a mix of tungsten photo lights along with strong window light. The photo lights are similar in color temperature to regular household incandescent bulbs while the daylight is very blue by comparison. In Automatic White Balance mode (on the left), the camera reacted to that daylight — which has a cool color cast — and applied too much warming, giving the original image a yellow tint. No problem: Just switching the White Balance mode from AWB to the Tungsten Light setting did the trick. The right image in Figure 8-16 shows the corrected colors.

Figure 8-16: Multiple light sources can result in a color cast in Auto White Balance mode (left); try switching to manual White Balance control to solve the problem (right).

Unfortunately, you can't access the White Balance setting in any of the point-and-shoot exposure modes, although you can sometimes address color issues via the Shoot by Lighting or Scene Type setting when you shoot in the scene modes. (Chapter 3 has details on that setting and its relative, Shoot by Ambience, which is also available in Creative Auto mode.) So your best bet is to shift to P, Tv, Av, M, or A-DEP modes, where you can not only choose different White Balance settings but also fine-tune each setting to precisely match the light that's illuminating your subject.

Changing the White Balance setting

Again, you can access the White Balance setting only in the P, Tv, Av, M, or A-DEP modes. Use either of these methods:

- ✒ **WB button (top cross key):** Press the WB button to display the screen shown on the left in Figure 8-17. Then highlight the setting you want to use and press Set.

  On this screen, as in the Shooting Settings and Quick Control displays, the various White Balance settings are represented by the icons listed in Table 8-1. You don't need to memorize them, however, because as you scroll through the list of options, the name of the selected setting appears on the screen. For some settings, the camera also displays the approximate Kelvin temperature (K) of the selected light source, as shown in the figure. (Refer to Figure 8-15 for a look at the Kelvin scale.) Press Set once more after you select the option you want to use.

- ✒ **Quick Control screen:** After pressing the Quick Control button to shift from the Shooting Settings screen to Quick Control mode, highlight the White Balance icon, found at the spot shown on the right in Figure 8-17. The selected setting appears at the bottom of the screen, and you can then rotate the Main dial to cycle through the various options.

  If you want to see all settings at one time, press Set again instead of rotating the Main dial. Then you see the screen shown on the left in Figure 8-17, and you can use the Main dial or cross keys to make your choice. Press Set to lock in the new setting.

White Balance setting

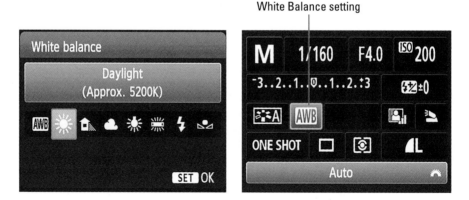

Figure 8-17: The WB button (top cross key) takes you to the White Balance setting.

Table 8-1	White Balance Settings
Symbol	*Setting*
AWB	Auto
☀	Daylight
⌂	Shade
☁	Cloudy
💡	Tungsten
▭	White Fluorescent
⚡	Flash
◢◣	Custom

A couple quick tips related to white balance:

- ✐ If the scene is lit by several sources, choose the setting that corresponds to the strongest one. The Tungsten Light setting is usually best for regular incandescent household bulbs, by the way. Selecting the right setting for the new energy-saving CFL (compact fluorescent) bulbs can be a little tricky because the color temperature varies depending on the bulb you buy.

- ✐ Your selected White Balance setting remains in force until you change it. To avoid accidentally using an incorrect setting later, get in the habit of resetting the option to the automatic setting (AWB) after you finish shooting whatever subject it was that caused you to switch from automatic to manual white balancing.

- ✐ Not sure which setting to choose? Try switching to Live View temporarily. As you adjust the White Balance setting, the live preview shows you the impact on your scene. See Chapter 4 for details on using Live View. Then use the Quick Control screen to adjust the White Balance setting (the WB button doesn't work in Live View mode).

- ✐ If none of the settings produce neutral colors, you can tweak the selected setting or even create a custom setting, as outlined in the next sections.

Creating a custom White Balance setting

If none of the preset white balance options produces the right amount of color correction, you can create your own, custom setting. To use this technique, you need a piece of card stock that's either neutral gray or absolute white — not eggshell white, sand white, or any other close-but-not-perfect white. (You can buy reference cards made just for this purpose in many camera stores for under $20.)

Position the reference card so that it receives the same lighting you'll use for your photo. Then follow these steps:

1. **Set the camera to the P, Tv, Av, M, or A-DEP exposure mode.**

   You can't create a custom setting in any of the fully automatic modes. (You can, however, select the custom setting you create when you record movies.)

2. **Set the White Balance setting to Auto (AWB).**

   The preceding section shows you how.

3. **Set the camera to manual focusing.**

   On the kit lens, just set the switch on the lens to MF and then twist the focusing ring.

4. **Frame the shot so that your reference card fills the center area of the viewfinder.**

   Make sure that at least the center autofocus point and the six surrounding points fall over the reference card.

5. **Make sure that the exposure settings are correct.**

   Just press the shutter button halfway to check exposure. If necessary, adjust ISO, aperture, or shutter speed to get a proper exposure; Chapter 7 explains how.

6. **Take the picture of your reference card.**

   The camera will use this picture to establish your custom White Balance setting.

7. **Display Shooting Menu 2 and highlight Custom White Balance, as shown on the left in Figure 8-18.**

Figure 8-18: You can create a custom White Balance setting from Shooting Menu 2.

8. **Press Set.**

Now you see the screen shown on the right in Figure 8-18. The image you just captured should appear in the display, along with a message that tells you that the camera will only display that image and others that are compatible with the custom white-balancing option. If your picture doesn't appear on the screen, press the right or left cross key to scroll to it.

9. **Press Set to select the displayed image as the basis for your custom white balance reference.**

You see the message shown on the left in Figure 8-19, asking you to confirm that you want the camera to use the image to create the custom White Balance setting.

Figure 8-19: This message indicates that your White Balance setting is stored.

10. **Press the right or left cross key to highlight OK and then press Set.**

    Now you see the screen shown on the right in Figure 8-19. This message tells you that the White Balance setting is now stored. The little icon in the message area represents the custom setting.

11. **Press Set one more time to finalize the custom setting.**

Your custom White Balance setting remains stored until the next time you work your way through these steps. Anytime you're shooting in the same lighting conditions and want to apply the same white balance correction, just press the WB button (top cross key) or use the Quick Control screen to access the White Balance settings and then select the Custom option.

Fine-tuning White Balance settings

As an alternative for manipulating colors, your Rebel T3i/600D enables you to tweak white balancing in a way that shifts all colors toward a particular part of the color spectrum. The result is similar to applying a traditional color filter to your lens.

To access this option, White Balance Correction, follow these steps:

1. **Set the Mode dial to P, Tv, Av, M, or A-DEP exposure mode.**

    You can take advantage of White Balance Correction only in these modes.

2. **Display Shooting Menu 2 and highlight WB Shift/Bkt, as shown on the left in Figure 8-20.**

    The first two numbers next to the option name indicate the current amount of fine-tuning, or *shift*, and the second value represents the amount of white balance bracketing enabled. (See the next section for details on that topic). In the figure, all values are 0, indicating that no fine-tuning or bracketing is enabled.

3. **Press Set to display the screen you see on the right in Figure 8-20.**

    The screen contains a grid that's oriented around two main color pairs: green and magenta (represented by the G and M labels) and blue and amber (represented by B and A). The little white square indicates the amount of white balance shift. When the square is dead center in the grid, as in the figure, no shift is applied.

4. **Use the cross keys to move the shift indicator marker in the direction of the shift you want to achieve.**

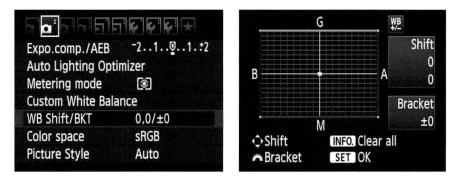

Figure 8-20: White Balance Correction offers one more way to control colors.

As you do, the Shift area of the display tells the amount of color bias you've selected. For example, in Figure 8-21, the shift is two levels toward amber and two toward magenta.

If you're familiar with traditional lens filters, you may know that the density of a filter, which determines the degree of color correction it provides, is measured in *mireds* (pronounced "my-reds"). The white balance grid is designed around this system: Moving the marker one level is the equivalent of adding a filter with a density of 5 mireds.

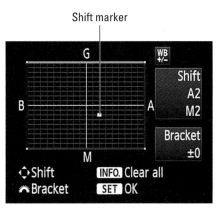

Figure 8-21: Press the cross keys to move the marker and shift white balance.

5. **Press Set to apply the change and return to the menu.**

   After you apply White Balance Correction, a +/– sign appears next to the White Balance symbol in the Shooting Settings display, as shown on the left in Figure 8-22. It's your reminder that White Balance Shift is being applied. The same symbol appears in the viewfinder, right next to the ISO value.

   You can see the exact shift values in Shooting Menu 2, as shown on the right in Figure 8-22, and also in the Camera Settings display. (To activate that display, remember to first display any menu and then press the Disp button. Chapter 1 provides more details.) For example, in Figure 8-22, the values indicate a shift two steps toward amber (A) and two toward magenta (M).

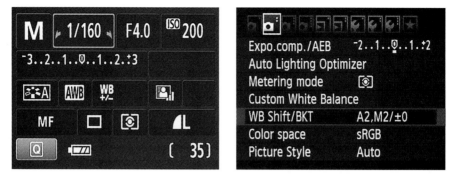

Figure 8-22: The +/– symbol lets you know that White Balance Shift is being applied.

Your adjustment remains in force for all advanced exposure modes until you change it. And the correction is applied no matter which White Balance setting you choose. Check the monitor or viewfinder before your next shoot; otherwise, you may forget to adjust the white balance for the current light.

6. **To cancel White Balance Correction, repeat the steps, set the marker back to the center of the grid, and then press Set.**

   Use the cross keys to move the marker back to the center of the grid. Be sure that both values in the Shift area of the display are set to 0.

   As an alternative, you can press the Info button after you get to the grid display. However, doing so also cancels White Balance Bracketing, which I explain in the next section. After you press Info, be sure to press Set to lock in your decision.

Many film photography enthusiasts place colored filters on their lenses to either warm or cool their images. Portrait photographers, for example, often add a warming filter to give skin tones a healthy, golden glow. You can mimic the effects of these filters by simply fine-tuning your camera's White Balance settings as just described. Experiment with shifting the white balance a tad toward amber and magenta for a warming effect or toward blue and green for a cooling effect.

Bracketing shots with white balance

Chapter 7 introduces you to your camera's automatic exposure bracketing, which enables you to easily record the same image at three different exposure settings. Similarly, you can take advantage of automatic White Balance Bracketing. With this feature, the camera records the same image three times, using a slightly different white balance adjustment for each one. You might try this feature to experiment with different color takes on a scene, for example.

Note a couple of things about this feature:

✔ Because the camera records three images each time you press the shutter button, White Balance Bracketing reduces the maximum capture speed that's possible when you use the Continuous shooting mode. See Chapter 2 for more about Continuous mode. Of course, recording three images instead of one also eats up more space on your memory card.

✔ The White Balance Bracketing feature is designed around the same grid used for White Balance Correction, explained in the preceding section. As a reminder, the grid is based on two color pairs: green/magenta and blue/amber.

✔ When White Balance Bracketing is enabled, the camera always records the first of the three bracketed shots using a neutral white balance setting — or, at least, what it considers to be neutral, given its own measurement of the light. The second and third shots are then recorded using the specified shift along either the green/magenta or blue/amber axis of the color grid.

If all that is as clear as mud, just take a look at Figure 8-23 for an example. These images were shot using a single tungsten studio light and the candlelight. White Balance Bracketing was set to work along the blue/amber color axis. The camera recorded the first image at neutral, the second with a slightly blue color bias, and the third with an amber bias.

| Neutral | +3 Blue bias | +3 Amber bias |

Figure 8-23: I captured one neutral image — one with a blue bias and one with an amber bias.

To enable White Balance Bracketing, follow these steps:

1. **Set the Mode dial to an advanced exposure mode (P, Tv, Av, M, or A-DEP).**

2. **Display Shooting Menu 2 and highlight WB/Shift Bkt, as shown on the left in Figure 8-24.**

3. **Press Set to display the grid shown on the right in Figure 8-24.**

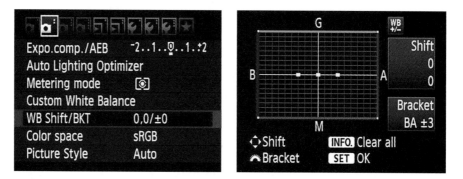

Figure 8-24: These settings were used to capture the bracketed candle images.

The screen is the same one you see when you use the White Balance Correction feature, explained in the preceding section.

4. **Rotate the Main dial to set the amount and direction of the bracketing shift.**

   Rotate the dial as follows to specify whether you want the bracketing to be applied across the horizontal axis (blue to amber) or the vertical axis (green to magenta).

   • *Blue to amber bracketing:* Rotate the dial right.

   • *Green to magenta bracketing:* Rotate the dial left.

   As you rotate the dial, three markers appear on the grid, indicating the amount of shift that will be applied to your trio of bracketed images. You can apply a maximum shift of plus or minus three levels of adjustment.

   The BKT area of the screen also indicates the shift; for example, in Figure 8-24, the display shows a bracketing amount of plus and minus three levels on the blue/amber axis. The settings shown in Figure 8-24 were used to record the sample images in Figure 8-23. As you can see, even at the maximum shift (+/–3), the difference to the colors is subtle.

If you want to get truly fancy, you can combine White Balance Bracketing with White Balance Shift. To set the amount of White Balance Shift, press the cross keys to move the square markers around the grid. Then use the Main dial to adjust the bracketing setting.

5. Press Set to apply your changes and return to the menu.

On Shooting Menu 2, the value after the slash shows you the bracketing setting, as shown on the left in Figure 8-25. (The two values to the left of the slash indicate the White Balance Shift amount.) The Shooting Settings screen also contains a White Balance bracketing symbol, as shown in Figure 8-25, and the Camera Settings display, which you bring up by pressing Info when any menu is visible, also reports the bracketing setting.

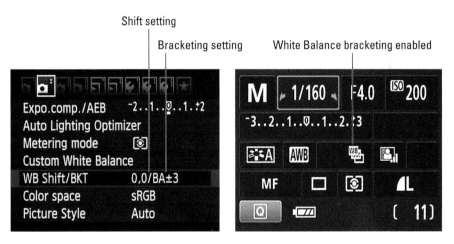

Figure 8-25: These symbols indicate that White Balance Bracketing is turned on.

The bracketing setting remains in effect until you turn off the camera. You can also cancel bracketing by revisiting the grid screen shown earlier, in Figure 8-24, and either rotating the Main dial until you see only a single grid marker or pressing the Info button. Either way, press Set to officially turn off bracketing.

Although White Balance Bracketing is a fun feature, if you want to ensure color accuracy, creating a custom White Balance setting is a more reliable idea than bracketing white balance; after all, you can't be certain that shifting the white balance a couple steps is going to produce accurate colors. Or, if you're comfortable with shooting in the Raw format, that's the best color safety net: You can assign a White Balance setting when you process the Raw images, whether you're after a neutral color platform or want to lend a slight color tint to the scene. See Chapter 2 for an introduction to Raw files; see Chapter 6 for help with the Raw conversion process.

Choosing a Color Space: sRGB versus Adobe RGB

Normally, your camera captures images using the *sRGB color mode,* which simply refers to an industry-standard spectrum of colors. (The *s* is for *standard,* and RGB is for Red, Green, Blue, which are the primary colors in the digital imaging color world.) This color mode was created to help ensure color consistency as an image moves from digital camera or scanner to monitor and printer; the idea was to create a spectrum of colors that all digital imaging devices can capture or reproduce.

However, the sRGB color spectrum leaves out some colors that *can* be reproduced in print and onscreen, at least by some devices. As an alternative, your camera also enables you to shoot in the Adobe RGB color mode, which includes a larger *gamut* (spectrum) of colors. Figure 8-26 offers an illustration of the two spectrums.

Which option is right for you depends on what you plan to do with your photos. If you're going to print your pictures without editing them, sRGB is probably the best choice because it typically results in the "punchy" colors that most people like. Some Internet printing services also request sRGB images.

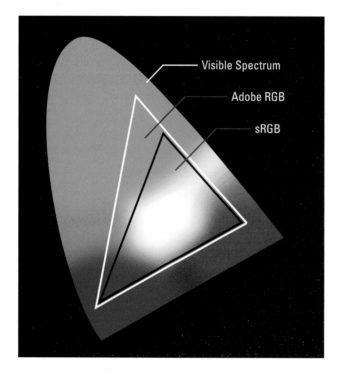

Figure 8-26: Adobe RGB includes some colors not found in the sRGB spectrum.

On the other hand, if you're a color purist or will be editing your photos or making your own prints, or all three, experiment with Adobe RGB. For the record, this route is the one that I take because I see no reason to limit myself to a smaller spectrum from the get-go. However, note that some colors in Adobe RGB can't be reproduced in print; the printer substitutes the closest available color when necessary. Additionally, you need photo software that offers support for Adobe RGB as well as some basic *color management controls,* which ensure that your image colors are properly handled when you open, print, edit, and save your files. You should plan to spend a little time educating yourself about color management, too, because you can muck up the works if you don't set all the color-management options correctly. Long story short: If you're brand-new to digital imaging, this option may be one to explore after you get more comfortable with the whole topic.

If you want to capture images in Adobe RGB instead of sRGB, you can make the adjustment via the Color Space option on Shooting Menu 2, shown in Figure 8-27.

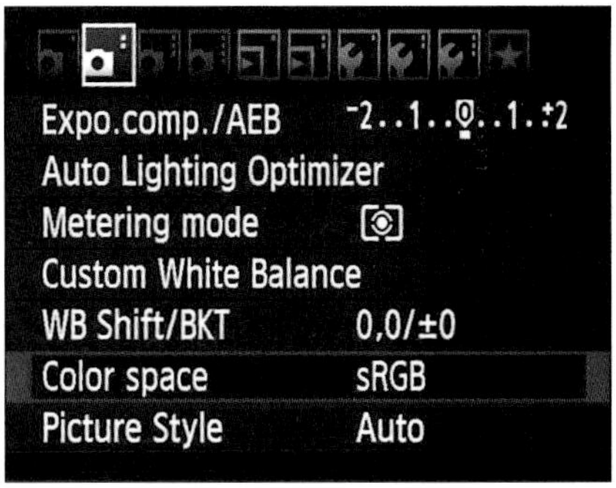

This color mode choice applies only when you shoot in the advanced exposure modes: P, Tv, Av, M, and A-DEP. In all other modes, the camera automatically selects sRGB as the color space. Additionally, your color space selection is applied to only your JPEG images; with Raw captures, you can select the color space as you process the Raw image. (See Chapter 6 for details about Raw-image processing.)

Figure 8-27: Choose sRGB unless you're savvy about image color management.

After you transfer pictures to your computer, you can tell whether you captured an image in the Adobe RGB color space by looking at its filename: Adobe RGB images start with an underscore, as in _MG_0627.jpg. Pictures captured in the sRGB color space start with the letter *I,* as in IMG_0627.jpg.

Taking a Quick Look at Picture Styles

In addition to all the aforementioned focus and color features, your Rebel T3i/600D offers *Picture Styles.* Using Picture Styles, you can further tweak color as well as saturation, contrast, and image sharpening.

Sharpening is a software process that adjusts contrast in a way that creates the illusion of slightly sharper focus. Sharpening is explained fully in Chapter 10, but the important thing to note for now is that sharpening cannot remedy poor focus, but instead produces a subtle tweak to this aspect of your pictures.

The camera offers the following six basic Picture Styles:

- **Auto:** This is the default setting; the camera analyzes the scene and determines which Picture Style is the most appropriate. For example, if you set the exposure mode to Portrait, the camera selects the Portrait Picture Style; if you use the Landscape exposure mode, the camera selects — guess what — the Landscape Picture Style. For all other exposure modes, the camera typically selects the Standard Picture Style.

- **Standard:** This option captures the image by using the characteristics that Canon offers as suitable for the majority of subjects.

- **Portrait:** This mode reduces sharpening slightly from the amount that's applied in Standard mode, with the goal of keeping skin texture soft. Color saturation, on the other hand, is slightly increased.

- **Landscape:** In a nod to traditions of landscape photography, this Picture Style emphasizes greens and blues and amps up color saturation and sharpness, resulting in bolder images.

- **Neutral:** This setting reduces saturation and contrast slightly compared to how the camera renders images when the Standard option is selected.

- **Faithful:** The Faithful style is designed to render colors as closely as possible to how your eye perceives them.

- **Monochrome:** This setting produces black-and-white photos, or, to be more precise, *grayscale images.* Technically speaking, a true black-and-white image contains only black and white, with no shades of gray.

If you set the Quality option to Raw (or Raw + Large/Fine), the camera displays your image on the monitor in black and white during playback. But during the Raw converter process, you can either choose to go with your grayscale version or view and save a full-color version. Or even better, you can process and save the image once as a grayscale photo and again as a color image.

If you *don't* capture the image in the Raw format, you can't access the original image colors later. In other words, you're stuck with *only* a black-and-white image.

The extent to which Picture Styles affect your image depends on the subject as well as on the exposure settings you choose and the lighting conditions. But Figure 8-28 offers a test subject shot at each setting (except Auto) to give you a general idea of what to expect. As you can see, the differences are subtle, with the exception of the Monochrome option, of course.

The level of control you have over Picture Styles, like most other settings in this chapter, depends on your camera's exposure mode:

Standard   Portrait   Landscape

Neutral   Faithful   Monochrome

Figure 8-28: Each Picture Control produces a slightly different take on the scene.

- ✒ **In Scene Intelligent Auto, Creative Auto, Flash Off, and the scene modes:** The camera sets the Picture Style for you.

- ✒ **In the advanced exposure modes (P, Tv, Av, M, and A-DEP):** You can not only select any of the preset Picture Styles but also tweak each style to your liking and create up to three of your own, customized styles.

- ✒ **Movie mode:** You can select any Picture Style, including any custom styles you create. (Want to shoot a black-and-white movie? Set the Picture Style to Monochrome before you start recording.)

For still photography, you can select a Picture Style in three ways:

- **Quick Control screen:** Press the Quick Control button to shift from the regular Shooting Settings display to the Quick Control screen and then highlight the Picture Style icon, as shown on the left in Figure 8-29. Rotate the Main dial to cycle through the available styles. (The figures show the normal Quick Control screen; in Live View mode, the settings appear on top of the image, as detailed in Chapter 4.)

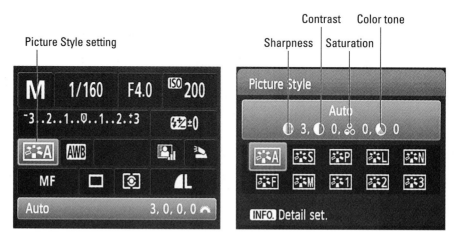

Figure 8-29: You can quickly select a Picture Style by using the Quick Control screen or pressing the bottom cross key.

The numbers you see along with the style name at the bottom of the screen represent the four characteristics applied by the style: Sharpness, Contrast, Saturation, and Color Tone. Sharpness values range from 0 to 7; the higher the value, the more sharpening is applied. At 0, no sharpening is applied. The other values, however, are all set to 0, which represents the default setting for the selected Picture Style. (Using certain advanced options, you can adjust all four settings; more on that momentarily.)

If you want to see all available styles, just press Set to display the screen you see on the right in Figure 8-30. Highlight the style you want to use, and the four style values appear along with the style name, as shown in the figure. Press Set to finish up.

- **Picture Style button (bottom cross key):** Press the key to display the same screen shown on the right in Figure 8-30. Again, just highlight your choice and press Set. (Notice that the label on the key is the same as the icon that appears with the Picture Style setting on the Shooting Settings and Quick Control screens.)

✔ **Shooting Menu 2:** Select the Picture Style option and press Set to display a menu full of all the styles, as shown in Figure 8-30. You again can see the values for the four style characteristics on the screen shown on the right in the figure. Highlight a Picture Style and press Set again to exit that screen.

For movie recording, you can select a Picture Style either from Movie Menu 3 or by using the Quick Control method. See Chapter 4 for help with the second option; it works a little differently than when you're shooting still photos.

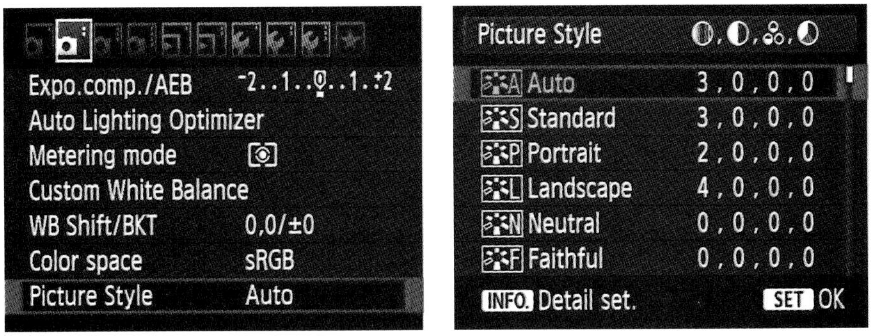

Expo.comp./AEB	-2..1..0..1..+2
Auto Lighting Optimizer	
Metering mode	
Custom White Balance	
WB Shift/BKT	0,0/±0
Color space	sRGB
Picture Style	Auto

Picture Style	
Auto	3 , 0 , 0 , 0
Standard	3 , 0 , 0 , 0
Portrait	2 , 0 , 0 , 0
Landscape	4 , 0 , 0 , 0
Neutral	0 , 0 , 0 , 0
Faithful	0 , 0 , 0 , 0
INFO. Detail set.	SET OK

Figure 8-30: You also can access Picture Style options via Shooting Menu 2.

This discussion touches on just the basics of using Picture Styles. The camera also offers some advanced Picture Style features, including the following:

✔ You also can modify each style, varying the amount of sharpness, contrast, saturation, and color tone adjustment that the style produces. After selecting a Picture Style — whether you're doing so from the Quick Setting screen shown on the right in Figure 8-29 or the menu screen shown on the right in Figure 8-30 — press Info to access a screen similar to the one you see on the left in Figure 8-31. Here, select one of the adjustment options, press Set, and then use the right/left cross keys to change the setting. After you finish tweaking the style characteristics, press Menu to exit the screen.

✔ You can create and store your own custom Picture Styles. The process is the same as for modifying a style, except that instead of starting with an existing style, you choose one of the three User Defined options, as shown on the right in Figure 8-31.

✔ For übergeeks (you know who you are), the CD accompanying your T3i/600D includes a software package named — are you ready? — Picture Style Editor, where you can create and save Picture Style files to your heart's content. You then download the styles to your camera via the memory card. And I would be remiss if I didn't also mention that some Canon user groups swap Picture Styles with each other online. (I'd be equally remiss if I didn't warn you to play at your own risk any time you download files from persons unknown to you.)

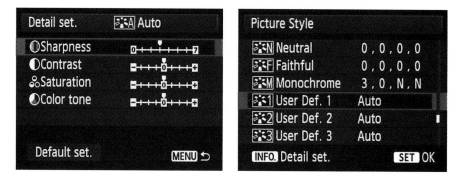

Figure 8-31: You can adjust the characteristics of one of the preset styles (left) or create your own custom style (right).

Unless you're just tickled pink by the prospect of experimenting with Picture Styles, I recommend that you just stick with the default settings. First, you have way more important camera settings to worry about — aperture, shutter speed, autofocus, and all the rest. Why add one more setting to your list, especially when the impact of changing it is minimal? Second, if you want to mess with the characteristics that the Picture Style options affect, you're much better off shooting in the Raw (CR2) format and then making those adjustments on a picture-by-picture basis in your Raw converter. In Canon Digital Photo Professional, which comes free with the camera, you can even assign any of the existing Picture Styles to your Raw files and then compare how each one affects the image. The camera tags your Raw file with whichever Picture Style is active at the time you take the shot, but the image adjustments are in no way set in stone or even in sand — you can tweak your photo at will. (The selected Picture Style does affect the JPEG preview that's used to display the Raw image thumbnails in Digital Photo Professional and other photo software.)

For these reasons, I opt in this book to present you with just this brief introduction to Picture Styles to make room for more details about functions that do make a big difference in your daily photography life, such as the white balance customization options presented earlier. But again, if you're really into Picture Styles and you can't figure out one of the advanced options from the descriptions here, the camera manual walks you step by step through all the various Picture Style features.

9

Putting It All Together

*E*arlier chapters of this book break down all the critical picture-taking features on your Rebel T3i/600D, describing in detail how the various controls affect exposure, picture quality, focus, color, and the like. This chapter pulls all that information together to help you set up your camera for specific types of photography.

Keep in mind, though, that there are no hard and fast rules as to the "right way" to shoot a portrait, a landscape, or whatever. So feel free to wander off on your own, tweaking this exposure setting or adjusting that focus control, to discover your own creative vision. Experimentation is part of the fun of photography, after all — and thanks to your camera monitor and the Erase button, it's an easy, completely free proposition.

Recapping Basic Picture Settings

For some camera options, such as aperture and shutter speed, the best settings depend on your subject, the lighting conditions, and, of course, your creative goals. But for many basic options, you can rely on the same settings for almost every shooting scenario.

Table 9-1 offers recommendations for these basic settings and lists the chapter where you can find details about each option. Figure 9-1 shows you where on the Shooting Settings screen you can find the symbols representing some settings; don't forget that you can adjust these options via the Quick Control screen. Just press the Quick Control button to shift from the Shooting Settings screen to the Quick Control display.

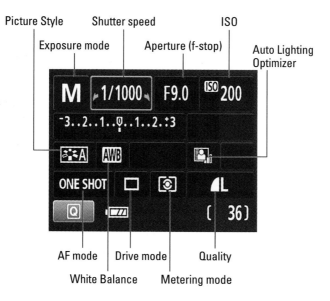

Figure 9-1: You can monitor these critical options on the Shooting Settings display.

One key point: Instructions in this chapter assume that you set the exposure mode to P, Tv, Av, or M exposure mode, as indicated in the table. These modes, detailed in Chapter 7, are the only ones that give you access to the entire cadre of camera features. In most cases, I recommend using Tv (shutter-priority autoexposure) when controlling motion blur is important, and Av (aperture-priority autoexposure) when controlling depth of field is important. These two modes let you concentrate on one side of the exposure equation and let the camera handle the other. Of course, if you're comfortable making both the aperture and shutter speed decisions, you may prefer to work in M (manual) exposure mode instead. P (programmed autoexposure) is my last choice because it makes choosing a specific aperture or shutter speed more cumbersome. A-DEP mode is not one I recommend because of the limitations I discuss in Chapter 7.

What's my beef with the other exposure modes — Scene Intelligent Auto, Flash Off, Creative Auto, and the scene modes? The problem with these point-and-shoot modes is that they prevent you from accessing certain settings that can be critical to capturing good shots of certain subjects, especially in difficult lighting. And if you're after a special effect, such as motion trails from car lights in a nighttime cityscape, forget it. You won't be able to produce that picture using any of the point-and-shoot modes — at least not without a lot of luck.

As you read through the rest of this chapter, also remember that it discusses choices for normal, through-the-viewfinder photography; Chapter 4 guides you through the options available for Live View photography and movie recording. (For Live View photography, however, most settings work the same as discussed here, with the exception of the autofocus options.)

Table 9-1	All-Purpose Picture-Taking Settings	
Option	*Recommended Setting*	*See This Chapter*
Exposure mode	P, Tv, Av, or M	2
Quality	Large/Fine (JPEG), Medium/Fine (JPEG), or Raw (CR2)	2
Drive mode	Action photos, Continuous; all others, Single	2
ISO	100 or 200 (available light permitting)	7
Metering mode	Evaluative	7
AF mode	Moving subjects, AI Servo; stationary subjects, One Shot	8
AF Point Selection	Moving subjects, Automatic; stationary subjects, Manual (single point)	8
White Balance	Auto	8
Picture Style	Auto	8
Live View	Disabled	4

Setting Up for Specific Scenes

For the most part, the settings detailed in the preceding section fall into the "set 'em and forget 'em" category. That leaves you free to concentrate on a handful of other camera settings that you can manipulate to achieve a specific photographic goal, such as adjusting aperture to affect depth of field. The next four sections explain which of these additional options typically produce the best results when you're shooting portraits, action shots, landscapes, and close-ups. You can discover a few compositional and creative tips along the way — but, again, remember that beauty is in the eye of the beholder, and for every so-called rule, plenty of great images prove the exception. As Ansel Adams so wisely said, "There are no rules for good photographs; there are only good photographs."

Shooting still portraits

By *still portrait,* I mean that your subject isn't moving. For subjects who aren't keen on sitting still long enough to have their picture taken, skip to the next section and use the techniques given for action photography instead.

Assuming that you do have a subject willing to pose, the classic portraiture approach is to keep the subject sharply focused while throwing the background into soft focus. This artistic choice emphasizes the subject and helps diminish the impact of any distracting background objects in cases where you can't control the setting. The following steps show you how to achieve this look:

1. **Set the Mode dial to Av (aperture-priority autoexposure) and rotate the Main dial to select the lowest f-stop value possible.**

   As Chapter 7 explains, a low f-stop setting opens the aperture, which not only allows more light to enter the camera but also shortens depth of field, or the range of sharp focus. So dialing in a low f-stop value is the first step in softening your portrait background.

   I recommend aperture-priority mode when depth of field is a primary concern because you can control the f-stop while relying on the camera to select the shutter speed that will properly expose the image. But you do need to pay attention to shutter speed also to make sure that it's not so slow that any movement of the subject or camera will blur the image.

   You can monitor the current f-stop and shutter speed in the Shooting Settings display, as shown in Figure 9-1. The settings also appear in the viewfinder readout; remember that shutter speed is shown as a whole number instead of fraction in the viewfinder. When the shutter speed reaches one second, you see quote marks after the number — for example, 1" means a shutter speed of one second.

2. **To further soften the background, zoom in, get closer, and put more distance between subject and background.**

As covered in Chapter 8, zooming in to a longer focal length also reduces depth of field, as does moving physically closer to your subject. And the greater the distance between the subject and background, the more the background blurs.

A lens with a focal length of 85–120mm is ideal for a classic head-and-shoulders portrait. But don't fret if you have only the 18–55mm kit lens; just zoom all the way to the 55mm setting. You should avoid using a much shorter focal length (a wider-angle lens) for portraits. They can cause features to appear distorted — sort of like how people look when you view them through a security peephole in a door.

3. **For indoor portraits, shoot flash-free if possible.**

Shooting by available light rather than flash produces softer illumination and avoids the problem of red-eye. To get enough light to go flash-free, turn on room lights or, during daylight, pose your subject next to a sunny window.

In the Av exposure mode, simply keeping the built-in flash unit closed disables the flash. If flash is unavoidable, see the list of flash tips at the end of the steps to get better results.

4. **For outdoor portraits in daylight, use a flash if possible.**

Even in daylight, a flash adds a beneficial pop of light to subjects' faces, as illustrated in Figure 9-2. A flash is especially important when the background is brighter than the subjects, as in this example; when the subject is wearing a hat; or when the sun is directly overhead, creating harsh shadows under the eyes, nose, and chin.

In the Av exposure mode, press the Flash button on the side of the camera to enable the built-in flash. For outdoor daytime portraits, disable the Red-Eye Reduction feature (Shooting Menu 1); you don't need it because the pupils are already constricted because of the bright ambient light.

One warning about using flash outdoors: The fastest shutter speed you can use with the built-in flash is 1/200 second, and in extremely bright conditions, that speed may be too slow to avoid overexposing the image even if you use the lowest ISO (light sensitivity) setting. If necessary, move your subject into the shade. (On some external Canon flashes, you can select a faster shutter speed than 1/200 second; see your flash manual for details.)

5. **Press and hold the shutter button halfway to engage exposure metering and, if using autofocusing, to establish focus.**

As spelled out in Table 9-1, the One Shot AF mode and Manual AF Point Selection options work best for portrait autofocusing. After selecting a focus point, position that point over one of your subject's eyes and then press and hold the shutter button halfway to lock focus.

No flash   With flash

Figure 9-2: To properly illuminate the face in outdoor portraits, use flash.

Chapter 8 explains more about using autofocus, but if you have trouble, simply set your lens to manual focus mode and then twist the focusing ring to set focus.

6. Press the shutter button the rest of the way to capture the image.

Again, these steps give you only a starting point for taking better portraits. A few other tips can also improve your people pics:

- **Before pressing the shutter button, do a quick background check.** Scan the entire frame for intrusive objects that may distract the eye from the subject. If necessary (and possible), reposition the subject against a more flattering backdrop. Inside, a softly textured wall works well; outdoors, trees and shrubs can provide attractive backdrops as long as they aren't so ornate or colorful that they diminish the subject (for example, a magnolia tree laden with blooms).

- **Frame the subject loosely to allow for later cropping to a variety of frame sizes.** Because your camera produces images that have an aspect ratio of 3:2, your portrait perfectly fits a 4-x-6-inch print size — but requires cropping to print at any other proportions, such as 5 x 7 or 8 x 10. The printing section of Chapter 6 talks more about this issue.

✔ **Pay attention to white balance if your subject is lit by both flash and ambient light.** If you use the automatic White Balance setting (AWB), as recommended in Table 9-1, photo colors may be slightly warmer or cooler than neutral because the camera can become confused by mixed light sources. A warming effect typically looks nice in portraits, giving the skin a subtle glow. Cooler tones, though, usually aren't as flattering. Either way, if you aren't happy with the image colors, see Chapter 8 to find out how to fine-tune white balance.

✔ **When shooting a group portrait, be careful that your depth of field doesn't get *too* shallow.** Otherwise, people in the front or back of the group may be beyond the zone of sharp focus. If you're using a long focal length (telephoto lens), select a very low f-stop value, and position yourself very close to your subject, depth of field may extend only a few inches, in fact. So it's easy to wind up with a wedding photo in which the bride's face is in sharp focus, for example, while that of her loving groom, standing just behind, is blurry. (Try explaining *that* to the mother of the groom. . . .)

✔ **When flash is unavoidable for indoor and nighttime portraits, try these tricks to produce better results:**

- *Indoors, turn on as many room lights as possible.* By using more ambient light, you reduce the flash power that's needed to expose the picture. This step also causes the pupils to constrict, further reducing the possibility of red-eye. (Pay heed to the preceding white-balance warning, however.) As an added benefit, the smaller pupil allows more of the subject's iris to be visible in the portrait, so you see more eye color.

- *Try setting the flash to Red-Eye Reduction mode.* Warn your subject to expect both a light coming from the Red-Eye Reduction lamp, which constricts pupils, and the actual flash. See Chapter 2 for details about using this flash mode, which you enable on Shooting Menu 1.

- *Pay extra attention to shutter speed.* In dim lighting, the camera may select a shutter speed as slow as 30 seconds when you enable the built-in flash in Av mode, so keep an eye on that value and use a tripod if necessary to avoid blurring from camera shake. Also warn your subject to remain as still as possible.

- *For nighttime pictures, try switching to Tv exposure mode and purposely selecting a slow shutter speed.* The longer exposure time enables the camera to soak up more ambient light, producing a brighter background and reducing the flash power needed to light the subject. Again, though, a slow shutter means that you need to take extra precautions to ensure that neither camera nor subject moves during the exposure.

• *For professional results, use an external flash with a rotating flash head.* Then aim the flash head upward so that the flash light bounces off the ceiling and falls softly down on the subject. An external flash isn't cheap, but the results make the purchase worthwhile if you shoot lots of portraits. Compare the two portraits in Figure 9-3 for an illustration. In the first example, the built-in flash resulted in strong shadowing behind the subject and harsh, concentrated light. To produce the better result on the right, a Canon Speedlite 580EX II was bounced off the ceiling.

Make sure that the ceiling or other surface you use to bounce the light is white; otherwise, the flash light will pick up the color of the surface and influence the color of your subject.

• *Invest in a flash diffuser to further soften the light.* Whether you use the built-in flash or an external flash, attaching a diffuser is also a good idea. A *diffuser* is simply a piece of translucent plastic or fabric that you place over the flash to soften and spread the light — much like sheer curtains diffuse window light. Diffusers come in lots of different designs, including small, fold-flat models that fit over the built-in flash.

Direct flash   Bounce flash

Figure 9-3: To eliminate harsh lighting and strong shadows (left), use bounce flash and move the subject farther from the background (right).

• *To reduce shadowing from the flash, move your subject farther from the background.* Moving the subject away from the wall helped eliminate the background shadow in the second example in Figure 9-3. The increased distance also softened the focus of the wall a bit (because of the short depth of field resulting from the f-stop and focal length).

Positioning subjects far enough from the background that they can't touch it is a good general rule. If that isn't possible, though, try going in the other direction: If the person's head is smack against the background, any shadow will be smaller and less noticeable. For example, less shadowing is created when a subject's head is resting against a sofa cushion than if he sits upright with his head a foot or so away from the cushion.

• *Study the flash information in Chapter 7 and practice before you need to take important portraits.* How the camera calculates the aperture, shutter speed, and flash power needed to expose your subject and background varies depending on the exposure mode you use. To fully understand how to create the flash results you want, you have to experiment with every advanced exposure mode, all covered in Chapter 7.

Capturing action

A fast shutter speed is the key to capturing a blur-free shot of any moving subject, whether it's a spinning Ferris wheel, a butterfly flitting from flower to flower, or, in the case of Figures 9-4 and 9-5, a hockey-playing teen. In the first image, a shutter speed of 1/125 second was too slow to catch the subject without blur. For this subject, who was moving at a fairly rapid speed, the shutter speed was all the way up to 1/1000 second to freeze the action cleanly, as shown in Figure 9-5.

Along with the basic capture settings outlined earlier (refer to Table 9-1), try the techniques in the following steps to photograph a subject in motion:

1. Set the Mode dial to Tv (shutter-priority autoexposure).

In this mode, you control the shutter speed, and the camera takes care of choosing an aperture setting that will produce a good exposure.

2. Rotate the Main dial to select the shutter speed.

In the Shooting Settings display, the option that appears highlighted, with the little arrow pointers at each side, is the one that you can adjust with the Main dial. (Refer to Figure 9-1.) In Tv mode (and M mode), the shutter speed is the active option. After you select the shutter speed, the camera selects the aperture (f-stop) necessary to produce a good exposure.

Figure 9-4: A too-slow shutter speed (1/125 second) causes the skater to appear blurry.

Figure 9-5: Raising the shutter speed to 1/1000 second "freezes" the action.

The shutter speed you need depends on how fast your subject is moving, so you have to experiment. Another factor that affects your ability to stop action is the *direction* of subject motion. A car moving *toward* you can be stopped with a lower shutter speed than one moving *across* your field of view. Generally speaking, 1/500 second should be plenty for all but the fastest subjects — speeding hockey players, race cars, or boats, for example. For slower subjects, you can even go as low as 1/250 or 1/125 second.

Remember, though, that when you increase shutter speed, the camera opens the aperture to maintain the same exposure in Tv mode. At low f-stop numbers, depth of field becomes shorter, so you have to be more careful to keep your subject within the sharp-focus zone as you compose and focus the shot.

TIP

You also can take an entirely different approach to capturing action: Instead of choosing a fast shutter speed, select a speed slow enough to blur the moving objects, which can create a heightened sense of motion and, in scenes that feature very colorful subjects, cool abstract images. I took this approach when shooting the carnival ride featured in Figure 9-6, for example. For the left image, I set the shutter speed to 1/30 second; for the right version, I slowed things down to 1/5 second. In both cases, I used a tripod, but because nearly everything in the frame was moving, the entirety of both photos is blurry — the 1/5 second version is simply more blurry because of the slower shutter.

1/30 second   1/5 second

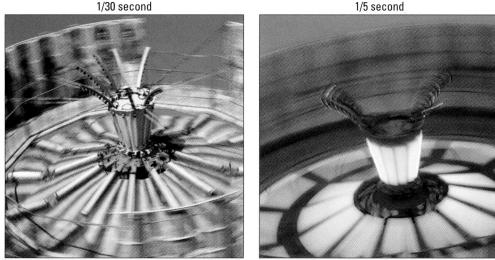

Figure 9-6: Using a shutter speed slow enough to blur moving objects can be a fun creative choice, too.

If the aperture value blinks after you set the shutter speed, the camera can't select an f-stop that will properly expose the photo at that shutter speed. See Chapter 7 for more details about how the camera notifies you of potential exposure problems.

3. **Raise the ISO setting to produce a brighter exposure, if needed.**

In dim lighting, you may not be able to create a good exposure at your chosen shutter speed without taking this step. Raising the ISO increases the possibility of noise, but a noisy shot is better than a blurry shot. (The current ISO setting appears in the upper-right corner of the Shooting Settings display, as shown in Figure 9-1; press the ISO button or use the Quick Control screen to adjust the setting.)

If auto ISO override is in force, ISO may go up automatically when you increase the shutter speed — Chapter 7 has details on that feature. Auto ISO can be a big help when you're shooting fast-paced action; just be sure to limit the camera to choosing an ISO setting that doesn't produce an objectionable level of noise. (Set that limit via the ISO Auto option on Shooting Menu 3.)

Why not just add flash to throw some extra light on the scene? That solution has a number of drawbacks. First, the flash needs time to recycle between shots, which slows down your shooting pace. Second, the fastest possible shutter speed when you enable the built-in flash is 1/200 second, which may not be fast enough to capture a quickly moving subject without blur. (You can use a faster shutter speed with certain Canon external flash units, however.) And finally, the built-in flash has a limited range, so unless your subject is within about 16 feet, you're just wasting battery power with flash, anyway. For more on all these issues, check out Chapter 7.

4. **For rapid-fire shooting, set the Drive mode to Continuous.**

In this mode, you can take almost four pictures per second. The camera continues to record images as long as the shutter button is pressed. You can switch the Drive mode by pressing the left cross key or using the Quick Control screen. The icon representing the current mode appears in the Shooting Settings display. (Refer to the labeling in Figure 9-1.)

5. **If possible, use manual focusing; otherwise, select AI Servo AF (autofocus) mode and Automatic AF Point Selection.**

With manual focusing, you eliminate the time the camera needs to lock focus in Autofocus mode. Chapter 1 shows you how to focus manually, if you need help. Of course, focusing manually gets a little tricky if your subject is moving in a way that requires you to change the focusing distance quickly from shot to shot. In that case, try these two autofocus settings for best performance:

- *Set the AF Point Selection mode to Automatic.* Press the button shown in the margin to adjust this setting. Then rotate the Main dial until all the focus points light up.

- *Set the AF (autofocus) mode to AI Servo (continuous-servo autofocus).* Press the right cross key or use the Quick Control screen to access this setting. The name of the current setting appears in the Shooting Settings screen. (Refer to Figure 9-1.)

Frame your subject under the center focus point, press the shutter button halfway to set the initial focusing distance, and then just reframe as necessary to keep the subject within the 9-point autofocusing area. As long as you keep the shutter button pressed halfway, the camera continues to adjust focus up to the time you actually take the shot. Chapter 8 details these autofocus options.

6. **Compose the subject to allow for movement across the frame.**

In other words, don't zoom in so far that your subject might zip out of the frame before you take the shot — frame a little wider than usual. You can always crop the photo later to a tighter composition. (Many examples in this book were cropped to eliminate distracting elements.) Chapter 10 shows you how to crop pictures.

Using these techniques should give you a better chance of capturing any fast-moving subject. But action-shooting strategies also are helpful for shooting candid portraits of kids and pets. Even if they aren't running, leaping, or otherwise cavorting when you pick up your camera, snapping a shot before they move or change positions is often tough. So, if an interaction or scene catches your eye, set your camera into action mode and then just fire off a series of shots as fast as you can.

One other key to shooting sports, wildlife, or any moving subject: Before you even put your eye to the viewfinder, spend time studying your subject so that you have a better idea of when it will move, where it will move, and how fast it will move. The more you can anticipate the action, the better the chance you have to capture it.

Capturing scenic vistas

Providing specific capture settings for landscape photography is tricky because there's no single best approach to capturing a beautiful stretch of countryside, a city skyline, or another vast subject. Depth of field is an example: One person's idea of a super cityscape might be to keep all buildings in the scene sharply focused. Another photographer might prefer to shoot the same scene so that a foreground building is sharply focused while the others are less so, thus drawing the eye to that first building.

That said, here are a few tips to help you photograph a landscape the way *you* see it:

- **Shoot in aperture-priority autoexposure mode (Av) so that you can control depth of field.** If you want extreme depth of field so that both near and distant objects are sharply focused, as shown in Figure 9-7, select a high f-stop value. An aperture of f/22 worked for this shot.

- **If the exposure requires a slow shutter, use a tripod to avoid blurring.** The downside to a high f-stop is that you need a slower shutter speed to produce a good exposure. If the shutter speed is slower than you can comfortably handhold, use a tripod to avoid picture-blurring camera shake. No tripod handy? Look for any solid surface on which to steady the camera. You can always increase the ISO setting to increase light sensitivity, which in turn allows a faster shutter speed, too, but that option brings with it the chance of increased image noise. See Chapter 7 for details. Also see Chapter 1 for details about image stabilization, which can help you take sharper handheld shots at slow shutter speeds.

Figure 9-7: Use a high f-stop value (or Landscape mode) to keep foreground and background sharply focused.

- **For dramatic waterfall and fountain shots, consider using a slow shutter to create that "misty" look.** The slow shutter blurs the water, giving it a soft, romantic appearance, as shown in Figure 9-8. Shutter speed for this shot was 1/15 second. Again, use a tripod to ensure that camera shake doesn't blur the rest of the scene.

In very bright light, using a slow shutter speed may overexpose the image even if you stop the aperture all the way down and select the camera's lowest ISO setting. As a solution,

Figure 9-8: For misty water movement, use a slow shutter speed (and tripod).

consider investing in a *neutral-density filter* for your lens. This type of filter works something like sunglasses for your camera: It simply reduces the amount of light that passes through the lens, without affecting image colors, so that you can use a slower shutter than would otherwise be possible.

✏ **At sunrise or sunset, base exposure on the sky.** The foreground will be dark, but you can usually brighten it in a photo editor, if needed. If you base exposure on the foreground, on the other hand, the sky will become so bright that all the color will be washed out — a problem you usually can't easily fix after the fact. You may also want to try some High Dynamic Range imaging techniques to produce an image that includes a greater range of shadows to highlights. Chapter 7 explains this creative option.

You can also invest in a graduated neutral-density filter, which is a filter that's clear on one side and dark on the other. You orient the filter so that the dark half falls over the sky and the clear side over the dimly lit portion of the scene. This setup enables you to better expose the foreground without blowing out the sky colors.

In the advanced exposure modes, experiment with enabling the Highlight Tone Priority option, too. Enabled via Custom Function 6 on Setup Menu 3, this feature can help you avoid blowing out highlights while still holding onto shadow detail. Chapter 7 offers more information.

✏ **For cool, nighttime city pics, experiment with a slow shutter speed.** Assuming that cars or other vehicles are moving through the scene, the result is neon trails of light, like those you see in Figure 9-9. Shutter speed for this image was ten seconds. The longer your shutter speed, the blurrier the motion trails.

Because long exposures can produce image noise, you also may want to enable the Long Exposure Noise Reduction feature. You access this option via the Custom Function option on Setup Menu 3; select Custom Function 4 and change the setting from Off to Auto or On. Chapter 7 discusses this option in more detail.

Figure 9-9: A slow shutter also creates neon light trails in city-street scenes.

✏ **For the best lighting, shoot during the "magic hours."** That's the term photographers use for early morning and late afternoon, when the light cast by the sun is soft and warm, giving everything that beautiful, gently warmed look.

Can't wait for the perfect light? Tweak your camera's White Balance setting, using the instructions laid out in Chapter 8, to simulate magic-hour light.

✏ **In tricky light, bracket shots.** *Bracketing* simply means to take the same picture at several different exposures to increase the odds that at least one captures the scene the way you envision. Bracketing is especially a good idea in difficult lighting situations such as sunrise and sunset.

Your camera offers automatic exposure bracketing (AEB) when you shoot in the advanced exposure modes. See Chapter 7 to find out how to take advantage of this feature.

Also experiment with the Auto Lighting Optimizer and Highlight Tone Priority options; capture some images with the features enabled and then take the same shots with the features turned off. You control Auto Lighting Optimizer on Shooting Menu 2; Highlight Tone Priority is found in the Custom Functions options on Setup Menu 3; see Chapter 7 for details. Remember, though, that you can't use both these tonality-enhancing features concurrently; turning on Highlight Tone Priority disables Auto Lighting Optimizer.

Capturing dynamic close-ups

For great close-up shots, start with the basic capture settings outlined earlier, in Table 9-1. Then try the following additional settings and techniques:

✏ **Check your owner's manual to find out the minimum close-focusing distance of your lens.** How "up close and personal" you can be to your subject depends on your lens, not on the camera body.

✏ **Take control over depth of field by setting the camera mode to Av (aperture-priority autoexposure) mode.** Whether you want a shallow or a medium or an extreme depth of field depends on the point of your photo. For the romantic scene shown in Figure 9-10, for example, setting the aperture to f/5.6 blurred the background, helping the subjects stand out more from the similarly colored background. But if you want the viewer to clearly see all details throughout the frame — for example, if you're shooting a product shot for your company's sales catalog — go in the other direction, stopping down the aperture as far as possible.

- **Remember that both zooming in and getting close to your subject decrease depth of field.** Back to that product shot: If you need depth of field beyond what you can achieve with the aperture setting, you may need to back away or zoom out, or both. (You can always crop your image to show just the parts of the subject that you want to feature.)

- **When shooting flowers and other nature scenes outdoors, pay attention to shutter speed, too.** Even a slight breeze may cause your subject to move, causing blurring at slow shutter speeds. (Chapter 7 offers some examples that illustrate this issue.)

- **Use fill flash for better outdoor lighting.** Just as with portraits, a tiny bit of flash typically improves close-ups when the sun is your primary light source. You may need to reduce the flash output slightly, via the camera's Flash Exposure Compensation control. Chapter 7 offers details about using flash.

Figure 9-10: Shallow depth of field helps set the subject apart from the background.

Keep in mind that the maximum shutter speed possible when you use the built-in flash is 1/200 second. So in extremely bright light, you may need to use a high f-stop setting to avoid overexposing the picture. You also can lower the ISO speed setting, if it's not already all the way down to ISO 100.

- **When shooting indoors, try not to use flash as your primary light source.** Because you're shooting at close range, the light from your flash may be too harsh even at a low Flash Exposure Compensation setting. If flash is inevitable, turn on as many room lights as possible to reduce the flash power that's needed — even a hardware store shop light can work in a pinch as a lighting source. (Remember that if you have multiple light sources, though, you may need to tweak the White Balance setting.)

- **To get *very* close to your subject, invest in a macro lens or a set of diopters.** A true macro lens is an expensive proposition; expect to pay around $200 or more. If you enjoy capturing the tiny details in life, it's worth the investment.

For a less expensive way to go, you can spend about $40 for a set of *diopters,* which are sort of like reading glasses you screw onto your existing lens. Diopters come in several strengths: +1, +2, +4, and so on, with a higher number indicating a greater magnifying power. In fact, a diopter was used to capture the rose in Figure 9-11. The left image shows you the closest shot possible with the regular lens; to produce the right image, a +6 diopter was attached. The downfall of diopters, sadly, is that they typically produce images that are very soft around the edges, as in Figure 9-11 — a problem that doesn't occur with a good macro lens.

No diopter   +6 diopter

Figure 9-11: To extend the close-focus ability of a lens, add magnifying diopters.

Coping with Special Situations

A few subjects and shooting situations pose some additional challenges not already covered in earlier sections. So to close this chapter, here's a quick list of ideas for tackling a variety of common tough-shot photos:

✏ **Shooting through glass:** To capture subjects that are behind glass, such as animals at a zoo, you can try a couple tricks. First, set your camera to manual focusing — the glass barrier can give the autofocus mechanism fits. Disable your flash to avoid creating any unwanted reflections, too. Then, if you can get close enough, your best odds are to put the lens right up to the glass. (Be careful not to scratch your lens.) If you must stand farther away, try to position your lens at a 90-degree angle to the glass. I used this approach in Figure 9-12.

✔ **Shooting out a car window:** Set the camera to shutter-priority autoexposure or manual mode and dial in a fast shutter speed to compensate for the movement of the car. Also turn on image stabilization, if your lens offers it. Oh, and keep a tight grip on your camera.

✔ **Shooting fireworks:** First off, use a tripod; fireworks require a long exposure, and trying to handhold your camera simply isn't going to work. If using a zoom lens, zoom out to the shortest focal length (widest angle). Switch to manual focusing and set focus at infinity (the farthest focus point possible on your lens). Set the exposure mode to manual, choose a relatively high f-stop setting — say, f/16 or so — and start at a shutter speed of 1 to 5 seconds. From there, it's simply a matter of experimenting with different shutter speeds. Also play with the timing of the shutter release, starting some exposures at the moment the fireworks are shot up, some at the moment they burst open, and so on. For the example featured in Figure 9-13, I used a shutter speed of about 5 seconds and began the exposure as the rocket was going up — that's what creates the "corkscrew" of light that rises up through the frame.

Figure 9-12: To photograph subjects that are behind glass, use manual focusing and disable flash.

Figure 9-13: I used a shutter speed of 5 seconds to capture this fireworks shot.

Be especially gentle when you press the shutter button — with a very slow shutter, you can easily create enough camera movement to blur the image. If you purchased the accessory remote control for your camera, this is a good situation in which to use it. (See Chapter 2 for more information about remote-control shooting.)

✔ **Shooting in strong backlighting:** When the light behind your subject is very strong, the result is often an underexposed subject. You can try using flash to better expose the subject, assuming that you're shooting in an exposure mode that permits flash. The Highlight Tone Priority feature, which captures the image in a way that retains better detail in the shadows without blowing out highlights, may also help. (Chapter 7 offers an example.)

But for another creative choice, you can purposely underexpose the subject to create a silhouette effect, as shown in Figure 9-14. Base your exposure on the brightest areas of the background so that the darker areas of the frame remain dark.

Figure 9-14: Experiment with shooting backlit subjects in silhouette.

Part IV
The Part of Tens

The 5th Wave   By Rich Tennant

"That's a lovely scanned image of your sister's portrait. Now take it off the body of that pit viper before she comes in the room."

In this part . . .

*I*n time-honored *For Dummies* tradition, this part of the book contains additional tidbits of information presented in the always popular Top Ten list format.

Chapter 10 shows you how to make minor picture touch-ups, such as cropping and adjusting exposure, by using the free software that shipped with your camera. Following that, Chapter 11 introduces you to ten camera functions that I consider specialty tools — bonus options that, though not at the top of the list of the features I suggest you study, are nonetheless interesting to explore when you have a free moment or two.

Ten Fast Photo-Editing Tricks

*E*very photographer produces a clunker image now and then. When it happens to you, don't be too quick to reach for the Erase button on your camera. Many common problems are surprisingly easy to fix using the tools found in most photo-editing programs.

In fact, you can perform many common retouching tasks using one of the free programs provided with your camera: ZoomBrowser EX (Windows) and ImageBrowser (Mac). This chapter shows you how.

Opening and Saving Images

For any of the photo alterations covered in this chapter, remember these editing basics:

- **Opening the photo:** After opening ZoomBrowser EX or ImageBrowser, track down the picture thumbnail. If you used the Canon software to download pictures from your memory card and didn't change the default download settings, the pictures should be stored inside a folder called My Pictures or just Pictures, depending on the operating system you use. Normally, the folder list appears on the left side of the program window. Figure 10-1 shows the Windows 7 version; Figure 10-2, the Mac variation as it appears in Snow Leopard.

  For simplicity's sake, I refer to ZoomBrowser EX and ImageBrowser from this point on as just "the browser."

Folder list   Thumbnail

Figure 10-1: To open a photo in the editing window, double-click its thumbnail (not the large preview).

After you find the picture thumbnail, check its file type. If you shot the picture using the Raw file format, you must process it using the raw-conversion instructions laid out in Chapter 6 before you can edit it using the software tools. If the picture is in the JPEG or TIFF format, double-click the thumbnail to open the picture in its own viewer window, as shown in Figures 10-3 (Windows version) and 10-4 (Mac). Then open the Edit list, as shown in the figures, and choose an editing tool. Your picture then opens inside an editing window, as shown in Figures 10-5 (Windows) and 10-6 (Mac). The figures show the tools related to red-eye removal, explained in the next section.

✏ **Navigating in the editing window:** The tools in the editing window vary depending on what editing task you selected. But you can always use the tools labeled in Figures 10-5 and 10-6 to zoom and scroll the picture display:

• *Windows:* Change the picture magnification by dragging the Zoom slider; scroll the display by clicking the Hand tool and dragging in the preview.

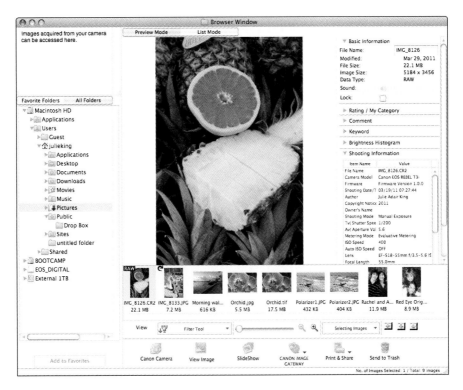

Figure 10-2: The Mac version of the software features the same basic layout.

- *On a Mac:* Zoom by choosing a magnification level from the Display Size drop-down list or by clicking the Zoom In and Zoom Out buttons. Use the scroll bars to scroll the display.

✔ **Saving the edited photo:** Whatever retouching task you do, your last step is to click OK to exit the editing window and then choose File⇨Save As to save your work. You may see a message saying that some shooting data may not be preserved in the edited file; click OK to go forward. Be sure to make the following choices in the file-saving dialog box that appears:

- *File type:* Use the TIFF format, which results in the best photo quality.

   Do *not* use JPEG. Every time you edit and save a picture in the JPEG format, you damage the picture quality slightly. Chapter 2 has details on this issue. If you need a JPEG version of an edited photo for online use, save it first as a TIFF file so that you will have a top-quality image for printing. Then follow the steps provided in Chapter 6 to create a JPEG copy of the TIFF file.

- *Filename:* If you started with a TIFF image, be sure to give the file a new name so that you don't overwrite the original.

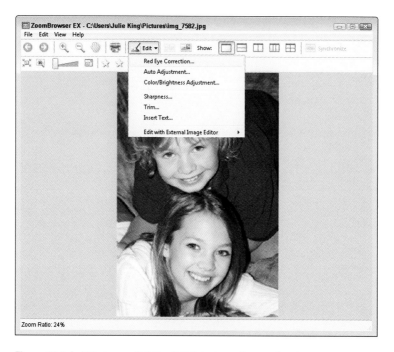

Figure 10-3: In Windows, click the Edit list above the preview to access retouching tools.

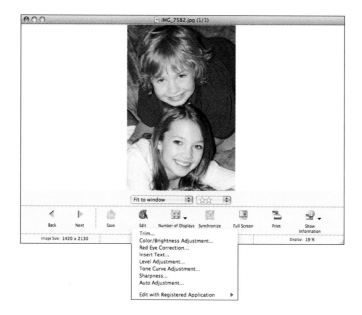

Figure 10-4: On a Mac, the Edit list appears at the bottom of the window.

Hand tool   Zoom slider

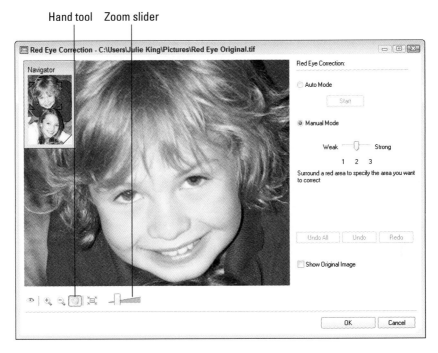

Figure 10-5: Use the Hand tool to scroll the display and the Zoom slider to change the display magnification.

Scroll bars   Display size   Zoom out/in

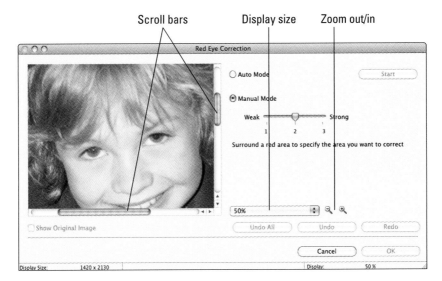

Figure 10-6: On a Mac, use these controls to adjust the preview size.

Removing Red-Eye

Red-eye usually isn't a major problem with the Rebel T3i/600D. But if you spot red-eye in your flash pictures, you can use the red-eye repair tool in the Canon browser software to fix the problem. Follow these steps:

1. **Open the picture in a viewer window, as explained in the preceding section, and choose Red Eye Correction from the Edit list.**

   Your photo appears in the Red Eye Correction retouching window, shown in Figure 10-7.

2. **Zoom in on your photo so that you can get a good view of the eyes.**

3. **Click the Manual Mode option.**

   In Auto mode, the red-eye correction tool can sometimes trip up, "correcting" red pixels that aren't actually in the eye, so stick with Manual mode, which enables you to specify exactly where you want the program to do its retouching work.

   After you select Manual, you gain access to a slider that enables you to adjust the strength of the correction. Set the slider to the middle position, as shown in the figure, for your initial red-eye repair attempt.

4. **In Windows, select the Red Eye tool, labeled in Figure 10-7.**

   The tool is ready to go if it appears highlighted, as in the figure. If not, click the tool icon. Mac users can ignore this step.

5. **Drag with your mouse to surround the first red eye with a white box, as shown in Figure 10-7.**

   A little OK box pops up near the rectangle, as shown in the figure.

6. **Click the little OK, as shown in the figure.**

   The program goes to work removing the red eye pixels. If you like the results, move on to the next eye. Or click Undo to get rid of the correction and then try again, adjusting the setting of the slider control if necessary.

7. **After you finish all eye repairs, click the OK button at the bottom of the editing window.**

   The Red Eye Correction window closes, and your repaired photo appears in the Viewer window.

8. **Save your picture in the TIFF file format, as outlined in the preceding section.**

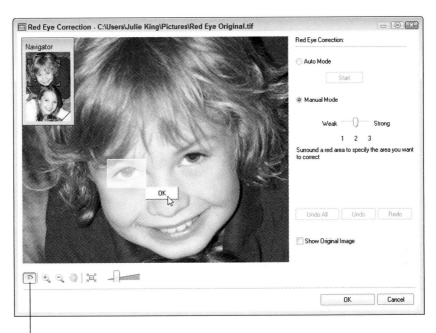

Red Eye tool

Figure 10-7: Drag to enclose the problem eye area with a small box; then click the little OK button that pops up.

Like most red-eye removal tools, the Canon version can do a good job in the right circumstances. But if the eyes are very bright, the tool may not be able to make the repair. In addition, no red-eye remover works on animal eyes; red-eye tools detect and replace only red-eye pixels, and animal eyes typically turn yellow, white, or green in response to a flash. The best solution is to simply paint in the correct eye colors.

Cropping Your Photo

To *crop* a photo simply means to trim away some of its perimeter. Removing excess background can often improve an image, as illustrated by the original frog scene, shown on the left in Figure 10-8, and its cropped cousin, shown on the right. In the original image, there's just too much going on — the eye has a hard time figuring out what's important. Eliminating all but a little of the surrounding foliage returned emphasis to the subject and created a stronger composition.

You may also want to crop an image so that it fits a specific frame size. As Chapter 6 explains, the original images from your camera fit perfectly in 4-x-6-inch frames, but if you want a 5 x 7, 8 x 10, or another standard print size, you need to crop your image to those new proportions. If you don't, the photo printer software or retail print lab crops for you, and the result may not be the composition you would choose.

Figure 10-8: Cropping creates a better composition, eliminating background clutter.

After opening your photo as outlined at the start of this chapter, choose Trim from the Edit drop-down list. Your photo appears in the Trim Image retouching window, and a dotted outline, or *crop box,* appears on the photo, as shown in Figure 10-9. Take these steps to do your cropping:

1. **Click the Advanced Options button to display all the crop-size controls.**

   Figure 10-9 labels the button and shows the controls that appear when you click it. (On a Mac, the panel that contains the controls pops out of the side of the dialog box instead of appearing within it.)

2. **Choose an option from the Select the Aspect Ratio drop-down list.**

   Your selection determines the proportions of the cropped image. You can go in three directions:

   • *Manual:* This option enables you to crop the image to any proportions. This option was used for the frog photo.

- *Maintain Original:* The program restricts you to cropping to the same proportions as your original.

- *Specific Aspect Ratios:* You also can select from specific aspect ratios: 1:1, 2:3, 3:2, 3:4, 4:3, 9:16, and 16:9. The first number in the pair indicates the width, and the second indicates the height.

3. **In Windows, make sure that the Trim button is selected. (Refer to Figure 10-9.)**

   It should be selected already unless you used the adjacent controls to zoom or scroll the preview. Just click the button to select it if needed. Mac users can skip this step.

Handle

Click to display advanced options

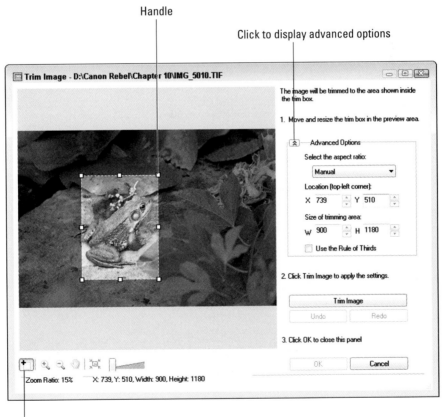

Trim button

Figure 10-9: You can specify a crop size via the Advanced Options controls.

4. **Adjust the size and position of the crop box as follows:**

   • *Move the crop box.* Drag inside the box.

   • *Resize the crop box.* Drag any of the *handles* — those little squares around the perimeter of the crop box, as labeled in Figure 10-9.

   As you drag the handles, the W and H boxes in the Size of Trimming Area portion of the dialog box reflect the new dimensions of the crop box, with the measurement shown in pixels. Keep in mind that pixel count is critical to print quality. Chapters 2 and 6 provide details, but the short story is that you need roughly 200 to 300 pixels per linear inch of your print. So if you have a finished print size in mind, monitor the W and H values as you adjust the crop box size to make sure that you aren't clipping away too many pixels.

   • *Set a specific crop size.* You also can enter specific pixel dimensions in the W and H boxes. The crop box automatically adjusts to the dimensions you enter.

   Using the third option is the easiest way to crop your photo to a size that doesn't mesh with any of the specific aspect ratio choices. Say that you want to produce a 5-x-7-inch print from your cropped photo and you want an image resolution of 300 pixels per inch. Just multiply the print dimensions by the resolution you want and then enter those values into the W and H boxes. For the 5 x 7 at 300 ppi example, the W and H values are 1500 and 2100, respectively. If the resulting crop boundary encompasses too much or too little of your photo, just keep adjusting the W and H values, making sure to always keep the two at the same proportions you originally entered.

5. **Turn on the Use the Rule of Thirds gridlines (optional).**

   A classic composition rule is to imagine that your image is divided into thirds vertically and horizontally and then position the subject at a spot where two dividing lines intersect. To help you visualize that concept, the Trim box can display those horizontal and vertical grid lines, as shown in Figure 10-10. Just click the Use the Rule of Thirds check box to toggle the grid on and off.

6. **When you're happy with the crop box, click the Trim Image button.**

   The cropped photo appears in the preview. If you don't like the results, click the Undo button and try again.

7. **Click OK to close the retouching window; then choose File⇨Save As to save your cropped image.**

   The first section of this chapter has file-saving tips.

When you shoot pictures using Live View, you do have the option to capture your originals at an aspect ratio of 4:3, 16:9, or 1:1. Chapter 4 explains how to make that bit of magic happen.

Display grid

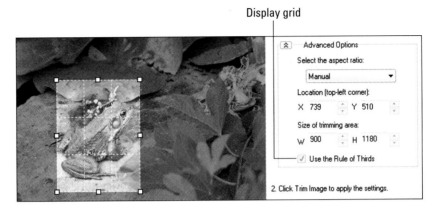

Figure 10-10: The Rule of Thirds gridlines offer a compositional guide.

Adjusting Color Saturation

Saturation refers to the intensity and purity of color. A fully saturated color contains no black, white, or gray. In other words, saturated colors are deep, rich, and bold.

On occasion, an image can benefit from a little saturation bump. Figure 10-11 offers an example. The cart and flowers had a nice mix of colors in the original photo, shown on the left, but there was something a bit anemic about the way the camera captured the scene. Increasing the saturation ever so slightly produced the better result shown on the right.

After opening the photo in a viewer window, as outlined at the start of this chapter, choose Color/Brightness Adjustment from the Edit list. Your image appears in the Color/Brightness Adjustment retouching window. The window contents vary depending whether you're using the Windows or Mac version of the program; Figures 10-12 and 10-13 show you both versions. Take the following steps to move forward:

1. **Set the Retouching mode to Color Adjustment.**

   • *In Windows:* Select Color Adjustment from the drop-down list at the top of the window (shown in Figure 10-12). After you do so, the window offers three sliders: Brightness, Saturation, and Contrast.

   • *On a Mac:* Click the Color Adjustment tab. The Mac version of the tool (see Figure 10-13) offers just Saturation and Brightness sliders.

One note about the Brightness and Contrast controls: These tools aren't the best options for adjusting exposure and contrast. You can get much better results by using the Level Adjustment and Tone Curve Adjustment tools, both explained later in this chapter.

Original   Increased saturation

Figure 10-11: Increasing saturation made the colors pop a little more.

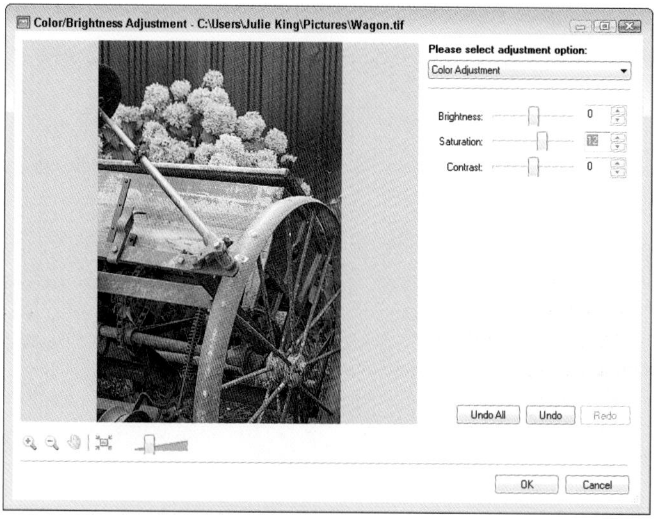

Figure 10-12: In Windows, select Color Adjustment from the top drop-down list.

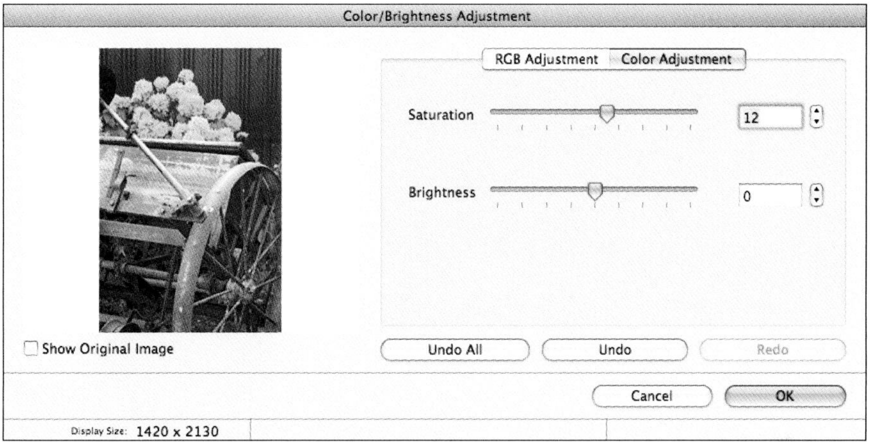

Color/Brightness Adjustment

RGB Adjustment | Color Adjustment

Saturation ──────────●────────── 12

Brightness ──────────●────────── 0

☐ Show Original Image   Undo All   Undo   Redo

Cancel   OK

Display Size: 1420 x 2130

Figure 10-13: On a Mac, click the Color Adjustment tab to display these options.

2. **Drag the Saturation slider to adjust the image.**

   Be careful about increasing saturation too much. Doing so can destroy picture detail because areas that previously contained a range of saturation levels all shift to the fully saturated state, giving you a solid blob of color.

3. **Click OK to apply the change and close the retouching window.**

4. **Save the edited image, following the steps provided at the start of this chapter.**

Tweaking Color Balance

Chapter 8 explains how to use your camera's White Balance and Picture Style controls to manipulate the colors in your pictures. You can also play with colors a little by using the Shoot by Ambience and Shoot by Lighting or Scene Type options, covered in Chapter 3. If you can't produce the results you want by using those features, you may be able to do the job after the fact by using the RGB Adjustment filter. In Figure 10-14, for example, an application of the filter toned down the amount of blue in the image and brought out the warm, yellow tones of the building instead.

To access the filter, follow the usual steps to open the photo in a viewer window (see the first part of the chapter if you need help) and choose Color/Brightness Adjustment from the Edit list. Then, in the editing window, choose RGB Adjustment to display the Red, Green, and Blue sliders, as shown in Figure 10-15. The top image shows the Windows version; the lower image, the Mac version.

Original   Colors Adjusted

Figure 10-14: Warming the colors emphasizes the buildings rather than the sky.

The filter is based on three color pairs: red-cyan, green-magenta, and blue-yellow. (Those six colors happen to be the primary and secondary colors of the RGB color world, which is the one in which all digital images reside.) When you move the sliders, you affect both the primary color and its secondary opposite, as follows:

- **Red:** As you drag the slider to the right, you increase red and decrease cyan. Drag the slider to the left to diminish reds and embolden cyans.

- **Green:** Drag this slider to the right to add green and reduce magenta. Drag to the left to produce the opposite result.

- **Blue:** Drag this slider to the right to increase the amount of blue and reduce the amount of yellow. Drag left to increase yellow and tone down blues.

In imaging lingo, tools of this type are *color balancing* filters because they shift the balance between the two opposite colors.

After adjusting your photo, click OK to close the editing window, and then choose File⇨Save As to save the altered image. See the first section of this chapter for some file-saving tips.

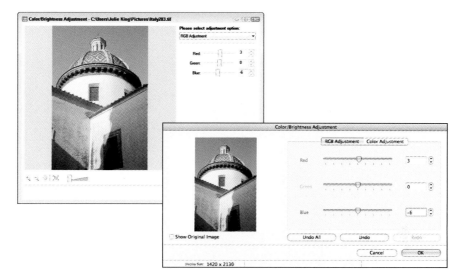

Figure 10-15: Select RGB Adjustment to tweak color balance.

Adjusting Exposure

Getting exposure just right is one of the trickiest aspects of photography. Fortunately, the Canon software gives you several tools for tweaking exposure. The next sections introduce the two most capable: the Level Adjustment filter and the Tone Curve Adjustment filter.

 Stay away from the exposure options that appear when you open the Color Adjustment filter (shown earlier, in Figures 10-12 and 10-13). In Windows, the filter offers a Brightness and Contrast slider; on a Mac, you see just the Brightness slider. The problem is that both sliders affect all pixels in your image; you can't brighten just the shadows, for example, without also brightening the *midtones* (areas of medium brightness) and highlights. For that reason, these sliders rarely produce good results.

Three-point exposure control with the Level Adjustment filter

With the Level Adjustment filter, you can adjust shadows, midtones, and highlights individually. Figure 10-16 shows the filter controls as they appear in Windows; the Mac version contains the same options in a slightly different layout.

You might be thinking: "Wow, that looks way too complicated for me." Don't worry; this filter really is easy to use. First, ignore everything but the graph in the middle of the box, known as a *histogram,* and the three sliders underneath, labeled Shadows, Midtones, and Highlights in Figure 10-17. See? Easier already.

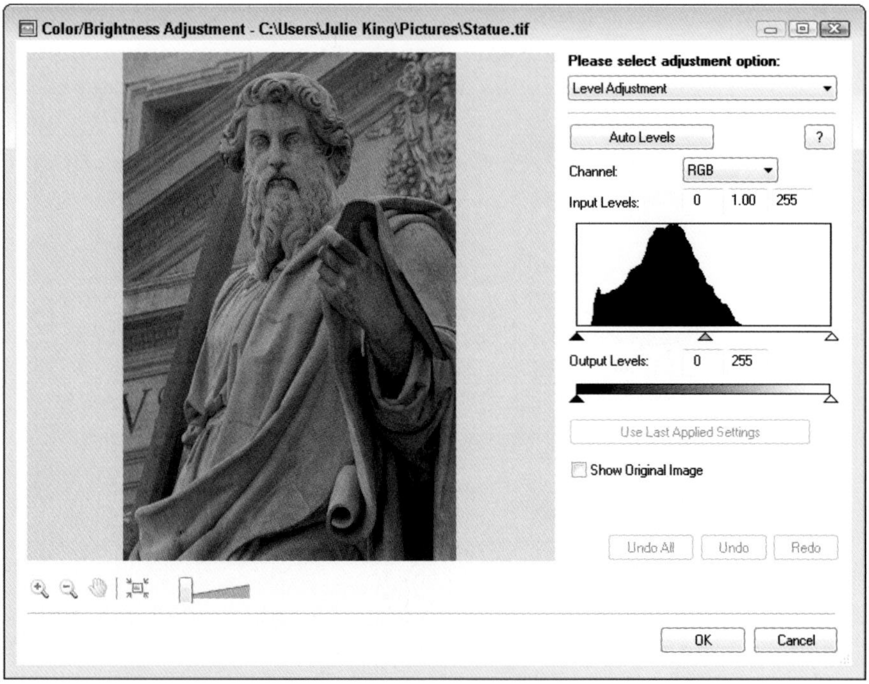

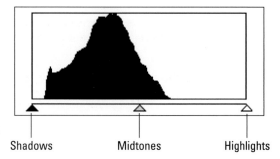

Figure 10-16: The Level Adjustment tool isn't nearly as difficult to use as it appears.

The histogram works just like the Brightness histogram that you can display while reviewing images on the camera monitor, a topic discussed in Chapter 5. The horizontal axis of the graph represents the possible brightness values in an image, ranging from black on the left side to white on the right. The vertical axis shows how many pixels fall at a particular brightness value.

Figure 10-17: All you need to worry about are these three sliders.

So if you have a tall spike in some part of the histogram, you have lots of pixels at that particular brightness value.

To adjust exposure, you just drag the three sliders underneath the histogram, depending on whether you want to shift shadows, midtones, or highlights. Follow these steps to try it out:

1. **In the browser, double-click the photo thumbnail to display the image in the viewer window.**

2. **Open the Level Adjustment editing window.**

   • *In Windows:* Choose Color/Brightness Adjustment from the Edit drop-down list. Then select Level Adjustment from the drop-down list at the top of the retouching window, as shown in Figure 10-18.

   • *On a Mac:* Choose Level Adjustment from the Edit drop-down list.

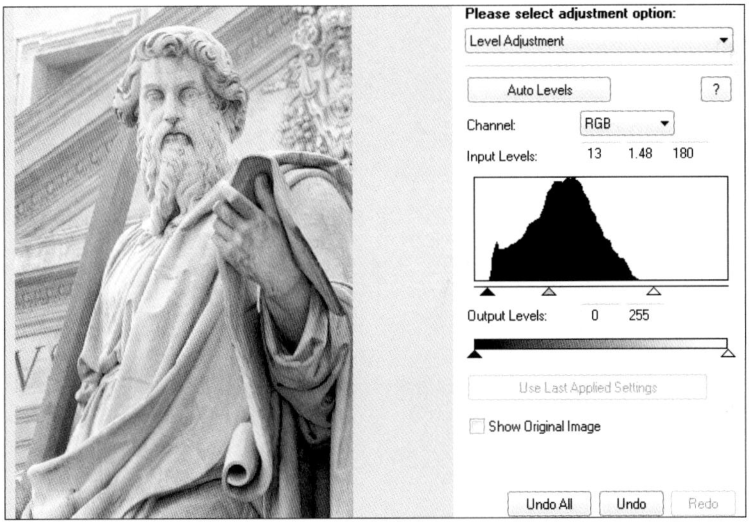

Figure 10-18: Levels were used to brighten highlights and midtones while darkening the shadows slightly.

3. **Set the Channel option to RGB.**

   On a Mac, the option is unlabeled; it's the pop-up list above the histogram.

4. **Drag the sliders underneath the histogram to adjust exposure.**

   • *To darken shadows:* Drag the Shadows slider to the right.

   • *To adjust midtones:* Drag the middle slider to the right to darken midtones; drag it to the left to brighten them.

   • *To brighten highlights:* Drag the Highlights slider to the left.

   When you drag the Shadows or Highlights slider, the Midtones slider moves in tandem. You may need to readjust that slider after you set the other two.

You can compare your original image with the adjusted one by toggling the dialog box preview on and off. In Windows, click the Show Original Image box to turn off the preview; click again to return to the preview. On a Mac, click the Preview box.

5. **Click OK to accept the changes and close the dialog box.**

6. **Choose File⇨Save As and save your image in the TIFF file format.**

   See the first section of this chapter to find out why.

Gaining more control with the Tone Curve Adjustment filter

When you use the Level Adjustment filter, you get three points of exposure-correction control: highlights, shadows, and midtones. The Tone Curve Adjustment filter takes things a step further, enabling you to manipulate specific values along the entire brightness spectrum.

Figure 10-19 offers a look at the Windows version of the Tone Curve Adjustment retouching window. The Mac version is slightly different in appearance, but it contains the same main components.

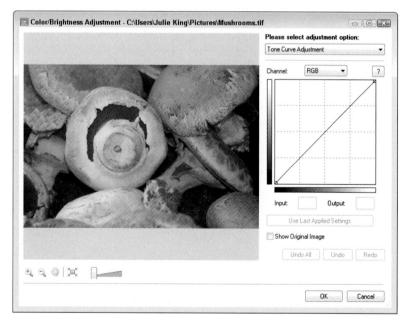

Figure 10-19: Using the Tone Curve Adjustment filter, you get even greater exposure control.

Again, the controls inside the window seem mighty perplexing at first. But here's all you need to know to take advantage of the filter:

✔ See the line that runs diagonally through the white grid? It's just another representation of the possible brightness values in a digital image. Black falls at the lower end of the line; white, at the top. (The shaded bars that run alongside the left and lower edges of the grid remind you of that orientation.) Medium brightness falls dead center on the line.

✔ To adjust exposure, click and drag at the spot on the line that corresponds to the brightness value you want to change. Drag up to brighten the image; drag down to darken it. For example, Figure 10-20 shows the center of the line dragged upwards. The resulting curve — *tone curve,* in imaging parlance — produced the exposure change shown in the preview.

✔ After a drag, a control point appears at the spot on the line you dragged to anchor that part of the tone curve, as shown in Figure 10-20.

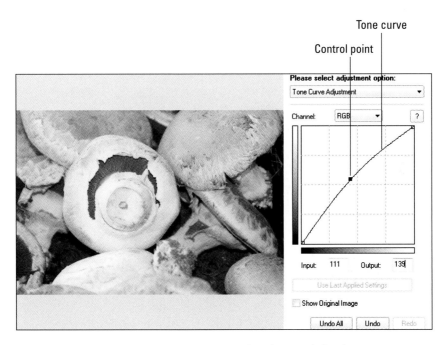

Figure 10-20: Drag upward to brighten the image; drag down to darken it.

✔ You can bend the tone curve as much as you want, in any direction you want. Just keep clicking and dragging to add control points. But understand that extreme curves or curves with tons of points can produce truly ugly results and odd breaks in color and brightness. A good policy is to aim for a gentle curve that has no more than six points, including the ones that are provided automatically at the black and white ends of the curve.

✏ To increase contrast, create an s-shaped curve; to decrease contrast, create a reverse-s shape. The gentle s-shaped curve, shown in Figure 10-21, produced the finished mushroom photo that you see in the preview. The curve resulted in a slight bump in exposure to medium and medium-bright pixels and a slight darkening of medium-dark and dark pixels. The white and black areas of the image remain unchanged.

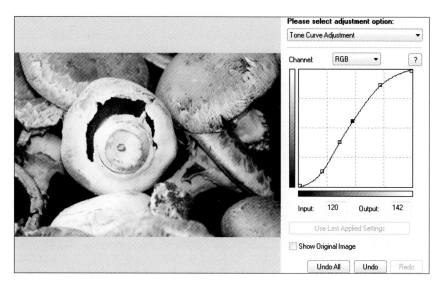

Figure 10-21: An s-shaped curve boosts contrast.

The best way to understand this filter is to try it. So take these steps:

1. **Open the image in its own viewer window.**

   You know the drill: Just double-click the thumbnail in the main browser window.

2. **Open the Tone Curve Adjustment retouching window.**

   • *In Windows:* Click the Edit drop-down list at the top of the browser window and choose Adjust Color/Brightness. When the retouching window appears, select Tone Curve Adjustment from the drop-down list at the top.

   • *On a Mac:* Click the Edit drop-down list underneath the image preview and choose Tone Curve Adjustment.

3. **Set the Channel option to RGB.**

   On a Mac, the option is the unlabeled pop-up list just above the grid.

4. **Bend the tone curve by adding and dragging control points.**

   See the preceding list for details on this step. If you need to delete a point, click it to select it and then press Delete. (The selected control point appears black.)

   If the image doesn't appear to change in the preview, check the status of the Show Original Image box. Deselect the box to turn on the dialog box preview.

5. **Click OK to apply the adjustment and close the retouching window.**

6. **Save the image in the TIFF file format, following the steps at the start of this chapter.**

Sharpening Focus (Sort Of)

Have you ever seen one of those spy-movie thrillers where the good guys capture a photo of the villain's face — only the picture is so blurry that it could just as easily be a picture of pudding? The heroes ask the photo-lab experts to enhance the picture, and within seconds, it's transformed into an image so clear that you can make out individual hairs in the villain's mustache.

It is with heavy heart that I must inform you that this kind of image rescue is pure Hollywood fantasy. You simply can't turn a blurry image into a sharply focused photo, even using the most sophisticated photo software on the planet. The digital process of *sharpening,* however, can *slightly* improve the apparent focus of pictures that are *slightly* blurry, as illustrated by the before-and-after images in Figure 10-22. Notice that I said *apparent* focus: Sharpening doesn't really adjust focus but instead creates the *illusion* of sharper focus by increasing contrast in a special way.

Here's how it works: Wherever pixels of different colors come together, the sharpening process boosts contrast along the border between them. The light side of the border grows lighter; the dark side grows darker. Photography experts refer to those light and dark strips as *sharpening halos.* You can get a close-up look at the halos in the right, sharpened example in Figure 10-23, which shows a tiny portion of the pencil image from Figure 10-22. Notice that in the sharpened example the yellow side of the boundary between the pencils received a light halo and the blue side received a dark halo.

A little sharpening can go a long way toward improving a slightly soft image — but too much sharpening does more damage than good. The halos become so strong that they're clearly visible, and the image takes on a brittle, sandpaper-like texture. Again, no amount of sharpening can repair a truly out-of-focus image, so all you do when you crank up sharpening is make matters worse.

Original   Sharpened

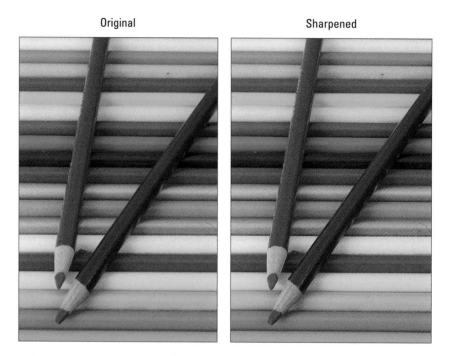

Figure 10-22: A slightly blurry image (left) can benefit from a sharpening filter (right).

Original   Sharpened

Figure 10-23: Sharpening adds light and dark halos along color boundaries.

Both the Windows and Mac versions of the Canon software offer a simple Sharpening tool, but the Windows version offers a second sharpening filter as well. Figure 10-24 shows the rudimentary sharpener in its Mac incarnation. To use this tool, just follow the usual steps: Double-click the image thumbnail to open it in its own window and then choose Sharpness from the Edit drop-down list. (See Figures 10-3 and 10-4 if you have trouble finding the list.) Drag the slider to the right to add sharpening and then click OK to finish the job.

Sharpness

Sharpness

0

Undo All   Undo   Redo

Show Original Image

Cancel   OK

Display Size: 1420 x 2130

Figure 10-24: The Mac version of the browser offers only a simple sharpening slider.

Windows users, however, have the option of using a more flexible sharpening tool, an Unsharp Mask filter. To switch to this filter, just click the Unsharp Mask tab at the top of the Sharpness retouching window, as shown in Figure 10-25.

The three sliders provided for the Unsharp Mask filter enable you to control where and how the sharpening halos are applied, as described in this list:

- **Amount:** This slider adjusts the intensity of the sharpening halos.
- **Radius:** This slider adjusts the width of the halos. Don't go too high, or the sharpening halos become quite noticeable.
- **Threshold:** Using this slider, you can limit the sharpening effect just to high-contrast color boundaries. Try raising the value a few notches from 0 when sharpening portraits, to sharpen the image without adding unwanted texture to the skin. This technique helped to keep the surface of the pencils smooth in the photo while sharpening the edges between them.

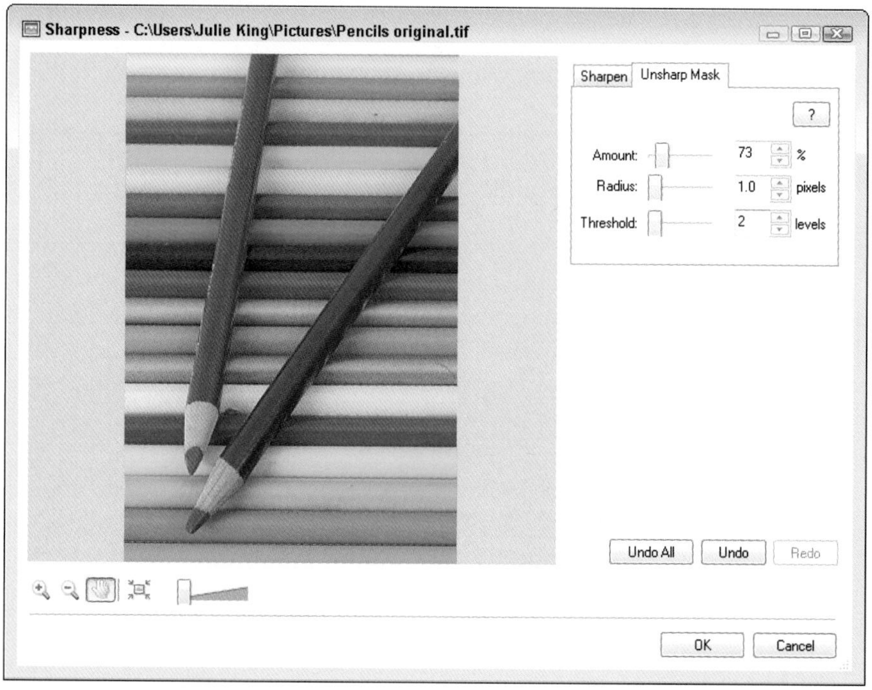

Sharpness - C:\Users\Julie King\Pictures\Pencils original.tif

Sharpen | Unsharp Mask

?

Amount: 73 %

Radius: 1.0 pixels

Threshold: 2 levels

Undo All Undo Redo

OK Cancel

Figure 10-25: The Unsharp Mask filter provides three levels of sharpening control.

Whichever sharpening filter you use, don't forget to save the altered image in the TIFF file format. The first section of this chapter explains this critical part of the retouching process.

Shifting to AutoPilot

You may have noticed, if you've explored the Edit drop-down list, the Auto Adjustment option. If you select this option, the program opens your image in a retouching window, as shown in Figure 10-26. Click the Auto Adjust Image button and sit back and wait. The program analyzes your image and then makes whatever changes it deems necessary. You can compare the "before" and "after" views of your photo by clicking the Show Original Image box on and off.

As a rule, this type of automatic image correction tool doesn't produce results as good as the ones you can create by using the manual filter controls. That said, if you aren't working on important images or you just don't have the time to use — or the interest in using — the more sophisticated tools, go ahead and give the Auto Adjust Image button a click. If you don't like what you see, click the Cancel button and do the job yourself, using the tricks laid out elsewhere in this chapter.

Figure 10-26: Click Auto Adjust Image to see what changes the program thinks are needed.

Adding Text

You know the saying "A picture is worth a thousand words." Well, you can increase that count by adding text to your photo. Follow these steps:

1. **Double-click the image thumbnail to open it in a viewer window. Then choose Insert Text from the Edit drop-down list.**

   Look for the list at the top of the window if you use the Windows version of the program and at the bottom if you're a Mac user. Either way, you see your photo in the Insert Text retouching window. Figure 10-27 gives you a look at the Windows version of the window. (Again, the Mac version is virtually identical.)

2. **Click in the preview at the spot you want to add the text.**

   In Windows, be sure that the Text tool, located under the preview, next to the Zoom tools, is selected before you click. After you click, a text box appears, as shown in the figure. At any time, you can resize the box as needed by dragging the little boxes that appear around its perimeter. To move the box (and any text inside), just drag inside the box.

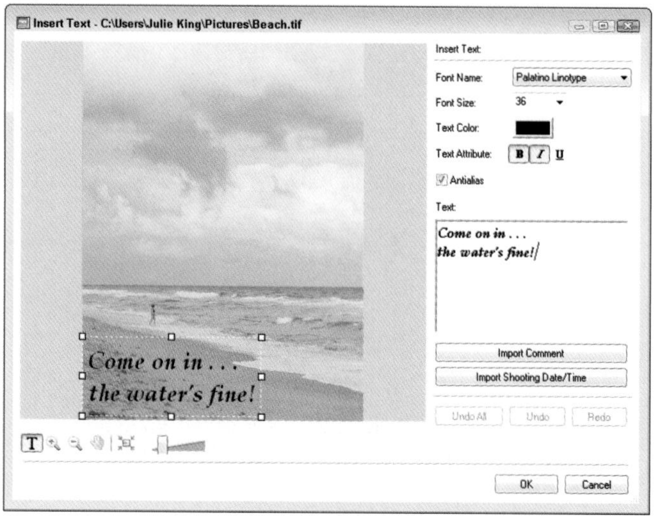

Figure 10-27: You can add captions and other text information.

3. Type some text.

The text appears in both the image preview and the Text area on the right side of the window.

To add the date and time you shot the picture, click the Import Shooting Date/Time button. Similarly, if you added comment text when organizing your pictures, clicking the Import Comment button enters that text for you. (You can add comments via the Comment pane that appears when you browse images in Preview display mode. For details, see the ZoomBrowser EX or ImageBrowser software manual, provided on one of the CDs that shipped with your camera.)

You can specify a font (type design), size, and color and add bold, underline, or italic formatting. The Antialias option smoothes the jagged edges that can occur when letters contain diagonal or curved lines. As a rule, keeping this option enabled is a good idea.

4. Click OK and then choose File⇨Save As to save your edited photo.

Choose TIFF as the file type; see the first section of this chapter for details.

Ten Special-Purpose Features to Explore on a Rainy Day

· ·

Consider this chapter the literary equivalent of the end of one of those late-night infomercial offers — the part where the host exclaims, "But wait! There's more!"

The camera options covered in these pages fit the category of "interesting bonus items." They aren't the sort of features that drive people to choose one camera over another, and they may come in handy only for certain users, on certain occasions. Still, they're included at no extra charge with your camera, so check 'em out when you have a few spare moments. Who knows; you may discover a hidden gem that provides just the solution you need for one of your photography problems.

Many features discussed here involve Custom Functions, a group of advanced options that you access via Setup Menu 3. If you're not familiar with how to navigate the Custom Functions, the next section spells things out.

Changing the Function of the Set Button

Normally, the main role of the Set button is to select items from the camera menus. When you're in shooting mode — that is, no menus are displayed and the Quick Control screen isn't active — pressing the button has no effect.

When you shoot in the P, Tv, Av, M, or A-DEP exposure modes, though, you have the option to assign one of the following additional tasks to the button:

✏ **Image Quality:** Pressing the button displays the screen where you can change the Quality settings.

✏ **Flash Exposure Compensation:** Displays the meter that enables you to adjust flash power.

✏ **LCD Monitor On/Off.** Performs the same monitor on/off function as the Disp button. Note that the Set button won't perform this chore when you shoot in Live View mode even if you select this option.

✏ **Menu display:** Brings up the menus. After the menus are onscreen, you use the button to select menu options.

✏ **ISO Speed:** Displays the screen where you can adjust the ISO Speed setting, just as if you had pressed the ISO button.

Follow these steps to customize the button:

1. **Set your camera to one of the advanced exposure modes (P, Tv, Av, M, or A-DEP).**

   You can't adjust the performance of the Set button in the other exposure modes. Nor does the button perform whatever alternative function you may assign when the camera is set to those modes.

2. **Display Setup Menu 3 and highlight Custom Functions, as shown on the left in Figure 11-1.**

   You use this menu item to customize 11 aspects of the camera's performance.

Custom Function category   Custom Function number

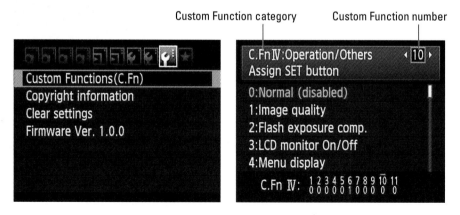

Figure 11-1: The Custom Function menu item provides access to 11 customization options.

3. Press Set.

The screen should look something like the one on the right in Figure 11-1, at least along the bottom of the screen. What appears in the rest of the screen depends on which Custom Function is selected.

The Custom Functions are grouped into four categories. The category number and name appear in the upper-left corner of the screen; the number of the selected function appears in the upper-right corner. The blue text indicates the current setting of the selected Custom Function. At the bottom of the screen, the top row of numbers represents the 11 Custom Functions, with the currently selected function indicated with a tiny horizontal bar over the number. The lower row shows the number of the current setting for each Custom Function, with 0 always representing the default.

4. If needed, press the right or left cross key to display Custom Function 10.

When you reach Custom Function 10, you see the options shown on the right in Figure 11-1.

5. Press the Set button.

Now the list of options for Custom Function 10 becomes accessible, and a highlight box appears around one option, as shown in Figure 11-2. Again, the option that appears in blue is the current setting — in the figure, Normal (disabled), which is the default setting for Custom Function 10.

Figure 11-2: You can configure the Set button to perform an extra function during shooting.

6. Press the up or down cross keys to highlight a setting.

7. Press the Set button.

8. To adjust another Custom Function setting, repeat Steps 4 through 7.

9. Press Menu to exit the Custom Function screens and return to Setup Menu 3.

Or to return to shooting mode, just press the shutter button halfway and release it.

Now whenever you shoot in the advanced exposure modes and press Set while no menus are displayed, the button takes on the function you just assigned to it. To go back to the default setting, repeat these steps and select option 0 in Step 6. The button then reverts to its original single-minded purpose, which is to lock in menu selections.

Customizing Exposure and Focus Lock Options

By default, you initiate autofocusing by pressing the shutter button halfway and lock autoexposure by pressing the AE (autoexposure) Lock button, which lives on the top-right side of the camera back and sports the label you see in the margin here. (Chapter 5 explains the AE Lock feature.) I recommend that you stick with this setup while you're still learning about your camera — otherwise, my instructions won't always work. But after you're feeling more comfortable, you may want to customize the locking behaviors of the two buttons.

To configure the buttons for still photography (more about movie recording options momentarily), set the Mode dial to one of the advanced exposure modes. You can enjoy full button control only in the P, Tv, Av, M, or A-DEP modes. Then head for Custom Function 9. As shown in Figure 11-3, you can choose from the following configuration options. (The first part of the setting name indicates what happens with a half-press of the shutter button; the second part indicates the function of the AE Lock button.)

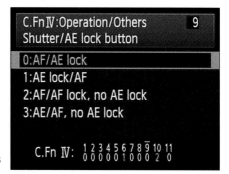

Figure 11-3: Adjust autoexposure and autofocus lock behavior via Custom Function 9.

- **AF/AE Lock:** This is the default setting. Pressing the shutter button halfway initiates autofocus; pressing the AE Lock button locks autoexposure.

- **AE Lock/AF:** With this option, pressing the shutter button halfway locks autoexposure. To initiate autofocusing, you instead press the AE Lock button. In other words, this mode is the exact opposite of the default setup.

- **AF/AF Lock, no AE Lock:** Pressing the shutter button halfway initiates autofocusing, and pressing the AE Lock button locks focus. Autoexposure lock isn't possible.

  Okay, I hear you: "Huh? Why would I want to use both buttons for autofocusing?" Well, this option is designed to prevent focusing mishaps when you use AI Servo autofocusing, explained in Chapter 8. In AI Servo mode, the autofocus motor continually adjusts focus from the time you press the shutter button halfway until the time you take the image. This feature helps you keep moving objects sharply focused. But if something moves in front of your subject, the camera may mistakenly focus on that object, which may leave your subject blurry.

To cope with that possibility, this locking option enables you to initiate autofocusing as usual, by pressing the shutter button halfway. But at any time before you take the picture, you can press the AE Lock button to temporarily stop the autofocusing motor from adjusting focus if an intruder moves into the frame. When you release the button, the autofocusing mechanism starts up again.

✓ **AE/AF, no AE Lock:** Similar to the preceding mode, this one also is designed to help you capture moving subjects in AI Servo mode. Pressing the shutter button halfway initiates autoexposure metering. Pressing the AE Lock button starts the autofocusing servo system; releasing the button stops it.

For Movie mode, you also can customize the shutter button/AE Lock button roles, but things work slightly differently:

✓ First, you customize the buttons via the Shutter/AE Lock Button option on Movie Menu 1, as illustrated in Figure 11-4.

✓ You get the same four options described above, but the third option — AF/AF lock, no AE Lock — is the one that comes in handy for taking a still picture during a movie recording. You press the shutter button halfway to autofocus as usual but then hold down the AE Lock button to lock focus. Now you can lift your finger off the shutter button if you like and, when you're ready to take a still shot, press it all the way down without causing the camera to reset autofocus again. (Okay, it's a little convoluted, but won't *you* be impressive when you demonstrate this trick at the next Canon Rebel user group.)

✓ The AE/AF, no AE Lock option enables you to use the shutter button to set autoexposure, which is adjusted continuously throughout the recording, and use the AE Lock button to set focus.

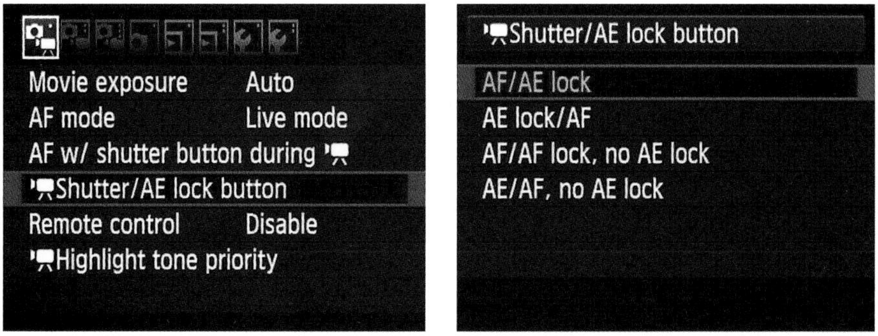

Figure 11-4: To customize the autofocus and autoexposure lock behavior during movie recording, use this option on Movie Menu 1.

Disabling the AF-Assist Beam

In dim lighting, your camera may emit an AF (autofocus)-assist beam from the built-in flash when you press the shutter button halfway — assuming that the flash unit is open, of course. This pulse of light helps the camera "see" its target better, improving the performance of the autofocusing system.

If you're shooting in a situation where the AF-assist beam may be distracting to your subject or to others in the room, you can disable it. Take these steps to control this aspect of your camera:

1. Set the Mode dial to P, Tv, Av, M, or A-DEP.

As with the other customization options discussed in preceding sections, this one is available only in these advanced exposure modes.

2. Display Setup Menu 3, highlight Custom Functions, and press Set.

You're taken to the main launching pad for adjusting all Custom Functions.

3. Press the right or left cross key as needed to select Custom Function 7.

4. Press the Set button.

Now the options shown in Figure 11-5 become accessible.

5. Press the up or down cross key to highlight a setting.

Here are your choices:

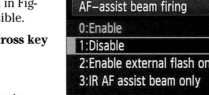

Figure 11-5: You can disable the autofocus-assist beam.

- *Enable:* This setting is the default and turns the AF-Assist Beam function on.

- *Disable:* I know you can figure this one out.

- *Enable External Flash Only:* Choose this setting to permit an external flash unit to emit the beam but prevent the built-in flash from doing so. (The idea is to save you the time and hassle of revisiting the Custom Function setting to enable or disable the beam every time you switch from the built-in flash to an external flash — two settings in one, if you will.) The external flash must be a compatible EX-series Speedlite unit.

- *IR AF Assist Beam Only:* This setting allows an external Canon EOS–dedicated Speedlite with infrared (IR) AF-assist to use only the IR beam to aid in focusing instead of pulsing a series of small flashes like the built-in flash does when it tries to play autofocus guide dog.

One note: An external Canon Speedlite has its own provision to disable the AF-assist beam. If you turn off the beam on the flash unit, it won't light no matter which Custom Function setting you choose.

6. **Press the Set button.**

   Your chosen setting affects all advanced exposure modes. In fully automatic modes, the autofocus assist beam continues to light from the built-in flash when the camera deems it necessary. If you use an external flash that offers the assist-beam control, you can disable or enable the function through the flash itself.

Without the aid of the assist beam, the camera may have trouble autofocusing in dim lighting. The easiest solution is to simply focus manually; Chapter 1 shows you how.

Enabling Mirror Lockup

One component involved in the optical system of an SLR camera is a tiny mirror that moves when you press the shutter button. The small vibration caused by the movement of the mirror can result in slight blurring of the image when you use a very slow shutter speed, shoot with a long telephoto lens, or take extreme close-up shots. To eliminate the possibility, your camera offers *mirror lockup.* When you enable this feature, the mirror movement is completed well before the shot is recorded, thus preventing camera shake.

Mirror lockup shooting requires a slightly different approach to taking a picture. To try out this feature, take these steps:

1. **Set the Mode dial to an advanced exposure mode.**

   Mirror lockup isn't available in the fully automatic exposure modes, so set the dial to P, Tv, Av, M, or A-DEP mode.

2. **Set Custom Function 8, Mirror Lockup, to Enable, as shown in Figure 11-6.**

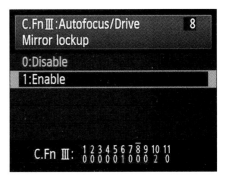

Figure 11-6: Mirror lockup prevents camera shake caused by the movement of the optical system's mirror.

3. **Frame your shot.**

4. **If you're using autofocus, press and hold the shutter button halfway to focus.**

   Or if you prefer manual focusing, twist the focusing ring as needed to focus the image.

5. **Press the shutter button all the way down to lock up the mirror. Then release the button.**

   At this point, you can no longer see anything through the viewfinder. Don't panic — that's normal. The mirror's function is to enable you to see in the viewfinder the scene that the lens will capture, and mirror lockup prevents it from serving that purpose.

6. **Press the shutter button all the way again.**

   The camera then takes the picture.

Using a tripod or another type of support is critical to getting shake-free shots in situations that call for mirror lockup. For even more protection, set your camera to the Self-Timer: 2 second mode, introduced in Chapter 2, and take your hands completely off the camera after you press the shutter button in Step 5. The picture is taken two seconds after the mirror lockup occurs. If you purchased the remote control unit for your camera, you instead can trigger the shutter button using it.

Adding Cleaning Instructions to Images

You've no doubt noticed that your camera displays a "Sensor Cleaning" message every time you turn off the camera. When you turn on the camera, a little "cleaning" icon flickers in the lower-right corner of the Shooting Settings display. These alerts tell you that the camera is automatically performing a maintenance step that's designed to remove from the sensor any dust particles that may have made their way into the camera interior.

If you don't see these alerts, open Setup Menu 2, choose the Sensor Cleaning option, and then press Set. Next, set the Auto Cleaning option to Enable. (I don't see any good reason to disable this feature unless you're continually turning the camera on and off, in which case the cleaning delay can be annoying.)

The automated sensor cleaning normally is all that's necessary to keep the sensor dust-free. But if you notice that small spots are appearing consistently on your images, you may need to step in and take action on your own. The best solution, of course, is to take your camera to a good repair shop and have the sensor professionally cleaned. I don't recommend that you take on this job yourself; it's a delicate procedure, and you can easily ruin your camera.

Until you can have the camera cleaned, however, you can use a feature on Shooting Menu 3 to create a custom dust-removal filter that you can apply in Digital Photo Professional, which is one of the free programs that ships with your camera.

The first step in creating the filter is to record a data file that maps the location of the dust spots on the sensor. To do this, you need a white piece of paper or another white surface and a lens that can achieve a focal length of 55mm or greater. (The kit lens sold with your camera qualifies.) Then take these steps:

1. **Set the lens focal length at 55mm or longer.**

   If you own the kit lens, just zoom in as far as possible, which sets the focal length at 55mm.

2. **Switch the camera to manual focusing.**

   On the kit lens, move the focus switch on the lens from AF to MF.

3. **Set focus at infinity.**

   Some lenses have a marking that indicates the infinity position — the symbol looks like a number 8 lying on its side. If your lens doesn't have the marking, hold the camera so that the lens is facing you and then turn the lens focusing ring clockwise until it stops.

4. **Set the camera to one of the advanced exposure modes (P, Tv, Av, M, or A-DEP).**

   You can create the dust data file only in these modes.

5. **Display Shooting Menu 3 and highlight Dust Delete Data, as shown on the left in Figure 11-7.**

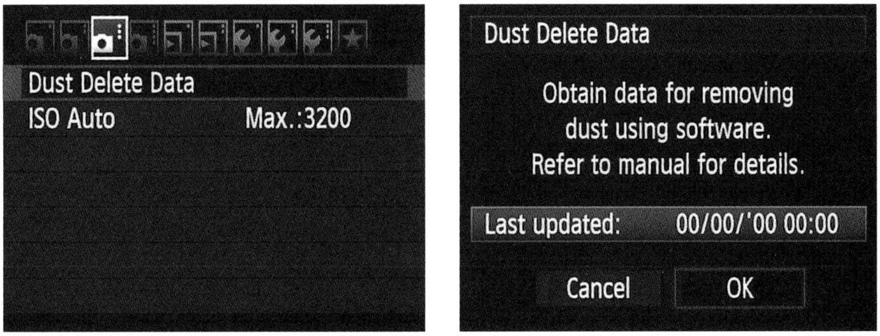

Figure 11-7: You can record dust-removal data that can be read by Digital Photo Professional.

6. Press the Set button.

Now you see the Dust Delete Data message. (Refer to the right side of Figure 11-7.)

7. Press the right cross key to highlight OK and then press Set.

The camera performs its normal automatic sensor-cleaning ritual, which takes a second or two. Then you see the instruction screen shown on the left in Figure 11-8.

8. Position the camera so that it's about 8 to 12 inches from your white card or piece of paper.

The card or paper needs to be large enough to completely fill the viewfinder at this distance.

9. Press the shutter button all the way to record the Dust Delete Data.

No picture is taken; the camera just records the Dust Delete Data in its internal memory. If the process was successful, you see the message shown on the right in Figure 11-8.

If the camera tells you that it couldn't record the data, the lighting conditions are likely to blame. Make sure that the lighting is even across the entire surface of your white card or paper and that the paper is sufficiently illuminated and then try again.

10. Press the Set button.

The current date now appears on the initial Dust Delete Data screen.

Figure 11-8: The Dust Delete Data is recorded when you press the shutter button all the way.

After you create your Dust Delete Data file, the camera attaches the data to every subsequent image, regardless of whether you shoot in the fully automatic or advanced exposure modes.

To clean a photo, open it in Digital Photo Professional and choose Tools⇨ Start Stamp Tool. Your photo then appears in an editing window; click the Apply Dust Delete Data button to start the automated dust-busting feature. The program's manual, provided on one of the two CDs that ships with your camera, offers details about this process; look for the Help entry related to using the Copy Stamp tool.

Turning Off the Shooting Settings Screen

When you turn on your camera, the monitor automatically displays the Shooting Settings screen. At least, it does if you stick with the default setting selected for Custom Function 11, which bears the lengthy name LCD Display When Power On.

You can prevent the monitor from displaying the screen every time you power up the camera, if you choose. The monitor is one of the biggest drains on the camera battery, so limiting it to displaying information only when you need it can extend the time between battery charges.

As with other Custom Functions, this option works only when the camera is set to one of the advanced exposure modes — in other modes, the screen still appears automatically. Still, any battery savings can be helpful when you're running low on juice.

To take advantage of this feature, take these steps:

1. **Set the camera to P, Tv, Av, M, or A-DEP mode.**

2. **Display Setup Menu 3, highlight Custom Functions, and press Set.**

3. **Use the cross keys to select Custom Function 11 and then press Set.**

   You see the screen shown in Figure 11-9.

4. **Press the up or down cross key to highlight Previous Display Status.**

5. **Press Set.**

6. **Press the shutter button halfway and release it to temporarily display the Shooting Settings screen.**

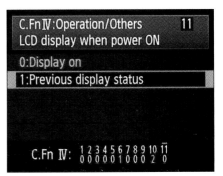

Figure 11-9: You can prevent the monitor from turning on automatically when you power up the camera.

7. **Press the Disp button to turn off the monitor.**

8. **Turn off the camera.**

When you turn on the camera again, the monitor doesn't automatically display the Shooting Settings screen — as long as the Mode dial is set to an advanced shooting mode, that is. To view the screen, press the Disp button; press the button again to return to monitor-off status.

However, note that if you turn the monitor on before shutting off the camera, the Shooting Settings screen *does* appear the next time you turn on the camera. Note the Custom Function setting name: Previous Display Status. It means what the name implies: The camera preserves the current monitor status even if you turn the camera off and then back on again. I don't know about you, but I'm already "memory challenged" — I don't need to add one more thing to the list of items to remember. So I leave this option at the default and just give the shutter button a quick half-press and release to dismiss the Shooting Settings screen when I fire up the camera.

Creating Your Very Own Camera Menu

Canon does a good job of making it easy to change the most commonly used camera settings. You can access many critical options by pressing the buttons on the camera body, and others require only a quick trip to the camera menus.

To make the process even simpler, you can create your own, custom menu containing up to six items from the camera's other six menus. Logically enough, the custom menu goes by the name My Menu and is represented by the green star icon, as shown on the left in Figure 11-10.

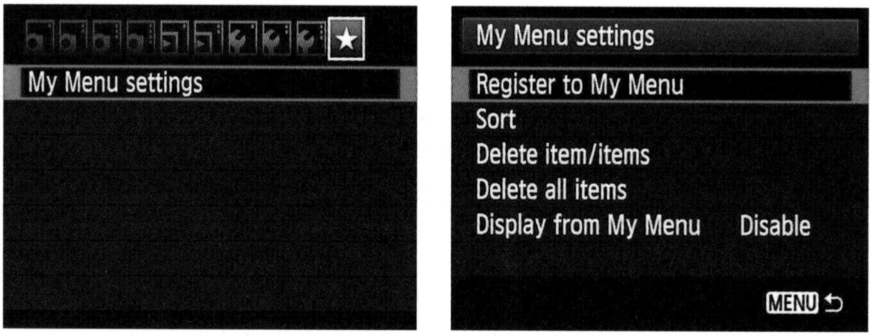

My Menu settings

My Menu settings

Register to My Menu
Sort
Delete item/items
Delete all items
Display from My Menu   Disable

MENU ↩

Figure 11-10: Group your favorite menu items by using the My Menu feature.

To create your menu, take these steps:

1. **Set the camera Mode dial to an advanced exposure mode.**

   Sadly, you can create and order from the custom menu only in P, Tv, Av, M, or A-DEP exposure mode.

2. **Press the Menu button and display the My Menu screen.**

   Initially, the screen shows only a single item, as shown on the left in Figure 11-10.

3. **Highlight My Menu Settings and press Set.**

   Now you see the screen on the right in Figure 11-10.

4. **Highlight Register to My Menu and press Set.**

   You see a scrolling list that contains every item found on the camera's other six menus, as shown on the left in Figure 11-11.

5. **Highlight the first item to include on your custom menu.**

   To add a specific Custom Function to your menu, scroll *past* the item named Custom Functions to find and highlight the individual function. (The item named Custom Functions simply puts the Custom Functions menu item on your menu, and you still have to wade through multiple levels of steps to reach your function.)

6. **Press Set.**

   You see a confirmation screen. (Refer to the right side of Figure 11-11.)

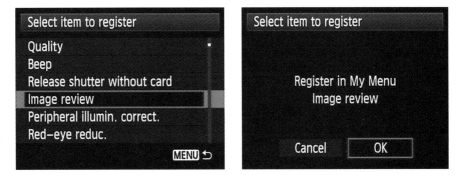

Figure 11-11: Highlight an item to put on your menu and press Set.

7. **Highlight OK and press Set.**

   You return to the list of menu options. The option you just added to your menu is dimmed in the list.

8. **Repeat Steps 5 through 7 to add up to five additional items to your menu.**

9. **Press the Menu button.**

   You then see the My Menu screen, where the items you added to the menu should appear.

After creating your menu, you can further customize and manage it as follows:

- ✓ **Give your menu priority.** You can tell the camera that you want it to automatically display your menu anytime you press the Menu button. To do so, select My Menu Settings on the main My Menu screen and then press Set. You then see the screen shown on the right side of Figure 11-10. Highlight Display from My Menu and press Set. Highlight Enable and press Set again.

- ✓ **Change the order of the list of menu items.** Once again, highlight My Menu Settings and press Set. Then highlight the Sort option (refer to the screen on the right in Figure 11-10) and press Set. Highlight a menu item, press Set, and then use the up or down cross keys to move the item up or down in the list. Press Set to glue the menu item in its new position. Press Menu to return to the My Menu Settings screen; press Menu again to return to your custom menu.

- ✓ **Delete menu items.** Display your menu, highlight My Menu Settings, and press Set. Then, to delete a single item, highlight Delete Item/Items and press Set. Highlight the menu item you want to remove and press Set again. Highlight OK and press Set again to confirm your decision. To remove all items from your custom menu, choose Delete All Items (refer to the right side of Figure 11-10), press Set, highlight OK, and press Set again.

Creating Custom Folders

Normally, your camera automatically creates folders to store your images. The first folder has the name 100Canon; the second, 101Canon; the third, 102Canon; and so on. Each folder can hold 9999 photos. If you want to create a new folder before the existing one is full, choose Select Folder from Setup Menu 1. You might take this organizational step so that you can segregate work photos from personal photos, for example.

After selecting the menu option, press Set, choose Create Folder, and press Set again. The camera asks for permission to create the folder; highlight OK and press Set one more time. The folder is automatically assigned the next available folder number and is selected as the active folder — the one that will hold any new photos you shoot.

To make a different folder as the active folder, choose Select Folder again, highlight the folder you want to use, and press Set.

Tagging Files with Your Copyright Claim

By using the Copyright Information option on Setup Menu 3, you can load copyright data into the camera's brain. Then, whenever you shoot a picture, your copyright information is added to the *metadata* (extra, invisible data) recorded with the image file. You can view the copyright information and other metadata in the free Canon software; the first section of Chapter 6 shows you how.

Including a copyright notice is a reasonable first step to take if you want to prevent people from using your pictures without permission. Anyone who views your picture in a program that can display metadata will see your copyright notice. Obviously, that won't be enough to completely prevent unauthorized use of your images. And technically speaking, you hold the copyright to your photo whether you take any steps to mark it with your name. But if you ever come to the point of pressing legal action, you can at least show that you did your due diligence in letting people know that you hold the copyright.

To turn on the copyright function, take these steps:

1. **Set the camera Mode dial to an advanced exposure mode.**

    You can create or modify copyright information only in P, Tv, Av, M, or A-DEP exposure mode. Rest assured, however, that your copyright information— after it's created — is stored in all images you shoot in either the advanced or fully automatic exposure modes.

2. **Display Setup Menu 3 and highlight Copyright Information, as shown on the left in Figure 11-12.**

3. **Press Set.**

    Now you see the screen shown on the right in Figure 11-12.

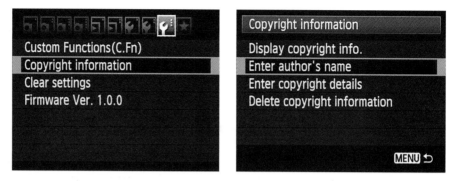

Figure 11-12: Tagging files with your copyright notice lets people know who owns the rights to the picture.

4. **Select Enter Author's Name and press Set.**

This step opens the data entry screen, as shown on the left side of Figure 11-13. Get comfortable as you go through the somewhat tedious steps of entering your name and other information — if you're an iPhone or Droid user, you'll feel like you've stepped back in time — but until touch-sensitive LCD screens (or voice recognition!) are standard features on digital SLRs, this is about as good as it gets for data entry.

5. **Enter your name into the box in the upper-left corner of the screen.**

Remember these text-entry tricks:

- Use the Quick Control button to alternate between the text box and the character-selection area below.

- The cross keys walk you from character to character in the list.

Figure 11-13: Enter your name and other copyright information that you want tagged to your images.

- Press Set to enter the current character in the text box.

- To delete a character, move the cursor just past the letter and press the Erase button.

6. **After you finish entering your name, press Menu.**

   You then return to the Copyright Information screen shown on the right in Figure 11-12.

7. **Highlight Copyright Information and press Set to add additional copyright data.**

   You might want to add the word Copyright and the year, for example, or your company name. Just repeat the same text entry process you used to enter your name.

8. **Press Menu to return to the Copyright Information screen.**

9. **To check the accuracy of your data, select Display Copyright Info and press Set.**

   You should see a screen similar to the one on the right in Figure 11-13.

10. **To wrap things up, press Menu one more time.**

If you tag your files with copyright data, you can later disable the tagging, if necessary, by using the Delete Copyright Information option (shown on the right in Figure 11-12).

Playing with the Creative Filters

Enough of the dry technical stuff — time for something a bit more entertaining. With the Creative Filters tool on Playback Menu 1, you can create some fun special effects before you even download photos to your computer. To try 'em out, follow these steps:

1. **Display Playback Menu 1 and highlight Creative Filters, as shown on the left in Figure 11-14.**

2. **Press Set.**

   You see a screen similar to the one on the right in Figure 11-14. The camera also briefly displays a brief message telling you that only images compatible with the Creative Filters tool are now accessible. In this case, only movie and video snapshot files are prohibited.

Figure 11-14: You can apply five special effects to photos on your memory card through the Creative Filters option.

3. **Use the right or left cross keys to scroll to the photo you want to alter.**

4. **Press Set.**

Now you see a screen similar to the one on the left in Figure 11-15. The icons at the bottom of the screen represent the five effects filters, which are:

- *Grainy B/W:* This filter turns your photos into old-fashioned, grainy, black-and-white photos like the one shown on the right in Figure 11-15.

- *Soft Focus:* This filter blurs the photo so it looks all soft and cuddly. It's great to use on photos of brides, babies, kittens, and teddy bears. And of course, it's ideal for making your water garden photo look like a Monet painting.

Figure 11-15: Select an effect and then press Set to tweak the results.

- *Fish-eye:* Choose this option to distort your photo so that it appears to have been shot using a fish-eye lens, as shown in the top-right example in Figure 11-16.

- *Toy Camera:* Creates an image with dark corners — called a *vignette* effect. Vignetting is caused by poor-quality lenses not letting enough light in to expose the entire frame of film (like in toy cameras). When you choose this effect, you can also add a warm (yellowish) or cool (blue) tint. For example, I applied the effect with a warm tint to create the lower-left variation in Figure 11-16.

- *Miniature:* This filter creates a trick of the eye by playing with depth of field. It blurs all but a very small area of the photo to create a result that looks something like one of those miniature dioramas you see in museums. I applied the filter to my city scene to produce the lower-right variation in Figure 11-16.

   This effect works best on pictures taken from a high angle, like the one featured in the figure.

5. **Use the cross keys to select a filter and then press Set.**

   Now you see controls for adjusting the effect, as shown on the right in Figure 11-15.

6. **Tweak the effect if desired.**

   Which controls appear depend on the effect, as follows:

   - *Grainy B/W:* You see a scale that lets you set the level of contrast to Low, Standard, or Strong. Press the right or left cross keys to change the value; the onscreen preview updates to show you the result.

   - *Soft Focus:* Again, press the right or left cross keys to set the amount of the blurring to Low, Standard, or Strong.

   - *Fish-eye Effect:* You can increase or decrease the distortion by choosing Low, Standard, or Strong.

   - *Toy Camera Effect:* Choose from three color tones: Cool, Standard, or Warm. Cool makes the photo look bluer, and Warm makes it look more golden.

   - *Miniature Effect:* This one's a little different: The little box that appears indicates the area that will remain in sharp focus when the rest of the image is blurred. Use the cross keys to move the box up or down. Or to rotate the box and change its orientation from horizontal to vertical, press the Info button. Then use the right/left cross keys to position the box.

Figure 11-16: I used the Creative Filters feature to create these variations on a city scene.

7. **Press Set.**

   You're asked to confirm that you want to save the adjusted image as a new file.

8. **Highlight OK and press Set again.**

   The camera creates a copy of your image, applies the effect, and then displays a message telling you the folder number and last four digits of the file number of the altered photo. If the original was captured using the Raw Quality setting, the altered image is stored in the JPEG format.

9. **Highlight OK and press Set one more time.**

   You're returned to the beginning filter screen. You can then apply additional effects if you want. Or press Menu to exit the Creative Filters screens altogether.

You can apply multiple filters to the same photo if you really want to go crazy. For example, you can go through the steps once to create a fish-eye effect and then apply the Grainy B/W filter to create a monochrome fish-eye photo.

Index

Apple & Macs

iPad For Dummies
978-0-470-58027-1

iPhone For Dummies,
4th Edition
978-0-470-87870-5

MacBook For Dummies, 3rd
Edition
978-0-470-76918-8

Mac OS X Snow Leopard For
Dummies
978-0-470-43543-4

Business

Bookkeeping For Dummies
978-0-7645-9848-7

Job Interviews
For Dummies,
3rd Edition
978-0-470-17748-8

Resumes For Dummies,
5th Edition
978-0-470-08037-5

Starting an
Online Business
For Dummies,
6th Edition
978-0-470-60210-2

Stock Investing
For Dummies,
3rd Edition
978-0-470-40114-9

Successful
Time Management
For Dummies
978-0-470-29034-7

Computer Hardware

BlackBerry
For Dummies,
4th Edition
978-0-470-60700-8

Computers For Seniors
For Dummies,
2nd Edition
978-0-470-53483-0

PCs For Dummies, Windows
7 Edition
978-0-470-46542-4

Laptops For Dummies,
4th Edition
978-0-470-57829-2

Cooking & Entertaining

Cooking Basics
For Dummies,
3rd Edition
978-0-7645-7206-7

Wine For Dummies,
4th Edition
978-0-470-04579-4

Diet & Nutrition

Dieting For Dummies,
2nd Edition
978-0-7645-4149-0

Nutrition For Dummies,
4th Edition
978-0-471-79868-2

Weight Training
For Dummies,
3rd Edition
978-0-471-76845-6

Digital Photography

Digital SLR Cameras &
Photography For Dummies,
3rd Edition
978-0-470-46606-3

Photoshop Elements 8
For Dummies
978-0-470-52967-6

Gardening

Gardening Basics
For Dummies
978-0-470-03749-2

Organic Gardening
For Dummies,
2nd Edition
978-0-470-43067-5

Green/Sustainable

Raising Chickens
For Dummies
978-0-470-46544-8

Green Cleaning
For Dummies
978-0-470-39106-8

Health

Diabetes For Dummies,
3rd Edition
978-0-470-27086-8

Food Allergies
For Dummies
978-0-470-09584-3

Living Gluten-Free
For Dummies,
2nd Edition
978-0-470-58589-4

Hobbies/General

Chess For Dummies,
2nd Edition
978-0-7645-8404-6

Drawing
Cartoons & Comics
For Dummies
978-0-470-42683-8

Knitting For Dummies,
2nd Edition
978-0-470-28747-7

Organizing
For Dummies
978-0-7645-5300-4

Su Doku For Dummies
978-0-470-01892-7

Home Improvement

Home Maintenance
For Dummies,
2nd Edition
978-0-470-43063-7

Home Theater
For Dummies,
3rd Edition
978-0-470-41189-6

Living the
Country Lifestyle
All-in-One
For Dummies
978-0-470-43061-3

Solar Power Your Home
For Dummies,
2nd Edition
978-0-470-59678-4

Available wherever books are sold. For more information or to order direct: U.S. customers visit www.dummies.com or call 1-877-762-2974.
U.K. customers visit www.wileyeurope.com or call (0) 1243 843291. Canadian customers visit www.wiley.ca or call 1-800-567-4797.

Internet

Blogging For Dummies,
3rd Edition
978-0-470-61996-4

eBay For Dummies,
6th Edition
978-0-470-49741-8

Facebook For Dummies, 3rd
Edition
978-0-470-87804-0

Web Marketing
For Dummies,
2nd Edition
978-0-470-37181-7

WordPress
For Dummies,
3rd Edition
978-0-470-59274-8

Language & Foreign Language

French For Dummies
978-0-7645-5193-2

Italian Phrases
For Dummies
978-0-7645-7203-6

Spanish For Dummies,
2nd Edition
978-0-470-87855-2

Spanish For Dummies,
Audio Set
978-0-470-09585-0

Math & Science

Algebra I For Dummies,
2nd Edition
978-0-470-55964-2

Biology For Dummies,
2nd Edition
978-0-470-59875-7

Calculus For Dummies
978-0-7645-2498-1

Chemistry For Dummies
978-0-7645-5430-8

Microsoft Office

Excel 2010 For Dummies
978-0-470-48953-6

Office 2010 All-in-One
For Dummies
978-0-470-49748-7

Office 2010 For Dummies,
Book + DVD Bundle
978-0-470-62698-6

Word 2010 For Dummies
978-0-470-48772-3

Music

Guitar For Dummies,
2nd Edition
978-0-7645-9904-0

iPod & iTunes
For Dummies,
8th Edition
978-0-470-87871-2

Piano Exercises
For Dummies
978-0-470-38765-8

Parenting & Education

Parenting For Dummies,
2nd Edition
978-0-7645-5418-6

Type 1 Diabetes
For Dummies
978-0-470-17811-9

Pets

Cats For Dummies,
2nd Edition
978-0-7645-5275-5

Dog Training For Dummies,
3rd Edition
978-0-470-60029-0

Puppies For Dummies,
2nd Edition
978-0-470-03717-1

Religion & Inspiration

The Bible For Dummies
978-0-7645-5296-0

Catholicism For Dummies
978-0-7645-5391-2

Women in the Bible
For Dummies
978-0-7645-8475-6

Self-Help & Relationship

Anger Management
For Dummies
978-0-470-03715-7

Overcoming Anxiety
For Dummies,
2nd Edition
978-0-470-57441-6

Sports

Baseball
For Dummies,
3rd Edition
978-0-7645-7537-2

Basketball
For Dummies,
2nd Edition
978-0-7645-5248-9

Golf For Dummies,
3rd Edition
978-0-471-76871-5

Web Development

Web Design
All-in-One
For Dummies
978-0-470-41796-6

Web Sites
Do-It-Yourself
For Dummies,
2nd Edition
978-0-470-56520-9

Windows 7

Windows 7
For Dummies
978-0-470-49743-2

Windows 7
For Dummies,
Book + DVD Bundle
978-0-470-52398-8

Windows 7 All-in-One
For Dummies
978-0-470-48763-1

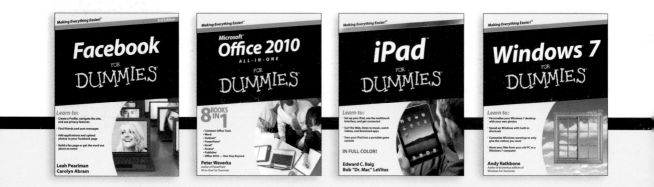

Available wherever books are sold. For more information or to order direct: U.S. customers visit www.dummies.com or call 1-877-762-2974.
U.K. customers visit www.wileyeurope.com or call (0) 1243 843291. Canadian customers visit www.wiley.ca or call 1-800-567-4797.